Writing in the
Arts and Sciences

Writing in the Arts and Sciences

ELAINE P. MAIMON   *Department of English*

GERALD L. BELCHER   *Department of History*

GAIL W. HEARN   *Department of Biology*

BARBARA F. NODINE   *Department of Psychology*

FINBARR W. O'CONNOR   *Department of Philosophy*

Beaver College

Winthrop Publishers, Inc.   Cambridge, Massachusetts

Library of Congress Cataloging in Publication Data

Main entry under title:

Writing in the arts and sciences.

Bibliography: p.
Includes index.
1. English language—Rhetoric.   2. Report Writing.
3. Exposition (Rhetoric)   4. Interdisciplinary
approach in education.   I. Maimon, Elaine P.
PE1478.W7   808'.042   80-25890
ISBN 0-87626-957-9

Cover and interior design by Susan Marsh
Illustrations prepared by Lyrl Ahern

Cover drawing from *Studies in Physiognomy* by Albrecht Dürer (1471–1528).
From the British Museum, Sloane Collection.

10 9 8 7 6 5 4 3 2

To our families, colleagues, and students, who have encouraged us in our assumption that writing is a metaphor for life.

Contents

WRITING TO LEARN

Writing in the Arts and Sciences

1   Studying the Academic Disciplines   4

Writing as problem solving 7 · *Getting started* 11
Writing the first draft 11 · *Revising* 14

QUESTIONS 16
EXERCISES 17

2   Writing to See and to Think   18

Some characteristics of private writing 19
The private journal 20 · *Academic problems* 22
Writing and reading as logical processes 37 · *Conclusion* 45

QUESTIONS 47
EXERCISES 47

3   Classroom Writing   55

Writing notes from lectures, discussions, and texts 55
Writing essay examinations 64

QUESTIONS 70
EXERCISES 70

4   Library Resources   71

The research process in the library 71
Resources in the humanities 78
Library research in the social sciences 81
Resources in the natural sciences 89 · *In summary* 97

QUESTIONS 97
EXERCISES 97

5   Writing in the Library   100

Recording 100 · Summarizing 102
Documenting 107 · Forms of documentation 110
Acknowledging 119

QUESTIONS 121
EXERCISES 121

LEARNING TO WRITE

Writing in the Humanities

✗ — 6   Research Papers in the Humanities   126

Getting started 128 · Writing the first draft 144
Revising 147

QUESTIONS 154
EXERCISES 154

7   Analyses and Reviews   155

Analyzing a poem 156
Analyzing stories, novels, and plays 162
Writing an analysis of a performance 163
Analyzing a painting or other graphic work 165
Book reviews 169

QUESTIONS 175
EXERCISES 175

8   Papers of Contemplation   176

Criticize or defend an author's view 178
Compare and contrast 191
The puzzle or problem paper 197
✗ —The speculative paper 201

QUESTIONS 204
EXERCISES 204

Writing in the Social Sciences

✕   9   Term Papers in the Social Sciences   208

Getting started 208 · *Writing the first draft* 210
Revising 215

QUESTIONS 220
EXERCISES 221

10   The Case Study Paper   222

Getting started 223 · *Writing the first draft* 226
Revising 229
The case history of a bill in Congress: HR1457 232

QUESTIONS 234
EXERCISES 234

11   Reporting Findings in the Social Sciences   236

Getting started 236 · *Writing the first draft* 238
Revising 252

QUESTIONS 253
EXERCISES 253

Writing in the Natural Sciences

12   Recording Observations in the Natural Sciences   256

Purpose of the laboratory notebook 257
Writing in the laboratory notebook 258
Revising and correcting the laboratory notebook 260
Format for the laboratory notebook 261
The research notebook 263

QUESTIONS 265
EXERCISES 265

13   The Laboratory Report in the Natural Sciences   266

Getting started 266 · *Writing the first draft* 268
Revising 273

QUESTIONS 275
EXERCISES 275

14 Review Paper in the Natural Sciences   276

Getting started 277 · *Writing the first draft* 287
Revising 289

QUESTIONS 292
EXERCISES 292

Appendix: Student Papers Written in Response to Assignments in
History, Sociology, Psychology, and Biology   295

History 134: Take-home essay 295
Assignment sheet: Small group study—Sociology 100 298
Psychology 101–102: The Mama Rat project 308
Biology 137 (animal behavior): Scientific review paper 319

Glossary   327

Index   331

Preface

Writing in the Arts and Sciences is an introduction to academic writing, reading, and studying. "The beginning writer," says Mina Shaughnessy, "does not know how writers behave." When students enter college, they are all beginners in the world of higher education. They must learn to cope with books, lectures, and papers assigned by scholars trained in a variety of fields. Each discipline has traditions that shape the reading and writing of its practitioners, but these scholarly traditions, with their specialized procedures, conventions, and terminology, may appear to the student as mysterious rites of passage. The purpose of this text is to cast light on those mysterious academic rites that until recently have been open to too few.

Although each academic discipline presents some constraints that are particular to itself, all areas of college study impose a number of subtle and unfamiliar expectations that may run counter to many students' previous experience. Even the most advanced high school student may be relatively unaccustomed to addressing absent strangers formally and at length in a tone of polite debate. Beginners in college need help in distinguishing what they already value—sincere expression—from what we must teach them to value—the communication of reasoned belief.

We have designed this textbook as a guide to these subtleties and pleasures. Learning the ins and outs of academic prose can mean the difference between success and failure not only in college but also in the larger world of professional and public activity. Most important, the traditions of liberal learning are valuable in themselves. These rites of passage may not always lead to ethical behavior, but they are still the best road to an examined life.

We believe that a composition course should be an introduction to "cultural literacy," a phrase used by the National Endowment for the Humanities to mean a literacy that enables one to participate fully in the life of our civilization. A composition course that uses this textbook will be shaped by the following principles:

1 Writing, like learning, is not an entity but a process.

2 Writing is a way to learn, not merely a means of communicating to others what has already been mastered.

3 Writing and learning are connected interactive processes. Students, therefore, need instruction and practice in cooperative procedures for learning from each other.

4 Writing in every discipline is a form of social behavior in that discipline. Students must learn the particular conventions of aim and audience within each discipline, and they must also learn to control the common conventional features of the written code: spelling, punctuation, conformity to standard English usage.

How to use this book

Writing in the Arts and Sciences is cross-disciplinary in its intention, conception, and authorship. But the book is designed for use in the English composition course, since it is there—or nowhere—that undergraduates can learn to see themselves as academic writers and readers. This textbook is designed to help you, the composition instructor, to draw on what you already know about language and the structure of discourse. When you use this book with your classes, you will still be teaching composition, not introductory courses in the disciplines, and you will be able to exemplify principles of good writing from a much broader range of material. You will also be better prepared to help students write effectively for more diverse audiences. In the past, many composition courses have depended on literary or belletristic material alone to exemplify scholarly modes of writing and thinking. This text also draws heavily on literary examples—Blake, Wordsworth, Dickens—but this literary material is juxtaposed to examples from history, philosophy, the graphic arts, dance, and from the social and natural sciences.

You may want to supplement this text with a cross-disciplinary anthology, or with just one or two additional readings—for example, Dickens's *Hard Times* or Antonia Fraser's *Royal Charles*—that would allow students to engage in further study based on the examples we introduce here. Nearly every instructor will want to supplement *Writing in the Arts and Sciences* with a concise grammar handbook. We believe that students should be taught to use such a handbook as a reference tool, like a dictionary. We believe further that grammatical terminology in and of itself is not an appropriate or useful focus for a writing course, especially not for a basic writing course. Instructors who arrange their composition syllabi according to the chapters in a grammar handbook may be neglecting the real basics of composition—the processes of academic writing and reading.

Writing in the Arts and Sciences is organized so that you can use it flexibly and creatively in your classroom. All chapters conclude with questions and exercises that present opportunities for short activities that can make writing an integrated part of every teaching and learning day. We have provided a glossary of specialized terms and four sample papers—from history, sociology, psychology, and biology—to exemplify various types of writing that college instructors expect. Those who prefer to organize their instruction in ways different from our chapter-by-chapter arrangement can consult the index. You may prefer, for example, to assign the various approaches to revision at the same time, rather than discussing revision as that topic comes up in each of the later chapters.

The text can be divided into two major sections. The first section (chapters 1–5), "Writing to Learn," focuses on writing as a way of learning. The second section (chapters 6–14), "Learning to Write," concentrates on writing as a means of communication within various disciplines.

Chapter 1, "Studying the Academic Disciplines," presents the key idea that disciplines are not differentiated so much by subject matter as by the special perspective that each discipline brings to experience. Chapter 2, "Writing to See and To Think," explains the uses of private writing and exemplifies procedures for transforming a topic into a problem to be solved. Here we deal with a variety of invention strategies, since we believe in presenting to students numerous possible activities that can help ease the anxiety of waiting for the Muse. Because students are diverse in their learning styles and interests, we present many things to try. We are aware that one person's heuristic can be another person's writer's block. So we recommend treating this material as a set of exercises, not as a list of rules. Chapter 2 also shows students how to apply logical principles, especially those articulated by Stephen Toulmin, to improving academic writing and reading.

Chapter 3, "Classroom Writing," presents practical procedures for taking notes and for writing essay examinations. Chapter 4, "Library Resources," provides access to reference materials, not only in literature, but in the other humanities and in the social and natural sciences. Chapter 5, "Writing in the Library," explains the processes of recording, summarizing, documenting, and acknowledging the ideas of others. Our approach here is to illuminate the typical caveat against plagiarism (usually expressed in language reminiscent of the surgeon general's warning against cigarettes) by explaining traditions of honest intellectual sharing—sharing in which students can learn to participate without exploitation. Here we also present and contrast two divergent forms of scholarly documentation: the footnote/bibliography format preferred in the humanities and the author/date format preferred in the natural and social sciences.

Just as the process of writing any single project is both recursive and self-contained, so the structure of our textbook is both recursive and self-contained. Chapter 1, in that sense, presents a self-contained, paradigmatic view of the writing process. That theme is then played with disciplinary variations in each of the nine chapters in the second section, "Learning to Write." The second section consists of three parts, "Writing in the Humanities," "Writing in the Social Sciences," and "Writing in the Natural Sciences." The chapters in each of these parts suggest strategies for writing apprentice versions of professional papers within the disciplines. Thus, we have written these parts as self-contained units so that you can select the material most appropriate to your own composition program.

Instructors at a polytechnic might teach chapters 1–5 and then go right on to chapters 12, 13, and 14, "Writing in the Natural Sciences." Instructors teaching a composition course that is coordinated with core courses in the humanities might supplement chapters 1–5 with chapters 6, 7, and 8, "Writing in the Humanities." Instructors who teach classes that include numerous social science majors might concentrate on chapters 9, 10, and 11, "Writing in the Social Sciences." Instructors teaching composition in professional programs might choose to emphasize the problem-solving papers discussed in chapter 8, the case studies taught in chapter 10, and the laboratory reports explained in chapter 13. Ideally, in a full-year composition course, instructors would concentrate on chapters 1–5 in the first semester and then on chapters 6–14 in the second. Students who work through the entire text will gain more than writing instruction: they will have an introduction to processes of thought in the liberal arts and sciences.

Pronouns

We struggled—agonized—over our policy on pronouns, to the point of irritating every one of our preliminary reviewers, all of whom are sympathetic to feminist principles. We have thus removed from the published text our democratic, but distracting, sprinkling of "she's," unless "she" refers specifically to a particular woman named in the text. We use the second person whenever possible and the third person plural most other times. But in those remaining instances when we are compelled to refer to a single unnamed student or teacher, we resolve our dilemma by reference to Mina Shaughnessy, who writes in *Errors and Expectations*, "After having tried various ways of circumventing the use of the masculine pronoun in situations where women teachers and students might easily outnumber men, I have settled for the convention, but I regret that the language resists my meaning in this important respect. When the reader sees *he*, I can only hope *she* will also be there" (p. 4).

Acknowledgments

We are indebted to Mina Shaughnessy for much more than her policy on pronouns. Her generous intellectual spirit was the earliest inspiration for this project. All five of us regard *Errors and Expectations* as a guide for college teachers in all disciplines, as we consider humane and rational higher education in the late twentieth century. Shaughnessy's work, along with that of James Kinneavy and Kenneth Bruffee, provides the theoretical framework for the practical activities exemplified in this book. We had opportunities to talk with Professors Kinneavy and Bruffee—and even more significantly to talk with one another across the disciplines—because of an institutional development grant awarded to Beaver College in 1977 by the National Endowment for the Humanities.

Several of the scholars who reviewed our manuscript in draft stages have enacted Bruffee's principles of collaborative learning. Frederick Crews, Paula Johnson, Richard Larson, and Harvey Wiener took time away from their own projects to write perceptively to us about ours. This book is immeasurably better because of their detailed suggestions and because of the comments offered by Margaret Belcher, Edward P. J. Corbett, Harry Crosby, Peter Hearn, Mort Maimon, Rob Mortimer, Calvin Nodine, and Barrie Van Dyck, who kindly looked at sections of our work in progress.

Several ideas in this text were clarified through discussions with Albert Anderson, Linda Flower, Maxine Hairston, John R. Hayes, E. D. Hirsch, Jr., Donald McQuade, Ellen Nold, Harriet Sheridan, and Richard Young. Our friends on the faculty and in the administration at Beaver College have provided an atmosphere in which a cross-disciplinary project could be carried forward without working at cross purposes to the institution. We are especially grateful in that regard to William Bracy, Helen Buttel, Josephine Charles, Helene Cohan, David Gray, Norman Johnston, and Bette Landman.

Among the many students who worked with us, we want to single out Karen Anderson, Jana Cohen, Elizabeth Czyszczon, and Kathy Mackin, who helped us as much by their enthusiasm for our project as they did by their assistance in our research. Patricia Kehoe and Linda Harrison typed various stages of the manuscript. Marie Lawrence coordinated our research assistants, typed and telephoned, but, most important, kept her good humor with five coauthors, some of whom could be absent-minded professors, misplacing on Thursday what had been carefully photocopied and collated on Wednesday.

John Wright, Richard Garretson, Richard Larson, Frederick Crews, Harvey Wiener, and Donald McQuade have taught us that the world of textbook publishing can share Mina Shaughnessy's commitment to humane values in teaching. And Paul O'Connell, John Covell, and the entire staff at Winthrop gave us the most valuable gifts of all: time, respect, and informed attention to the integrity of a new and challenging project.

As anyone who has ever been a coauthor knows, the greatest challenge of all was to the friendship that existed among the five of us. Finally, we want to thank each other for being even better friends today than we were in those other days when we retreated daily into the territoriality of our academic departments.

Writing in the Arts and Sciences

ocie
cat
als
But
ge
th
sity

ainst the king's Ch

urt vs. the count

ouse of Commons

ss, which include

hat seemed to the

erties. They didn

ere directed again

kes, dissolved his

ers. An angry and

Writing in the
Arts and Sciences

1 Studying the Academic Disciplines

Consider for a moment the nude. Stop to think how you regard the unclothed human body. An image from the pages of *Playboy* or *Playgirl* might come to mind, or a beautiful Rubens painting, or a frail, limp body on an operating table. What could you write about your image of the nude? Throughout the history of civilization, scholars have written in countless ways about the nude. Today, the various academic disciplines reflect the different ways that a nude—or any object—can be perceived:

- To the artist the nude is an object of beauty to be appreciated aesthetically.

- The biologist might categorize the nude in the phylum Chordata, the class Mammalia, the order Primates, the genus *Homo*, the species *sapiens*.

- The physiologist might be concerned with the nude's pallor. Is the poor peripheral circulation a reaction to cold or an emotional response to being caught in the nude?

- To a philosopher, the nude suggests nudism and might well raise questions about the power of the state: Should the state have the right to control when and how its citizens are obliged to wear clothes?

- An economist might well regard the nude as a marketable commodity controlled by the laws of supply and demand.

- A sociologist would probably consider the nude to be only naked and wonder if this naked person was being antisocial or was, in fact, eccentric or deviant.

- A psychologist might wonder what needs are fulfilled by this display of nudity.

- To a mathematician, the nude is a topological structure, defined by angles and planes, and transformable by rules of topology into many other shapes with the same mathematical properties.

- The anthropologist is interested in understanding different societies, and attitudes toward the wearing of clothes provide data on cultural mores. The nude may represent a unique and interesting culture.

- The historian, naturally, will put the nude into known historical contexts and will try to discover if those examples help to explain this nude.

- To other scholars in the arts and sciences the nude might be a metaphor for nature or a model of an intricate complex of marvelously efficient mechanisms or a combination of common chemicals.

During the next four years, instructors in your college courses will ask you to look at the world in ways as diverse as the ways the scholars above view the nude. The reading and writing that you do in each course will differ from what you do in other courses in more than just subject matter. In your earlier years you may have assumed that teachers taught different subjects: in history, you considered such topics as George Washington and Abraham Lincoln; in science, you thought about molecules and chemical compounds. But subject matter is only the most obvious difference among the courses that you take. Your instructors consider themselves members of different academic disciplines, not just because they sometimes study different subject matter, but because they have developed different systems for looking at and organizing experience. In the broadest sense, all courses have the same subject matter—the world—but as you study each discipline, you will look at that subject matter from a slightly different angle.

As you move from class to class, you will also be shifting your perspective. These shifting perspectives will be reflected in the different questions that your instructors ask and in the different research methods that you will use to answer these questions. As a student of the arts and sciences, you will be asked to play different roles as you study different disciplines. The most dramatic differences will be between the roles you are asked to play in your humanities courses and those you are asked to play in your courses in the social and natural sciences. These roles are the outcome of different traditions, although these traditions are still evolving. One of your most important tasks in college is to understand these traditions of liberal learning well enough for you to play a part, and even to contribute to advances.

In your science courses you will learn how to formulate and test hypotheses. You will learn systematic and objective approaches to explanations of cause and effect. In science courses, your role demands that you perform rituals that establish distance between you and the material you are studying. In that sense, the methods that you will learn for performing and recording experiments are theatrical techniques to help you maintain your objective stance. Effective writing in the sciences is impersonal without being frigid. The best scientific writers are the best actors; they understand the complexities of the scientific role.

The stance of the humanist is also complex. In the humanities—

literature, philosophy, language, religion, art and music criticism—the human viewpoint is important. Scholars in the humanities are personally engaged in intellectual confrontations with the world. They search for reasons, values, and interpretations in all areas of human concern. Even though their perspective is less impersonal than that of their colleagues in science, their approach is equally impartial. Their pursuit of values must transcend emotional involvement. Effective writing in the humanities is engaged without being distorted.

Although scientists and humanists ask different questions, both groups share an attitude of fair-minded inquiry. When these people function in their roles as scholars, they are liberated for a time from their own inhibitions and prejudices. They are able to study and to learn about all that exists in the wide world.

When we use the term "liberal arts" in this book, we mean the kind of learning that liberates the mind to ask questions, that emphasizes questions more than answers. In the Middle Ages the liberal arts (*artes liberales* in Latin) referred to the branches of study befitting a freeman. The liberal arts contrasted with the *artes serviles*, the servile arts, because only freemen—those whose were not servants—were permitted to study the liberal arts.

Today the liberal arts continue to be distinguished from more technical subjects because of their emphasis on questions. Learning is liberal or free when students understand the processes through which they can learn more on their own. Procedures in the liberal arts are consequently open-ended. When you learn a technical skill, typing for example, you learn the basic procedure once and for all, and then you work for increased speed and accuracy with this set procedure. The process of typing will not lead you to discover new processes or new knowledge unless your familiarity with the machine and your inclination toward liberal learning encourage you to invent a better typewriter. Technical areas of study emphasize performance; liberal areas of study emphasize invention.

But liberal learning does not permit us to hold on to any single answer for too long. As soon as you find one answer, you discover that that answer leads to other questions. Liberal learning can be unsettling. People like certainty, the right answer, the only way. Because of this desire for certainty and security, people can find themselves living with answers that other people have imposed upon them. In a free society, people learn to cultivate inquiring minds. They see that in broad areas of life there are no single right answers, that knowledge has a peculiar way of generating more questions, and that the world is more ambiguous than it appears. Liberal learning frees the mind to experience a sense of wonder at this ambiguous and fascinating world. F. Scott Fitzgerald writes, "The test of a first-rate intelligence is the ability to hold two opposed ideas in the mind at the same time, and still retain the ability to function." A liberally educated person learns to use this first-rate intelligence to function—even to prevail—in the midst of ambiguity.

Writing can help you to illuminate ambiguous situations, not to find certainty, but to find better ways to exist without certainty. Writing is an intellectual activity that helps you to develop <u>flexibility</u>, to create ways to test out your own responses and ideas, rather than merely to accept the ideas of others. You may have heard the story of the military leader who hired an instructor to teach his enlisted men to read and his officers to write. Writing can mean power.

The idea of writing as power may sound strange to you because most beginning students do not see writing as power at all. In fact, they often feel powerless and intimidated as they confront a bewildering array of college writing tasks, all sounding different and all seeming to represent the different whims of individual teachers in each classroom. College writing assignments, in this context, have been compared to a variety of new games in which no one seems ready to explain the rules to students. Academic writing can seem like a trap; you're expected to play, but you are not told how to win. In this book we propose to introduce you to the many types of writing assignments that you may confront in college and to prepare you to do these assignments successfully.

Writing as problem solving

As you use this book, we hope that academic writing will no longer seem a trap. But writing will still be a problem. A problem is a question for which you do not have an answer. Problems with a single correct answer, problems in multiplication for example, have methods that insure solution. Either you know the method for reaching the solution or you don't know it. And if you don't know the appropriate method, you can learn it.

Problems are more difficult to solve when there is not a single correct solution, and writing a paper is an ambiguous problem of this difficult kind. It is always helpful to begin with a careful definition and interpretation of the problem. In academic writing it helps to define the problem first in terms of *aim*, or *purpose*, and of *audience*. Whether you are taking notes in a lecture class, writing a book review, or putting together a term paper, your first question should be "why?" Why are you writing whatever it is you are writing? Is your major aim to express your feelings, to play with language, to communicate information to others, or to persuade others to accept your point of view? James Kinneavy, in A *Theory of Discourse*,[1] divides different sorts of academic writing into categories according to their major aim: expressive (writing to express your feelings); literary (writing to play with words); informative (writing to communicate information to others); and persuasive (writing to convince others).

Most of the writing that you are asked to do for college credit is either informative or persuasive; thus, most writing for college credit requires

[1] 1971; rpt. New York: Norton, 1980.

you to imagine "the others" that you are supposed to be informing or persuading. These others are your audience, and you have to make them up according to the conventions of the discipline and the kind of paper that you are writing. As we will say many times throughout this text, it is not sufficient to imagine your instructor as your audience; you must go further and imagine your instructor playing a particular role—representative of scholars in a discipline or representative of people who hold the view opposing the one you are arguing.

Writing involves many complex choices, and in this text we suggest a number of heuristics, or strategies, for making these choices. *Heuresis* is the Greek term (*inventio* is the equivalent Latin term) for discovering ideas in the mind and then making something out of them. Throughout this text we suggest procedures for helping you to discover what you think about a topic. We provide you with heuristics, some of which may work for you, others of which may not, to find out what you think and then to clarify these ideas for yourself and others. Heuristics and *eureka* come from the same Greek root. Strategies for inventing questions will sometimes lead to that flash of insight that makes us shout, "Eureka, I've found it!"

Please remember that a heuristic is a strategy, not a rule. No one can provide you with a simple set of rules for writing. You can learn the conventions of Standard Written English usage and then consult a handbook when you need to refresh your memory, but writing according to those conventions will produce only correct writing, not good writing. Because there are no rules for good writing, it cannot be taught in the same way that multiplication is taught. Once students learn the principles of multiplication, they can do any problem in multiplication, if they concentrate and keep their minds on what they are doing. Writing is different. Students can know the principles of good writing—clarity, logical development, attention to audience—and still have a great deal of difficulty on a particular writing task. The heuristics presented in the next chapter and the suggestions that we make throughout this text will help you to find strategies suited to your own style of working. We also hope that you will develop flexibility in selecting different strategies to solve different problems.

Chapter 2 deals specifically with private writing, the writing that you do to clarify ideas for yourself. This text as a whole emphasizes the value of using writing as a mode of discovery. The second section of chapter 2 shows you how to use logic to find ideas and to test the ideas that you find. In subsequent chapters we give significant attention to communicating your discoveries to others; once we identify communication as a major goal, writing becomes a much more complex task.

The writer is bombarded with numerous considerations, all vying for his attention simultaneously. Table 1.1 presents a list of the various elements involved in any act of public writing. The elements at the top of the list—ideas, audience, and genre—require the most thought because

TABLE 1.1
*Priorities of choice and
convention in the
writing process*

Choices

Thematic focus and ideas	Choose subject, modes of discourse, and thematic design for generating and organizing ideas; integrate details or examples from observation, reading, or other sources of knowledge.
Rhetorical aims and attitudes	Have specific readers or audience in mind and their expectations regarding the subject and writer; be consistent in your point of view, tone, and style.
Genre or type of writing project	Determine the kind of writing required for the subject, circumstances, and audience; complexities may range from a simple personal note to intricacies of artistic form, such as short story or sonnet.
Structural format and coherence	Use transitional devices, paragraphing, subsections, subheads, typeface, or other reader-based structural devices, composition components, and manuscript conventions.
Syntax	Maintain logical word order, grammatical structure, coordination, subordination, and effective closure of independent or sentence units.
Diction	Choose words that convey meaning and style accurately and effectively; refer to a standard college dictionary.
Standard written English	Use the dialect and conventions of standard written discourse as distinguished from idiom or irregular patterns of speech.
Spelling and punctuation	Use standard orthography and conventional graphic devices of mechanics and punctuation; do not neglect final editing.
Copying and proofreading	Use legible handwriting or accurate typing, the motor skills of written composition, and proofread the final draft or copy for scribal errors.

Conventions

Source: This table was adapted from the work of Professor Ellen Nold of Stanford University by Professor William Bracy, chairperson of the Beaver College English Department.

these are the areas of widest choice. As the arrows indicate, the next three items—format, syntax, and diction—allow for more limited choice, since these matters are determined in part by customs within each discipline, by the constraints of the language, and by the writer's other choices about genre and audience. At the bottom of the list are those elements that are governed entirely by conventions—rules that every writer accepts about usage, spelling, punctuation, and typing. Writing would be much easier if we could deal with each element in its turn, but we can't. No one writes according to a nine-step linear procedure, but in any act of public writing we must manage all nine considerations of choice and convention.

As you can probably verify from your own experience, the human mind rebels against dealing with so many diverse problems simultaneously. Psychologists refer to the situation as "cognitive overload." When you look carefully at the various factors that any writer must juggle, it seems remarkable that anybody can write at all.

One reason that people can write at all is that they have learned to make routine a number of the elements in the writing process. No one could drive a gear-shift car safely if he had to think about the process with every change of gears. And no one could write anything worth reading if he had to think about how many loops to make in an *m*. Most college writers, for example, mastered penmanship long ago, or if they have not mastered it to the point that they don't have to think about it, they have learned to type.

Penmanship and typing involve very few choices. We have to learn the accepted ways to write or type legibly, and that's that. Spelling and punctuation also offer very little room for choice. Practice helps, but even those who have mastered spelling, punctuation, and the conventions of standard grammar will sometimes make mistakes. Expert writers in the throes of creativity have been known sometimes to forget the proper agreement between subject and verb.

Other elements in the writing process can also be made a matter of routine. If you are filling in printed forms, then you do not have to make decisions about structure, format, or coherence. On the other hand, some writers make the mistake of regarding their thematic focus and ideas as matters of routine, and they consequently produce a series of prefabricated phrases that they have written many times before and that no one, including themselves, wants to read again.

Routine does not always work for reducing the cognitive overload in the writing process. It is, therefore, very important to learn how to pay attention to just a few things at a time, to organize your efforts so that you are not always trying to juggle nine things at once. In the second major division of this text, chapters 6–14, we assume that you will be writing *multiple drafts* of important projects. We divide our discussions of each type of paper into sections entitled "Getting Started," "Writing the First Draft," and "Revising." Few writers arrange their activities in a neat linear way, not even according to the suggestions presented in this book. Still, we believe that it might be useful to refer to the sample procedures presented here whenever you are confronted with a writing task of some complexity. We define below the considerations that might draw the major portion of your attention at each stage.

Getting started

You have just heard the news that a paper is due. First decide, or ask your instructor, what kind of paper it is. You know what course the paper is assigned for, so begin by turning to the appropriate section of this book: the humanities, the social sciences, or the natural sciences. If the assignment is to write a term paper, you will want to consult chapters 6, 9, or 14. If the assignment is to write a case study or to report findings, consult chapters 10, 11, or 13. If the assignment requires you to analyze or to critique a literary, graphic, theatrical, or musical work, consult chapter 7. If you are asked to write a book review, the latter part of chapter 7 should help. The papers of contemplation described in chapter 8 are frequently assigned in philosophy and history courses, so we have classified them with assignments in the humanities, but these papers may also be assigned in any course in which the instructor wants you to take a philosophical approach to your material. Whenever you are asked to examine a specific problem, check to see if chapter 8 might help. Instructors in business administration, political science, economics, sociology, and anthropology often assign papers of contemplation without calling them by that name.

Once you have determined the nature of your assignments, read the appropriate "Getting Started" sections. If the assignment is to do a term paper, you will need to consult chapters 4 and 5 for help in finding and using library resources. You will also begin to refine your topic to a manageable problem for research. The invention techniques discussed in chapter 2, "Writing to See and to Think," will help you to clarify your thinking at this stage. These heuristics will also help you to get started on the tasks that require careful observation: case studies and reports of findings. Getting started on papers of analysis and contemplation may be the most difficult of all, so instead of staring at a blank sheet of paper, try some of the aids to seeing and thinking described in chapter 2.

Writing the first draft

What are the processes that writers use to transform lists of observations, summaries of library research, and fragments of brilliant ideas into the sentences and paragraphs of connected discourse? Of all the procedures we describe in this text, we find it most difficult to illuminate the mysteries of writing a first draft. Some writers use fully formed sentences and paragraphs as a heuristic. They write what we might call a zero, or discovery, draft because in the process of seeking ways to connect sentences, these writers discover the structure of their ideas. Other writers need to try out possible connections by treeing their ideas (see chapter 2) or by making a rough outline. Still others like to shuffle, rearrange, and otherwise manipulate their notecards, almost as if their paper were a jigsaw puzzle.

Whatever method you use, your main task in writing a first draft is to find connections and to write something that seems to have a beginning, middle, and end. We say "seems to have" because very few writers can write an adequate introductory paragraph in a first draft. Before you can introduce your paper successfully you first have to write your paper. A first draft is usually a version of the middle of your paper. Students often waste many agonizing hours trying to write the perfect first paragraph. In most instances it is better simply to begin writing with the assumption that you will eventually throw out or rework your first few paragraphs.

Your finished paper will be much more readable if you can restrain yourself from investing too much time and energy too early in the drafting process. Successful papers are not written; they are rewritten. You will have more time and energy left to rewrite if you have not tried to write perfect prose on your first draft. You will also be more willing to cut and paste your manuscript if you have not tried to make it look neat and beautiful too early. Most beautiful things have looked messy in their early stages. Ask any studio art major!

It is most important to remember, as you push out the first draft, that you are involved in a creative process. Students sometimes make a false distinction between academic writing and "creative" writing. They assume that only the writing of fiction, poetry, or drama is a creative activity. And frequently the literary writing of these students is more fanciful than creative. Imagining purple elephants on Broadway is much easier than imagining the preconceptions that practicing sociologists might bring to the reading of your paper on race relations. Writing academic papers is a challenging and rewarding process. Beginning writers do not realize that professional writers often take a long time to get started on a project and that they expect to revise many times. Beginners and professionals both must craft their meaning stage by stage in the creative process of getting thoughts down in words.

In academic writing, as in other creative processes, it is important to plan a period of incubation, a time when you simply stop writing and do something else while you let your mind continue to work on the problems of the paper. Students frequently neglect to allow enough time for incubation, or they go to the other extreme and count too much on the powers of the mysterious unconscious. Once again, the key to an efficient use of time is planning. Allow enough time for your project so that you can stop and do other things after a period of sustained work. It is best to stop at a point in your draft where you have explicitly articulated the next problem that you must deal with. Then, while you engage in other activities, your unconscious mind can be working on that problem. When I wrote the first draft of this chapter, I stopped after the section that discusses academic writing as a creative process. At that point, I wrote this note to myself: "Go on to discuss incubation. Connect idea of incubation to idea of academic writing as creative." Then, as I made breakfast for my children, my mind could work on that point, with no conscious effort on my part. As a result, I was eager to return to my desk, for I knew quite specifically what was to be done next, and I found that I could write more fluently on this next point because of the brief period of unrelated activity.

A period of rest is particularly important after you have completed a first draft, because a lapse in time will help you to see your writing as others might see it. There is nothing wrong about using a first draft to clarify your ideas for yourself. In fact, a helpful way to get yourself to write the connected sentences and paragraphs of a first draft is to admit to yourself quite candidly that your purpose at this stage is to talk to yourself. Professor Linda Flower of Carnegie-Mellon University uses the term "writer-based prose" to refer to egocentric writing of this kind. She points out that egocentrism at this stage is not selfishness, but instead a strategy of first expressing ideas in a form accessible and useful to the writer before trying to transform these ideas to meet the needs of a reader.[2] On complex projects you should permit yourself some early egocentrism, which will pay off later in a more readable finished paper.

Writer-based prose focuses more on the writer—his feelings, his discovery process—than on the information or on the needs of a reader to understand that information. Nearly all formal, academic writing must finally focus on the communication of information and concepts, but recording your responses and telling about your procedures will give you a chance later to manipulate your information in written form. Too often beginning writers tax their short-term memory by trying to do complicated verbal manipulations without the aid of pencil and paper. These same students would not be ashamed at all to ask for pencil and paper if they were presented with a problem in long division, but when confronted with a writing task, which is more complex because it is less well defined than a problem in numerical calculations, students try too hard to skip steps, to do long division in their heads.

Many students need to learn to let the writer-based prose flow freely on their early drafts, which are not written to be assessed by readers anyway. A draft of writer-based prose can be mined very productively for hidden structures which can serve as organizing principles for later drafts. Writer-based prose also tends to be filled with the writer's own private language. Just as writers need to search through first drafts for personal abbreviations and then on later drafts write out these words in full, writers should also look for conceptual abbreviations, concepts that are merely referred to rather than explored, and write these out in full for the reader.

2 "Writer-Based Prose: A Cognitive Basis for Problems in Writing," *College English*, 41 (September 1979), 19–37.

First drafts are often, quite legitimately, lacking in sufficient context, structured as narratives (simply telling what you did or what the book said in a chronological order), or even structured according to associations that are meaningless to anyone but you. The important point is not to feel guilty if your first draft is writer-based. Just leave yourself enough time for revision.

Revising

To revise means literally "to see again." The key task during the revision process is to see your paper as others will see it. Courses in oral communication always emphasize that a speaker must anticipate the needs of an audience. You should imagine an audience for academic writing, too, but that audience is less concrete and specific than the group of faces that a speaker confronts. Since your instructor will read and assess your finished paper, you may decide to imagine him as your only reader. If you limit your imagination of audience in this way, you will immediately encounter difficulties. How can a writer convey information to a reader who already has more information than the writer? Unless you expand your idea of audience, you will at best tend to gloss over important points because the teacher has fully explained them in class, or at worst, you may find yourself too intimidated to write at all.

In most cases you will be better off if you imagine a group of readers that includes your instructor and your classmates in the course. The imagined presence of the instructor should keep you from lapsing into slang and remind you to follow the conventions of the appropriate academic discipline, and the imagined presence of your classmates should keep your explanations clear and sufficient.

If you are lucky, your instructor may give you an official opportunity to share your preliminary drafts with classmates. Few things are more valuable to a writer than hearing readers' responses. But if your class uses a system of peer collaboration, you may sometimes feel frustrated because some of your classmates are "misreading" your paper. Don't be defensive. Listen attentively to all comments and then decide later which comments to accept and which to reject. In writing, as in life, you will get some good advice and some bad advice, and it's helpful to use the composition classroom to practice discriminating between the two.

The responses of a real audience will help you to see quite clearly the differences between writer-based and reader-based prose. You will find that there is frequently a subtle battle going on between a writer and a reader, with each one trying to expend the lesser amount of energy. When you have a stake in getting your information or ideas across, you are entering a buyer's market, and you should learn all that you can about accommodating the needs of your buyers, your readers.

Your readers, above all, want to know your point in writing, and they want to know this point as efficiently as possible. They do not want to wade through a chronological account of your research process. They need to be reminded frequently of what you are talking about. If you want them to connect two ideas, you have to do the work of forming the connection. Finally, they do not want to be distracted by clumsy sentence structure, misapplied marks of punctuation, inaccurate spelling, or careless proofreading.

Here are some techniques to try when you revise your paper. In later chapters we provide advice that is especially useful in revising particular kinds of papers, but the following procedures may be generally useful:

- Go through your early draft and "interview" each paragraph by asking, "What is the point of this paragraph?" Write that idea in the margin.

- Use these points, which you have abstracted from your early draft, to make an outline showing the hierarchy of your ideas.

- Sometimes these points simply have to be added to the paragraph as it is already written, or perhaps you will have to write an additional paragraph. Sometimes you will discover that a paragraph has no point; get rid of the paragraph.

- After a careful reading of your early draft, you will frequently see possibilities for reorganization. Photocopy your draft and then use a scissors to cut it apart and rearrange the pieces on another sheet of paper. This process will also give you a chance to try out some new connections.

- Do not be reluctant to repeat key words, especially words that name concepts. Avoid using "this" or "that" without a following noun. Avoid: "King Charles soon discovered this." Prefer: "King Charles soon discovered this plot."

- Use a conveniently indexed handbook of grammar and usage. You will discover in such a handbook that the semicolon, for example, has a finite and predictable number of uses. If you have a problem with semicolons, you can check your use of semicolons in the handbook.

- Proofread carefully for spelling. Even if you have special problems with spelling, you may be surprised to discover that your errors fall in certain predictable categories. Learn your own pattern of error.

- Proofread carefully for typographical errors. You may not be a super typist, but it is your responsibility to find and correct all typing errors. Very few instructors will object to neatly penned-in corrections. Remember, too, that it is difficult to see typographical errors in a paper that is by now nauseatingly familiar to you. Professional writers often read their final draft aloud. Some even force themselves to read it backwards so that they have a chance to find those errors that, as Professor Mina Shaughnessy says, "carry messages that writers can't afford to send."[3]

3 *Errors and Expectations* (New York: Oxford Univ. Press, 1977), p. 12.

In chapters 3 and 12 we discuss classroom writing, which does not necessitate all the steps listed above. In chapters 4 and 5 we present suggestions for using writing to make efficient and effective use of academic resource materials. But in chapters 6–11 and 13–14, when we discuss those major writing assignments that are presented to you to help you to learn what it means to be a scholar in each discipline, you will find that we give specific advice for "Getting Started," "Writing the First Draft," and "Revising." As you read those chapters, you may want to look back again at this one.

Our focus on the writing process and on strategies for making choices at each stage of composition is, we think, consistent with the spirit of the arts and sciences. Experienced writers are not dogmatic. They do not try to follow a rigid formula for every writing task. They do not move in a regimented fashion from getting started to writing the first draft to revising. Experienced writers think about their readers at every stage of the writing process. Those unseen readers influence the selection of topic and controlling question as well as decisions that are made later on. But experienced writers will even temporarily abandon their audiences at moments when an inspired turn of phrase launches a flight of creative thought. In short, experienced writers feel free to make choices about how they write best in each situation, dependent mainly on the purpose of a particular act of writing.

The single most important aim of this volume is to help you to become a more confident, experienced writer, free to develop your own style of composing. Inexperienced writers, says Mina Shaughnessy, do not know how writers behave. Scholars in different disciplines behave in different ways when they write, but they all share some common characteristics. They think in terms of problems, rather than topics. Because they are always aware of their audience and its needs, they think more about effects than intentions. They seek structure and order. Consequently, they perceive significance, rather than mere sequence. They are sensitive to the nuances of language; in fact, they like to play with words. They have a tolerance for criticism and understand that an evaluation of a piece of writing is not a personal attack. Because they are not defensive, they frequently take risks.

Our hope for you as you work with this book is that you will become a more experienced writer, that through writing you will explore how various scholars think within the traditions of the arts and sciences. We believe that practice in writing throughout your curriculum will help you to play the diverse roles adopted by scholars in different disciplines. And finally, we hope that these diverse experiences in writing and reading will give you the freedom to put together for yourself your own view of the arts and sciences.

QUESTIONS   1 What are some differences between the sciences and the humanities?

2 What are your most important responsibilities before beginning to write a paper?

3 What are the main reasons for writing a rough draft?

4 What tasks deserve particular attention when you revise a paper?

5 What circumstances might legitimately require you to write only one draft of a paper?

EXERCISES **1** Suppose that you are a legislator charged with drafting a law to allow the use of genetic engineering for the purpose of reducing the number of violent and antisocial people in society. You choose to hear testimony on the law from:

> **a** a biologist
>
> **b** a historian
>
> **c** a political scientist
>
> **d** a philosopher
>
> **e** a psychologist
>
> **f** a criminologist.

Identify the perspective that you would expect each of them to adopt when addressing the problem. What questions would you ask each scholar?

2 Suppose you are a television station manager who is arranging a special discussion on whether or not marihuana should be legalized. What academic disciplines would you want represented on the panel to insure a full and fair discussion? Explain your choices.

3 In this chapter we have drawn a distinction between those skills that are entirely rule-governed (typewriting, multiplication) and those that are best learned by devising strategies and employing them creatively. Compare and contrast writing with playing chess, driving a car, playing bridge, and putting together a model airplane from a kit.

4 You are scheduled to address four different groups on the topic of feminism. Although you will present essentially the same information to each of the groups, identify the ways that you would change your presentation in each case. The groups are:

> **a** your classmates, who are also working on individual research projects
>
> **b** the National Organization for Women
>
> **c** the Society of American Historians
>
> **d** the National Anti-Feminist League.

2 Writing to See and to Think

Learning about a subject means more than memorizing axioms, dates, and formulas. You need also to develop general intellectual skills that will allow you to understand your discipline in its entirety, that is, to approach it intelligently, knowing what questions to ask, where to discover answers to those questions, and, finally, how to develop and organize your own ideas about the subject. A body of knowledge about the discipline is fundamental, but a student of any subject should also learn how to acquire and interpret additional knowledge. This chapter describes and discusses the ways in which writing can help you to learn, to think about, and to understand the disciplines in the arts and sciences.

To use facts and ideas, you must store them in your memory in a way that allows you to retrieve them when you need them. The complex working of the human memory remains to a considerable extent mysterious, but we do know some facts about memory, and these are important to how you ought to study. We know that the number of isolated facts that can be remembered is quite small. We know that they can be remembered only if they are constantly gone over, rehearsed. We also know that new material can be learned only by absorbing it into material and concepts already held in the memory. These facts, provided by cognitive psychology, suggest the value of writing to learning, for writing can be the tool by which you can engage in the constant rehearsal necessary for successful integration of new material into old.

The new understanding of learning that we have gained from cognitive psychology—that to learn is to absorb new information into preexisting patterns of thought—stands in opposition to the older view that students, like robots, can learn just by sitting down and memorizing several chapters at a time. We now believe that to learn new material, you must work with it, must give it some kind of structure. You must represent it to yourself in some way, whether it be visually or metaphorically or just in an outline. What is essential is some active involvement with the material. Writing about the material provides the active involvement.

Another characteristic of memory is that embedded within it is both a great deal of factual information and the capacity for organizing that information. Locked away in your gray matter are assets you are probably not aware of and, therefore, are not using. The strategies discussed in this chapter can help you to get into that "great raveled knot" and use its resources.

In short, writing is one of the most important intellectual activities that you do in college, for writing is not simply a method of communicating what you know about a subject; it is an extremely useful tool for assisting you in a variety of academic tasks, from observation to argument. From making simple lists to analyzing and synthesizing complex data, intellectual functions, especially the more complex ones, "seem to develop most fully only with the support system of verbal language—particularly, it seems, written language."[1] The most useful writing in this kind of learning is what we call "private" writing, that is, writing that you do for yourself.

Some characteristics of private writing

To appreciate fully the value of writing to your education, you may have to overcome some prejudices that exist in most students. Foremost among these is the belief that writing is a one-dimensional skill to be learned only for the purpose of communicating what you know so that an instructor can grade it. This view is not only limiting, it is destructive, for it reinforces patterns that make writing a chore to be avoided or, at best, tolerated. It is important to think of private writing as you would think of a painter's sketchpad. Before many painters apply paint to canvas, they sketch out some ideas in draft form. They use their sketchpad to try out many different ways of seeing and shaping their material.

Private writing, like the sketchpad, will be of little use, however, unless you appreciate its value and learn how to use it effectively. There are ways to increase the usefulness of your private writing. First, you should always keep in mind that writing to see and to think is intended for your eyes only. It will not be graded, so suspend the rules of writing. Don't worry about spelling and grammar; don't stop to rewrite parts, not even those that you know would be unacceptable to an instructor. It has been said, "Your editorial instinct is often much better developed than your producing instinct."[2] You might be one of the people who have to concentrate consciously on "turning off your internal editor," that nagging voice reminding you of all the possible things that you might do wrong.

1 Janet Emig, "Writing as a Mode of Learning," *College Composition and Communication*, 28 (May 1977), 122.
2 Peter Elbow, *Writing Without Teachers* (New York: Oxford Univ. Press, 1973), p. 25.

One way to gain a reprieve from this voice is to practice "freewriting," that is, writing whatever comes to your mind without going back to read, edit, or correct any of it. The purpose of this practice, at least ten minutes a day if possible, is to help you become more comfortable with writing and to begin to think of it as a natural part of your academic skills. Freewriting will also help you to associate writing with thinking.

Second, make writing a part of your regular study habits. Too often students think that by copying, paraphrasing, or working through an assignment on paper they are adding another step to an already time-consuming process. In fact, thinking on paper does take time, but it is time well spent. And if you learn to form and organize your thoughts more effectively, the time will justify itself.

Last, to encourage yourself to develop your private writing abilities, make space for these informal jottings. For each course, set aside a separate part of your notebook or carry with you a notepad to be used exclusively for freewriting. You will find it more useful to keep all your private writing for a course in one place since you can then look through it all together, and you can turn to it quickly when you want to write. There may be greater frustrations than not remembering where you wrote something down, but few are as irritating.

The private journal

The best way to create thinking space is to keep a journal. For a long time instructors in some disciplines have required students to keep these informal written records. Composition teachers use them to teach students to write down thoughts and observations that might be turned into essays, as places for "expressive" writing or "reflective" writing. Subjects such as sociology, psychology, and education often rely on logs, running records by students of their observations in the field. But journals, separate notebooks for your private writing, need not be used only for assigned academic tasks. Their real value may well be as permanent, cumulative records of your thoughts as you work through intellectual problems.

Journals are not class notebooks, where you record others' ideas; nor are they diaries, where the emphasis is largely on one's personal experiences and reactions to the day-to-day world. They are places where you can generate and think through ideas for paper topics, work out a problem presented in class, log experiences that are a part of a course, record thoughts and insights that you think might be useful, but are not exactly sure how. Journals are kept to record dialogues you have with yourself in your academic life.

Naturally, the degree to which and the ways in which you use a journal are up to you, but experience has taught that the more one writes, the more useful a journal is. If you record observations, you may notice over weeks or months patterns forming that may stimulate you to think freshly about the subject observed; if you jot down questions that come to you in lectures or in your reading, you may well come back to them for paper topics later in a semester. In short, journals can be used to keep records of the ideas, reactions, questions, and random thoughts that come up during any semester.

Another use of a journal is to copy passages from materials you read. It is, of course, time consuming to copy a great deal of material, but especially difficult parts of articles, book chapters, or poems can profitably be copied. The simple act of slowly recording the exact words of an author can often impart meaning that you did not see when you first read them. A journal can also serve as a permanent repository of your favorite lines and passages.

Beyond copying, you might find summarizing a useful way to understand a difficult written piece. Summarizing, like copying, has often been overlooked as a way of learning, probably because in addition to being more time consuming than underlining, it appears to be an old-fashioned form of busywork devoid of real value. Quite to the contrary, summarizing fits almost all of the requirements of a good intellectual exercise: it forces you to make hard choices, to find the essence of an argument, to identify and select from among the subordinate parts of the argument, and to reduce the piece to manageable proportions without either directly quoting or losing the tone of the author. (See chapter 5 for suggestions on summarizing.) These are challenging tasks, but the rewards are considerable. To create a helpful summary, you will have to understand what you are reading quite thoroughly. Since thorough understanding is the purpose of most reading assignments in the arts and sciences, the summary can be a good aid to learning. And when it is time to review the book or article for an examination or recitation, your summary may be the only review you need.

Use your journal to record your responses to things you have read or to conferences or discussions you have just finished. Our responses to the world are of two kinds, immediate and delayed. Often when a reader finishes a piece of writing, he has already developed some immediate responses. They may be emotional or seemingly illogical, but they will almost certainly get lost as the piece is either forgotten or thought about in more organized ways. These responses should be recorded. You may have occasion to wonder later what you thought of the piece, or you may get feedback from others and wish to incorporate that into your understanding. You may find your initial responses very useful when you go back to write about the piece in a more organized fashion. You can remember only so much; you need a written record. Similarly, after returning from a conference with your instructor, or when reading his comments on an essay or paper, record your responses to his responses. This record will be especially helpful when you write your next exam or paper.

Journals also give you a place to write out ideas from sources or from forms of presentation that are unfamiliar to you. For example, if you are primarily a verbal person working with visual materials, try to verbalize in your journal what you see. Visual information (drawings, graphs, charts, tables) needs to be interpreted to be useful. Try writing out what you see, describing, establishing relationships, seeing patterns. Having to choose adjectives and verbs may provide keys to understanding the direction of lines or the differences between two colored bars. Describing a flow chart or an organizational table forces you to identify relationships, movement, and purpose that might otherwise flow by you. This translation into connected discourse will also allow you to see gaps in your understanding.

Academic problems

While you will spend much of your time in college acquiring new information, you will spend at least as much time trying to interpret and understand that material. Many of your assignments will be designed to make you think about the subject matter presented. Thinking seriously about an academic subject requires you to do something meaningful with your material. Generally, your task is to make sense of the material, to draw conclusions about it. To develop your own understanding of facts, you need to be able to discover relationships between facts and to make assertions about those relationships.

Discovering relationships and making assertions are important steps in solving academic problems as they were defined in chapter 1. Academic problems range from assessing the impact of the French desertion from NATO to determining the composition of a chemical compound to discovering the symbolism in Yeats's "Sailing to Byzantium." Problems are focused questions. To answer these questions, you need to gather information and to think. Frequently, students gather enough information, but they do not think about it in ways that yield acceptable or complete solutions. Some of the strategies below can help you think about academic problems.

Another common difficulty students often encounter is an inability to identify or create academic problems. While the purpose of many essay examinations (chapter 3) is to pose problems for solution, one of the main purposes of paper assignments is to encourage students to formulate the problems they themselves wish to solve. Too often students try to write on a "topic," when they should be writing on a problem. A topic is a static entity, a thing, and it is possible to write anything at all about a thing. The topic "Charles II, King of England," for example, encourages unfocused research and random, wide-ranging thinking. To take as your focus a topic results in meandering, disconnected papers. One important academic ability is to generate a question out of a topic. Some of the strategies below can help you to shift your focus from what you know about a subject to what you want to know about it. For example, you could ask, "What do I want to find out about Charles II?" This movement away from your present state of knowledge to goals for future knowledge is the beginning point for the development of a problem.

Strategies The following strategies are creative ways to help you define and solve problems. Experienced writers employ them routinely and naturally. Here we have defined them and described them perhaps too formally. They are, simply, ways of thinking, of recasting and redefining problems so that they lend themselves to solutions. If these strategies seem artificial at first, it is probably because they are so structured. As you learn them and use those most helpful to you, they will become natural parts of your thinking processes.

Brainstorming Select a topic: Charles II, the Republican party, free will, *Great Expectations*, the periodic table, Athens, Expressionism, Wallace Stevens, the Panama Canal, inflation, the Bronx. Now for five minutes write down anything that comes to mind about the topic. You might begin by writing down all the possible questions you would like to ask and the fragments of knowledge you already possess about the topic. These jottings need not be organized—you just want to get your thinking down on paper.

A sheet of paper on which a student was brainstorming about Charles II might look like the notes in figure 2.1. These notes and ideas were gleaned from reading an English history textbook. The student is recording important topics and asking questions about them. Such a brainstorming sheet might produce some ideas if studied by itself, but there are several ways to use such a sheet to help organize random writing into a problem. The important point is that you have these items down in writing so that you can study them, add to them, underline them, and extract from them.

Your next step is to try to see relationships among the items recorded, for it is in relationships that you will probably discover a problem worth investigating. Here are some strategies for finding connections.

Lists Go back through your notes and pull out the key words or concepts, that is, those items that seem to be the most interesting ones to explore. A list from the sheet above (figure 2.1) might be as shown in figure 2.2.

Try to see relationships. Ask questions. For example, as a king, Charles was lazy, was a ladies' man, didn't get along with Parliament, and had secret relationships with Louis XIV of France. Why didn't he like Puritans and Parliament? Was Parliament made up of Puritans? How could he be lazy and enter into those secret relationships with Louis XIV? Did Louis XIV help him against Parliament and the Puritans?

This writer is moving toward some questions that are at once more concrete and complex than those on the brainstorming sheet.

Explaining statements of fact Select a fact. Then see if you can create a list of items that might explain it. For example, you might select the item, "Charles II was restored to his

Charles II, was he a good king?
Catholicism. Louis XIV of France. He was
supposed to be a ladies' man. Restoration
to his throne 1660. Where was he before?
Was 30 years old in 1660 — Two wars against
Dutch. Why? Didn't like the Puritans. Why
not? Textbook said he was lazy, wasn't a
strong king. I wonder why not? What did
he do until he was 30 years old? Married
a Portugese princess? Clarendon Code against
Puritans. Did not get along with Parliament?
Why not? Took bribes from Louis XIV. Popish
plot against Anglicanism. Treaty of Dover 1670
— Meet with Louis XIV, etc., etc. Did this
meeting lead to Popish plot? Was Louis XIV
Catholic?

FIGURE 2.1

FIGURE 2.2

good king
ladies' man
Restoration —
　30 years old
against Puritans

lazy
did not get along
　with Parliament
bribes from Louis XIV
secret treaty of Dover

throne in 1660, when he was 30 years old," and then try to relate other
items to it by forming questions such as: Was he lazy because he became
king when he was thirty years old? Was his attitude toward the Puritans
caused by what happened before the Restoration? Was his attitude towards
Parliament and Louis XIV caused by what happened during his first thirty
years? Such questions lead to other questions: How was Charles II restored

FIGURE 2.3

to his throne? What happened during his first thirty years? What was the effect of those thirty years on his rule when he was restored?

Treeing a topic Since you are interested in trying to find relationships, you might try creating a topic tree, the purpose of which is to see the connections among several items and to establish dominant and subordinate relationships. The working out of a topic tree can help you see different kinds of relationships and can be especially valuable if you are a visually oriented person. (You do not need to explain the relationship, just that it might exist.)

A tree generated from the brainstorming sheet on Charles II might look like figure 2.3. This tree is based on a simple question: "Who were the people with whom Charles II worked?" The tree contains very little information, but even with just these four entries, you can begin to ask further questions about the connections among them. Do they all belong in the same category? Can you find differences in Charles's relationships to the others? Well, an obvious difference is that he was hostile to the Puritans and to Parliament but friendly with Louis XIV. You now have subcategories to add to the tree (placed in parentheses in the tree in Figure 2.4). These subcategories encourage you to ask a further question: Are there others with whom Charles II was friendly or hostile? Looking over your brainstorming sheet, you might want to add that Charles seemed to be friendly with Catholics. The tree is beginning to fill up (figure 2.4).

You now have a basis for asking a "why" question. Why was Charles hostile towards the Puritans and Parliament and friendly to Louis XIV?

Charles II

(hostile)   (friendly)

Puritans   *Parliament*   *Louis XIV*   *Catholics*

FIGURE 2.4

Are the causes related? Looking back over the material you have written down, you try to pick out possible causes (Dutch wars, exile, Restoration, Catholicism) and fit them into the tree. Some additional directed reading to find if relationships between these items and those on the tree exist may be necessary for a better understanding of the topic. A revised tree (figure 2.5) might reflect the discovery that the Puritans in Parliament had forced the young Charles II into exile and had lopped off his father's head and also that the secret Treaty of Dover with Louis XIV called for a Dutch war and the establishment of Catholicism in England.

These known relationships generate a lot of questions, among them, why did Charles think that siding with Louis XIV and with Catholics in England would protect him against Parliament? If you were aware of Charles's experiences in exile, you might wonder how they influenced his performance as king. The revised tree—the plan for your paper—looks like figure 2.6.

The topic tree allows you to develop an overview of Charles II's reign. Having worked out some basic relationships, you will see a problem in Charles's policies. You might pose the problem in a variety of ways:

1 Why did Charles II establish a close relationship with Louis XIV when his Parliament was hostile to Louis XIV?

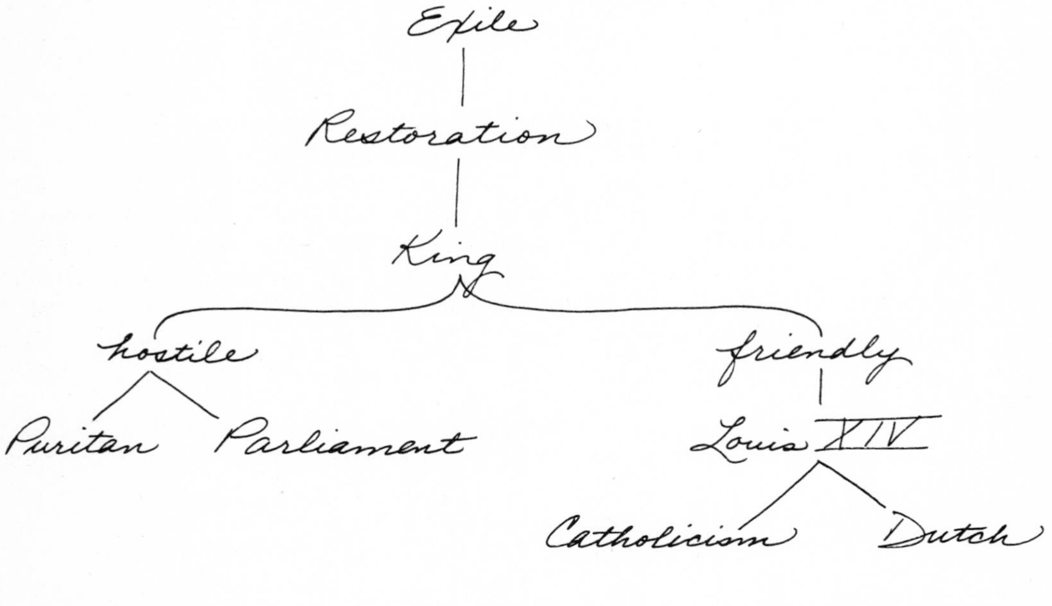

FIGURE 2.5

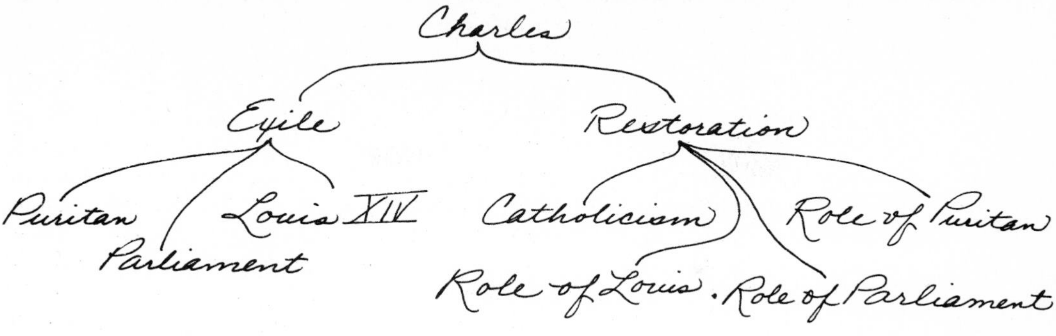

Charles

Exile   *Restoration*

Puritan Parliament   *Louis XIV*   *Catholicism*   *Role of Puritan*

Role of Louis · *Role of Parliament*

FIGURE 2.6

2 What was the role of foreign policy (or religious policy) in Charles II's relationship with Parliament?

Seeing another relationship, you might form the question: "In what ways were Charles II's foreign and religious policies as king of England influenced by his experiences while in exile?"

Word associations, analogy, metaphor

Another useful way to think about a topic is to compare it to something else. You will find a source for an analogy in word associations. Let us say that you are trying to write on the topic of the American presidency in the seventies. Your train of word associations might look like this: *presidents, Nixon, Ford, Carter, peanuts, Watergate, power, charisma, celebrity.* With the word *celebrity* you have the possibility for an analogy. You might learn something about the informal powers of the American president by comparing the president's role, point by point, with the role of a public figure from the sports or entertainment worlds. The responsibility of the president differs greatly from that of others who appeal to the multitude, yet viewing the American president as a crowd-pleaser, a *People* magazine figure, may help you to see your topic from a new angle.

When your general topic involves an abstract concept, look for a concrete comparison. Sometimes you will discover new ideas about your topic if you set out on purpose to compare it to something that seems quite different on the surface. Is there any common ground, for example, between learning to write and learning to ski? Both are complex processes that involve coordinating a great diversity of activities. Both processes involve taking risks. And with enough motivation and dedication, most individuals can learn both processes, although individuals will differ greatly in the degree of agility that they will eventually develop. By seeing the abstract intellectual process of learning to write in terms of the concrete, physical process of learning to ski, you give yourself a chance—through metaphor—to develop fresh ideas on the subject.

Seeing a topic as a particle, wave, or field

Young, Becker, and Pike, in *Rhetoric: Discovery and Change*,[3] suggest that you look at a topic as a particle (a thing, or a static entity); as a wave (a process); and as a field (a system of relationships). We suggest their excellent book for a full discussion of this idea, but we will introduce this heuristic as a way of helping you to see and think about a topic.

These three perspectives help you to see your topic in a new way and to generate fruitful questions for your research or contemplation. Consider again the topic of King Charles II of England. An experienced historian is trained to explore this topic from a variety of angles. Particle, wave, field questions give you a structure by which you can discover questions that a historian asks naturally.

Particle. What are the implications of viewing Charles II as a particle? First of all, you are interested in him alone. What kind of a king was he? What were the effects on him of his father's execution or his subsequent exile for ten years? What was his private life like? What kind of personality did he have? Any of these problems, if researched, could be organizational ideas for a paper or could become part of a larger paper on Charles II.

Wave. Thinking of Charles II as a wave is trying to see him as part of a continuum or a process. Where does he fit into that which went before or came after him. How did his foreign policy compare with that of Oliver Cromwell? How successful was his reign in comparison to other Stuart kings? Where does Charles II's reign fit into the English struggle for civil liberties? What was his role in the development of the English empire?

Field. To see Charles as part of a field is to look at him in a context, as part of a network. What was his relationship with Louis XIV of France? What was the opinion of Charles among European monarchs? What was his relationship with Puritanism and Catholicism? What were his political or foreign policies?

Asking who? what? where? when? and why? about a topic

If you have studied journalism or worked on your school newspaper, you have already been introduced to the questions that are the journalist's tools of the trade: Who? What? Where? When? Why? You may not have realized that these questions are heuristics, strategies to help the journalist record and organize the facts about an event. These questions have wide applications to your thinking about all your academic subjects. Even though they are familiar and obvious, these questions can still be useful.

The problems explored below in our description of Kenneth Burke's pentad are similar to the journalist's questions, although Burke combines Where? and When? into a single question about *scene* and then adds the question of how? (which he calls the *means,* or *agency*).

3 Richard E. Young, Alton L. Becker, and Kenneth L. Pike, *Rhetoric: Discovery and Change* (New York: Harcourt Brace Jovanovich, 1970).

Seeing a topic as an action, actor-agent, scene, means, purpose

Kenneth Burke, a twentieth-century rhetorician, has developed a way of looking at a topic in dramatic terms. Because his plan involves five different perspectives, he calls it a pentad. You may want to read Kenneth Burke's own explanation of this system in his "Introduction" to A *Grammar of Motives*.[4] You may also want to look at William F. Irmscher's explanation and application of Burke's system in *The Holt Guide to English*.[5] W. Ross Winterowd, in *The Contemporary Writer: A Practical Rhetoric*,[6] applies the pentad specifically to the analysis of published pieces of writing. Here we intend to present only a brief overview of Burke's suggestions for viewing a topic as a dramatic action.

Burke's dynamic view of topics forces you to add a predicate to any topic name. When you employ the pentad, you can no longer write generally on Charles II. You first have to think of an *action* involving Charles II. Then you can look at the *actors* or *agents* (the people performing the action). You can next look at the *scene* (the setting in which the action takes place), the *agency*, or *means* (the ways that the actors have used to achieve their purposes), and finally, at the *purpose* itself (the point of all this activity).

If, for example, you have decided to write a history paper about Charles II, you must begin by thinking about an action involving Charles II. A likely choice might be the signing of the secret Treaty of Dover in 1670. As you think about that action, you will recognize that you must consider an additional agent. Charles II of England signed the Treaty of Dover with Louis XIV of France. Just this initial consideration of *action* and *actors* raises fruitful questions to help you to generate ideas. The image of the two actors leads to questions about characterization. What kind of person was Charles II? Louis XIV? What kind of people were they when they interacted? Consideration of the action, the signing of the secret treaty, leads to questions about the specific details of the event. But questions about an action involve more than what was done in deed. What was done in thought? What sort of planning, conspiring, or imagining took place as part of this event?

Questions about the *scene* lead you to focus on the time and place of the action. What was England like in 1670? What was Dover like? What else was going on as the backdrop to this historic event?

Questions about the *means* or *agency* will lead you to study the bargaining that went on between Charles and Louis to insure Charles an annual income from France and to encourage Louis to look forward to the establishment of Catholicism in England.

4 Berkeley, Calif.: Univ. of California Press, 1969.
5 *The Holt Guide to English: A Contemporary Handbook of Rhetoric, Language, and Literature*, 2nd ed. (New York: Holt, Rinehart & Winston, 1976), pp. 27–45.
6 New York: Harcourt Brace Jovanovich, 1975.

Finally, your question about *purpose* will help you to explore Charles's determination to free himself from Parliament and Louis's desire to encourage the spread of Catholicism. You may suspect other purposes as well. Did each king believe that this treaty would extend his own personal power?

This pentad provides a structure for you to pursue an idea to a logical conclusion. Instead of simply deciding to write about Charles II or about the Treaty of Dover and then reading about the topic with no specific questions in mind, the pentad can help you to organize your thinking and your notecards. You will be better prepared to read actively, to think through the situation to causes, means, and implications. The questions in the pentad will help you to organize what you read and then to discover what you still need to know. Even after pursuing all the questions in the example, you still need to find out whether the Treaty of Dover was ever put into effect. What happened? But now at least you have developed a specific line of inquiry, and you can apply the pentad again to explore the resulting actions.

Seeing your topic as X and then asking questions about it

Burke's dramatic view of a topic requires active questioning, and this active questioning is a necessary step in seeing and thinking about your topic. In chapter 1 we suggested that different disciplines define themselves in terms of the questions that they pose about experience. Knowing the appropriate questions to ask about a topic displays your understanding of the approaches within a particular discipline. In our companion anthology, *Readings in the Arts and Sciences*, you will find an essay by Professor Bernard Mausner entitled, "The Nature of Social Science."[7] In that essay, Professor Mausner looks at Eugene O'Neill's play *Mourning Becomes Electra* from the points of view of various disciplines. In the questions listed below, substitute *Mourning Becomes Electra*—or anything else of your choice—for X, to see some of the questions that different disciplines pose about a topic.

Literary criticism
What is X about?
What are the themes of X?
What is the structure of X?
Can we view X symbolically?
What is the genre of X?
What are the sources for X?
What have other literary critics said about X?
What effect does X have on an audience?

Psychoanalysis
What does X tell us about the emotional development of children?

7 Bernard Mausner, *A Citizen's Guide to the Social Sciences* (Chicago: Nelson-Hall, 1979), pp. 1–16.

Anthropology

What does X tell us about a particular society and culture?

Sociology

What does X tell us about the interactions of social classes in a particular country at a particular time?

Political science

What does X tell us about the sources of power and the ways in which power is exercised in a particular community?

Economics

What does X tell us about the ways people work, exchange the products of their labor, and use money as a vehicle for these exchanges?

Seeing your topic graphically　　We really know very little about the way people think and see. The mind of another person is a mystery, unknowable in many fundamental ways. Different people use different means to generate and invent ideas. For some writers, invention most frequently requires words, and most of the suggestions in the preceding pages involve verbal thinking. But some people may need to see experience graphically before they can translate that experience into words. Others may need to see things numerically before they can write connected discourse. It is important to experiment with different procedures in the preliminary stages of the composing process. In this way, you will get to know your own cognitive style, your individual way of seeing and thinking about experience. In this section and in the two sections that follow, we offer some suggestions for using pictures and numbers to find out what you think and know about a topic.

Sometimes studio art majors are unnecessarily intimidated by a composition course. If you are a studio art major, try sketching your rough draft in pictures, rather than in words. Or try making a *story board* on your topic. A story board involves several graphically presented scenes, each one with a caption of a sentence or two. Most rough drafts, whether in words or pictures, tend to be episodic, anyway. You may be one of those writers who need to see your material graphically before you can write connected discourse. Reread the material on Burke's pentad. A story board necessarily treats a topic dramatically. Combine your creation of a story board with perspectives derived from Burke's view of a topic as dramatic actions.

If you are basically a visual thinker, making a *collage* may help you to generate ideas on your topic. Let us suppose that you have to write a paper on the impact of primary elections on the American system of nominating a president. It may help you to get interested in the topic if you begin by looking at or collecting pictures from old magazines of volunteers working in New Hampshire and of candidates campaigning in California.

No political science instructor or composition instructor will accept this collage in place of a paper, just as no studio art instructor will accept a paper in place of a collage. The story board, the collage, and indeed all the invention techniques suggested so far are merely means to an end, ways of getting started on the process of generating ideas on a topic.

Static and dynamic diagrams If you choose to represent a situation graphically, then the form chosen should be appropriate to the material. First we will indicate how you might diagram Aristotle's theory of government in a static diagram or table, and then how you might represent Plato's more dynamic theory in a flow chart.

Aristotle believes all states can be classified into six types depending on two considerations: the number of persons who rule the state and whether they rule well or badly. Table 2.1 shows the six types.

Plato, too, has a theory that classifies states by their form of government. But in addition his theory purports to account for how one form of government changes into another; that is, Plato's theory is a process theory. To represent this theory adequately in a diagram it would not be sufficient to give a list of his classification of states (aristocracy, timocracy, oligarchy, democracy, despotism). To show the changes his theory permits you should use a flow chart, in which arrows are used to express change. For example, see figure 2.7. So if you were assigned a paper on Plato or Aristotle, their theories could be usefully summarized in similar diagrams or tables. Of course, you would also need to define what Plato means by each term; and for this explanation you might have another diagram—see figure 2.8.

The full value of a flow chart appears when the process to be described has "feedback loops," that is, when the process does not travel just in one direction and when it can return to earlier states. Consider figure 2.9. This diagram tells you that an aristocracy can change into either a timocracy or an oligarchy. If it takes the left-hand branch, then from a timocracy it will change into despotism, then an oligarchy, then democracy, and will then return to aristocracy to oligarchy, from that to democracy, and from that back to aristocracy, where the process begins again. Notice the "feedback" from democracy to aristocracy. The diagram tells you that democracies always are preceded by oligarchies; that democracies are always followed by aristocracies; that timocracy can come

TABLE 2.1
Aristotle's classification of states

Number of rulers	True	Corrupt
One	Monarchy	Tyranny
Few	Aristocracy	Oligarchy
Many	Polity	Democracy

Source: W. T. Jones, A History of Western Philosophy, vol. 1 (New York: Harcourt, Brace & World, 1969), p. 291.

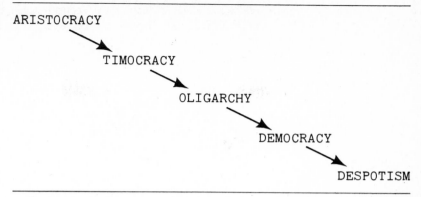

FIGURE 2.7
Plato's theory of the state.

ARISTOCRACY

TIMOCRACY

OLIGARCHY

DEMOCRACY

DESPOTISM

FIGURE 2.8
Plato's classification of states.

```
Aristocracy = rule by the best
Timocracy  = rule by the ambitious
Oligarchy  = rule by the wealthy
Democracy  = rule by the many
Despotism  = rule by a tyrant.
```

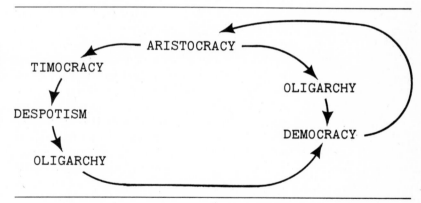

FIGURE 2.9
Flow chart of political change.

ARISTOCRACY

TIMOCRACY

OLIGARCHY

DESPOTISM

DEMOCRACY

OLIGARCHY

only from aristocracy. But an oligarchy can be preceded by either aristocracy or despotism.

Flow charts are valuable, then, in representing processes. But we will give another example of a flow chart that does not depict a process. We give it to illustrate how very complicated information can be translated from a verbal description to a diagram. The example is taken from a regulation of the U.S. Internal Revenue Service concerning whether or not you are obliged to pay social security taxes for domestic services performed by relatives. Here is the regulation:

Social security taxes now apply if you pay cash wages for domestic services to your mother or father, or your spouse's mother or father, if you meet the following conditions for at least 4 continuous weeks in a quarter: (1) you have a son or daughter (including an adopted child or stepchild) in your home who is under age 18, or who has a physical or mental condition that requires the personal care of an adult; and (2) you are either a widow (widower) or a divorced person who has not remarried; or you have a spouse in your home who, because of a physical or mental condition, is not capable of caring for the son or daughter.

What makes this difficult to read is that although it seems to have just two conditions that, if satisfied, oblige you to pay social security taxes, in fact, each of the conditions has qualifications and alternatives. To interpret it, it is best to break it down into a series of questions, each corresponding to one of the conditions mentioned in the passage, and show in a diagram (figure 2.10) the consequences of answering each question "yes" or "no." In this case there are only two consequences that count—you must pay social security taxes or you are not obliged to pay them.

In reading this chart you need only proceed until you come to a question whose answer leads you directly to the consequence on the bottom. Thus, if you answered the second question ("Do you have a child in your home?") by a "no," then you go immediately to the consequence that you are not obliged to pay. This arrow shows that having a child in the home is a necessary condition of having to pay these taxes. By contrast, the two questions on the third level—Is the child under 18?" and "Does the child have a condition that requires the care of an adult?"—are neither of them individually necessary conditions; that is, you could answer "no" to one of them and still be liable to taxation. They are jointly necessary; one of them must be answered "yes" if you are to be liable to taxation. The same is true for the questions on the fourth level of the diagram. And notice that no one of these questions represents a sufficient condition of being liable to taxes; a "yes" answer to any individual question is not by itself sufficient to make you liable.

When you are writing a paper from library sources, you will not be able to find ideas to write about until you organize the source material into forms that are usable to you. For some students the flow chart on social security taxes may be harder to read than the paragraph about the regulations. For other students, the visual form will help to clarify the information.

In this section we are concerned primarily with techniques to help you organize your information. Diagramming it in one of these ways (or one of the other ways mentioned later in chapter 11) forces you to organize

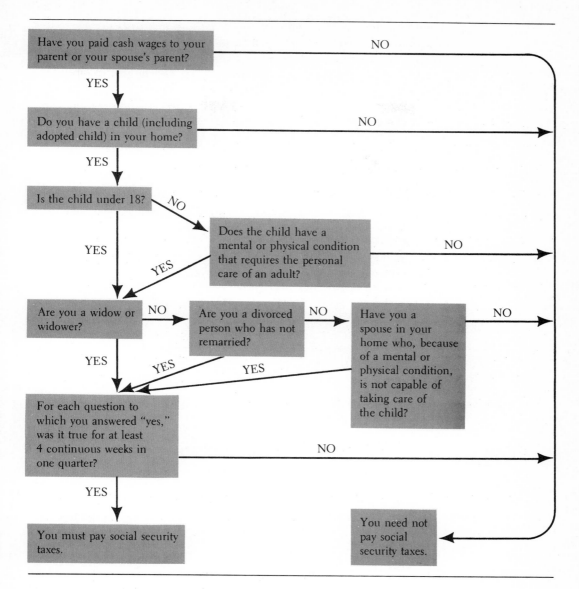

Have you paid cash wages to your parent or your spouse's parent? — NO

YES

Do you have a child (including adopted child) in your home? — NO

YES

Is the child under 18? — NO

Does the child have a mental or physical condition that requires the personal care of an adult? — NO

YES

YES

Are you a widow or widower? — NO

Are you a divorced person who has not remarried? — NO

Have you a spouse in your home who, because of a mental or physical condition, is not capable of taking care of the child? — NO

YES

YES

For each question to which you answered "yes," was it true for at least 4 continuous weeks in one quarter? — NO

YES

You must pay social security taxes.

You need not pay social security taxes.

FIGURE 2.10
Flow chart for tax regulation.

it for yourself. But you might also consider that if these diagrams help you understand the material you are working with, they may be helpful also to readers of your paper.

Seeing your topic in numbers and tables Some writers need to see a topic in unadorned numerical form before they can put together any sentences on the subject. Let us suppose that you are reading in preparation for doing a paper on "Teaching Writing to the Gifted and Talented." You have decided that you can't get far with this project until you have figured out at least a working definition of *gifted* and *talented*. You know that simple Stanford-Binet IQ scores will not be enough, but you also know that you are the sort of writer who needs to see your material first in numbers. Figure 2.11 is a first step toward writing a definition. When you actually write the first draft, you may decide not to use this numerical representation at all. The important point is to write facts and ideas down initially in the way that helps you to see and think about them.

If you do decide to use the numerical definitions in your actual paper, you must not assume that the simple presentation of numbers will be self-evident to your readers. You would have to take the additional step of translating these numbers into words and then drawing appropriate inferences from the data. For example, you might write:

> In <u>Teaching the Gifted Child</u> (1960), Gallagher identifies the academically talented, gifted, and highly gifted in terms of their scores on the Stanford-Binet IQ test. The talented are those

Talented	IQ 116+	15-20% of school pop.
Gifted	IQ 132+	2-4% of school pop.
Highly gifted	IQ 140+	0.1% of school pop.

Figures from Gallagher (1960)

FIGURE 2.11

who score 116 or above on the test, and this group includes 15–20 percent of the school population. The gifted, those who score IQ 132 or above, constitute 2–4 percent of the school population, while the highly gifted (IQ 140 or above) make up only .1 percent of the school population. Since many school systems use the Stanford–Binet test as an initial screening device, understanding the scores on this test is a first step to defining the special category of student: the gifted and talented.

Sometimes a writer who thinks numerically will present tables even more complicated than the one above, without any accompanying verbal explanation. If you are a numerical thinker, remember that many of your readers are not. You should use numbers freely to help you to see and think about your topic. Then learn to generate verbal explanations to help your readers. (See chapter 11 for help in devising tables and graphs and for developing sentences and paragraphs to explain them.)

Writing and reading as logical processes

Each of the techniques recommended in the preceding sections are ways or organizing or making sense of information you have gathered. Each encourages you to ask specific questions of the material with the purpose of revealing relationships that may not be obvious. The relationships you might find within your information are of many kinds, for the kinds of questions your readers might have in mind will vary. Thus, the heuristic used by novice journalists—who? what? where? when? and why?—helps them to keep in mind the kinds of questions their readers are likely to ask about any news item. Similarly, in academic writing, there are many different kinds of relationships to find among the items you discover. You might relate them by time (which came before the other?), or causally (which caused the other?), by classification which item is an instance and which the class?), by motivation (what motivated an action?), by function (what does a process do?), and so on.

By contrast, there is just one relationship in which logicians are interested: the relationship of evidence to a conclusion. The focus of logic is on arguments, where an argument is defined as a set of statements such that one (called the "conclusion") is said to "follow from" or to be "supported by" the others (called the "premises"). A fully explicit argument, then, has three components: the evidence (premise or premises), the conclusion, and (not to be forgotten) the claim that it is an argument. Here is an example of a simple argument that has all three components: "The butler's fingerprints were found on the murder weapon. Therefore, the butler is the murderer." The first sentence is the premise; the second is the conclusion; and the word "therefore" communicates that the relationship between them is an argument. The person writing or saying this is accusing the butler on the basis of the fingerprint evidence. To a logician, this assertion is equivalent to making two claims: the butler's fingerprints were on the weapon—that is, the premise is true; believing the premise true is a good reason for also accepting the conclusion—that is, the relationship between the premise and the conclusion is such that the evidence makes the conclusion more likely to some degree.

So of any argument you can ask two questions: Are the premises true? Does the conclusion follow from the premises? The defense attorney for the butler can defend the butler in two ways. He can reject the premise, by showing the butler's fingerprints are not on the weapon. Or he can reject the inference, by showing that the fingerprints are not sufficient evidence to convict the butler. If the attorney succeeds at either one of these, the argument is not a good one.

When you are dealing with an argument you are confronted by two problems. The first is simply to identify the argument: as a reader of another's argument, to figure out what the author intends the argument to be; or as a writer, to communicate the argument clearly to your reader. The second problem facing you is how to construct a *good* argument, or how to assess whether a stated argument is a good one or not. On the first problem, we offer here a strategy useful for identifying arguments, and we will draw from it a lesson for writing your own arguments so that your reader can understand what you are doing. A complete treatment of the second problem would take a course in logic, but we will offer some suggestions on how you might evaluate arguments as well.

The identification strategy is very similar to the method of treeing a topic. It depends upon the fact that any argument has a structure, and that the structure can be represented by arrows, so that to each arrow there corresponds an inference. Thus, the argument given above can be represented as

The butler's fingerprints are on the murder weapon.
↓
The butler is the murderer.

Nothing very illuminating is gained by building a "tree diagram" for a simple argument like this one. But take a more complicated one:

After examining the locks and the windows carefully we found no reason to believe they were forced. So it must have been an inside job. The only two people who had access to a key were Mark and Joan. So one of them must have done it. But we know that Joan could not have done it, for she was out of town that weekend—we have several witnesses to testify to that. Consequently, Mark did it.

If you represented this argument in a tree diagram, you would get figure 2.12. This diagram allows you to see that there are seven inferences made in the argument (one for each arrow), and that the whole argument depends on three basic premises, the three statements that do not have arrows leading into them. The structure indicates the questions that are appropriate to ask of each sentence. Of the three basic premises, you need to ask, "Is it true?" Of each sentence connected by an arrow to another sentence, you need to ask whether the statement at the top of the arrow is a good reason for you to believe the statement at the bottom of the arrow.

But how do you construct this diagram? You do it in two steps. First you make as much use as you can of the structural information the author gives. Then you fill in the rest of the diagram by your sense of what a

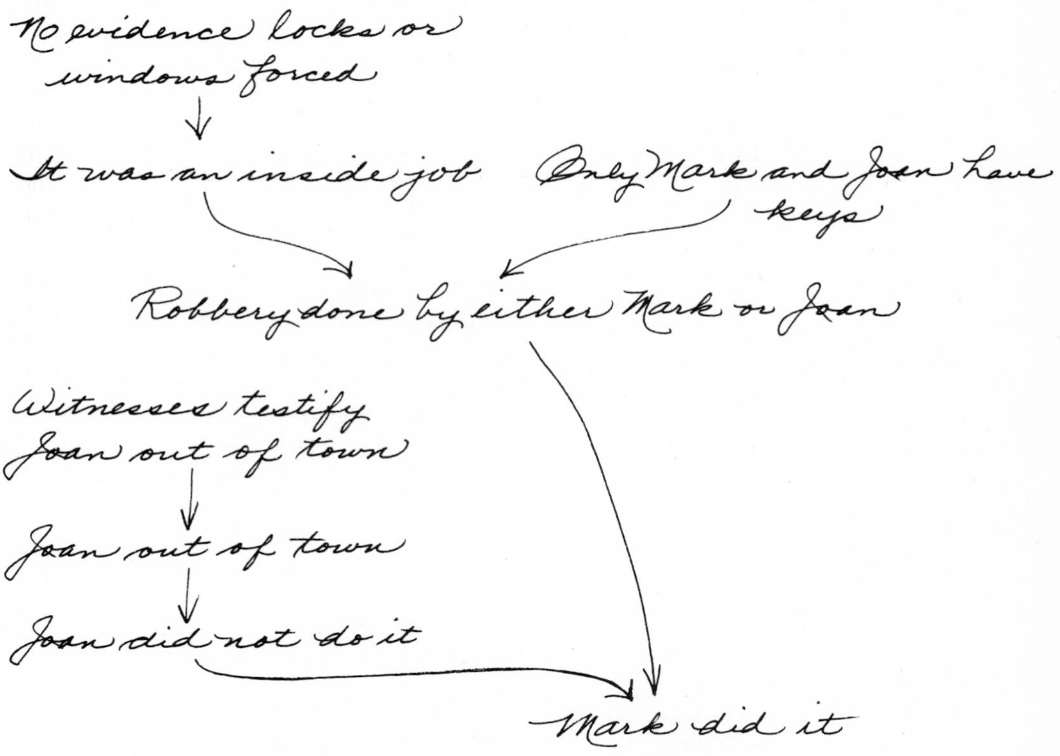

No evidence locks or windows forced
↓
It was an inside job   Only Mark and Joan have keys

Robbery done by either Mark or Joan

Witnesses testify Joan out of town
↓
Joan out of town
↓
Joan did not do it

Mark did it

FIGURE 2.12

good argument is. The structural information is contained in the small transitional words like these:

Premise indicators	Conclusion indicators
Because . . .	Thus . . .
Since . . .	Hence . . .
In view of . . .	Therefore . . .
Inasmuch as . . .	Consequently . . .
For . . .	So . . .

The first step in argument identification is to pick out these words and begin to place arrows accordingly. Suppose we take the argument given above and number the different sentences and circle the words that give structural information (figure 2.13). Of the words we have circled, "so" comes before a conclusion, so the end of an arrow must point to statements 2 and 4. "For" comes before a premise and "consequently" comes before a conclusion, so 6 must be a premise for something, and 8 a conclusion. Thus far this is the information you have extracted:

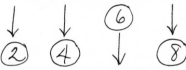

Now you go back to the argument and see if you can fill in the other end of each arrow. Some of it you can do mechanically. For example, there is but one sentence that precedes 2, so 1 has to be the other end:

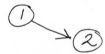

Then use other structural information. Notice the "but" that introduces 5. The "but" indicates an interruption in the natural flow of the argument. In this case the evidence points toward Joan. The sentence introduced by "but" rebuts the conclusion that Joan did it by giving reasons that go counter to the implicit accusation against Joan. Consider how natural it would be for someone who wishes to defend Mark to start the rebuttal

---

FIGURE 2.13
(1) [After examining the lock and the windows carefully we found no reason to believe they were forced.] (So) [it (2) must have been an inside job.] (3) [The only two people who had access to a key were Joan and Mark.] (So) [one (4) of them must have done it.] But we know that [Joan could not have done it,] (for) [she (6) was out of town that weekend,] (7) [we have several witnesses to testify to that.] (Consequently) [Mark did it.]

---

with: "But Mark could not have done it because. . . ." There are many other words and phrases that give information about the intended logic of the argument. For example, "although" and "despite the fact that" indicate that the writer is conceding a point against what he is about to say. A defender of Mark who wishes to concede that the evidence against Mark is strong will say, for example, "Although it might seem that Mark alone could have done it, in fact he was out of town that weekend too."

Still, it would be unusual to find an argument in which all the logical relationships among the sentences are indicated by some words or phrases. When you have exhausted the search for argument-indicator words, you must go to meaning and ask which arrangements make the better argument. You must go to meaning to see further connections: Is it to be read as

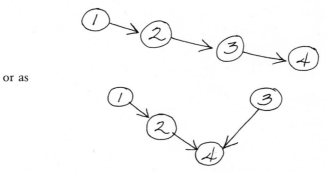

or as

You resolve this difficulty by your view of which interpretation makes more sense: is the fact that it was an inside job—2—a good reason to believe that only two persons had access to a key—3? Is the fact that it was an inside job a reason to believe Joan or Mark did it—4? These decisions are not mechanical, for you are now beyond the structural information provided by the author. You have to see that 2 and 3 together give a good reason for 4. In the end, your diagram should be this:

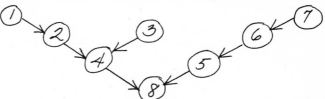

The most important lesson to be drawn from this example is how significant the small transitional words are in communicating to the reader what the argument is. By omitting them, you tax the reader. Notice also the variety of usages through which structural information is communicated—in this passage, by the "but" and by the dash. If the "so" before the second sentence had been omitted, the use of "must" should tell you an inference is being drawn. You could write out the same information by using these forms over and over again: "My first conclusion is. . . .

My evidence for that is. . . . My second conclusion is. . . . My evidence for that is. . . ." and so on. But such writing would be mechanical and dull. So good writers vary the forms and vary the direction. Notice how the first two sentences are ordered: premise-conclusion. But see how in the fourth sentence, which combines our 5, 6, and 7, the order is: conclusion-premise-premise.

The value of a tree diagram is that it allows you to see the logical relationships: that 1, 3, and 7 are the basic statements that are not further supported; that 4 depends on 2 and 3; that 5 depends on 6 and 7. But the tree diagram is very sparse in the information it provides. It gives you only the bare skeleton of the argument.

A second value of forcing yourself to do such a diagram is that it forces you to "chunk" the information contained in the argument: you try to pick out just the essential information to put into the diagram. Here is an example from Charles Darwin's *On the Origin of Species:*

As many more individuals of each species are born than can possibly survive; and as, consequently, there is a frequently recurring struggle for existence; it follows that any being, if it vary slightly in any manner profitable to itself, under the complex and sometimes varying conditions of life will have a better chance of surviving and thus be naturally selected. From the strong principle of inheritance, any selected variety will tend to propagate its new and modified form.

In this passage Darwin uses "as" twice ("as" comes before a premise); "consequently," "it follows that," and "thus," once each (they indicate a conclusion); and the underlined "from" in the last sentence, although not usually an argument indicator, here signifies that the strong principle of inheritance is a premise. "As P, and as, consequently Q, it follows that R, thus S" means "Because of P, it follows that Q; because of Q, it follows that R; because of R, it follows that S." (P is his first sentence; Q, his second sentence; R, his third; and S, his fourth.) Its tree diagram is shown in figure 2.14.

The tree diagram method of analysis need not be confined to sentences, as we have done here.[8] You can use it also on whole chapters of a book or on paragraphs of a chapter. It is useful at the editing stage of your paper to see if you can draw a tree diagram of the relationship between the sections or paragraphs of your paper. If your paper is intended to be an argumentative paper and you cannot do a tree diagram of it, then something is wrong.

8 For more on the method, consult Monroe C. Beardsley, *Thinking Straight: Principles of Reasoning for Readers and Writers*, 4th ed. (Englewood Cliffs, N.J.: Prentice-Hall, 1975) and Michael Scriven, *Reasoning* (New York: McGraw-Hill, 1976).

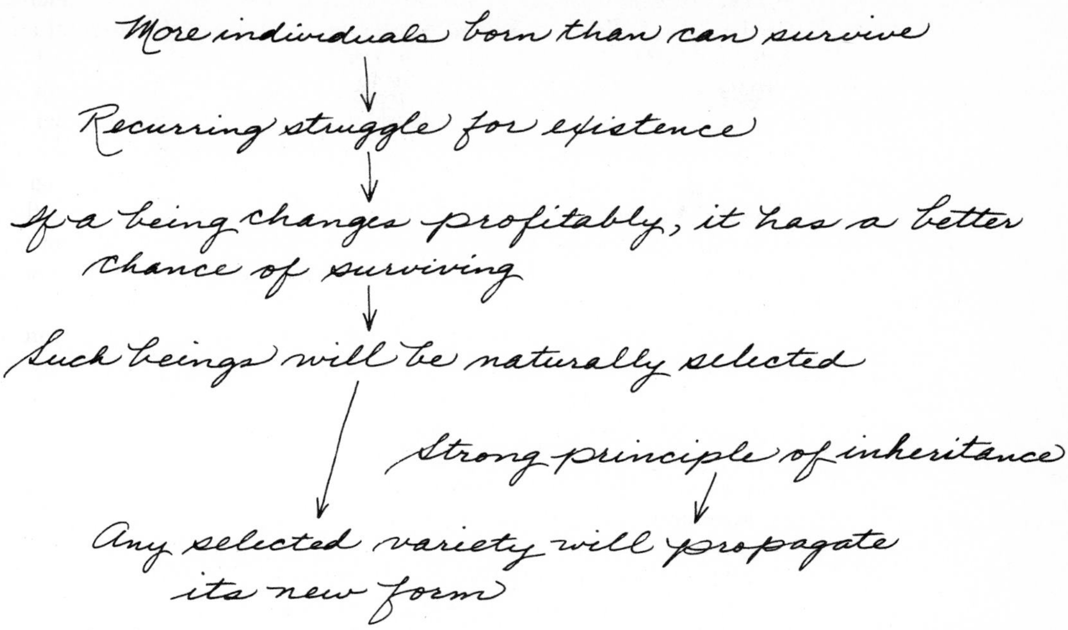

More individuals born than can survive

↓

Recurring struggle for existence

↓

If a being changes profitably, it has a better chance of surviving

↓

Such beings will be naturally selected

Strong principle of inheritance

↓   ↓

Any selected variety will propagate its new form

FIGURE 2.14

Stephen Toulmin has suggested an alternative method for analyzing arguments.[9] He believes any good argument has at least three elements: a ground, a claim, and a warrant. The relationship between the ground and the claim is similar to the relationship of the premise (ground) to the conclusion (claim). It is his notion of "warrant" that introduces something new. Its significance can be seen from the questions each element is intended to answer. Imagine the following dialogue:

Q: Who do you think is guilty?
A: The butler.   (*Claim*)
Q: How do you know? What is your evidence?
A: His fingerprints were on the murder weapon.   (*Ground*)
Q: So what?

Reflect for a moment on what an appropriate answer is to this last question. It does not call for you to justify the ground. It does not question whether the fingerprints were on the weapon. Nor does it ask for additional

9 *The Uses of Argument* (New York: Cambridge Univ. Press, 1958) and Stephen Toulmin, Richard Rieke, and Allan Janik, *An Introduction to Reasoning* (New York: Macmillan, 1979). It should be noted that Toulmin analyzes arguments into six components, of which we mention only three.

evidence, as would the question "Do you have any other evidence against him?" To be told the murderer also had a motive does not answer "So what?" The question asks that you establish the link between your evidence and the conclusion you want to draw from it. What it calls for is a "warrant," some general principle of inference which when applied to this case, justifies your inference from this ground (premise) to this claim (conclusion).

The search for a warrant will uncover, if it is successful, what else you are committed to if you want to draw the inference. But you need to choose a warrant that is neither too strong for the case nor so weak as to be trivial. Thus, "If the butler's fingerprints are found on the murder weapon, then he is guilty" is too weak; it is too specific to the case. It just says there is a link between the claim and ground, which is the question at issue. On the other hand, "Whenever a person's fingerprints are found on a murder weapon, we may infer that that person is guilty of the murder" is too strong. We know there are other explanations for the fingerprints being on the weapon. So the criteria for a good warrant are that it be strong enough to explain the inference but not so strong that it is false or implausible. In our example, you can find a plausible warrant either by weakening the relationship between ground and claim ("If a person's fingerprints are found on a murder weapon, then very possibly that person is the murderer") or by adding restrictions to the circumstances under which you think guilt may be inferred from fingerprints. Thus, for example, it seems plausible to say, "Whenever a murder has been committed and there is one suspect who has a motive and opportunity and whose fingerprints are on the weapon, and when we have eliminated other candidates, then we may infer that that person is very likely to have committed the crime." But now notice that if this is the route you take to find a plausible warrant, you need to get more information on the case: Did the butler have a motive and opportunity? Are the other candidates really eliminated? In effect, to search for a warrant is to search for other *relevant* facts about the case. The warrant shows the relevance of the ground to the claim.

The importance of the distinction between warrants and grounds for academic writing in particular is this: Because most academic assignments are intended as exercises in the particular techniques of some discipline, instructors are usually interested not so much in the facts you accumulate but in how you use them. In other words, instructors are interested in how well you can use the warrants of that particular discipline. The warrant may be a definition (for example, the ground that a poem has fourteen lines is relevant to literary analysis because of the warrant that defines sonnets as poems with fourteen lines). The warrant may be a scientific law, or a particular technique of statistical inference, or a principle of experimental procedure. In history a warrant might be a principle of historical interpretation, or it might be a generalization about what motivates human beings in particular situations. In law a warrant might be a statute or a rule of evidence. (Consider, for example, how the principle that a person is innocent until proven guilty "warrants" the conclusion that a person is innocent when the case against him is insufficient.)

These warrants are substantive principles to be learned in courses in these disciplines. Logic can tell you only that you need a warrant. Logic by itself cannot always tell whether a given warrant is acceptable or not. The diagnosis of an illness, for example, is an argument in which a list of symptoms takes the place of the grounds, and the statement that the patient has a particular illness is the claim. The diagnosis is justified—that is, the argument is a good one—only if there is a plausible warrant that connects those symptoms to that illness. You need to study medicine to find out whether there are such warrants. But by logic alone you can tell what the warrant should look like: People with S_1, S_2, S_3 . . . S_n are likely to have illness X. So this method of analysis can point you in a direction, although it may not give you the final answer.

The lesson from this analysis is that for each inference you draw in your paper, you should ask yourself whether the reader has an answer in the paper to the question "So what?" Have you shown the link between the claim and the ground? Or is it so obvious that it need not be stated?

Two final points about this technique are worth making. The first is that the technique can be used generatively, to find gaps in your information before you write your paper. After the research phase of your paper, when you are trying to organize your information, for each claim you propose to make you can ask what else are you committed to if that inference is to be justified. The second point is based on the fact that there is a difference in the order of generality between the warrant and the ground: in going from grounds to warrant, you go from a set of facts to some more general principle. It is a characteristic of academic papers that they all move within the paper itself between the general and the specific. A paper entirely on the same level is a bad paper. If you keep in mind the distinction made here it will help you to vary the level of reasoning within the final paper.

Conclusion

As you are probably aware by now, the strategies discussed in this chapter can be overwhelming if you think of them all together. Their application must be selective. You should try them as they seem to apply to the particular problem you are working on. All of the strategies represent ways of thinking about or seeing problems that occur at any stage in the writing process. Before you begin to write, you may, for example, need to generate a list or develop a table to clarify in your own mind the relationships between parts of a problem. But the table can also be used in the paper to illustrate the same point for your reader. During the drafting stage you might arrive at a point at which your ideas run out. To get started again, you should try one or more of these heuristics. For example, if a draft of a paper on a political group bogs down after you have described and evaluated the group, where do you go next? You might consider the group as a "wave" (Where did it come from? Within what political tradition does it belong?), or as a part of a "field" (What is its relationship with political groups of its ideological orientation? Where does it fit into the current political power structure?). Even as you revise a paper you may need to think about your problem in a new way, especially if you want your conclusion to be more than a summation. At the end of your writing process you can still make use of strategies like brainstorming or asking questions (What are the implications of X?).

In fact, we are faced here with the question "How do we end this chapter?" Brainstorming on this problem might look like the notes in figure 2.15.

What can we say that doesn't merely repeat, but which follows from and adds to this chapter? Already discussed the strategies — Can say that they will all be used and illustrated in more detail when we discuss individual paper assignments. No — sounds too bland. What is more important to add? What are some of the implications of this chapter? Well, they're useful — too obvious. Could say that in the writing process you will most likely not only be generating new ideas at all stages, but will be doing other tasks at all stages. Good! Need to discuss recursive nature — "messy." Nature of writing — that the process is not neat and sequential — the conclusion of this chapter would be a good place to do that.

FIGURE 2.15

Writing is not a process, but a series of processes. That is, writing does not often move smoothly from generating ideas and making a plan to revising, editing, and proofreading. You will find yourself doing various subtasks at every stage of writing a paper. While you are trying to develop an organization, you may well be formulating your topic sentence. While you are writing a draft, you will also still be discovering and working out new ideas. While you are editing for punctuation, you may still be rewriting parts or reorganizing your paragraph sequence. The needs of your readers should rarely be far from your mind. Writing by process means that at each stage of your development you should be focusing your attention on a few things at a time. In fact, this orderly way of organizing your writing will help to make you aware of particular problems as you write and will encourage you to move back and forth among the various subtasks until you are satisfied that the paper reflects your plan clearly and completely. We suggest that you use this chapter for reference as you proceed through the various writing assignments in the rest of the book. But to prepare yourself to use these thinking devices, it would be a valuable exercise to practice them in your journal. Select a topic from one of your courses and "play" with it on paper. Try as many of the strategies as you can to see how they actually work. You may be surprised to discover how creatively you can see and think about the topic.

QUESTIONS 1 In what specific ways can writing be an aid to learning?

2 How does private writing differ from writing for someone else?

3 What are some uses of a personal journal?

4 How is a topic tree different from an outline?

EXERCISES 1 Without stopping or editing, for ten minutes each day write in a private journal. At the end of a week review your journal. How could such a journal be useful to you?

2 Figure 2.16 illustrates an example of brainstorming on the topic of television. Draw up a list of the key ideas and try to establish relationships between some or all of those ideas. Transform one or more of the relationships you discover into a thematic paragraph.

3 Consider the following analogies and metaphors. In each case, make a list of the implications that follow if the analogy is true; that is, make a list of what you can know or assume about the first item by transferring to it those things you know about the second item. Compare your lists with those of others in the class.

a The Teapot Dome scandal was the Watergate of the 1920s.

b The atom is very much like a mini solar system.

T.V. — children waste too much time watching — too much violence? Effects on homework, can't be good — does it make kids antisocial? — Can be educational — why isn't it? T.V. is more harmful than useful — is that true? Parents need to exercise control — advertising directed toward children puts a lot of pressure on parents to buy things — whose fault? Why so many ads directed toward children? — what happens when children watch too much T.V.? One study showed that they become immune to violence — makes them passive — what are bad effects of this? They become irritable after too much watching.

FIGURE 2.16

c The Boer War was to England at the turn of the century what Vietnam was to America in the 1960s and 1970s.

d A cerebral stroke is like a short circuit in an appliance.

4 Consider each of the following topics as a particle, a wave, and a field. Make a list of each category for each topic. Compare your lists with those written by classmates.

a your college

b the Beatles

c the United States Government

d your favorite friend

5 Each of the following topics is followed by three questions. Identify each question as representing a particle, wave, or field approach to that topic.

Socrates:

a What was Socrates' ethical theory?

b What contributions did Socrates make to the history of ethics?

c In what ways did Socrates' ethics differ from the ethical views of his contemporaries in the fifth century B.C.?

Darwin:

a What impact did Darwin's theory of evolution have on nineteenth-century England?

b Was Darwin really the first evolutionist in the history of biology?

c What does Darwin actually say about the value of his voyage on the *Beagle*?

6 Following is a list of items from an American history textbook. Using all of these items, write a short, focused paragraph establishing relationships among the items:

Declaration of Independence, 1776
Yorktown, British surrender, 1783
American colonies
first shots fired, Concord, 1775
King George III of England
George Washington
United States of America

7 You are a parent who has advertised in the local newspaper for a full-time housekeeper and babysitter for your three-year-old son so that you can work. You have received the following short note from a person named Deborah Draft. After reading the note carefully, make two lists, one containing your positive reactions to the application, the other, your negative responses. What positive and negative inferences do you draw from the application? Would you hire Deborah Draft? Why or why not?

```
    I am interested in your advertised job for a
housekeeper. I am experienced at routine
housekeeping chores since I have had to take care
of our five-room house since the age of twelve,
when my mother left us. I have also had three
positions in housekeeping while in high school.
The letters of reference from those jobs are
inclosed. This kind of day work will also allow
me to finish my undergraduate degree at night
school where I am studying elementary education.
I think that my courses in childcare and pre-
school learning will also help me in this job.
```

Thank you,

Debbie
Debbie Draft

8 Following are some facts about a student who is running for election as president of the student government. You are editor of the student newspaper. Write two lead paragraphs for two different newspaper stories about him. One of the lead paragraphs must be favorable (to help him gain election); the other should be unfavorable (to convince people not to vote for him). The success of the two paragraphs will depend on your selection and interpretation of the facts. Keep in mind that the apparent reason for the paragraphs is to announce his candidacy.

Name: John Prose, junior, Clearwriting State College

Offices held: Junior class president

Activities: Basketball (3 years), captain (junior year); Alpha Rho Alpha social fraternity, social chairman (freshman and sophomore years); volunteer, municipal youth athletic league (junior year).

Academic record: cumulative grade point average 2.3 on a scale of 4.0; academic probation (freshman year); academic warning (sophomore year); began as a chemistry major, switched to business administration in sophomore year, and to physical education in junior year.

Social record: social probation (sophomore year) for organizing parties without a college permit; suspended for four basketball games (sophomore year) for partying after curfew.

Campaign platform: Pledges to advocate the abolition of the fraternity system on campus.

9 Following is a series of seven facts presented in simple chronological order. Write a sentence that presents a claim based on these facts. Explain the warrant for your claim.

a John Smith, graduate student, married Maggy Olsen, 1945.

b John Smith, Ph.D. in political science, was hired by Central University as an assistant professor, 1947.

c John Smith published major book, promoted to associate professor, 1950.

d Announcement made that he was being investigated as a Communist by the House Un-American Activities Committee, 1952.

e His wife divorced him, 1953.

f He married one of his students, 1953.

g He was fired by the university, 1954.

10 Figure 2.17 is a tree diagram of an argument, the numbers in the diagram corresponding to the sentences given immediately below. Try to write the argument in paragraph form, using number 1 as the thesis statement.

1 Americans should eat less meat.

FIGURE 2.17

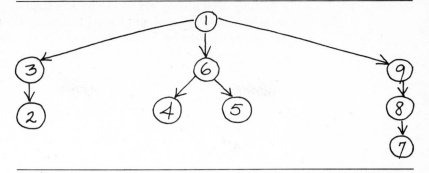

2 It takes twenty pounds of grain protein or more to produce one pound of meat.

3 Meat is a wasteful source of food.

4 Americans now eat twice as much meat as Americans did twenty-five years ago.

5 Americans twenty-five years ago were healthier than are Americans now.

6 A diet with less meat in it would be a healthy change for most Americans.

7 Protein consumed in the form of meat is far more expensive than grain protein.

8 Decreasing the proportion of meat in the American diet would result in a smaller proportion of family income going to food.

9 If American families spent less on food, then more money would be available to stimulate the economy and attack inflation.

11 Suppose the following were regulations that governed whether or not a person is entitled to vote in an election. Devise a flow chart with two outcomes, one reading, "You are not entitled to vote" and the other reading, "You are entitled to vote."

Only citizens of Patagonia are entitled to vote in national elections, but not all citizens are entitled to vote. A person younger than eighteen years of age may not vote, nor may convicted felons vote, unless they have been pardoned and their right to vote reinstated by the court that found them guilty of a felony. Married couples have only one vote, although they may choose for themselves which one will exercise the vote. Only persons who have paid income tax within the previous five years may vote, and no person is permitted to vote more than once in any given election.

12 Figure 2.18 is a simplified version of a flow chart which the Internal Revenue Service uses to explain to prospective taxpayers whether or not they are obliged to file a tax return for a given year. Please answer the following questions by referring to the flow chart.

a Keith Larson is seventy-six, unmarried, and has an income of $4,000. Is he obliged to file a return?

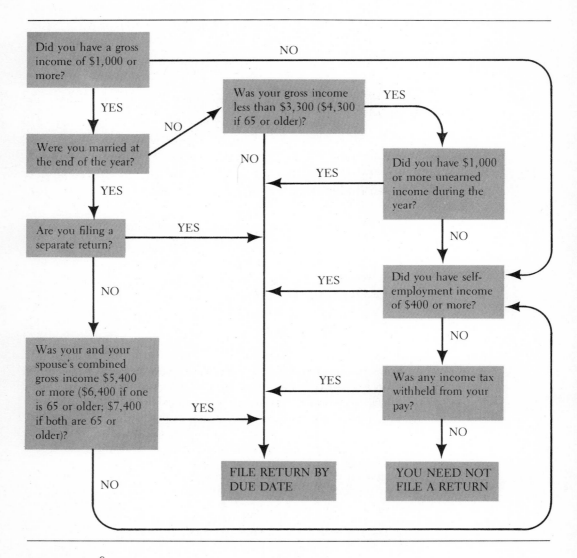

FIGURE 2.18

b Lois and David Cohen are married to one another. David is forty-three; Lois is forty-five. Their combined income for the year is $23,500. Are they obliged to file a return if they file separate returns? If they file a joint return?

c Sally O'Brien is sixty-six and unmarried. Her income for the year is $4,000, of which $2,200 is unearned income. Must she file a return?

d Sam and Reina Mortimer are a married couple with a combined income of $7,000. They are both seventy-two. Of the $7,000 income, $800 is unearned income and $900 is self-employment income. Must they file a return?

Write two paragraphs that state the conditions under which a person must file a tax return. Begin the first paragraph with the words "You must file a tax return if . . ." and the second paragraph with the words "You need not file a tax return if. . . ." Hand your paragraphs to another student in the class and have that student answer the questions above on the basis of your rewriting of the conditions.

13 What generalization would *warrant* the inference from these premises to these conclusions?

a There are more neutrinos in the universe than was previously thought. Therefore, the Big Bang theory is false.

b The number that solves a puzzle is divisible by three. Therefore, the number must be odd.

c *Hard Times* was written by Charles Dickens. Therefore, *Hard Times* is a Victorian novel.

d Gertrude promised she would come to my party, so it was discourteous of her not to come.

e The ceiling of the basement was more scorched than any other part of the house. Therefore, the fire started in the basement.

Discuss how you would find out if the warrant is true.

14 Using the information below, apply Burke's pentad. Write a sentence on the topic "Socrates" that transforms the topic into an *action*. Then write a sentence that views the topic as an *actor-agent*, as a *scene*, as a *means*, and as a *purpose*.

In 399 B.C. Socrates accepted the verdict of an Athenian court that condemned him to death. He took hemlock in the presence of his friends and died. He had been prosecuted for corrupting the youth of Athens and for introducing new gods. Because of an Athenian law that banned executions during one month of the year, Socrates had to wait for about a month after the trial before the sentence could be carried out. During this time his great friend Crito tried to persuade Socrates to flee from prison, but Socrates rejected the plea on the grounds that at seventy years of age he had no reason to fear death; in fact, he welcomed it. Death, he said, is what a true philosopher spends his life preparing for. And so, obeying the law, he drank hemlock and died.

3 Classroom Writing

The writing that you do most regularly in the college classroom falls into two categories: writing notes and writing tests. These two types of writing aim toward very different purposes and require different strategies. When you write notes from lectures, discussions, and texts, you are recording information and ideas from an outside source, but you are writing primarily for yourself, to supplement your memory and to help you synthesize and understand the material. When you write answers for essay examinations, you are presenting information and ideas that represent your understanding of the material you have learned. You are not writing for yourself, but for a reader who represents scholars in a particular field and who will evaluate your answers by scholarly standards. In fact, understanding the requirements of your audience in an essay test sometimes helps to make an adequate answer into a superior one.

The sections that follow treat the various kinds of classroom writing, the reasons why such types of writing are an important part of learning, and strategies for making these types of writing an integral part of your learning process.

Writing notes from lectures, discussions, and texts

Like most forms of writing, note taking is a skill that evolves from experience. Individuals develop methods that they have found to be most effective, methods that are efficient and that contribute to learning. Often students' note-taking styles will change during college until they find the right balance between effort expended and results gained. Such a trial-and-error process may result in effective methods, but many courses may have to be taken before a satisfactory method emerges. The purpose of the following sections is to speed up this process by acquainting you with some legitimate goals for note taking, and to offer some techniques to try to improve your note taking in all courses.

Note taking from lectures

Many students go through college never using class time wisely or never organizing for the most efficient use of their study time. For example, taking down everything an instructor says in class may appear conscientious, but for many students this method is actually an impediment to learning. Writing for an entire class period, head down, hand moving, prevents some students from listening to what is being said. Also, pages of notes in which illustrations and anecdotes crowd out the points they were intended to support make reviewing those notes a tedious and sometimes not very useful exercise. How often have you had to ask yourself, after your notes have sat unexamined for a few weeks, "Now why did I write that down?"

On the other hand, sitting idly in class with the excuse that you are listening to and absorbing a lecture (and don't want to be distracted by writing) is also an ineffective way to learn for most students. Like the days of our lives, class lectures become fuzzy and indistinct with the passage of a surprisingly short period of time. Working memory is capable of retaining about seven "chunks" of information. Even though you may be thrilled by a lecture, you do not have the cognitive capacity—no one does—to retain it and all of the others that you hear in a week. You need to leave every class with something down on paper. Writing extends short-term memory. It allows you not only to keep a record of others' ideas, it allows you to study them later, to learn them exactly, to react to them and connect them with your own experience and information.

Besides helping your memory, taking notes can also help you pay attention to the lecture by keeping your mind actively involved with what the instructor is saying. Psychological studies have demonstrated that in the average college classroom, at any given moment one out of every three students is daydreaming, a high percentage of them about sex. While pleasantly diverting, such lapses contribute little to your understanding of the course material. You cannot learn something that you haven't even heard. Taking notes reinforces your concentration, physically as well as mentally.

But the main purpose of class notes is to give you a *summary* of what happened in class. This summary will be most useful to you later if it reflects and emphasizes the main points that the instructor made. Remember, the instructor has a purpose in presenting the material he selects for each class period. If you can figure out the purpose you will have established the major organizing principle around which to take your class notes. A good question to go into class with is "Why is today's lecture being given?" Figuring this out requires you to make judgments, to be sensitive to what goes on in class. Some students can do this during the lecture itself; others cannot concentrate on listening and evaluating at the same time. Naturally, the better you understand the intentions of an instructor, the more organized and concise you can make your notes. If you are not sure what a lecture is about, it is better to play it safe and take more notes than you usually would. Taking time after class to organize your notes will then accomplish your main purpose, which is to understand the material at the level the instructor wishes.

There is no answer to the question "How many notes should I take in a class?" But the strategies given below can help you discover the most effective use that you can make of your class time. You will probably find that some of them work for you and some do not, but we urge you to experiment with each of them to find out, early in your college experience, how you take notes most successfully.

The best way to prepare yourself to "understand" a lecture is to anticipate it. Always consult the course syllabus, which often will list the topics for each lecture, and read the assigned reading for that class period. The text assignment usually provides clues as to what the general topic for a class period will be. In class, then, you will have certain advantages. You will already know key words, concepts, people, or ideas. You will have a context into which you can place the material from the lecture.

Once in class, the best guide to what to record is your professor. Generally, most college lectures are not delivered in simple narrative fashion ("first this happened . . . then this occurred . . .). Most professors construct their lectures around pivotal points and, overtly or subtly, will share these main organizing ideas with you. So, look for cues in class and build your notes around the most obvious points made. Here are some cues to look for:

▪ What is said during the first few minutes: Often at the beginning of a lecture the instructor will give an introduction that will include the main points to be covered that day, or will provide an overview of the topic. It pays to be especially alert during these early minutes. It pays to be there at the beginning. Lateness is more than a breach of etiquette.

▪ Overt directions: Typical of remarks put into a lecture as cues are: "The major point is . . ."; "This is central to our understanding of . . ."; "It is important to note that. . . ." Any comment introduced by this sort of direction should be written down.

▪ Anything written on the chalkboard: Instructors' use of the chalkboard ranges from complete outlines of the day's lecture to words written hastily. But whenever an instructor takes the time to record a word or an idea, it should be assumed to be important.

▪ Points repeated during the lecture: This is an especially valuable way of spotting the organizing principles of a lecture in which there are no overt cues, for often an instructor will return to important material to reinforce it from different directions. Look for the signals "As I said before . . ."; "This, you will remember, is . . ."; and "We saw this in another context. . . ."

Your instructors may give none of these cues; they may give them all; they may give others. Individual lecture styles vary so much that you should consciously look for the ways your instructors emphasize the major points or the organizing principles of their lectures. If you cannot learn to pick them out while you are listening and taking notes, you should try to do so as soon after the end of class as possible, while the lecture is still fresh in your mind. A few summary sentences pulled out and written in the margin may well help you organize the lecture later during your study of the notes.

Lecture styles are not the only variables you have to contend with as you move from class to class. Another factor that will affect your note taking is the course material itself. Different subjects are taught differently. Just as you will have to take different kinds of notes for different instructors, so will you have to record differently for different subjects. For example, in the humanities and in many of the social sciences, concepts are often more important than information in organizing lectures. As one writer said of history, "Facts are merely hooks on which to hang concepts." In such courses, the organizing ideas for lectures will generally be observations that emphasize a principle or general condition. Examples of such organizing principles are: "Most European monarchs in the late seventeenth century wanted to emulate Louis XIV of France," or "Impressionism was the most dynamic movement in art in the last decades of the nineteenth century," or "At its core, Marxism is not an economic, but a philosophical system." In such situations, examples and data will usually be given, but almost always as illustrations and evidence. The important parts to record are the organizing principles. You should take notes on the supporting material only as you need it to fix the organizing idea in your mind. A good rule of thumb is to write down the evidence that the instructor indicates is the strongest proof or the most vivid illustration.

Conversely, in certain courses, especially in the physical sciences, the factual material itself is the essence of a lecture and, therefore, needs to be recorded completely. If an instructor in anatomy gives a lecture on the parts of the human gastrointestinal tract or a chemist talks on the components of DNA, the facts, all of them, are crucial.

The above examples from the humanities and the sciences are, however, only guidelines showing tendencies or general characteristics of disciplines. In most subjects and within single courses, the lectures will vary, with some centering on theory and others on data that you need to have. Your job is to be sensitive to what kind of lecture is being given in each individual class period. Experience alone will make you confident in your courses, but, as usual, looking for cues will help. Do the facts being given in a lecture illustrate a point, or are they themselves the focal point? If, for example, an instructor says, "There are many examples of monarchs who tried to emulate Louis XIV," you may need to record material about one or two kings to fix the point. But if an instructor says, "DNA is composed of the following materials," you should be ready to write them all down.

However you finally decide to take class notes, whether outlines, fragments, lists, complete sentences, or full, or developed paragraphs, try not to write on the entire page of your notebook. Even though it may take more paper, leave wide margins and gaps between your sections of notes. In short, leave spaces. Remember, your notes are working papers, not inviolate prose that is to be graded. Sacrifice neatness for utility. Dense notes, packed in from top to bottom and margin to margin are neither easy to read nor to use. Leave space to fill in new information as you get it, examples from your text or more complete data. Keep space available for your comments as you study the notes and are forming your ideas and making connections with other knowledge. You may, upon reflection, disagree with a point in your notes. You will want space to pen in a question to ask in class regarding the problem. Cherish the value of words, but recognize the value of white space.

Notes from class discussions   The purpose of class discussions is to encourage you to be an active participant, not a passive recorder. Much of the emphasis in a discussion is on getting students involved in thinking, reacting, and responding. These are important intellectual activities in the learning process, for through them you are supposed to discover and express your opinions. Writing is an invaluable tool for accomplishing these tasks.

Unfortunately, too many times, when class discussion begins, pens and pencils go down. Admittedly, it is considerably more difficult to take notes from discussions than from lectures, for, unlike lectures, discussions tend to be disorganized and difficult to follow. Also, students usually don't know how much of what other students are saying is important. And if you are an active participant, it is not easy to take notes and formulate what you want to say. But note taking in discussions is not only manageable, it is important. Note taking helps to keep you active and alert; it allows you to impose some organization on the discussion; and it can prepare you to speak.

As with lectures, there is no sure guide to note taking in discussions, but the best preparation, as before, is in anticipating the discussion. Think about the assigned readings. Ask yourself, "Why is this discussion scheduled? Do I have any views on the topic?" When you give some attention to the topic before class, you will be better able to follow and to join in the conversation in class.

Use your notes to record important points made. You may not know what will be important at first, so you may record more at the beginning than you will as the discussion progresses. For your later reference, write down points reinforced by the instructor, for his interjections will usually be intended to guide the discussion toward his goals. Note all points that are generally agreed upon or mentioned repeatedly.

While you probably will take down some points for later reference, you should concentrate your attention on writing for purposes of thinking and responding. What is your opinion of what others are saying? Keep a running record of your ideas. If you respond on paper first, even if it is just a few words or a phrase, you may discover that when you speak, your contribution will be organized and directly related to the topic. What happens in this sequence—responding, writing, speaking—is that you will have organized your thoughts better by the act of writing them down. We have mentioned before that writing is thinking on paper. In the case of class discussions you can use writing almost as an instant monitor. "What is it I want to say? Is it worth saying?"

If you are not particularly active in class discussions, this type of writing may help you to contribute. Brief, written notes may give you more courage to speak up. A few reference words, and, of course, your quick reflection on your ideas as you write them, may help to defuse some of your fears that you will say something stupid, that you will forget some of the points if there are several, or that you will embarrass yourself in some other way. Even if you choose not to respond to the discussion, these notes on your ideas and reactions are valuable. They will help to insure that you follow the discussion, that you think about what is being said, and that you try to form opinions.

Discussion notes will probably be messy. Don't worry about it or try to take neat, ordered notes. Discussions are messy. At every stage you will have to indicate who said what. This is especially important for two participants, your instructor and you. Be sure to write in "my opinion" or put your ideas in brackets. Don't be hesitant to draw arrows to the recorded comment to which you are responding. Any technique that makes the notes useful for you, in class and later when studying, is a valuable technique.

Studying from class notes   Too often students do little with their class notes beyond reviewing them before an examination. Such a practice deprives them of a chance to learn their material. It has been estimated that students forget about three-quarters of what they learn in college. This forgetting is due to many reasons, but among them is the widespread tendency to study for specific examinations rather than for understanding. Even if this transient goal is met and students have stored enough material in memory to pass a test, they probably will not do as well as they could. Last-minute memorizing does not always result in a grasp of information sufficient to allow one to use information effectively in an essay examination.

Learning must take place over a period of time. Give yourself enough time to absorb and understand your class notes. Strategies for the effective studying of notes always involve an investment of time over a period of days or weeks. You should become more than familiar with the material in your notes; you should be on intimate terms with it. The first necessary step is to put your notes in a form that corresponds to your studying needs. If rewriting or typing them helps you to learn them, then the time copying will be well spent. However, most students have neither the time nor the need to recopy notes. Many have found it more valuable to reorganize their notes in some way, since the act of reordering raw, unedited notes, unlike copying, requires active intellectual involvement. Following are some strategies, arranged sequentially, to assist you in learning your course content.

Reducing and restructuring your notes. The major problem in studying for an examination in a course is that you are confronted with large masses of material, the accumulation of weeks or months of note taking. How is it possible to learn dozens or hundreds of pieces of information? As you probably already know from experience, memorizing is not only unproductive but counterproductive, because it detracts from real study. The best answer, offered by psychologists and confirmed by experience, is organization and structure. It is important to fit information into larger contexts, to relate it to other information, and to see it in some kind of a structure. This process of structuring your lecture notes, you will remember, began in the classroom with your identification of organizing principles. As you study, write your comments on the relationships within your material and between this new material and what you already know. The structure to which you attach information may come from the course, from other courses, from ideas that you have known for a long time. One characteristic of intellectual maturity is a need to impose order on seemingly unrelated objects or to give meaning to information. Establish an intellectual principle of order in your notes. Developing the ability to create order from chaos is one of the purposes of a college education, and during your early undergraduate years chaos may still seem to be winning.

How do you begin? The best strategy is to find some way to reduce your material. The only requirement of the method is that it allow you to reduce systematically, each reduction providing key concepts, ideas, or words that trigger associations in your mind. Some students prefer to outline their class notes. Others prefer to pick out one or two points from each class session under which to organize the lesser points. Many students have reported to us that their best study strategy consists of extensive reduction of notes, finally to lists of just a few words. Built into those words are numbers of associations with other concepts, ideas, or categories. And each of these represents whole groupings of other facts. This kind of reducing is an ongoing process throughout study so that at examination time you are so familiar with your course material that a few references— key words or categories—allow you to recall by association large blocks of material.

Reinforcing your knowledge of your notes. Reducing your notes requires that you go over them periodically to learn them by reinforcement as well as by association. Familiarity breeds understanding, and it is only with this kind of understanding that you will be able to think about your course material in constructive, associative ways. One of the problems with studying notes is that it is usually a lonely, tedious job, sitting in your room rereading. These circumstances contribute to that common academic malaise, mind wandering, the feeling that you would rather be doing something with friends. We suggest very strongly that whenever possible you study with the friends who are in your courses.

What you need to do is to get together with others and, quite literally, compare notes. Even the best note takers will miss material. Not only does collective studying help you fill in the gaps in your own knowledge or understanding, the process itself is inherently beneficial. Collaborative learning within a community of scholars is a respected academic tradition. It works. Different people not only bring different perspectives to a learning project; their presence can also make studying more enjoyable. To make such sessions productive, however, you must follow some basic ground rules. You must all agree that the purpose of getting together is to study. Set a time limit after which you can socialize. To read notes to each other and discuss course material for two hours is more useful than spending an entire evening talking about life and occasionally saying, "Hey, we had better get back to work." The second rule is to take notes or add to your own. Do not leave such sessions without something written down.

Reflecting on your notes. One of the primary advantages of studying your notes over a period of time is that increasing amounts of material begin to lodge themselves in your brain. The more you know your material, the more material you carry around in your head. Whether or not you are aware of it, you will probably think about this material. Consciously or unconsciously you will mull over these facts and ideas. An incubation period is as important to learning as it is to writing. Do you ever remember a time when you were trying to think of someone's name and you couldn't, but that night in bed, when you were thinking about cleaning your room in the morning, the name popped into your mind? Looking at your notes for the first time the day before an examination robs you of a chance to get valuable insights.

Taking notes from readings

Taking notes from books and articles poses fewer difficulties than taking class notes. Unlike lectures, which exist as a permanent record only in your notes, the printed page may be consulted again and again. This characteristic is both a strength and a weakness. Material in a book or article lends itself to careful analysis and, consequently, can be learned with accuracy. On the other hand, the existence of the material in a book can give you a false feeling of security. It is always there. You can learn it at your leisure. One of the most pervasive difficulties in studying is the postponement of learning textbook material, primarily because a text does not possess the immediacy of a lecture. For example, many students underline or highlight passages in their textbooks. This strategy, in itself, is not a bad way to read the first time through. However, you should recognize underlining for what it is, a way to organize to study. In effect, what you are saying to yourself is, "This is important. I must come back later to learn it." And too often "later" means the day before an examination, too late to digest the material or to learn parts of it that are troublesome. It is also quite possible to underline large portions of a page and to get to the bottom with no idea of what you have read.

The primary way to insure your active involvement in reading is to take notes. Note taking requires you to think about the material you are reading, because to keep a few notes you have to make choices about what is important and what is not. The written exercise forces you to be selective. People who only underline tend to underline too much material; they don't need to force themselves to make choices, and, therefore, they rarely do. Figure 3.1 is a paragraph that a student has underlined indiscriminately.

The example below of a Grand Central Station of underlinings will be useless to the student when he studies. If the student were to read carefully, his notes might look like figure 3.2.

This brief set of notes might be enough to jog this student's memory about the important details because he has followed the lead of the author and concentrated on what the author thought was important. It is all right not to underline or record the parts about James's background, his disappointment, and what historians formerly thought. These observations need not be ignored, but they need not be given the same attention as the organizing ideas of a paragraph.

What then could one usefully write in the book while reading the above paragraph? In the books that you own, marginal notations are a valuable form of note taking. (Of course, you would never mark up a library book!) But you can make the books that you have purchased your

---

Too much underlining

The prestige of the English monarchy declined greatly under James I, 1603–1625. As a Scotsman who had lived his adult life in poverty, he came to the English throne expecting to control vast fortunes. He was greatly disappointed. The parsimony of parliament and the suspicion of royal authority that he discovered, forced him to resort to ill-advised schemes to raise money, including the sale of offices, peerages, and monopolies. These policies divided the nation. Formerly, historians argued that he divided his nation along the lines of religion—the puritans against the king's Church. But the major division was always the court vs. the country. The focal point of opposition was the House of Commons, the instrument of the landed gentry. This class, which included puritans and Anglicans, organized against what seemed to them to be royal encroachments against their liberties. They didn't approve of his church, but their efforts were directed against his pocketbook. They blocked his new taxes, dissolved his monopolies, and, finally, impeached his ministers. An angry and militant parliament was James' bequest to his son.

FIGURE 3.1

> *Thesis: major division in England under James I — court and country. He wanted increased income. Opposition, led by gentry in H of C said no, and stopped him.*

FIGURE 3.2

own indeed by using the margins to organize, summarize, and respond, as shown in figure 3.3.

Notice how little is underlined and how each underlined segment is annotated. When this student comes back to review this passage, reviewing is all he will have to do. He will not have to read fifteen or twenty underlined lines. Notice also that he has made notes to himself to find out words or ideas with which he is unfamiliar. He can make a point of looking these up. They are not lost in an indiscriminately drawn maze of lines. In short, this student understands the paragraph that he has read, and that, after all, is the purpose of studying.

Writing essay examinations

The purpose of any essay examination is to determine if you know the course material well enough to use it in a controlled situation. The instructor will ask you to do something with the knowledge you have been exposed to, so the first requirement for taking an essay examination is to understand your instructor's directions. Knowing what type of question you are answering will help you to determine the nature and focus of your responses and to set limits. Following are the general categories into which essay questions fall. They are not mutually exclusive, and some essay questions may ask for more than one type of response, but these categories are illustrative of the types of questions you should look for when taking an examination.

The information question	This question type is the most common form of essay question. It asks for nothing more than information and is the most direct way for an instructor to find out how much you know about a subject. Table 3.1 lists key words that will help you to identify an information question.
Compare, contrast, or choose between two things	This type of question, discussed in detail in chapter 8, seeks to find out how much you know about two or more topics. Remember that you must connect the two topics, not just discuss them separately. Table 3.2 lists key words to look for.
Questions that ask you to argue a point of view or to develop an interpretation	These types of questions often have no right answers, and while some answers can be wrong, most answers fall into the reasonable or unreasonable category. Remember the definition of an argument presented in chapter 2. Table 3.3 shows the key words in questions of argument and interpretation.

James began on the wrong foot

what were these?

look up this word

The prestige of the English monarchy declined greatly under James I, 1603–1625. As a Scotsman who had lived his adult life in poverty, he came to the English throne expecting to control vast fortunes. He was greatly disappointed. The parsimony of parliament and the suspicion of royal authority that he discovered, forced him to resort to ill-advised schemes to raise money, including the sale of offices, peerages, and monopolies. These policies divided the nation. Formerly, historians argued that he divided his nation along the lines of religion—the puritans against the king's Church. But the major division was always the court vs. the country. The focal point of opposition was the House of Commons, the instrument of the landed gentry. This class, which included puritans and Anglicans, organized against what seemed to them to be royal encroachments against their liberties. They didn't approve of his church, but their efforts were directed against his pocketbook. They blocked his new taxes, dissolved his monopolies, and, finally, impeached his ministers. An angry and militant parliament was James' bequest to his son.

thesis

their reason →

their method →

TABLE 3.1
*Key words in questions
of information*

Words	What they ask	Example
Define	Give the exact meaning of the topic. How is it different from everything else of its type?	Define Marx's concept of alienated labor.
Describe, Discuss	Tell what happened or what the topic is. Concentrate only on primary or most important features.	Describe the conditions on the ships that brought slaves to America and discuss one rebellion that took place on a slave ship.
Explain why	Tell the main reasons why the topic happened or happens.	Explain why the ocean tides are not at the same time every night and why they are not always the same height.
Illustrate	Give one or more examples of the topic, relating each to the topic.	Primitive tribes usually have rigid family systems. Illustrate this point, using one of the tribes studied this semester.
Relate	Show how the topic has an effect on something else; the connection(s) between two things.	Relate the evolution of the horse to the changes in its environment.
Summarize	To give all the main points of a topic; to reduce it without changing it.	Summarize Galileo's main discoveries.
Trace	Give a series of important steps in the development of a historical event or a process or any sequence of happenings.	Trace the events that led up to the Civil War.

Source: Adapted from Harvey S. Wiener and Charles Bazerman, The English Handbook: Reading and Writing *(Boston: Houghton Mifflin, 1977), pp. 311–15. Copyright © 1977 by Houghton Mifflin Company. Used by permission.*

TABLE 3.2
*Key words in questions
of comparison/contrast*

Words	What they ask	Example
Compare	Show how two things are both alike and different.	Give two examples of biological polymers and compare them.
Contrast	Show only the differences between two things.	Contrast the sculpture of Renaissance Italy with that of Baroque France.

Questions of application and speculation

These are among the most difficult essay questions, for they ask you to apply what you know to solve a problem. In addition to knowing the subject matter, you must be able to "use" it in a creative but logical way, analyzing the problem and thinking through the solution. You must not only reason out a solution, but show why your solution is reasonable. The key words for this type of question are often not as evident as in other questions, so you may have to read a question several times before you recognize it. Table 3.4 gives some words to look for.

Although all of these question types ask for different kinds of responses, they share common traits. Instructors know the characteristics of good answers, and these include a clear statement of purpose (your thesis or response), the reasons why you responded as you did, and support for your answer. Theses without supporting evidence are unacceptable; facts unrelated to each other or to the thesis are useless facts. You need to direct your answer toward the exact question asked and to respond to it concisely, but sufficiently, in the time allowed. If you are wondering how to do all of this, you share a concern with almost every undergraduate student.

Answering an essay examination question

Following are some guidelines for taking essay examinations. Some of them may seem obvious, but under the pressure of time the simplest tasks can be forgotten or, worse, ignored in an attempt to cut corners.

Read the question—all of it. One difficulty with looking for key words to give you your direction is that you may skip too quickly over the rest of the question. Many essay answers are unsuccessful because they miss the point of the question. Make sure you understand not only what type of question it is, but what the specifics are, and what all of your obligations are. Many essay questions have two or more parts, and it is a common mistake for students to answer the first very capably, the second in less acceptable fashion, and to ignore the third. Before you begin to write, make sure that you are aware of all of your responsibilities.

Make notes on what you know about the subject. Although it takes a few minutes to jot down a few words and phrases, taking the time to do so can result in a better answer than if you immediately begin writing.

TABLE 3.3

Key words in questions
of argument and
interpretation

Words	What they ask	Example
Agree or Disagree	Give your opinion about a topic. You must express either a positive or a negative opinion. Support your opinion from appropriate sources.	The first six months of a child's life are the most important period in its emotional development. Agree or disagree.
Analyze	Break down the topic into its parts and explain how the parts relate to each other and to the whole topic.	Analyze the structure of Beethoven's Fourth Symphony.
Critique, Criticize	Break the topic into its parts (analyze); explain the meaning (interpret); and give your opinion (evaluate).	Critique Peter Singer's argument that all animals are equal.
Evaluate	Give your opinion about a topic. You may make both positive and negative points, but you must come to some conclusion about the relative weight of good and bad points.	Evaluate the importance of protein molecules in a cell.
Interpret	Explain the meaning of the topic. Give facts to support your point of view.	Interpret the meaning of the election statistics given on page 12 of your textbook.
Justify, Prove	Give reasons to show why the topic or assertion is true. Use examples.	Justify, from a Southerner's point of view, the need for slaves in the ante bellum South.

These notes will help you to make decisions about the question. In a "compare" or "contrast" question, do you know which approach you want to take? Should you criticize or support a thesis in a question? What *do* you think of Steinbeck's *Grapes of Wrath*? You need to know before you begin. A common problem with timed essays is lack of focus, caused often because students discover what they want to say as they write and, consequently, change directions in midcourse. A few minutes at the

TABLE 3.4
*Key words in questions
of application and
speculation*

Words	What they ask	Example
Could . . . ?	Determine if the topic is capable of what is being asked. Your response should include a yes or no answer.	Could Hitler have won World War II if he had defeated Great Britain in 1940?
How would . . . ?	Determine the probable reaction to the topic in the circumstances provided.	How would President Truman have reacted upon discovering the Watergate break-in?
What would happen . . . ?	Based on what you have already learned, determine the probable outcome of a new set of circumstances.	Concentrated solutions of urea (8 M) act as denaturing agents for proteins by disrupting noncovalent bonds. What would happen to the configuration of a protein dissolved in 8 M urea?

beginning spent making your decisions, organizing your notes into coherent groups, and putting these groups into a logical order will save you valuable writing time, for you will be writing purposefully.

Write the answer. Be direct. The instructor is not hunting for elegant phrases or meticulously chosen words in a timed essay. He wants to know the state of your knowledge or your powers of analysis or your ability to synthesize data. As a rule—which you are allowed sometimes to break— try to begin with a clearly stated topic sentence in which you set down the scope and direction of your answer. Follow it with your reasons and supporting materials. Handle each part of the question separately and indicate at all times what you are doing.

"How long should the answer be?" Your instructor will give you guidelines. Stay within them. It is just as easy, and just as tempting, to write too much as too little. Theses not supported by facts, evidence, detail, or argument are not going to be received very well. On the other hand, do not put in everything you know about a topic with the expectation that your instructor will pick out whatever he wants. Selection is your job, not his. Concrete, supporting detail is very important, but only if relevant. Remember that your answer is not supposed to be a multiple-choice exam for your instructor.

The requirements of a timed examination almost always prevent the writing of a second draft, and your instructor understands that your essay will not be as good as it could be if you had more time. Nevertheless, your essay must be adequately written without glaring errors that will distract and annoy the reader. Spell words as well as you can (and especially do not misspell any of the words you had to learn for the exam), punctuate carefully, and use proper grammar. Make your handwriting legible. It is in your own interest to present your essay, the product of thorough study and careful thought, in a form worthy of its content. The studying that you have done in preparation for the examination will help to make some elements of the writing process routine. If you understand the concepts well before you come to the exam, you won't have to worry about generating ideas. The format of the essay is also pretty much determined by the exam questions. So plan to leave a few minutes at the end of the exam to proofread your answers.

So far in this book we have dealt with ways to use writing to think, to organize ideas, to record, and to write in classroom contexts. The rest of the book discusses the preparation for and writing of papers outside of class. Although these out-of-class assignments are designed to develop additional skills, keep in mind the strategies you have encountered so far. They can be helpful in a wide variety of writing tasks.

QUESTIONS

1 What is the value of reducing your class notes to lists or outlines?

2 What are your major responsibilities when writing a timed, in-class essay examination?

3 What are the main problems with underlining or highlighting material in your textbook?

4 What are the major differences between questions that ask you to argue a point of view and questions that ask you to speculate?

EXERCISES

1 Immediately after you leave a lecture, meet with several of your class-mates to "compare notes." Each of you should take several minutes to write down what you believe to have been the main points of the lecture. Discuss your impressions and try to resolve your differences.

2 Monitor your own study techniques. How do you study or use class notes? What strategies for studying do you think you could profitably try?

3 Practice reducing each paragraph in one of your reading assignments to one or two sentences.

4 Summarize in your own words the textbook entry in figure 3.1. In what ways is your summary different from the underlining in the text? Which do you believe will be more useful? Why?

4 Library Resources

The library and its resources are central to a liberal education. Writing a research paper is inevitably a part of the college experience, and the research typically done by college students starts within the walls of the library. To write a research paper based on library materials requires learning two skills: finding pertinent material, and shaping that material into a coherent paper. This chapter discusses resources that are available in the library, first the resources generally useful to all disciplines and then some specialized resources useful to particular disciplines. In the following chapter we explain methods for recording, summarizing, documenting, and acknowledging what you find. These two chapters, then, deal with the basic skills needed for library research. In later chapters (6, 9, and 14) we discuss how to use these skills (and others) to put together a complete term paper in the humanities, the social sciences, and in the natural sciences.

The research process in the library

Much student library research is hit or miss. If you start by looking in a card catalog for books or by browsing at random in the stacks, the research that results is almost inevitably incomplete and insufficient for a good paper. If the sources you do find are not related to one another, the problem of organizing your material becomes enormous. In addition, students often tend to be too content oriented in their library searches; they concentrate on finding information on the topic and pay too little attention to the quality, quantity, or nature of the sources they use. Papers written as a result of such haphazard searches are marked by blandness, lack of substance, overgenerality, and overdependence on too few sources.

To avoid these traps, library research should be systematic and follow a carefully conceived strategy. In designing such a strategy for a particular project it is helpful to keep in mind two general characteristics of library research. The first is that in the library, topics are explored at two different levels. One deals with content, using materials that give you information directly on the topic. The other level is bibliographical, the objective of which is not so much to get information on your topic as it is to find out what materials are available on the topic and some indication of the value of these materials. Efficiency in the use of your time in the library is a function of the interplay of these two levels. People who confine themselves to trial-and-error browsing in the stacks operate entirely at the content level. If they should find good sources, it is accidental, and they have no way of knowing if there are better sources available. It is more efficient to discover by a bibliographical search that a given book is not worthwhile than to spend time reading the whole book before you know. On the other side, of course, excessive time can be spent discovering what is available; at some point you must come to the content level and read on the substance of the topic.

Library research is made complex by the fact that these two levels are not completely successive. You do not typically first do a bibliographical search and then go to content. Library search should be thought of as a simultaneous, two-task process. The material that you are reading for content will also lead you to additional items for your bibliography, and items on your bibliography will lead you to new ideas about your subject matter. The process is continuing and self-perpetuating. An initial bibliographical search may indicate the name of a significant book. You read the book (content level) and find further references to other material (bibliographical level), which you then follow up. In addition, as you pursue the topic on the content level you may modify your understanding of the topic itself in a way that suggests new areas in which to conduct the bibliographical search.

A second characteristic of library research is that it typically proceeds from the general to the specific. As you proceed through the search, you will find your focus becoming increasingly narrowed until you finally get to the topic or aspect of the topic about which you will write. You can visualize the books and articles you need to read for your paper as contained in a circle surrounded by a series of concentric circles, each of which represents bibliographical aids of an increasing order of generality. If your topic is Dickens's *Hard Times*, then in the center circle are books and articles on *Hard Times*. The next circle out represents works on Dickens, more general than works on a novel by Dickens. The next circle would be bibliographies on Dickens—guides to materials on Dickens— then bibliographies of Victorian literature, and so on. The outermost circle represents guides to what is in the library (figure 4.1).

The research task is to get from the outermost circles to the innermost. Once the innermost has been reached, the bibliographical search is ended. If you know nothing about the library, you start at the outermost circle. If you don't need that, but you know little about Dickens, then start with the next circle—encyclopedias. Obviously, the farther in you can start, the faster the search, and where you start is dictated by your prior knowl-

FIGURE 4.1
*Order of generality in
a search for literature
on Dickens's* Hard
Times.

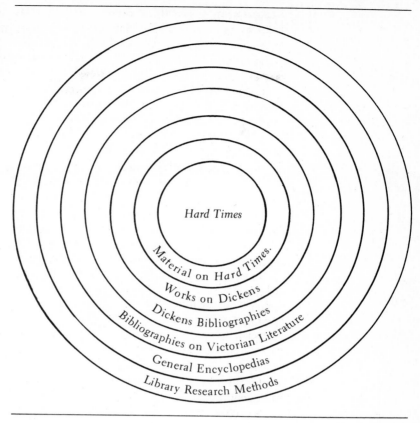

edge of the topic. In this respect, bibliographies are like maps. If you are looking for a small town in western Pennsylvania, and you know it is in Pennsylvania, it is more efficient to start with a map of Pennsylvania than with a map of the United States.

Before we describe the materials the library contains, it is worth mentioning a resource that you may overlook: the reference librarians. These are a special group of librarians whose sole function is to help you find what you need. They are best at telling you what reference works you can consult, particularly the more specialized reference materials.

The reference section *General encyclopedias. Encyclopaedia Britannica, Encyclopedia Americana,* and *Collier's Encyclopedia* are general reference works organized alphabetically and usually in many volumes. They contain articles on a wide range of topics, but although they give bibliographies at the end of each entry, they are not designed primarily as a bibliography. Their purpose is to cover the subject of the entry as completely as possible within the given space, and the references they make are usually to classic rather than to up-to-date works. Consequently, their primary use in library research is to give a very general overview of a topic. If you need a perspective on your topic, you might try an encyclopedia.

Using encyclopedias intelligently can yield more than a basic outline of information on the topic. For example, the most recent *Encyclopaedia Britannica* is divided into two parts, the Micropaedia and the Macropaedia. In the Micropaedia you will find brief information with directions on where to find more information in the Macropaedia. If you were researching Charles Dickens (see the Humanities section later in this chapter), you would discover in the Micropaedia a reference to "Dickens 5; 706" (meaning look up p. 706 of vol. 5 of the Macropaedia for the main entry on Dickens) and seven other references to related topics dealt with in the Macropaedia: English literature of the nineteenth century; the novel's attack on social abuses, and so on. These references collectively give you a good background from a variety of angles for your further reading and help you to begin to focus the topic.

Remember, your library search has two prongs: content and bibliography. While an encyclopedia can give you an introduction to a topic, it can also supply information on sources to read on the topic, that is, other places to search for information. The *Encyclopaedia Britannica* entry on Dickens, for example, lists four categories of books you may wish to consult: bibliographies, or books containing further lists of books on Dickens; biographies of Dickens; books of criticism of his works; and anthologies, or collections of essays on Dickens and his work. Consulting this general reference work gives you a good start.

Specialized encyclopedias. The *International Encyclopedia of the Social Sciences, Encyclopedia of Education Research, The Encyclopedia of the Biological Sciences, Encyclopedia of World Art, Encyclopedia of Philosophy, New Oxford History of Music, Encyclopedia of Bioethics* are examples of specialized encyclopedias. Like general encyclopedias, these are arranged in essays on topics of particular relevance to their field. The entries tend to be more complete than in the general encyclopedias and more detailed in their treatment of topics. The bibliography can be only as up to date as the date of the encyclopedia itself. Another useful aspect of these encyclopedias is the fact that they are indexed and have cross-references at the end of each entry. But as with the general encyclopedia, these volumes provide an overview of a topic rather than extensive bibliographies. If you are lucky, you may find that the entry you consult has an annotated bibliography in which the author of the piece makes a judgment about each reference and what it might be used for.

Other reference works. Almanacs, atlases and biographical dictionaries such as *the World Almanac and Book of Facts, The Times Atlas of the World, Dictionary of American Biography*, and *Who's Who* are used to check facts.

Bibliographies, indexes, and abstracts

In this category are all those materials that deal primarily with bibliographical information. There are general indexes and ones devoted to special fields, such as *Social Sciences Index, Humanities Index, New York Times Index, Reader's Guide to Periodical Literature, Book Review Index, Statistical Index, Books in Print, Dissertation Abstracts, The Philosopher's Index, Biological Abstracts, MLA Bibliography*. This category of materials is somewhat confusing because it contains several different terms. "Bibliography" means merely a list of books and other sources. An index "points to" where books or articles are to be found.

Some bibliographies, referred to as annotated bibliographies, provide a brief description or evaluation of the citation. These comments ("a reliable historical study"; "a new interpretation") are to be treasured as guides. These abstracting journals are usually published monthly and bound in annual volumes with a subject index and author index. Articles referred to are grouped by topic, and the entry includes complete bibliographic material and a summary of the article. Books are also entered in the abstracts. Since the abstracts survey hundreds and hundreds of journals, some or many of the articles abstracted will be unavailable, depending upon the size of your library. After reading the abstract, you must decide whether the article is important enough to your paper for you to read the article itself. Some indexes provide complete abstracts or summaries of the article or book cited.

In order to use indexes you must know the category under which to look, the key word. Thus, obviously, in a search for an essay on Dickens's *Hard Times*, the two key words are "Dickens" and "*Hard Times.*" But a topic will not always have an obvious key word. If so, you must be creative. The information you derive from the encyclopedia or other general reference works should give you several leads, or the books you have on the topic may give you ideas for entry words.

Citation index

One strategy is the forward search using the *Science Citation Index* or *Social Science Citation Index* or *Humanities Citation Index*. Unlike a search using *Biology Abstracts* or any other abstract series, where you search back through the literature for articles on your topic, the citation indexes are arranged so that you can search forward in the literature from a given reference to all the more recent articles that cite the given reference in their bibliographies. This indexing system is based on the assumption that research reports announcing new discoveries will cite previous research reports on the same topic. Let us say that you are working on a psychology paper on short-term memory. Your psychology textbook says that George Miller's article "The Magical Number Seven, Plus or Minus Two" is an important article. After reading this article, you can look up the author and article in a citation index. There you will find a list of all the articles published in a designated one-year period that have cited "The Magical Number Seven, Plus or Minus Two." You can in this way find more recent articles about short-term memory. Since Miller's article was first published in 1956, you would consult only those volumes published after 1956, giving particular attention to the more recent annual indexes. A citation index is an effective way to locate up-to-date information.

Books The organization of books in library stacks is based on one of two systems: the Dewey Decimal System or the Library of Congress System. The number systems they use—that is, the codes by which they classify books—are different. The older Dewey system classifies books according to subject category (a number) and author (a letter). The system has proved inflexible for many new subject areas, so most libraries have switched to the Library of Congress System, illustrated in the example cards in figure 4.2, which assigns to each subject area a letter or combination of letters (European history D and DR) followed by numbers that designate subdivisions within the categories. College librarians will be happy to provide you with a breakdown of the classification system used in your library.

When looking in a card catalog for books, it is wise to look under as many different topics or references as possible. Remember our advice and keep a list of key words, that is, words that relate to your topic and might themselves be classified separately in bibliographies or the card catalog. Such a list not only allows you to approach your topic from different directions, it may also lead you to books in sections of the stacks you might not find if you restrict your search. You may discover other related books. For example, for a topic on King Charles II of England, key words you may come across are: England; Stuart, Monarchy (found in political science section), Cabal, London, Louis XIV (found in the history of France section). Browsing in these other sections may produce still more books containing pertinent information. Although browsing in itself is not an adequate research strategy, it can help you to uncover information that has eluded your organized search. Besides, browsing is fun.

Periodicals Periodicals include journals, newspapers, and magazines. Depending on your topic, you may find some or all of these periodically issued publications useful, for they contain short, theme-oriented pieces. Particularly in the specialized journals in your field of research, the articles often present types of writing you may not get from books. For example, journals contain articles outlining a new direction in a field, containing the latest research on a subject, or discussing debates that exist on your topic.

Journals are classified by their title in a special card catalog, not usually the same card catalog described above. Early in your research you should check your own library's holdings of those journals that seem to be frequent sources of articles on your subject. Then you can look at recent issues of the journal to find up-to-date material. The best way to search for articles when you don't know which journals to look in is to use the indexes described above.

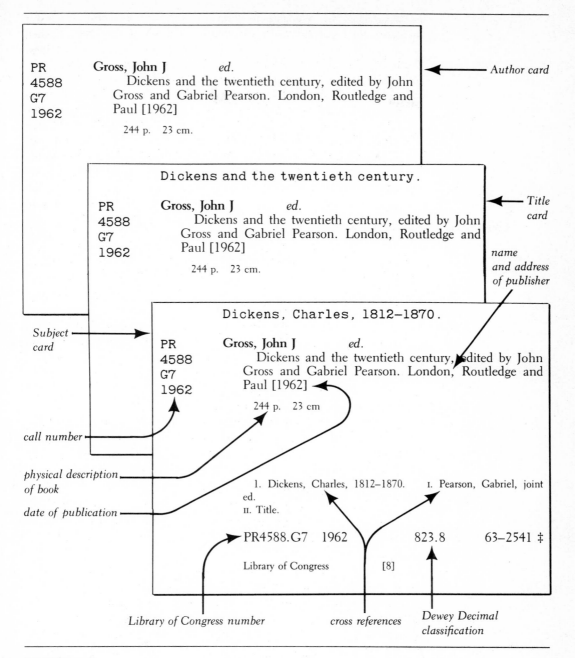

Author card

PR
4588
G7
1962

Gross, John J   *ed.*
Dickens and the twentieth century, edited by John
Gross and Gabriel Pearson. London, Routledge and
Paul [1962]

244 p.   23 cm.

Title card

name and address of publisher

Dickens and the twentieth century.

PR
4588
G7
1962

Gross, John J   *ed.*
Dickens and the twentieth century, edited by John
Gross and Gabriel Pearson. London, Routledge and
Paul [1962]

244 p.   23 cm.

Subject card

Dickens, Charles, 1812–1870.

PR
4588
G7
1962

Gross, John J   *ed.*
Dickens and the twentieth century, edited by John
Gross and Gabriel Pearson. London, Routledge and
Paul [1962]

244 p.   23 cm

call number

physical description of book

date of publication

1. Dickens, Charles, 1812–1870.
ed.
II. Title.

I. Pearson, Gabriel, joint

PR4588.G7   1962

Library of Congress   [8]

823.8   63–2541 ‡

Library of Congress number   *cross references*   *Dewey Decimal classification*

FIGURE 4.2
How to read cards in the card catalog.

77   *Library Resources*

Periodicals are available in three forms: current issues, which are located in the current periodical section of the library; bound past volumes; and some form of microfilm, such as microfiche or microcards. Periodicals should be used with caution. *Newsweek*, for example, is not sufficiently scholarly for many research projects, while it is usually futile to struggle through journals intended for advanced professionals. Your instructor may provide a list of journals that are most useful for your level of research and for your topic.

Not the least value of consulting periodicals is that they give you models for the tone and style of the discipline in which you are working, for organization, and for footnoting style (chapter 5). Articles are, in a sense, professional term papers.

Other library resources   In small colleges, if the library does not have a copy of a book you need, you can order it through interlibrary loan. Most libraries have this service. You can also order copies of articles that your library does not have. (You must pay for a photocopy of the article, so it is especially important that you be able to assess the probable value of something before you order it.)

You might also want to consider using a computer search of a topic. The computer provides a list of materials on the topic requested. When using a computer, you must carefully select a key word for the categories you want searched, for you want a list of a reasonable size. You limit what the output is by the key words you choose, by the dates you want searched, and by the characteristics of the materials you want. A computer search is of greatest value when the paper demands information as current or as comprehensive as possible.

Up to this point we have been discussing the library as it can be used by students in all disciplines. The following three sections of this chapter deal with the specialized resources that exist for three major areas of study: humanities, social sciences, and natural sciences. In each case we will take you through a hypothetical search to provide a model of how searches can be done. You should not think that library research is always conducted in a neat, sequential order as presented (general background, bibliographical search, specialized research). Actual library research is messy. We hope that the following procedure will help make it less messy and more productive.

Resources in the humanities

Assume you are assigned to do a research paper on Charles Dickens's *Hard Times*. The twofold task of researching this topic in the library requires that you find out useful information about *Hard Times* and find out where that information exists. As we have suggested in the first section of this chapter, your research begins at the most general level and progresses to the more specific sources.

Encyclopedias and specialized encyclopedias

If you begin with the *Encyclopaedia Britannica*, you will find that the article on Charles Dickens is seven pages long, followed by two columns of bibliography. In addition to getting an overview and chronology of his life, you will also read some conflicting opinions about him and a statement of the controversies that surround him and his work. In the bibliography, you will find listed several different types of literature used in compiling the encyclopedia entry: biographies, criticism, and anthologies. In addition, the list contains citations for other bibliographies from which to continue and expand your search.

Books

If you look in the card catalog under the subject category *Dickens*, you will find not only the editions of *Hard Times* possessed by the library but also books on *Hard Times*. An example is a book called *Twentieth Century Interpretations of Hard Times*, edited by Paul Gray. In a search for material on *Hard Times*, the discovery of a book like this is of enormous value. It is exactly on your subject with a set of essays by different people, so you ought to be able to get a wide perspective on the novel from it. Books like this also typically are very helpful for bibliographies. This collection of essays will help you with both of your purposes: to find useful content and to seek out appropriate additional sources.

Bibliographies in books like this also are typically selective and often usefully annotated. If you find this book, you will discover at the end of it two pages entitled "Selected Bibliography," which give you further references to material on *Hard Times*, with comments indicating why the editor is recommending them:

Carnall, Geoffrey, "Dickens, Mrs. Gaskell, and the Preston Strike," *Victorian Studies*, VIII (1964), 31–48. A specialized but informative study of the influence of contemporary events on the composition of *Hard Times*. [1]

Book reviews

Book reviews are useful for several reasons. They provide a quick way of determining what is in a book. They give you information on how the book has been received, especially by other people in the field. The reviews in the more scholarly periodicals provide a critical commentary on the book, sometimes challenging the author on important matters. Thus, on one level, reviews are valuable in being convenient and quick, telling you right away whether the book is worth getting. This information is especially useful when the book is not immediately available. But at another level, book reviews in scholarly journals may have the same status and authority as a periodical article; it is perfectly acceptable to quote from book reviews as you do from periodical articles.

1 Paul Gray, ed., *Twentieth Century Interpretations of Hard Times* (Englewood Cliffs, N.J.: Prentice-Hall, 1969), p. 122. © 1969. Reprinted by permission of Prentice-Hall, Inc.

If you want a quick look at the contents of the book, the best source is *Book Review Digest,* which arranges its entries by author, title, and subject, alphabetically. It is called a digest because it prints excerpts from some of the reviews, which give you a sense of the book quickly. Other book review indexes include *An Index to Book Reviews in the Humanities.*

According to the *Encyclopaedia Britannica,* Edgar Johnson's *Charles Dickens: His Tragedy and Triumph* is "now the standard biography." Suppose you want to check on that judgment. Then look up Edgar Johnson in the relevant year of the *Book Review Digest* (for 1953, its first year of publication). You will find data on the book, a brief description of the content of the book, and whether it contains a bibliography or index. Then follow references to reviews in some twenty-one periodicals.

When there is a good article on your subject printed in a book whose title does not indicate it, look in the *Essay and General Literature Index.* If you look up Dickens in the 1975 edition, you will find that it indexes some articles on Dickens generally and also articles specifically on *Hard Times*:

Dickens, Charles
       About
 Frye, N. Dickens and the comedy of humors. *In* Wimsatt, W. K. ed. Literary criticism: idea and act p537–59
 Quirk, R. Charles Dickens, linguist. *In* Quirk, R. The linguist and the English language p1–36

    About individual works
      Hard times
 Haberman, M. The courtship of the void: the world of Hard times. *In* The Worlds of Victorian fiction p37–55[2]

This entry tells you there is an essay dealing with *Hard Times,* entitled "The Courtship of the Void; The World of Hard Times," printed in a book called *The Worlds of Victorian Fiction,* the essay appearing on pages 37 to 55.

Articles in periodicals To find what articles on a subject have been published or to find more information on an article whose reference you already have, you consult a periodical index, such as *Reader's Guide to Periodical Literature, Social Sciences and Humanities Index, Humanities Index, International Index,* or *British Humanities Index.*

More specialized indexes, useful on other topics in the humanities, include *The Art Index, The Philosopher's Index, Music Index, Index to Reproductions of American Painting, Index to Reproductions of European Painting, Historical Abstracts.*

2 *Essay and General Literature Index.* Copyright © 1975 by The H. W. Wilson Company. Material reproduced by permission of the publisher.

A specialized bibliography in English is the *MLA Bibliography*. It is not selective, so it includes references to everything published in a given year on, say, Dickens. In the 1977 edition, for example, there are 113 items on Dickens, only six of them mentioning *Hard Times* in the title. This is not to say that only six articles discuss *Hard Times*; as we already saw, articles and books can be significant for a subject without that fact being reflected in the title. Thus, the following entry might well deal with *Hard Times*, but from the title one cannot tell:

> 5040. Feltes, N. N. "To Saunter, To Hurry: Dickens, Time and Industrial Capitalism." VS 20:245–67.[3]

To find out whether the article does deal with *Hard Times*, you must either read it or find an abstract of it. (See next section.) Specialized bibliographies are therefore not a good *initial* bibliographical source. It is reasonable however, to consult the most recent editions to find material too recent for other bibliographies. It would not be a reasonable enterprise, however, for an undergraduate term paper on *Hard Times* to take, say, the last ten editions of the *MLA Bibliography* and note down all the pieces that have *Hard Times* in their title (or related words or phrases that you should recognize from reading the novel, such as the Gradgrind School or Fact or Fancy.) You should notice which journals seem to be the ones significant articles appear in: *Nineteenth Century Fiction, Dickensian, Victorian Studies*. You can also look in *The New Cambridge Bibliography of English Literature* (CBEL) and in *Year's Work in English Studies*.

Abstracts of articles   Abstracts of articles summarize the content of the article and should be used to decide whether to read it or not, not as a substitute for reading it. From 1970 to 1975, the *MLA Bibliography* published a volume of abstracts of selected articles. You can also consult *Abstracts of English Studies*, which, since 1958, has published summaries of articles.

Library research in the social sciences

Social science materials can be searched by level of generality, as described in the first half of this chapter. We will describe materials at three levels of generality: encyclopedias and handbooks, books, and journal articles and indexes. A search conducted on any single topic will introduce only a subset of reference works in the social sciences. In these pages we select one topic—autism, a psychotic disorder characterized by emotional aloofness and delayed or absent speech—and we follow that topic through all reasonable reference materials. Although our search for information on

---

[3] Reprinted by permission of the Modern Language Association of America from the *MLA Bibliography 1977*. Copyright © 1978 by the Modern Language Association of America.

autism will introduce a wide range of reference materials, at times we will point to related reference works that cover additional areas in the social sciences.

Encyclopedias, dictionaries, handbooks, and yearbooks in the social sciences

These references provide the most general level of information. They contain summaries of topics in the social sciences and are a good starting place for your research. The *International Encyclopedia of the Social Sciences* is written to help students and social scientists keep abreast of developments outside their specialties. The entries provide an historical perspective and sometimes also give some indication if controversies exist. The editors include some research contributions from outside the United States. But it is unlikely that the material found here would be of any more use, and might possibly be of less use, than that found in a good textbook.

In the section on childhood mental disorders in the *International Encyclopedia of the Social Sciences*, you find a paragraph on autism embedded in an eight-page article on childhood mental disorders. (See figure 4.3.) From this paragraph you obtain a reference to a book by Kessler, published in 1966. Since Kessler's definition is cited in this very general reference work, you can assume that her book as a whole is important to your search.

Reviews of the field

There are three series in the social sciences, *The Annual Review of Anthropology*, *The Annual Review of Psychology*, and *The Annual Review of Sociology*, and similar series in biology, chemistry, and medicine. Each annual volume contains about a dozen articles written as a review and perspective on the topic for professionals in the field. These reviews are highly regarded by social scientists, although students will find them a little more difficult to use than the *International Encyclopedia*. If the topic of your paper happens to be one in an area covered by a review article, an annual review will be an immensely useful addition to your bibliography. Below are examples of selected chapter titles from three recent annual reviews.

Annual Review of Anthropology
Anthropological Economics: The Question of Distribution
Apes and Language
Dance in Anthropological Perspective

Annual Review of Psychology
Prevention: The Clinical Psychologist
Facial Expression of Emotion
Individual Differences in Cognitive Abilities

Annual Review of Sociology
The Sick Role: Assessment and Overview
The Social Organization of the Classroom
Urban Density and Pathology

FIGURE 4.3
Excerpts from Britton
K. Ruebush,
"Childhood Mental
Disorders," in
International
Encyclopedia of the
Social Sciences, *ed.*
David L. Sills,
Macmillan/Free Press.
Copyright © 1968.

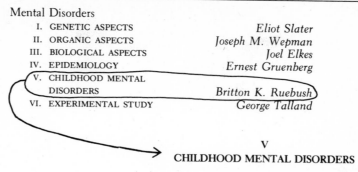

Mental Disorders

I.	GENETIC ASPECTS	*Eliot Slater*
II.	ORGANIC ASPECTS	*Joseph M. Wepman*
III.	BIOLOGICAL ASPECTS	*Joel Elkes*
IV.	EPIDEMIOLOGY	*Ernest Gruenberg*
V.	CHILDHOOD MENTAL DISORDERS	*Britton K. Ruebush*
VI.	EXPERIMENTAL STUDY	*George Talland*

V

CHILDHOOD MENTAL DISORDERS

Early conceptions of mental disorders in children are reflected in several clinical papers on child-rearing practices from the sixteenth, seventeenth, and eighteenth centuries (see Kessen)

. . .

Autism and symbiotic psychosis. Childhood psychoses do not tend to crystallize into as many varieties or subtypes as is the case with adult psychoses (Kessler 1966). Two major subtypes have been defined in early childhood: infantile autism and symbiotic or interactional psychotic disorder. Age of onset in infantile autism is the first few months of life as the infant fails to develop a normal emotional attachment to a mother figure. He remains emotionally aloof, speech development is delayed or absent, feeding and sleeping problems and stereotyped motor and motility patterns are prominent, and the

look this up

symptoms

Each volume (except the sociology series) contains a subject and author index, with page numbers for each entry. The following entries on autism were found in the subject index of a recent volume of the *Annual Review of Psychology*.

Audition
  and sleep surround, 227
Australia
  nutrition studies in, 162
Autism
  and behavioral genetics, 477
  in children
    and behavioral intervention, 451
Aversion
  and classical conditioning
    588–91, 595–96
  therapy
    and behavioral intervention, 451–54
Aversive consequences
  and counterattitudinal

hallucinations to self-destruction and simultaneously the enhancement of positive, socially appropriate behaviors.

Two developments of particular note described in the above reviews are the

. . .

not much on autism in this article

Behavioral interventions with autistic children typically must overcome particularly severe deficits of perception and responsivity to environmental contingencies and deficits in appropriate expressiveness, notably language. Reported interventions have often taken the form of case studies of experimental analyses of behavior in individual patients. See Lovaas & Newsom (171) for a comprehensive review.

Behavioral interventions with chronic psychiatric patients involve problems both in the initial training of behavior and in ensuring generalization and maintenance of behavior. The reinforcement history of these patients has been shown to render

this looks very useful

171. Lovaas, O. I., Newsom, C. D. 1976. Behavior modification with psychotic children. In *Handbook of Behavior Modification and Behavior Therapy*, ed. H. Leitenberg, pp. 303–60. Englewood Cliffs, NJ: Prentice-Hall. 671 pp.

Human Studies

During the years 1973 through 1976, there were many significant advances in human behavioral genetics. Our telescopic overview of this research can be supple-

. . .

The amount of research in psychopathology has been especially impressive during this period, as indicated by the appearance of three books focused on the genetics of psychopathology (91, 206, 286) and by the large number of reviews of specific areas: schizophrenia (83, 108, 109, 275, 306, 333), affective disorders (104, 234, 304), neuroses (211, 241, 246), autism (113, 291), homosexuality (245), hyperactivity (34), criminality (40), and chromosome anomalies (213). The methodologically sophisticated XYY study recently reported by Witkin et al (330) substantiates the possible

113 Hanson, D. R., Gottesman, I. I. 1976. The genetics, if any, of infantile autism and childhood schizophrenia. *J. Autism Child. Schizophr.* 6:209–33

291. Stabenau, J. R. 1975. Some genetic and family studies in autism and childhood schizophrenia. In *Mental Health in Children*, ed. D. V. S. Sankar, 1:31–60. Westbury, NY: PJD Publications

The pages referred to, which were in two separate articles, are presented in figure 4.4. The numbers indicate references at the end of the chapter.

Education yearbooks

Handbooks are published every few years and provide excellent summaries and perspectives on diverse topics in education. For example, the *Second Handbook of Research on Teaching*, edited by R. M. Travers, contains forty-two chapters, each written by experts in the field, who summarize the cumulated state of knowledge and the impact of research in education. Topics include methodological issues; early education; mentally handicapped; gifted; reading, math and other content areas; teacher education. *The Teacher's Handbook*, edited by Dwight Allen and Eli Seifman, covers topics concerned with various aspects of the teacher's role; the instructional process; the development of the learner, both normal and exceptional; curriculum and content areas; and theoretical, sociological, and ethical issues confronting education. In these education yearbooks you will find references to the teaching of autistic children.

Political science and economics yearbooks

In your search for information on autism, you would not be likely to use materials in political science, economics, or business, but you should know that these fields also produce many handbooks and yearbooks. *The Annual Register of World Events: A Review of the Year* discusses world events by geographic region and includes documents and maps as well as chronology; *Demographic Yearbook* provides statistics for 250 countries; *Yearbook of the United Nations* presents the activities of the United Nations and its agencies. The Government Printing Office publishes thousands of documents annually, which are listed in the *Monthly Catalog of United States Government Publications*. A selective and more useful list is provided in *Public Affairs Information Service Bulletin*.

Students of political science and economics and business will need to use newspapers to obtain up-to-date information on their topics. The *New York Times* and the *Wall Street Journal* both publish indexes that guide the student to the location of articles on a topic. The *New York Times Index* provides a summary of news events with references to individual articles.

Books

After reviewing yearbook and encyclopedia material on your topic, you should turn to books and monographs. The card catalog entry for autism might yield the entries shown in figure 4.5.

When browsing through the stacks you frequently will find other useful books. In this case, a student looking for the Davids's book in the RJ section discovered that another book, *Annual Progress in Child Psychiatry and Child Development* by Stella Chess and Alexander Thomas, had two chapters on autism.

Following up on the reference to the book by Kessler cited in the encyclopedia article, we find in the foreword to the Kessler text that it is "addressed to people seriously interested in the general areas of child

FIGURE 4.4
(on facing page)
Entries in Annual Review of Psychology. *Reprinted by permission of the authors and Annual Review, Inc.*

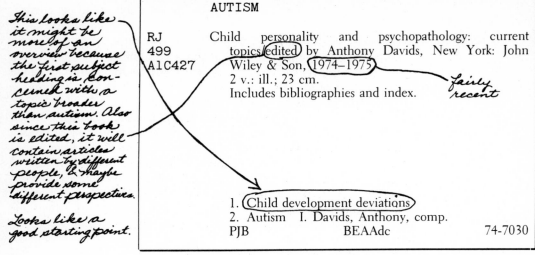

This looks like it might be more of an overview because the first subject heading is concerned with a topic broader than autism. Also since this book is edited, it will contain articles written by different people, & maybe provide some different perspectives.

Looks like a good starting point.

AUTISM

RJ 499 A1C427 · Child personality and psychopathology: current topics (edited) by Anthony Davids, New York: John Wiley & Son, (1974–1975) 2 v.: ill.; 23 cm. Includes bibliographies and index.

fairly recent

1. (Child development deviations)
2. Autism   I. Davids, Anthony, comp.
PJB   BEAAdc   74-7030

This seems to be written for parents.

Maybe good for filler or examples — don't want to start with this.

Autism.

RJ 506 A9D46 · **Des Lauriers, Austin M** Your child is asleep; early infantile autism: etiology, treatment, (parental) influences [by] Austin M. Des-Lauriers [and] Carole F. Carlson. Homewood, Ill., Dorsey Press, 1969
xiv, 403 p. 24 cm. (The Dorsey series in psychology)

Bibliography: p. 385–391.

1. Autism.   i. Carlson, Carole F., Joint author.   ii. Title.

RJ506.A9D46   618.92′8′9   68-56869
Library of Congress   [5]   MARC

FIGURE 4.5
Card catalog entries.

Autism

RJ 506 A9B4   **Bettelheim, Bruno.**
    The empty fortress; infantile autism and the birth of the self. New York, Free Press [1967]

    xiv, 484 p. illus. 24 cm.

    Bibliography: p. 461–468.

Autism

RJ 499 R54   **Rimland, Bernard, 1928–**
    Infantile autism; the syndrome and its implications for a neural theory of behavior. [New York, Appleton-Century-Crofts [1964]

    xi, 282 p. 22 cm. (The Century psychology series)

    Bibliography: p. 237–265.

    1. Autism. I. Title.

RJ499.R54   135.37   64–12897
Library of Congress   [4–1]

Autism

RJ 506 A9C6   **Coffey, Hubert S.**
    Group treatment of autistic children [by] Hubert S. Coffey [and] Louise L. Wiener. Collaborators: Carter Umbarger [and others] Englewood Cliffs, N.J., Prentice-Hall [1967]

    xii, 132 p. illus. 22 cm. (Prentice-Hall psychology series)

    Bibliography: p. 131–132.

AUTISM – CASES, CLINICAL REPORTS, STATISTICS.

RJ 506 A9S79   **Stuecher, Uwe.**
    Tommy: a treatment study of an autistic child. Arlington, Va., Council for Exceptional Children [1972]

    xi, 52 p. illus. 21 cm.

    Bibliography: p. 47–52.

    1. Autism—Cases, clinical reports, statistics. I. Title.

RJ506.A9S79   618.9′28′98209   72–94299
                                        MARC

psychopathology." The book contains chapters on different types of pathology in children and includes a section on diagnosis of infantile autism.

Journal articles, bibliographic indexes
The most sophisticated level of research material is found in the journals, so it is unwise to read individual journal articles until you have looked at books, encyclopedias, or yearbooks first. Journal articles assume that the reader knows something about the subject already, and so they may use terms or discuss data without providing a context. If you have done background reading first, then journal articles provide up to date and very specific information that cannot usually be obtained elsewhere.

The way to find journal articles on your topic is to use the abstracts. Here is a list of major indexing or abstracting publications.

Psychological Abstracts
Child Development Abstracts and Bibliography
Sociological Abstracts
Resources in Education
Developmental Disability Abstracts
Women's Studies Abstracts
Abstracts in Anthropology
Crime and Delinquency Literature

In one year of *Psychological Abstracts,* the following entries were found under the key words *autism* and *early infantile autism* in the subject index. This search must be repeated in each years' subject index as far back as it is productive to search.

Authoritarianism 11798, 12099
Authoritarianism (Parental) [See Parental Permissiveness]
Authority 11099, 11531, 11798, 11806
Autism [See Early Infantile Autism]
Autistic Children 10747, 11816, (11841,) 12069, 12088, 12178, 12217, 12273, 12702
Autohypnosis 10994
Automated Information Processing 12822

Early Infantile Autism 11815, 11816, 11840

Locating the numbers listed under the subject index yields the abstracts of articles. One abstract is shown in figure 4.6.

A search in one year of *Developmental Disabilities Abstracts* yielded several items in the subject index (figure 4.7). Notice that the summaries of these articles include the address of the author, a piece of information not available in *Psychological Abstracts.*

You can even find research reports that have not yet been published but that have been presented orally at professional meetings. A source of information for timely education-related reports is ERIC, standing for Educational Resources Information Center. The journal *Resources In*

Now that I know there is a whole journal on autism, I can just look through that for good articles.

Since journals usually have one volume number per year, I cleverly deduce that this journal must have begun in 1970.

11841. Cantwell, Dennis P.; Baker, Lorian & Rutter, Michael. (U California Medical School, Los Angeles) **Families of autistic and dysphasic children: II. Mothers' speech to the children.** *Journal of Autism & Childhood Schizophrenia,* 1977(Dec), Vol 7(4), 313–327. —Tested various hypotheses about deviance in the communication of mothers to their autistic children. The language of mothers of 13 autistic boys was compared to the language of mothers of 13 boys with developmental receptive dysphasia. The 2 groups of boys were of similar age (mean ages 9 yrs 0 mo and 9 yrs 7 mo, respectively), nonverbal intelligence (IQ at least 70), and language level. The language samples came from hour-long taped interactions between the mothers and their children in their homes. Aspects of maternal communication examined included the following: amount of language used, frequency usage of different types of utterances, syntactic complexity of utterances, grammaticality of utterances, clarity of communication, and tones of voice used. No differences were found between the 2 groups of mothers in level of language usage, pattern of functional interaction, or in overall clarity of communication. Findings provide *no* support for the suggestion that autism is due wholly or in part to deviant patterns of mother–child communication. (43 ref)—*Journal abstract.*

FIGURE 4.6
Entry in Psychological Abstracts. *Copyright © 1978 by the American Psychological Association. Reprinted by permission.*

Education (RIE) contains summaries and subject and author indexes for ERIC, as well as an institution index. Unlike the articles in other abstracting indexes, these articles are not published in journals, but are available from the ERIC Document Reproduction Service. Articles come in microfiche (film), which can be read on the library's microfiche reader, or in hard copy, which means on paper. Which form to order depends on its importance to your paper and your note-taking style. The microfiche is harder to read, but it is also much cheaper than the printed copy. Because most journals have a long time lag between first submission of an article by the author and its publication in the journal (two to two and a half years), ERIC is one way that authors disseminate their research more rapidly. You should therefore use the most recent issues of *RIE* in your effort to be up to date.

Resources in the natural sciences

Papers in the natural sciences are usually review papers and therefore must be up to date, comprehensive, and authoritative. Most references more than fifteen years old will be out of date and should be used only for historical purposes. Also, you should avoid nontechnical references (*Newsweek, Reader's Digest, The New York Times*), since these are generally popularized versions of the original, more complete research reports.

This seems very valuable — a complete search of the literature up to 1975. Although it would cost me $4.00, it would provide me with very complete information. I wonder if I can get it in time... the reference librarian probably knows how long it takes to get things from ERIC.

2426 *Autism. A Selective Bibliography. Exceptional Child Bibliography Series No. 603.* Reston, Virginia: Council for Exceptional Children, 1976. 32 p. Available from CEC Information Services and Publications, Council for Exceptional Children, 1920 Association Drive, Reston, Virginia 22091. Price $4.00.

Approximately 125 abstracts and associated indexing information are provided for documents or journal articles published from 1966 to 1975 and selected from the computer files of the Council for Exceptional Children's Information

. . .

for ordering microfiche or paper copies of the documents through the ERIC Document Reproduction Service.

2385 KIERNAN, CHRIS. Alternatives to speech: a review of research on manual and other forms of communication with the mentally handicapped and other noncommunicating populations. *British Journal of Mental Subnormality,* 23, Pt. 1(44):6-28, 1977.

The available evidence on alternatives to speech as means of communication suggests that nonco munication and a tistic state throug manual systems. How the whether the speech acqui tion is preferable or alternative ma ual cognitive dev tion be answered particular, the alt native understan ing supported

None of these journals are the same as the ones cited in Psychological Abstracts — the two abstracting journals must search different types of journals. It's probably a good thing I looked in both.

2449 KELLY, JOHN B.; & SAMUELS, MARIAN. A new look at childhood autism: school-parent collaboration. *Journal of School Health,* 47(9):538-540, 1977.

Special prolo autistic child schools can b ents, and son ents, school s in honor. Spe prolonged au child schools

2342 HAYES, R. W.; & GORDON, A. G. Auditory abnormalities in autistic children. *Lancet,* 2(8041):767, 1977. (Letter)

Hearing tests administered by means of the electroacoustic impedence meter to 16 autistic children 8-15 years of age with no records of an

FIGURE 4.7
(on facing page)
Entries in Developmental Disabilities Abstracts. (DDA *ceased publication in 1978, after appearing for ten years.)*

The process of locating references on a topic in the natural sciences is divided into three levels. First, you identify appropriate search words to help you locate information on your topic. Second, you identify and use textbooks, encyclopedias, data books, dictionaries, and/or monographs to learn the background information appropriate to your topic. Third, you identify and use recent review articles and research reports to learn the current state of knowledge on your topic. Here we use the topic of the relationship between marihuana and the female hormone estrogen to exemplify the search process, and in chapter 14 we use the same topic to show the process of writing a review paper in the natural sciences.

Background research

Discovering the conceptual framework in your subject area and determining exactly where your topic fits into this framework requires a considerable effort with relatively little visible results. That is, much of what you learn about your topic will not be converted directly into paragraphs in a term paper, but your understanding of the context will be crucial to the quality of your paper. Acquiring background knowledge is especially difficult in the sciences because of the dense technical quality of scientific information. But thorough background research assures in-depth understanding and confidence, which in turn inevitably shows up in your written work. Since the purpose of a textbook is to provide an overview of a discipline, your best starting point is often a search through the relevant textbooks you already own.

One of the most persistent problems in scientific literature searches is the successful selection of key words or search words that will lead to information on a given topic. Unfortunately, scientists do not always remember to put seemingly obvious key words into the titles of their research reports and books. Consequently, you will have to create a list of potential search words. Without these search words, it would be virtually impossible to locate specific information on your topic in all the thousands of books and hundreds of thousands of research reports published annually.

In the sample search on the marihuana-estrogen problem, you must identify search words that will produce information on the possibility that the active ingredient in marihuana may interact with or imitate estrogen. Working from the obvious search word "marihuana" and its alternate spelling, "marijuana," you can expand your search words by referring to the background reading:

marihuana
marijuana
    (alternate spelling)
tetrahydrocannabinol
    (active ingredient)
THC, Δ^9-THC, Δ'-THC
    (abbreviations of tetrahydrocannabinol)

Cannabis
(Latin name of marihuana plant)

The importance of multiple search words should be obvious when you discover that many scientists refer to the active ingredient, tetrahydrocannabinol, rather than the name of the plant, marihuana.

You should also write down some more general terms that include your primary topic, just in case the specific topic is not listed. In this case, those terms could be "hallucinogen," "toxicology," and "pharmacology." Colloquial terms are generally not used in scientific writing, and therefore your search words need not include "pot" or "grass."

General encyclopedias You might want to consult one or two of the general encyclopedias for background information on your topic. These sources, however, do not make very impressive references for your supposedly up-to-date paper, because a five-year or greater lag time occurs between the announcement of new discoveries and their inclusion in general encyclopedias. High-school students typically base their science papers on encyclopedia entries; college students begin to use monographs and technical journals as the major sources of information for their papers. Experienced college-level writers omit the general encyclopedias entirely from their search and instead concentrate their efforts on more up-to-date resources.

Specialized encyclopedias Certain specialized encyclopedias also can be useful if they include your topic. An example of such an encyclopedia is a new thirteen-volume reference on animals, *Grzimek's Animal Life Encyclopedia*. This encyclopedia is an outstanding source of information on animals, especially the vertebrates and is also useful because it has substantial, although not always conveniently arranged, bibliographies.

Both scientific dictionaries and regular unabridged dictionaries might help you understand unfamiliar words not found in your textbook, although these definitions will almost never be recent enough to be quoted directly in your paper.

Data books and handbooks Technical information on a variety of scientific subjects is frequently organized into data books. The best known reference of this type in the field of biology is the *Biology Data Book*. This three-volume work is part of a series, and the other books in the series (for example, *Respiration and Circulation* and *Metabolism*) can be helpful in searching for information on specific topics.

Other handbook references are useful in many science searches. The *Merck Index* provides chemical information that explains, for instance, why some articles call Δ^9-THC the active ingredient of marihuana while others mention Δ'-THC instead. A second handbook reference is the *Handbook of Chemistry and Physics*, which has many tables of chemical compounds.

Books If you are lucky, you might find in the card catalog a very recent book or collection of articles on your topic. If these books were published further back than two or three years ago, they will only add to your collection of slightly out-of-date background information and are therefore best eliminated. For example, a search through a typical college library card catalog under the search word "marihuana" revealed many well-thumbed cards, but only one book that was recent enough and sufficiently technical to seem even vaguely promising, and even this reference was several years old, so it probably would not have much recent information. Remember, in the natural sciences, information in books is never as up to date as information in periodicals. Books take a long time to be published, and in the meantime the information they present becomes somewhat out of date.

Periodicals The scientific periodicals are your most important source of up-to-date information. These journals publish articles (research reports) that announce the discovery of new scientific information. Some of these journals, like *Science* and *Nature*, contain research reports from a wide range of scientific disciplines, while others have reports from only a single discipline, like *Anatomical Record* and *Journal of Plant Physiology*.

Most research reports are written entirely by the scientists who did the research. But some scientists, often working with professional editors, write articles about their research intended for a general audience. These articles are valuable and can be used easily by undergraduates. The best-known sources for such articles include the journal *Scientific American*, the more technical journals *American Scientist* and *Bioscience*, and the less technical journals like *National Geographic* and *Smithsonian*. These journals are adequate source materials for most freshman classes. More advanced students should consult actual research reports.

Most published research reports are intended for the enlightenment of other scientists working in the same field, and these articles assume that the reader is already familiar with a specialized vocabulary. If you are going to understand these articles, you will need the vocabulary learned during your background reading, and you will have to cultivate a slow, deliberate, and thorough reading style.

Your most critical problem when doing library research on a scientific topic is to locate the most significant and recent five or so research articles on your topic. This is no small task, since more than a million scientific research reports are published each year. Fortunately, a variety of indexing and abstracting services can help you retrieve appropriate articles limited to your topic. As a beginning, students feel compelled to consult *Reader's Guide to Periodical Literature*, but this index includes only two or three (*Science*, *Scientific American*) of the thousands of journals publishing scientific research articles.

A relatively new indexing service, *General Science Index*, began in 1978. It indexes articles from approximately ninety major journals in the natural sciences and follows the *Reader's Guide* format. Although relatively shallow in its coverage, *General Science Index* is a reasonable starting point, especially for freshman or sophomore searches. For more in-depth searches, a specific and more complete index will produce the best results.

The numerous specific indexes differ both in their format and in the subject areas they include. The *Science Citation Index*, for example, includes articles from all the natural sciences. Most other indexes cover only one scientific discipline. For example, *Biological Abstracts* and its companion index, *Bioresearch Index*, as well as the *Biological and Agricultural Index* (a companion to *Reader's Guide*) and the *Biology Digest*, all index articles on topics in biology. Some indexes are even more limited; *Zoological Record* restricts its coverage to articles on the biology of animals.

Some of the more frequently used indexes for various scientific disciplines are:

Astronomy and Astrophysical Abstracts
Biological Abstracts
Chemical Abstracts
Bibliography and Index of Geology
Index Medicus
Physics Abstracts

In the marihuana-estrogen search we would select *Biological Abstracts* as an appropriate index. *Biological Abstracts* indexes and abstracts the biology articles contained in approximately 8,000 different journals. The abstracts themselves, which are short summaries of individual research reports, are arranged by topic and then numbered consecutively. To help you find the particular abstracts that you need, there are five different indexes: author, biosystematic, generic, concept, and subject. Most students find the subject index easiest to use.

Locate a key word in the subject index. Stop to examine the format of the index (figure 4.8). The most important words from the title and from the article itself have been condensed to a single, somewhat confusing line of type. A slash indicates the beginning of the title. The reference number in the right-hand column gives the number of the abstract. For example, in this list, only the twelfth article appears to deal with the relationship between marihuana and the estrogen hormones:

AXIS IN THE RAT PLASMA   GONADOTROPIN RELEASING   18350

Now look in the appropriate book of abstracts to find number 18350 (see figure 4.9) and read the abstract. Notice, by the way, that the actual title of the article has neither the term "marihuana" nor "gonadotropin." Repeat this process until you have about ten promising abstracts. Then locate these relevant original articles in the journals indicated. The article abstracted in figure 4.9 was originally published in volume 23 of *Neuroendocrinology*.

Subject Context	MARGIN ▼ Keyword	Ref. No.

Subject Context	Keyword	Ref. No.
OMAS AT THE PUPILLARY	MARGIN CAUSING SPONTANEOUS HYPHE	5533
SMALL SIZE OF RESECTION	FOR THIN CUTANEOUS MELANO	28314
OSYNTHESIS OF ORBITAL	FRACTURES VIA THE TRANS CON	19208
NASTANDLEY REFLEXED	MORPHOLOGY FERN TAXONOMY	13109
TENED LAMINA TOOTHED	MORPHOLOGY FOSSIL/ LEAVES	72375
S DIFFERENTIATION LEAF	MORPHOLOGY OF CERCIDIPHY|	
ICATORS AND THEIR	OF ERROR HUMA^	
FIES NEAR THE SUPERIOR	OF THE ...u	60370
TEAU IN THE NORTHERN	...ER CELANDIN	17391
C BASIN IN THE FA^**	....s MAINTAINED FROM E	66542
SEAL A^^ ^	SPINACH CAULIFLOWER CABB	73075
^...u.LLANO	FOR THIN CUTANEOUS MELANO	41625
..c uF DISEASE IN	MARIGOLDS CALENDULA-OOFFICINALS CUL	29505
SMOKE CIGAR/CIGARETTE	MARIHUANA /CHEMICAL STUDIES ON TOB	18285
JOINT SMOKING PARSLEY	/OUT PATIENT CLINICAL EXP	73298
OF THE CHRONIC USE OF	A REVIEW ANIMAL HUMAN T	23666
PERTENSION CIGARETTES	ALCOHOL ASPIRIN/ EXPERIE	30165
ONE DEMONSTRATION OF	AND COLA LEAF IN ILLICIT C	42123
ITION MEMORY HUMAN/	AND MEMORY IMPAIRMENT	23694
SSOCIATION REHEARSAL/	AND MEMORY INTRUSIONS H	61398
EN DEMAND/ EFFECT OF	AND PLACEBO MARIHUANA S	73297
LOR MATCH MID POINTS/	AND VISION AFTER 10 YEAR	4847
ION TIME/ ETHANOL AND	EFFECTS ON EVENT RELATED	17416
IS SATIVA SOUTH AFRICA	GALACTITOL CYSTEIC-ACID S	29638
AXIS IN THE RAT PLASMA	→GONADOTROPIN RELEASING	18350 ←
YORK STATE USA HUMAN	GOODMANS LOG LINEAR ME	61405
SEDATIVES ANALGESICS	HALLUCINOGENS STIMULAN	61397
DRAWAL/ TOLERANCE TO	HEART RATE AND SUBJECTIV	36297
PHORUS AND POTASSIUM	HEMP AMMONIUM NITRATE	12471
HITE COLLEGE STUDENTS	HEROIN COCAINE AMPHETA	4860
SCRIMINATION OF	INTOXICATION HUMAN/ THE	4821
UME FRAGRANCE SAFETY	MUTAGENESIS CARCINOGEN	12219
OVEMENTS/ EFFECTS OF	ON HUMAN REACTION TIME	67425
SE NEW YORK STATE USA	PSYCHOTROPIC DRUGS/ RUR	11748
OUTH AFRICA CELL WALL	SERINE O GALACTOSIDE LINK	29639
FECT OF PENICILLIN G BY	SMOKING CANNABIS DOG SU	74320
ARIHUANA AND PLACEBO	SMOKING ON PSYCHOLOGIC	73297
AN PLASMA FOLLOWING	SMOKING UV MONITORING/	42112
UNIVERSITY USA HUMAN	TOBACCO ALCOHOL/ DRUG	67427
ELATES OF ADOLESCENT	USE AS RELATED TO AGE SE	29859
ARIABLE/ DIMENSIONS OF	USE IN A MIDWEST CATHOLI	61391
OF LONG-TERM CHRONIC	USE ON NEURO PSYCHOLOG	42104
MATICAL MATRIX MODEL	MARINE /A MODEL FOR THE DYNAMIC ST	69651
IAN OCEAN FRESH WATER	/A TEMPORAL AND GEOGRAPHIC	44617
SKS ECOLOGY BEHAVIOR	/AN ANNOTATED BIBLIOGRAPHY	8857
ROWTH RATE BRANCHING	/MORPHOLOGY OF SORELLA IN N	56698
O CLIMATE FRESH WATER	/OXYGEN AND CARBON ISOTOPI	21478
GEOGRAPHY PALEOZOIC	/PALEONTOLOGY AND BIO STRAT	14612
MIDDENS	/RADIO CARBON DATING OF SHE	16440
ECOLOGY MORPHOLOGY	/REVISION OF THE ORDOVICIAN C	15555
IN HETERONEMA-ERECTA	/THE CARBON-13 NMR SPECTRU	46677

*promising-
looking article*

*articles on
marihuana —
29 of them!*

FIGURE 4.8
Excerpt from the subject index of Biological Abstracts, *vol. 65, showing the listing of articles on the subject of "marihuana." Copied with permission of* BioScience Information Service.

Even with *Biological Abstracts'* subject index and those thousands of abstracted articles, you will still spend a considerable amount of time on your search and yet miss some good references. Because of this problem, the computer-assisted search is becoming increasingly popular and certainly offers several advantages if properly designed. First, you will save some time, although designing the search takes several hours. Second, you will get a more thorough search since the computer usually includes several different indexing services in its data base. But you should also weigh the drawbacks: the computer search does cost more, and if you

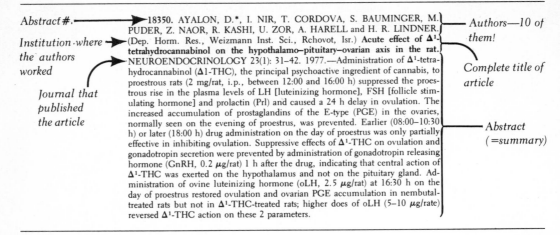

Abstract #. — 18350. AYALON, D.*, I. NIR, T. CORDOVA, S. BAUMINGER, M. PUDER, Z. NAOR, R. KASHI, U. ZOR, A. HARELL and H. R. LINDNER.

Institution where the authors worked

Journal that published the article

Authors—10 of them!

Complete title of article

(Dep. Horm. Res., Weizmann Inst. Sci., Rehovot, Isr.) Acute effect of Δ¹-tetrahydrocannabinol on the hypothalamo–pituitary–ovarian axis in the rat. NEUROENDOCRINOLOGY 23(1): 31–42. 1977.—Administration of $\Delta 1$-tetrahydrocannabinol ($\Delta 1$-THC), the principal psychoactive ingredient of cannabis, to proestrous rats (2 mg/rat, i.p., between 12:00 and 16:00 h) suppressed the proestrous rise in the plasma levels of LH [luteinizing hormone], FSH [follicle stimulating hormone] and prolactin (Prl) and caused a 24 h delay in ovulation. The increased accumulation of prostaglandins of the E-type (PGE) in the ovaries, normally seen on the evening of proestrus, was prevented. Earlier (08:00–10:30 h) or later (18:00 h) drug administration on the day of proestrus was only partially effective in inhibiting ovulation. Suppressive effects of $\Delta 1$-THC on ovulation and gonadotropin secretion were prevented by administration of gonadotropin releasing hormone (GnRH, 0.2 μg/rat) 1 h after the drug, indicating that central action of $\Delta 1$-THC was exerted on the hypothalamus and not on the pituitary gland. Administration of ovine luteinizing hormone (oLH, 2.5 μg/rat) at 16:30 h on the day of proestrus restored ovulation and ovarian PGE accumulation in nembutal-treated rats but not in $\Delta 1$-THC-treated rats; higher does of oLH (5–10 μg/rate) reversed $\Delta 1$-THC action on these 2 parameters.

Abstract (=summary)

FIGURE 4.9
Excerpt from Biological Abstracts, vol. 65, showing a single abstract of a research report. Major parts of the abstract are labeled. Copied with permission of BioScience Information Service.

design the search poorly, you can waste a lot of money. Also, only some of the references will have abstracts, and some will clearly be irrelevant. The information you present on the form is crucial to a successful search. For example, a request asking for all articles on the physiological effects of marihuana published in the last five years and giving no sample references produced a list of thirty marihuana references, but none on the particular problem of estrogen mimicry. When we redesigned the request to be more specific, the results were more satisfying: thirty-seven articles, thirty-two of which were directly relevant to the specific paper topic.

Review articles In addition to writing research reports, scientists also occasionally produce articles summarizing the state of knowledge in their particular field of research for the benefit of scientists outside that specialty. Most of these review articles appear in annual volumes with helpful titles like *Annual Review of Biochemistry* or *Recent Advances in Phytochemistry*, although some review articles can be found in regular scientific journals.

The most common method for discovering these articles is in the list of references of your up-to-date research reports. Otherwise, you will have to consult the *Bioresearch Index*, a companion indexing service to *Biological Abstracts*, which does index the articles in review series, or you would have to prepare a list of the likely looking review series (for example, in the sample search, *Annual Review of Pharmacology and Toxicology*, *Advances in Pharmacology and Chemotherapy*, *Advances in Drug Research*, and *Pharmacological Reviews*) and then check the table of contents for the last three volumes of each series for a useful review article.

These review papers can help you by organizing and summarizing the important research reports on your topic, but they also have three drawbacks: they may be out of date, since they are based on already published research; they may be biased, emphasizing the author's own opinions and research; and they may discourage you from independently organizing and summarizing the original research reports.

In summary

No matter what your discipline, your use of the library will have several common features. For all searches, there is the twofold process of generating a bibliography on a topic at the same time that the topic is being defined and refined by the content you are accumulating. For all disciplines, as we have seen, the search proceeds best from the general to the more specific. In using the library for a research problem, you have to make numerous decisions.

Always try to determine the specific expectations of your readers, whom you should usually presume to be scholars in the field of your research. These scholars will hold you to standards that are appropriate for apprentices in their field, so you don't have to worry about becoming an expert. Ask your instructor about the primary expectation for the particular paper you are working on. Is it more important, for example, that the paper be comprehensive or argumentative? Your readers' differing expectations will guide your choices of resources for research. In table 4.1 we list, on the left, various expectations for research papers and, on the right, the major research resources for each expectation.

QUESTIONS 1 Describe how you might use series of abstracts to save time in your research.

2 In a paragraph describe how you would find book reviews of a book that you have consulted during your research.

3 What do you do if your college library does not have the book you need to complete research on your topic?

4 Why are periodicals usually more useful than books for research on scientific topics?

EXERCISES 1 Select a topic, preferably a topic on which you are going to write an assigned paper, and read about it in the *Encyclopaedia Britannica*. What leads do you find from a proper use of this research aid?

2 Think of the categories of reference materials that you might consult for a paper on animal rights. Study figure 4.1 and then label concentric circles for the references you would use.

3 Using your response to exercise 1 as a beginning, make a list of key words suggested by your topic. Look these words up in your library's card catalog. Did you discover possibly useful books under the different entries?

TABLE 4.1 Research resources for various expectations for research papers	*Expectations*	*Resources*
	Up to date	Look for journals; use the most recent references. Find out if something important has happened to or on your topic which makes all previous work outdated. If so, this new development gives you a limit to the search. In books, look for recent symposia, particularly if they include bibliography.
	Comprehensive	Look for a book that has your topic as its primary focus. This is the best place to begin, for it makes the boundaries of the topic clear. Bibliographical search is especially important here.
	Authoritative	Look for material to certify the authority of your source. In a paper on the biology of DNA, it might be all right to quote *Newsweek* as an example of what the media are saying about the issue, but not as an authoritative source on an issue in biology. If you use a source heavily and authoritatively, you should find out how authoritative it is, in the case of books, by consulting book reviews (in an authoritative journal!) and in the case of periodicals by consulting specialized indexes if they are available (ask reference librarian) or by checking the biographies of the authors. Use the *Dictionary of American Scholars* (for scholars in the humanities) or *American Men and Women of Science* (for natural and social scientists). Or ask your instructor.
	Representative	The key here is to look for material that is one level above the example you are working with. For example, if you are to write about a school of writers or a school of art, you should not take one case and write as if that was representative of the school unless you have good reason to believe that this case is exemplary. If you are writing about Manet as an Impressionist, then you must read a book on Impressionism.
	Argumentative	Find controversy by looking in journals for articles with titles like "A Reply to . . ."; "In Defense of. . . ."

4 Select one of the three areas of study discussed in the sections entitled "Resources in . . ." and find out which of the resources discussed are in your college library.

5 Imagine that you have decided to write a paper on one of the following problems:

 a The evolutionary relationship between gorillas and humans

 b How the Viet Nam War affected the 1968 presidential campaign

 c The reasons for the attractiveness of religious cults.

Conduct a limited library search for books and articles that would be most useful to you. Limit yourself to the five best references. Explain briefly how you found each one.

5 Writing in the Library

Library work involves finding and reading, but just as important, it involves writing. Writing provides a record of your search. When you are ready to draft your paper, many days of work in the library will be represented by a few inches of 3 × 5 cards and several inches of 5 × 8 cards or notebook paper. This written record of your search enables you to organize wide-ranging resources into a manageable form.

But the writing you do as you search in the library provides more than a mere record. Your activity of writing, as you select, record, summarize, and comment, helps you to synthesize and structure the material as you find it. As we have said earlier, writing does more than help you to remember; writing helps you to see and to think.

Recording

Your procedures for recording library information should reflect the two different levels of any research process: the content level and the bibliographical level. You should distinguish between these two levels by the physical form of your notes: 3 × 5 cards for bibliography, 5 × 8 cards or notebook paper for content notes. Since your bibliographical search intermeshes with your content search, your note-taking system should reflect those connections.

During early stages of your library search, when you are compiling a working bibliography, you may want to jot down a short—very short—comment right on the bibliography card to remind yourself why a particular item looks promising. If you are dealing with an annotated bibliography, you may want to record the description on your card.

As you proceed with your bibliographical search, be sure to make a 3 × 5 card to record the precise reference for each source, even for those that you are almost certain you will not use in your final paper. Use the exact format that you will have to employ later in the final draft of your research paper. (For the two most frequently used formats for bibliographies and reference lists, see the end of this chapter.) It really doesn't take much more time to record complete bibliographical information. Removing a card from an alphabetized stack takes no time at all, but finding missing bibliographical information can take hours or days. When it comes time to prepare the final draft, your typist (especially if you are your typist) will appreciate having your reference items recorded in an appropriate and consistent form.

You will find 3 × 5 cards too small for your content notes, so use larger cards or notepaper. Although these notes are not just bibliographical, you should still record the source of each note. You need not repeat the full bibliographical information. Thus, "Smith, p. 232" would be sufficient if there is just one book by Smith in your working bibliography. You might construct a code to provide a key to each source. For example, you might number each bibliographical card and place that number on every page of notes you take from that source. Be sure to record the page numbers for every note you take, putting "pp." before them to distinguish them from code numbers or other numbers in your notes.

At the next stage of the process you are narrowing the working bibliography to those items that will be of greatest use to you. (Implication: You should walk out of the reference section of the library with a longer list of references than you think you will eventually use. Much of what you have on the first list is probably repetitive.) At the end of this stage you want to be in a position to go back over the notes you have taken and decide what you should read more carefully. While these notes do not have to be complete, you should develop a set of categories by which to judge each article or book: "looks comprehensive"; "technical"; "up to date"; and so on. Then you go back and take more extensive notes on the material.

The notes you take at this later stage should be in a form to make them useful to your specific purpose. If you see a passage that might make a good quotation, then write it out fully and carefully with quotation marks. Check that you have not omitted words and that you have punctuated the sentences precisely as the original author has done. There are few things more frustrating than trying to track down a quotation you remember but cannot pinpoint, or than wanting to use the exact words of an author when all you have recorded are your own abbreviations.

Your own abbreviations are most useful for recording facts or general information that you will not need to quote exactly. If you have developed a convenient system for taking notes in class or from your textbook, then use that system for recording information in the library. (See chapter 3 for some suggestions on taking notes.)

Whether you are quoting exactly, writing abbreviated notes, or summarizing, you should also be generating your own comments, ideas, and judgments on the material. As you write these reactions, be sure to distinguish them clearly from your record of an author's thinking. You may want to use a different color ink to record your own responses, or you may want to preface your own judgments with "My comment:" or something else of the sort. (See figure 5.1.)

Photocopy machines, which are widely available in libraries, make it possible for you to retain an exact copy of important sources and to mark what you read. But even if you own the source, you should write some notes on it. Photocopying an article is not reading it. For students with lots of pocket change, photocopying can equal procrastination.

Summarizing

As you work with library materials, it is often necessary to summarize lengthy passages into a form that you can later use. Even if you photocopy an important article, writing a one-paragraph summary of its key points helps you to understand the material. The summary may even remind you later why you thought the article important in the first place. But whether you make extensive use of summaries during your research process or not, you will certainly be required to condense and rephrase source

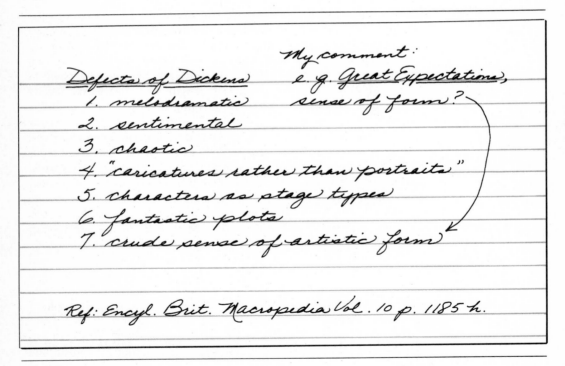

FIGURE 5.1
Sample content card.

material and then to embed this summarized information or opinion into the structure of your own paper. It is rarely appropriate in any discipline to present numerous lengthy quotations from a source. Identifying, selecting, and recasting the main ideas from your research materials are essential to the success of your project.

Before you read an article or chapter, you should decide why you are reading it. If you are writing a paper on the response of contemporary Victorians to *Hard Times,* and you read "Disinterested Virtue: Dickens and Mill in Agreement," it is your own question that dictates how you summarize the article. You can omit all reference to material not pertinent to your topic. This focused reading and summarizing speeds up the research process.

It is always a good idea to read a chapter or article completely and carefully before attempting to summarize it. Sometimes a writer delays stating the dominant idea until the end of the essay. You cannot see how all the parts fit together until you have read the whole thing. Having read it, remember that summarizing is an active process. You do not just list what each paragraph is about. Instead, you rearrange the parts to select the important ideas. Begin by stating in one sentence what the main point of the essay is. Then return to the passage to identify the parts and to determine how each part relates to the main point.

You may have been told that to summarize means to put something in your own words. That advice can be misleading. It is all right to use key words and even sets of two or three words from the original. You should not try to "translate" the passage into other words by looking up synonyms in the dictionary. A good summary is not so much putting something in your own words as it is putting something *into your own paragraph and into your own sentences.* The structure of your paragraph will look like no paragraph in the original essay, since your paragraph will summarize the ideas contained in several paragraphs of the original. No sentence in your summary should resemble any sentence in the original. It is not appropriate to copy a sentence with a word changed here and there.

The following is a passage from an introductory statistics text written by H. L. Levinson. Read this passage and then write a one-paragraph summary of it:

The World of Superstition

In games of chance there are bound to be runs of luck *for* and *against* the individual. This much is understood by everyone. No sane person sits down to a game of bridge with the expectation that all hands will be of about the same strength, nor does he expect the numbers in roulette to appear regularly in some order, so that, for instance, number 5 never would appear a second time until all the other numbers had had an opportunity to appear once. He expects these fluctuations due to chance—or luck, if he prefers to call it that—but he may see in them verifications of superstitions that he has previously acquired.

Quaint though the idea of looking to the stars for tips on the fall of a roulette marble may seem to some of us, it is a form of superstition which you may have encountered in some of your daily affairs without recognizing it! For instance: You are a businessman waiting at your office for a certain Mr. Jones to come in and sign a contract for a large order of your product. He phones at last to say that he will be unable to get in today. But before the day is ended Mr. Jones unexpectedly runs across other arrangements that seem more advantageous to him, and your contract is never signed. The true story of what happened is this: On that particular morning Mr. Jones spilled the salt at the breakfast table. At once he made up his mind to be extremely cautious that day, and above all not to sign the contract. Then came the other arrangements. Mr. Jones believes that the salt spilling was a special warning sent by a kind providence to prevent him from entering into a disadvantageous contract. In fact he says, if he had never believed in such signs before, a clear-cut case like this would have converted him at once.

What is the significance of such actions, examples of which could be multiplied almost indefinitely? Why are these superstitious beliefs still so widespread and deep-rooted in a period like the present one, which is called the *scientific era*?

In the days when science was virtually the exclusive property of a few isolated individuals, it could not be expected that popular beliefs would be much influenced by it. Today the case is radically otherwise; as everyone knows, we have been fairly bombarded with scientific products and by-products. Home, office, street, and farm are teeming with them. No one can say that he has not been exposed more or less directly to the influence of science, or that he has not had a chance to "see the wheels go around." And the man in the street believes in science, or at least claims to. He has seen it work and, almost without realizing it, trusts his life daily to the accuracy of its predictions. When he sits down before his radio for an evening's entertainment he does not say, "I hardly think it will work tonight, as I just saw the moon over my left shoulder." If it does not work he examines the electrical connections, or looks for a faulty tube. It never occurs to him to connect the mishap with the number of black cats he has recently met. He knows very well that the difficulty is in the radio, and that if he cannot fix it the repairman will, regardless of the moon and the black cats. Yet this same man will sit down to a game of cards and find it perfectly natural to attempt to terminate a run of bad hands by taking three turns around his chair.

These superstitious beliefs are a heritage from a past, in which magic and the black arts, witchcraft, sorcery, and compacts with the devil were among the common beliefs of the people. Today many of them have passed away, especially those more obviously contra-dicted by the findings of modern science. It has been a long time since the last trial for witchcraft at Salem. The onetime fear of charms and curses, laid upon one person by another, is now a mark of a primitive stage of civilization. Curses, says Voltaire, will kill sheep, if mixed with a sufficient quantity of arsenic.

Although there is no denying that the modern form of superstition is a milder manifestation than previous ones, yet in a sense it is a much less excusable belief. For the increase in our knowledge of the natural world during the last three hundred years is immense. Where there was chaos and mystery there is now order and mystery. Science has not taken away the ultimate mystery, but it has added a good deal of order. It is more of an intellectual crime to see the world today through the dark glasses of superstition than it once was.

Superstition would be less prevalent if more people realized that there is only one set of natural laws, that things work only *one* way, not half a dozen ways. Nature abhors a contradiction. If a deck of cards really does take account of the fact that I dropped and broke my mirror this morning and distributes itself accordingly, why should I not expect my automobile to begin climbing telegraph poles under like circumstances? The one is a collection of fifty-two printed slips of paper, which operates according to the laws of chance, the other a steel mechanism that operates according to the laws of mechanics and thermodynamics. The distinction is less striking the more closely it is examined.

The fact is that if things really work in the way presupposed by these superstitious beliefs, then the reasoning of science is wrong from the bottom up, its experiments are delusions, and its successes merely happy accidents. As the successes of science number in the millions, this view of the world requires us to believe in millions of remarkable coincidences.[1]

Here is an adequate summary of the Levinson passage:

```
    If a scientific view of the world implies
there is just one set of natural laws that impose
some order on a mysterious universe, then,
according to H. C. Levinson, superstitious
beliefs can have no reasonable place in this
scientific era. Still, many people who have no
trouble believing in the laws of mechanics and
thermodynamics have a great deal of difficulty in
understanding the laws of chance. Although people
seldom believe that a poorly functioning radio
has any relationship to a black cat passing by,
people may believe that the same black cat has
```

1 H. C. Levinson, *Chance, Luck and Statistics* (New York: Dover, 1963), pp. 17–21. Reprinted through the permission of the publisher.

some influence on their inability to win a hand
of cards. Many people persist in believing in
luck rather than in the mathematical
probabilities involved in the laws of chance.
They do not understand that superstitions are
incompatible with the reasoning of science.

Notice that the summary focuses on the *relationship* between two complex ideas—science and superstition. The writer of the summary has recognized that the first five paragraphs of the original are composed almost exclusively of examples and anecdotes. The summary writer omits all examples but one—the poorly functioning radio and the black cat— and that one example is retained to give a single concrete instance of an abstract relationship. Notice also that the summary begins with the main idea in the passage, even though in the original that idea is withheld until the end.

The successful summary does not depend on direct quotations from the original, but it does use a few brief phrases, just as Levinson uses them. These phrases—"one set of natural laws"; "view of the world"; "superstitious beliefs"—are used without quotation marks, since they are sets of words that might appear anywhere and do not belong to the author of any one piece. Yet it would be difficult to imagine how anyone could adequately summarize the original passage without using at least one or two of those phrases. Searching for synonyms would be time misspent.

On the other hand, the summary in figure 5.2 takes too much material from the original and by doing so actually *misses* the author's major point.

WRONG

Only one or two words changed from the original.

This sentence is taken word-for-word from the original.

In games of chance there are bound to be runs
of luck for and against the individual. And in
everyday life there are runs of luck for and
against individuals. But the difference is in
games the world depends on superstitions, and in
everyday life they depend on science. For
example, when a man sits down before his radio
for an evening of entertainment he does not say,
"I hardly think it will work tonight, as I just
saw the moon over my left shoulder." If it does
not work he examines the electrical connections,
or looks for a faulty tube. It never occurs to
him to connect the mishap to the number of black
cats he has met recently.

FIGURE 5.2

The student who has written the above "summary" may be in very serious trouble, even if he follows the paragraph with a footnote number and documents the source. It is never right to copy a full sentence that someone else has written, unless you quote the material precisely and enclose the whole in quotation marks. It is also never appropriate to do what the student has done in the last sentence of his summary: "It never occurs to him to connect the mishap to the number of black cats he has met recently." The sentence in the original, in the fourth paragraph, read, "It never occurs to him to connect the mishap with the number of black cats he has recently met." Changing a "with" or "to," making minor changes in word order, omitting or adding a few descriptive words does not serve for putting the material in your own words. In fact, you are in double jeopardy when you mutilate quoted material. Since you change the wording, you may not use quotation marks. You also fail to digest the material in order to abstract the main ideas in your own context. At best, you risk a low assessment of your understanding of the source. At worst, you risk a low assessment of your honesty.

Careful summarizing and accurate quotation (always enclosed in quotation marks) during your research process will help you to avoid problems when you use your notes to write a draft of your research paper. The care that you take as you work in the library will help you later to draw on the work of others to develop your own ideas.

Documenting

Although instructors in different disciplines may expect you to use various formats for documentation, all instructors agree on the sort of material that must be documented:

1 direct quotations

2 other people's judgments, ideas, opinions, and inferences, even if you rephrase this material

3 facts that other people have discovered and that are not generally known by the reading public

4 experiments performed by other people.

Sometimes students believe that the essence of library research is in knowing *how* to document, how to use footnotes. At the end of this chapter, we will show you the two most frequently used forms of documentation. But much more important to you as an apprentice scholar are the issues of *what* and *why* to document.

One of your major jobs is to make sense of the ideas of other people, to sort, sift, weigh, assess, and finally to *connect*. Understanding the what and why of documentation and acknowledgment will help you move with confidence through the best that has been thought and said and to connect yourself to a tradition of learning.

Direct quotations Quotations are known by everybody to be the kind of sentence that must be documented. Why should a writer use a direct quotation from another writer? There is no simple answer, for we have varying purposes for repeating word for word what another has said or written. Sometimes we quote because what we quote is funny, moving, or wise, or simply a clear explanation of a position. In these cases our aim is to credit the other person, for it is a matter deserving praise to have constructed language in a way that makes it worthy of being quoted. It is also a matter of truthfulness, for otherwise who could tell which were your own thoughts? In these cases, the emphasis is on the content of the quotation rather than on the author. In other cases of quotation, we emphasize the author; it is surprising that he (of all people) should have said it. Or it may be important to the paper to show this person does in fact believe this. For example, if you are writing a paper on Jefferson's views of slavery, to quote from Jefferson on the subject is to provide evidence relevant to a thesis on what Jefferson thought. In other cases, we quote because we want the author of the quotation to be persuasive to the audience. You use quotations for support when you appeal to a quotation from Gandhi, whose reputation for wisdom may be persuasive to the audience; or when you quote a scientist, who knows more than the audience; or when you simply make an appeal to a person with more experience in the area under discussion.

When you use a direct quotation in your own paper, you should also make clear why you are using it. Introduce and follow up quotations with your own explanation.

Other people's judgments, ideas, opinions, and inferences Frequently, you will draw on the ideas of other writers without actually using their exact words. For example, you may be writing a paper about the architecture of Le Corbusier's Carpenter Center for the Visual Arts at Harvard University. You may have read *Architecture Boston*,[2] edited by the Boston Society of Architects, in which the editors criticize the building because it makes little practical or visual sense in the Cambridge climate or landscape. Even if you do not quote directly from *Architecture Boston*, as we have consciously avoided doing above, you must still indicate the source for your judgment of the Le Corbusier building. Even if you did not like the building at all long before you read *Architecture Boston*, you still must cite the text if your reading has helped you to clarify and articulate the reasons for your distaste.

Just so, if you read Robert Langbaum's *The Poetry of Experience*[3] and then find that Langbaum's idea about the tension between sympathy and

2 Barre, Mass.: Barre Publishing, 1978.
3 New York: Norton, 1963.

judgment in the dramatic monologue informs your reading of that sort of poem from then on, then you must mention Langbaum each time you base an interpretation of your own on his idea. Your reference to Langbaum's work does not diminish your own creativity or originality. In fact, you demonstrate your ability to connect your own ideas to a tradition of scholarship. Few ideas are nurtured in isolation.

Sometimes your instructor will advise you to concentrate on either primary or secondary sources. These terms are relative. Depending on your topic, the same material can be primary or secondary. For example, if your topic for a history paper is "Propaganda During the Period of the Second World War," then newspapers would be primary material for this research. If, however, your topic is "Decisions of the Cabinet During the Second World War," then newspapers would be secondary sources.

In the natural and social sciences, in most cases, primary sources are considered to be direct reports of experiments or of original theoretical thinking. Secondary sources are books derived from other more basic material; they summarize, digest, organize, and integrate original writings of others. Textbooks are usually secondary sources.

In literature, fine arts, philosophy, and religion, primary sources are the works of art (*Paradise Lost*); original philosophical writings (Plato's *Republic*); or original religious texts (the *Upanishads*). Secondary sources in these fields include critical and historical commentaries, books *about* Milton, Plato, and the *Upanishads*.

Facts that other people have discovered

When you are doing research in an unfamiliar area, all facts may be news to you. One sign that you have done thorough research in the areas designated in your library paper is that you come to know by the time you write your final draft which facts need to be documented and which do not. For example, you may read in Nancy Milford's *Zelda*[4] that Zelda met Scott Fitzgerald in July 1918. Even if you did not know the fact before you read it in Milford's biography, you do *not* have to document that information in your own research paper. If your research has been wide enough, you will have discovered that there is no debate about the month and year of this famous meeting.

On the other hand, if you refer to Zelda's infatuation during the summer of 1924 with a young French aviator named Edouard Jozan, you *do* need to cite Nancy Milford as your source. You will know from reading other biographies that Milford was the first researcher to track down and interview Jozan. In fact, she was the first one even to spell his name accurately.

Experiments performed by other people

In papers written for the natural and social sciences, you must refer to empirical research done by other people. To report your own laboratory work, your own data, or your own case study without reference to other

4 New York: Harper & Row, 1970.

researchers who have done similar work is a very serious error. Science proceeds through the publication of activities and through the replication of experimental research. When you refer to the scientists whose work has preceded yours, you do more than confirm your honesty: you identify yourself as a scientist.

Forms of documentation

There is no one universally accepted way to document the sources you use in your paper, but each system, although different in detail, provides roughly the same information, which is sufficient to allow the reader to check the original sources of the quotations, opinions, and facts used in the paper: the name of the author, the title of the publication, and facts about the publication—place of publication, publisher, date, pages. Below we present two generally accepted forms, one recommended by the MLA (Modern Language Association) and the other recommended by the APA (American Psychological Association). Check with your instructors to determine which form they prefer, or to ask if they prefer some other form. As a rule, instructors in the humanities will prefer the MLA format, while instructors in the natural and social sciences and in education will prefer the APA format.

In both of these formats there are two stages of documentation. First, there are the specific references you make in the text of the paper. In the MLA format you make references by placing a number at the end of the appropriate sentence, and then you give the details either at the bottom of the page (a "footnote") or in a numbered list at the end of the paper (an "endnote"). In the APA format, sometimes called the "author-date" method, you give the reference by placing the name of the author and date of the publication in parentheses at the appropriate place in the text of the paper. The second stage of documentation is a list of sources you have used, collected at the end of the paper and ordered alphabetically. In the MLA format this is called a "bibliography," and in the APA format it is called a "reference list." The differences are outlined in table 5.1.

MLA format   *Footnotes/endnotes.* Number footnotes consecutively, starting from 1. Do not use asterisks or other symbols; use arabic numerals without period, parentheses, or slashes. Successive quotations in one paragraph usually may be documented in a single note.

Type footnote numbers slightly above the line, after any punctuation, and always after the quotation or passage to which they refer. Place the first footnote at the bottom of the page, separated from the last line of the text by triple spacing, indenting the first line three spaces from the margin and placing the reference number just above the line. Leave one space between the footnote number and the first letter of the footnote. Single space each footnote, bringing all lines after the first back to the margin,

	In the text of the paper	Alphabetical list of sources
MLA	numbers and footnotes or endnotes	Bibliography (sometimes includes works that you have read in addition to those cited in footnotes)
APA	author and date in parentheses	Reference List (never includes works that are not cited in the text of the paper)

TABLE 5.1
Comparison of MLA and APA documentation formats

but double space between footnotes to allow space for the number above the line.

The footnotes below include most of the types you will need in papers you write in college. Follow each type exactly, and be sure to read explanatory comments in parentheses following most footnote examples. Use abbreviations of dates and cities by all means, but use them correctly and consistently: don't write "March" in one place and "Mar." in another. Note that in footnotes the author's first name comes first.

[1] Louise Bogan, <u>Achievement in American Poetry, 1900–1950</u> (Chicago: Regnery, 1951), p. 352.

[2] Henry James, <u>The Future of the Novel</u>, ed. Leon Edel (New York: Vintage, 1956), p. 35.

[3] Bogan, p. 81.
(This note refers to the book in footnote 1. Do not repeat a full reference—abbreviate it, and add the correct page. Note: op. cit. ["Bogan, op. cit., p. 81"] is not generally used anymore.)

[4] Angel Flores, ed., <u>An Anthology of French Poetry from Nerval to Valery in English Translation</u> (Garden City: Doubleday, 1958), p. xviii.
(An editor of an anthology will be named first when you are referring to *his* contribution: in, for instance, the Preface, as in the example above, or in his notes. See footnotes 2 and 5.)

[5] William K. Frankena, "The Concept of Social Justice," in <u>Social Justice</u>, ed. Richard B. Brandt (Englewood Cliffs, N.J.: Prentice-Hall, 1962), p. 21.
(When you cite an article written by an author who is not the editor of the book, you cite the author's name first. The editor's name follows the title of the book.)

⁶ Samuel French Morse, "The Native Element," _Kenyon Review_, 20 (1958), 446.

(This is an article in a journal, volume 20, published in 1958, and the reference is to page 446. The volume number may be given on the publication itself either in roman or arabic numerals, and either is acceptable in footnote references. The page number is always given in arabic numerals and must follow the volume number and year of publication. When both volume and page numbers are given, do not write out or include abbreviations for "volume" and "page.")

⁷ William H. Gass, "The Case of the Obliging Stranger," _Philosophical Review_, 66 (1957), 193.

(Volume 66, published 1957, ref. on p. 193, but do not write out "vol.," "no.," or "p.")

⁸ _Ibid._, p. 194.

(This Latin abbreviation, underlined, means reference is to same article as immediately preceding, but to a different page. It is often easier simply to repeat the author's name before the page—Gass, p. 194—than to write and underline _ibid._)

⁹ "Colleges Prodded on Support for Underprivileged Students," _New York Times_, Oct. 30, 1963, p. 5.

(This is the way to cite newspapers and popular magazines.)

¹⁰ Henry James, _The American_ (London: Macmillan, 1921), p. 303.

¹¹ James, _The Future of the Novel_, pp. 92–93.

(If you have two books or articles by one author and you refer to them more than once, be careful to make clear in the second and later references which one you mean, but do not write out full references again. (See footnote 2.)

¹² _The Complete Works of Algernon Charles Swinburne_, ed. Sir Edmund Gosse and T. J. Wise (London: William Heineman, & New York: Gabriel Wells, 1925), III, 125.

(There are three volumes of this book, and the footnote reference is in volume III, p. 125. See comment about placement of editor, footnote 4. Since the name of the poem quoted is not given in the footnote, it is assumed that it has been given in the text of your paper. Don't repeat in the footnote any material given in text.)

¹³ Thomas Babington Macaulay, "Bunyan, John," _Encyclopaedia Britannica_, 11th ed., 4, 805.

(There is no need to name the editors of encyclopedias, nor place and date of publication. When the initial or name of the author of the article is given, use it. Otherwise, begin with the title of the article. Some encyclopedias, i.e., *Americana*, list editions not by number as above, but by dates: 1960 ed.)

[14] Dorothy Van Ghent, The English Novel: Form and Function (1953; rpt. New York: Harper & Row—Harper Torchbooks, 1961), p. 127.

(Use this format for a modern reprint of an older edition.)

[15] Interview with Richard Wilbur, Beaver College, Glenside, Pa., October 6, 1977.

(Use this format for a personal interview.)

[16] F. Scott Fitzgerald, The Great Gatsby (1925; rpt. New York: Scribners—Scribner Library, 1960), p. 15. Henceforth, all references to this work will be to the above edition and will be cited in the body of the paper.

(If you are using a single literary source for a paper of critical analysis, you may use a single footnote to identify the edition you are using. You may then document additional references to that source by citing page numbers in the body of your paper according to the following format: "At his lips' touch she blossomed for him like a flower and the incarnation was complete" (p. 112).

[17] Alfred Hitchcock, dir., The Lady Vanishes, with Michael Redgrave, Rank Organization, 1938.

(Use this format to cite a film. Notice that you begin with the director's name. Then the title of the film is underlined. Next include additional information—performers, producers, writers—any facts that you think might be helpful to the reader. The citation must include the distributor and the date.)

[18] Harold Pinter, Betrayal, dir. Peter Hall, with Blythe Danner, Raul Julia, Roy Scheider, Trafalagar Theater, New York, 2 April 1980.

(When you cite a theatrical performance, you may place either the playwright or the director first. Your choice depends on your emphasis. Also include the theater, city, and date of performance.)

[19] William Blake, The Four and Twenty Elders Casting Their Crowns Before the Divine Throne, Tate Gallery, London.

(Cite works of art in the text of your paper if possible. If you must cite a graphic work in your notes, follow the above format. Underline the title. Identify the location of the work.)

[20] <u>Son-Rise: A Miracle of Love</u>, prod. Richard
M. Rosenblum, NBC, 14 May 1979.

(Use this format for a radio or television program.)

[21] James Mason, <u>Charles Dickens, A Tale of Two
Cities</u> (excerpts), Caedmon, TC 2079, 1976.

(Use this format for a recording. The performer [or in some cases the
composer] goes first, then the title of the record, the manufacturer,
catalog number, and year of issue.)

[22] Letter received from Harvey S. Wiener, 28
July 1980.

(Use this format to cite a personal letter.)

Bibliography. The differences between bibliography and footnotes are
few but important. First, the bibliography is an alphabetical listing, by
authors, of all works cited in your paper. Many instructors in the humanities will want you to include also those works read but not cited in
the paper itself. The author's last name is placed first, followed by his
initials or his first name. Second, instead of indenting the first line, as
with footnotes, indent the second, so that the alphabetical list of authors'
last names stands out. Third, the punctuation is different, as you will see
below. Fourth, pages referred to in books are omitted; however, for specific
articles or poems referred to in periodicals or books, you will type in the
inclusive pages of the poem or article rather than the specific pages of the
poem or article referred to in your paper. Use abbreviations consistently
and see that they are the same ones used in footnotes.

▪ Sequence. Arrange the elements in the following order: Author. Title.
Facts of Publication. For author, give surname, then first name. Give
title. For journals, give journal name, volume number, issue number,
date, inclusive pages of article. For books, give place of publication,
publisher's name, date of publication.

▪ Punctuation. For *books,* use a period between author and title and
between title and facts of publication and at end of entry. (Edition is
always punctuated by period: "ed."). Use a comma between other divisions, except for a colon between place of publication and name of
publisher. Use parentheses for dates of journals.

For *journals,* use a period between author and title of article, and at
end of entry. Place title of article in quotation marks. Underline name of
journal. Use a comma between title of article and name of journal,
between volume number and issue number, and between date and pages.

▪ Capitalization. Capitalize the initial letters of all major words in the
title of a book, article, journal, and the proper names of author, publisher,
and place of publication.

- Form

Author's Surname, Author's First Name(s). *Book Title.* Place of Publication: Name of Publisher, year.

Author's Surname, Author's First Name(s). "Title of Article." *Journal Title*, volume number (date), page numbers.

Sample Bibliography

Blake, William. The Four and Twenty Elders Casting Their Crowns Before the Divine Throne. Tate Gallery, London.

Bogan, Louise. Achievement in American Poetry, 1900–1950. Chicago: Regnery, 1951.

"Colleges Prodded on Support for Underprivileged Students," The New York Times, Oct. 30, 1963, p. 5.

Fitzgerald, F. Scott. The Great Gatsby. 1925; rpt. New York: Scribners–Scribner Library, 1960.

Flores, Angel, ed. An Anthology of French Poetry from Nerval to Valery in English Translation. Garden City: Doubleday, 1958.

Frankena, William K. "The Concept of Social Justice," in Social Justice, ed. Richard B. Brandt. Englewood Cliffs, N.J.: Prentice–Hall, 1962, pp. 21–33.

Gass, William H. "The Case of the Obliging Stranger." Philosophical Review, 66 (1957), pp. 193–204.

Hitchcock, Alfred, dir. The Lady Vanishes. With Michael Redgrave. Rank Organization, 1938.

James, Henry. The American. London: Macmillan, 1921.

———. The Future of the Novel, ed. Leon Edel. New York: Vintage, 1956.

(Do not repeat author's name. Handle other titles by that author as indicated here.)

Macaulay, Thomas Babington. "Bunyan, John." Encyclopaedia Britannica, 11th ed.

Mason, James. Charles Dickens, A Tale of Two Cities (excerpts). Caedmon, TC 2079, 1976.

Morse, Samuel French. "The Native Element,"
  <u>Kenyon Review</u>, 20 (1958), 446–465.

Pinter, Harold. <u>Betrayal</u>. Dir. Peter Hall. With
  Blythe Danner, Raul Julia, Roy Scheider.
  Trafalgar Theater, New York. 2 April 1980.

<u>Son–Rise: A Miracle of Love</u>. Prod. Richard M.
  Rosenblum. NBC. 14 May 1979.

Swinburne, A. C. <u>The Complete Works of Algernon
  Charles Swinburne</u>, ed. Sir Edmund Gosse and
  T. J. Wise, Vol. III. London: William
  Heineman, & New York: Gabriel Wells, 1925.

Van Ghent, Dorothy. <u>The English Novel: Form and
  Function</u>. 1953; rpt. New York: Harper & Row–
  Harper Torchbooks, 1961.

Wiener, Harvey. Letter to author. 28 July 1980.

APA format

The author-date method. In the body of your paper cite the appropriate sources by giving the author's name and the date of the publication. These author and date citations are embedded in the sentence where the work is discussed, as the examples below show.

In a recent study of reaction times (Smith, 1970), it was reported that. . . .

(Use the name of the author and the date of publication, separated by a comma)

Smith (1970) compared reaction times. . . .

(When the name of the author occurs naturally in the textual discussion, only the year of publication is necessary.)

In 1970 Smith compared reaction times. . . .

(In the rare case where both year and author are given in the text, no further reference is required.)

When the experiment was repeated (Brown, 1973b), it was discovered that. . . .

(If in 1973 Brown has two publications that you use in your paper, you designate the first one in alphabetical order as "Brown, 1973a" and the other "Brown, 1973b" to eliminate ambiguity. These letters after the year must also appear in the reference list with full details of publication.)

Williams, Jones, and Smith (1963) found. . . .

(If the work cited has two or more authors, all the surnames of the authors are given the first time it is cited. If the work has just two authors, you always give both names.)

Williams et al. (1963) found. . . .

(If the work cited has three or more authors, then although the first time it is cited you give all the names, for subsequent citations include only the surname of the first author followed by "et al." and the year.)

There is evidence that the developmental view is false (Jones, 1957, pp. 10–19).

(Because material within a book is often difficult to locate, you should, wherever possible, give page numbers to assist readers. Citation of a page, a chapter, figure, table, or equation should be made at the appropriate point in the text rather than in the reference list. Page numbers should always be given for quoted material.

It has been argued (Smith, 1960, chap. 3) that. . . .

(Citation of a chapter in a book.)

Reference lists. At the end of your paper, list all citations on a page entitled "References."

■ Sequence. Arrange the elements in a reference entry in this way: Author. Title. Facts of Publications. For author, give surname, then initials (not first name). Give title. For journals, give journal name in full, date of publication, volume number, inclusive pages of articles. For books, give place of publication, publisher's name, date of publication.

■ Punctuation. Use periods to separate the three major subdivisions of a reference citation: author, title, and facts of publication. Use commas within the subdivisions (e.g., between date and volume number in a journal entry). Use a colon between the place of publication and the book publisher. Use parentheses for extensions, qualifications, or interpretations of each subdivision or the entire entry. Punctuate accurately and uniformly.

■ Capitalization. Capitalize the initial letter of *only* the first word of book titles, articles, or chapters. Make exceptions according to common usage, such as capital letters for proper names, German nouns, first word after a colon or dash. For the name of a journal, capitalize the initial letter of all major words. Underline book and journal volume numbers to indicate italics. Titles of journal articles and chapter titles appear without quotation marks.

■ Form

Author's Surname, Author's Initials. *Book title*. Place of Publication: Publisher's Name, date.

Author's Surname, Author's Initials. Title of article. *Journal Title*, year, *volume number*, pages.

Ordering references in the reference list. When writing the reference list, list all names in inverted order, last names followed by initial or initials. In the case of multiple authorship, use the inverted order for all names, separating each name from the preceding name with a comma. Use a comma and an ampersand (&) before the final name, even with two authors. Occasionally a work will have as its author an agency, an association, or institution, or it will have no author at all. Alphabetize corporate authors, such as associations or government agencies, by the first significant word of the name. Full official names should be used (American Psychological Association, not APA). If there is no author, the title moves to the author position, and the entry is alphabetized by the first significant word of the title.

Sample References

The blood business. Time, September 11, 1972, pp. 47–48.

Magazine article without author.

Harlow, H. F. Fundamental principles for preparing psychology journal articles. Journal of Comparative and Physiological Psychology, 1962, 55, 893–896.

Journal article.

Riesen, A. H. Sensory deprivation. In E. Stellar & J. M. Sprague (Eds.), Progress in physiological psychology (Vol. 1). New York: Academic Press, 1966.

Article in an edited book.

Strunk, W., Jr., & White, E. B. The elements of style (2nd ed.). New York: Macmillan, 1972.

Book.

Several of the above citations have been adapted from the *Publication Manual of the American Psychological Association*, 2nd ed., 1975.

Variants on the APA style. One variant on the APA style is the numbered reference. A number which can be checked in the reference list is introduced first in the body of the text. For example:

The composition of letters, memos, essays, and technical reports is widespread, time–consuming, and often difficult (1). Although most people write. . . .

1. E. T. Klenmer and F. W. Snyder. <u>J. Commun</u>. 22, 142 (1972).

There are other forms which your instructor may prefer, so ask.

APA and MLA compared In tables 5.2 and 5.3 we illustrate the differences between the MLA style and the APA style. To highlight their different requirements, we present a simple model of a book reference and a journal reference in each style. The model includes the appropriate sequence, capitalization, underlining, and punctuation. (Thus, in the MLA model, *"Book Title"* indicates that the title should be capitalized and underlined, while in the APA model, *"Book title"* indicates that the title should be underlined but only the first letter of the title should be capitalized.)

Acknowledging

Many of your ideas and most of your inspiration may not come from the library at all. Something that your instructor says in a lecture may spark the idea for a paper. A bull session in the dormitory may finally illuminate

	MLA style: *"footnotes/endnotes"*	APA style: *"author-date method"*
Book	Author's First Name(s) Surname, *Book Title* (Place of Publication: Name of Publisher, year), pages.	(Author's Surname, date, sometimes pages)
	Example:	Example:
	¹²John Rawls, <u>A Theory of Justice</u> (Cambridge: Harvard University Press, 1971), p. 35.	(Rawls, 1971) (Rawls, 1971, pp. 35–39)
Journal article	Author's First Name(s) Surname, "Title of Article," *Journal Title*, volume number (year), pages.	Same as above.
	Example:	Example:
	¹⁴John Rawls, "Justice as Fairness," <u>The Philosophical Review</u>, 67 (1958), 173.	(Rawls, 1958)

TABLE 5.2
References in the text of paper

	MLA *style: "bibliography"*	APA *style: "references"*
Book	Author's Surname, Author's First Name(s). *Book Title.* Place of publication: Name of Publisher, year.	Author's Surname, Author's Initials. *Book title.* Place of Publication: Publisher's Name, date.
	Example:	Example:
	Rawls, John. <u>A Theory of Justice</u>. Cambridge: Harvard Univ. Press, 1971.	Rawls, J. <u>A theory of justice</u>. Cambridge: Harvard Univ. Press, 1971.
Journal article	Author's Surname, Author's First Name(s). "Title of Article." *Journal Title,* volume number (date), page numbers.	Author's Surname, Author's Initials. Title of article. *Journal Title,* year, *volume number,* pages.
	Example:	Example:
	Rawls, John. "Justice as Fairness." <u>The Philo-sophical Review</u>, 67 (1958), 164–194.	Rawls, J. Justice as fairness. <u>The Philo-sophical Review</u>, 1958, <u>67</u>, 164–194.

TABLE 5.3
Alphabetical list of
sources at end of paper

Plato's *Republic.* One reason for attending college rather than studying on your own is to learn from other people—your instructors, classmates, and friends. The phrase "a community of scholars" really does mean something.

Some students still feel reluctant to discuss their work-in-progress with others because they are afraid of "stealing" other people's ideas or of having their own ideas stolen. Professional writers behave quite differently. Look in the front sections of any book that happens to be on your desk (including this one) and read the page of acknowledgments (sometimes included in the foreword or preface). You will find long lists of people who are thanked for reading and commenting on a manuscript in various stages.

An acknowledgment page can be a liberating document. If you are open about the help you receive, you can feel free to connect your own thinking to the ideas of others. Remember, too, that you have an ethical obligation to acknowledge help, whether it comes from a roommate or from a tutor in your college's writing center.

An expression of gratitude, however, *never* justifies exploitation. You must not seek or accept any help with the actual phrasing of sentences in your paper. Nor should you ever copy anything written by a classmate.

Professional authors have been taken to court when it turned out that they copied the work of colleagues whom they had duly thanked in an acknowledgments page.

Format for acknowledgment There are few fixed conventions for an acknowledgments page, so you can be as creative or playful as you like. Acknowledgments should be typed on a separate page right after the title page. Here is a sample:

```
    Many thanks to Professor Norman Johnston, who
suggested that I read the articles I have
included on prison conditions in colonial
America. Professor Johnston also permitted me to
discuss some of the ideas in this paper with him.
My roommate, Carolyn Wooden, spent many dinners
listening to my opinions about colonial America.
Many thanks to her for her suggestions and for
her patience. Kathy Mackin of the Beaver College
Writing Center responded to early drafts of this
paper. I want to thank her also for helping me
keep my perspective in this project when, like
Hester Prynne at the prison door, I felt as if I
was drawing on energy that I didn't know I had.
```

QUESTIONS

1 What are the most important rules to remember when taking notes?

2 What is the role of summarizing in research?

3 In what circumstances should you footnote or cite a source in a research paper?

4 What purposes are achieved by putting an acknowledgments page in your research paper?

EXERCISES

1 Reread pp. 100–102 in chapter 1 of this book. Write a one-paragraph summary of this material. What is the most important point in your summary? Where does the point appear in your summary?

2 Assume that you have received the following help while you were working on a term paper entitled "Sun and Moon Imagery in *The Rime of the Ancient Mariner*":

a At every stage of the project you discussed your ideas with your boy friend, Michael Maizel.

b During a peer review session you shared an early draft with three classmates. Two of them, Leslie Bronfien and Laurel Hertzler, gave you valuable comments that helped to shape the paper. One of them, Olga Martinet, quibbled over every line and made you feel like a failure as a writer, but she did help you to find four or five spelling errors.

c. You had several conferences with your instructor, Professor William Bracy.

d When you happened to mention your project to your geography instructor, Professor Edward Wolff, he helped you to understand why the sun came up on the left in one stanza and on the right in another.

e Your school's reference librarian, Josephine Charles, used interlibrary loan to order many books and articles for you.

f Your friend, Debbie Derrickson, who is an English major, suggested that you read the following article: Robert Penn Warren, "A Poem of Pure Imagination," *Selected Essays*, ed. Robert Penn Warren (New York: Random House, 1951). On p. 218 of that essay you found the idea that clarified the whole project for you. Warren says there that Coleridge uses symbols as a focus for a wide range of meaning, not as a point-to-point representation of a concrete idea. You do not quote Warren directly in your paper.

g Your father typed the paper for you.

Write an acknowledgments page to express thanks for the help you have received. What portion of this help must be documented in the text of your paper? Write an appropriate footnote, according to the MLA format, as described in this chapter.

3 Begin keeping a record of help you receive on a paper that you are currently writing. As your list grows, draft an acknowledgments page.

4 As a class, discuss the different purposes of the MLA and the APA styles of documentation.

5 Using the six examples of card catalog entries in chapter 4, develop two bibliographies, one according to the APA style and the other according to the MLA style.

6 Assume that you are citing p. 35 of the first card catalog entry in chapter 4. Write the citation according to the APA and MLA styles.

7 Select an article from a scholarly journal in a discipline that interests you, perhaps in the discipline of your anticipated major. Find the original source for every footnote. Use interlibrary loan if you need to. Check all direct quotations. Has the author quoted accurately? How does the author use ellipses (. . .)? Does the choice of omitted material distort the meaning of the quoted passage? Does the author ever quote out of context? To what effect? How many direct quotations does the author use? How are these quotations introduced and followed up? What besides direct quotations does the author document? Check his paraphrases and summaries with the material in the source. Has the author remained faithful to the meaning and tone of the original? If your instructor permits, work on this project with a partner. Then compare notes.

8 Read the acknowledgments in every textbook that you are using this semester. (Sometimes the acknowledgments appear as the last few paragraphs of the preface or foreword.) What kinds of help do most authors receive while they are writing their books?

Writing in the Humanities

Note th
in paren
should
referenc
bibliogr

Immedi
of the c
the stat
— who
when? T
way to

consider that his
claration to Boun
n is . . . the or
which education
ed" (HT 27), is
There is also a
motional life (th
ch he has neglect
e opposition betw
m of the Head" an
the Heart" is an

6 Research Papers in the Humanities

The term paper, or the library research paper, is a standard assignment of liberal arts courses. It is liberating in the sense that more than most assignments in the classroom, it allows you considerable flexibility in choosing your topic or your approach to your topic. You take the responsibility for more decisions in writing a term paper. At the same time it calls for a sophisticated response on your part, for it is bound by quite strict conventions and requires you to bring together many academic skills, including: bibliographical and library research; careful note taking; organizing and synthesizing data and opinion; developing and arguing a thesis consistent with your evidence; and writing a clear, cohesive, and persuasive paper. In the research paper you are expected to become familiar in depth with some problem related to the course and to form your own views of that problem. As such, the term paper marks a rite of passage in many humanities courses, for you are being asked to perform, in microcosm, the tasks that scholars in the field engage in to produce articles in professional journals.

The assignment of a term paper is based on the reasonable and widely held assumption that a discipline is best introduced at two levels. At one level, you need to get a feel for the field, to find what kinds of problems it deals with and what methods it uses. This wide view of the field is represented by the reading assignments in the class. The other level is the pursuit of some narrow problem in depth, and it is this pursuit that the assignment of a research paper is designed to accomplish. It is not an empty exercise.

Term papers in the humanities are distinct from other papers by virtue of three important characteristics. The first is that they require research, but it is not easy to explain just what research in the humanities involves. To many, the term "research" evokes images of a white-coated scientist manipulating liquids in tubes at a laboratory bench. The analogous image for a researcher in the humanities is less clear cut, perhaps a person reading and taking notes in a dusty library corner. What makes this image less definitive is that the person might well be a scientist reviewing the literature on some topic, so although scientists have an image to themselves, researchers in the humanities do not.

To get a handle on what makes research in the humanities distinctive, you must first get rid of the common view that papers fall into just two classes: research papers and opinion papers. Students often assume that they are supposed to write about fact in their science classes and opinions in their humanities classes. If everybody has a right to his own opinion in the humanities, what is the point of research? The answer is that between facts and opinions there is a realm of *reasoned* beliefs, conclusions, claims, and interpretations which, although not just a matter of fact, are still disputable and capable of rational assessment. You do indeed have a right to believe what you want, but you have no right to expect others to believe it unless you can back it up in some way.

The answer to the question "When did Charles II reign in England?" is not an opinion; it is a fact. The answer to the question "In what ways was Charles II's foreign policy as king of England affected by his experiences while in exile?" is also not an opinion—at least not in the way that many students define the word. When students ask, "Should I give my opinion?" they usually are asking whether they should express their own preference on the matter. A proper answer to the question about Charles II's foreign policy is not an issue of personal inclination. A proper answer should be based on a reasoned interpretation of a set of events and circumstances, such as what Charles II thought before and during the time he became king, his experiences on the Continent, the influence on him of the king of France, and so on. You may feel one way or another about these events and circumstances, and that preference may affect your interpretation, but in a history class you are obligated to back up your interpretation with the kind of evidence that historians will accept. They will not accept as a decisive answer, for example, what Charles II said about his own foreign policy. But historians may disagree on what the answer is, not because it is a mere matter of taste but because the range of facts to be considered in forging an answer is so great. Nor is a disagreement among historians on the subject just a matter of knowledge, of one knowing more about the period than another. The facts known equally to both historians may be open to several equally plausible interpretations. In such a case, there are certainly answers that are plainly wrong—inconsistent with the facts—but several answers that are *reasonable*, worthy of belief.

This example, drawn from history, is typical of the kinds of problems dealt with in the humanities. When doing research on a topic, you have a responsibility to find out what kinds of evidence are acceptable to the discipline, that is, what counts as a plausible answer, and also to find out the range of disagreement that exists in the discipline on this topic. Both require reading other scholars, but not for the purpose of eliciting *the* right answer. You are seeking a plausible answer, a respectable answer. If in a philosophy class you decide to write on whether animals have rights, you need to read philosophers to find out what is at stake in giving a negative or positive answer to the question. You must discover what else you are committed to if you say animals do have rights. Once you find it out, you decide whether you are prepared to accept the commitment. For example, you need to find out whether extending rights to animals commits you intellectually to vegetarianism, to the abolition of hunting, or to the abolition of zoos. It is the purpose of the discipline of philosophy to examine these kinds of connections, and to engage in research on the topic is to discover the kinds of considerations philosophers find persuasive in establishing these connections.

In doing a research paper, then, you are attempting to discover what the nature of evidence is in the discipline and also to follow your question to the answers that the discipline finds plausible.

Because the term paper is built on thorough, careful research, a second important characteristic is that it requires more extensive preparation time than most other pieces of writing you will be asked to do in college. The word "term" paper itself conveys time; it takes time to complete a major research project. So you should begin compiling a bibliography and reading in the general area of your topic soon after you receive the assignment. Even if you do not yet have a definite topic, reading in the area from which you might select a topic will provide context and will help you to define a specific area for your paper. Many research papers fail ultimately because the writer has not taken the time to familiarize himself with the larger area in which his topic is embedded. No amount of last-minute heroics can save a paper if insufficient research is the difficulty.

The third characteristic of research papers is that they are governed by rules and conventions that need to be learned. This kind of paper, above all, follows prescribed forms. Some are standard universal conventions, such as the necessity to document and give a bibliography. Other conventions vary from field to field, for example, forms of documentation (chapter 5) and the use of direct quotations in the body of the paper. Before writing your draft you should become familiar with the conventions of the discipline and the specific preferences of your instructor.

Getting started

To illustrate strategies for writing a term paper in the humanities we have chosen a paper on a literary work—*Hard Times*, by Charles Dickens—for two reasons. First, it is an example where there is a distinction between the primary text, the novel, and secondary sources, books and articles on the novel. Not all humanities projects have this distinction. If your topic were, for example, the implications of a principle of equality of opportunity for women, you would not have a primary text on which to work. But many projects do involve a primary text. When your project does, the first step in getting started is always to read the primary text; in this case, read *Hard Times*. Our second purpose in choosing this example is to illustrate the differences between doing a literary analysis of a text (chapter 7), where the emphasis is on what *you* see in the text, and a research paper on a text, where you are expected to test your impressions and add to them by reviewing what others have seen.

It should be emphasized that research *on* a novel does not replace your close and critical reading of it as if for a literary analysis. It is to your advantage in doing research to have already formed some ideas of what you might say about it. Thus, the strategy of the first step is the same as that recommended in chapter 7 for a literary analysis: as you read, take notes on features of the novel that strike you as interesting or important. If there are passages you think might be candidates for quotation in your paper, write them out in full. Note down striking images, paraphrase themes, notice unusual words or combinations of words, and don't forget to record stray thoughts as they occur to you. Where the passage seems too long for full quotation, you should still note its existence so you can retrieve it if you decide to use it. Thus, Dickens's description of Coketown, the dreary industrial town in which the novel is set, runs half a page. Figure 6.1 shows how your notecard might read.

It is advisable to give a card to each separate entry, for when you are finished you will want to go over them and put them into categories if you can. You will then see connections you had not previously seen.

It is a general principle of efficient research that you should narrow your topic. But don't be too eager to limit your thinking in this first stage of reading your primary text. Even if halfway through your reading you have found what you think may be your thesis, or have generated a controlling question, you still have to read the whole text, so there is little advantage in choosing subsequently only those passages that relate to your question. At this stage you are getting ideas and information that may only later in your project turn out to be significant. You should notice as much as you can. It is true that at this stage of the research, as at any stage, you must also be selective in the notes you take—otherwise you would transcribe the whole novel word for word. But you are relatively less selective at this stage than at any later stage.

So while you are still reading, stay alert to many ideas that could serve as a thesis. When you have finished reading the text, you can then select among the various possible theses. Whatever thesis you choose, whatever aspect of the novel you wish to write about, you will still have to read some general material on *Hard Times* in order to put your idea into context. So the logical next step is to find books and articles that locate the novel in an historical framework. Where you will go from there, to more specific material, will depend on your narrowing the focus for your search. You must now be very selective in the material for which you search.

After you have read and taken notes on the novel and after you have read some general material on *Hard Times*, you should work out a

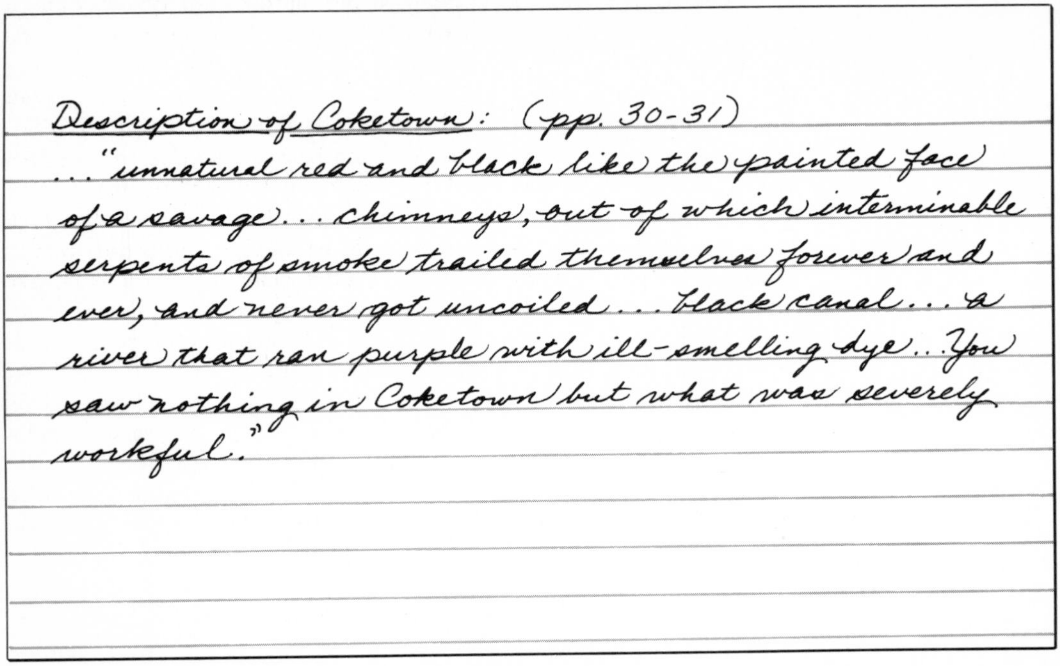

> *Description of Coketown:* (pp. 30-31)
>
> ... "unnatural red and black like the painted face of a savage ... chimneys, out of which interminable serpents of smoke trailed themselves forever and ever, and never got uncoiled ... black canal ... a river that ran purple with ill-smelling dye ... You saw nothing in Coketown but what was severely workful."

FIGURE 6.1
Notecard with quotation from Hard Times.

controlling question for your paper. This is a question to which the paper will be an answer. You may have generated a number of possible questions as you read the novel and as you conducted your preliminary research, but now is the time to refine the question. The purpose of refining such a question is twofold. First, it forces you to decide what you already have discovered and to make some initial sense of it, thereby calling a halt to a useless accumulation of facts. The second purpose is to provide you with a principle of selection for the rest of the material you will read.

Given these two purposes, you have three criteria for a good controlling question:

1 The question must be sufficiently narrowing to make some of the published material on *Hard Times* irrelevant to your purpose. (Otherwise, it will not be a principle of selection.)

2 It must require research for its answer.

3 It must be realistic; that is, you must be capable of doing it with the information and time you have available.

Although it is possible that a question you ask of *Hard Times* might be too narrow to be useful, problems arise more commonly from not having any such question or from having one that is too general. (The question

"When was *Hard Times* published?" is too narrow, although to ask of a Platonic dialogue when it was written would not be too narrow, for it is an issue of dispute among scholars and leads you to important questions of historical scholarship.) A controlling question is to research papers somewhat as a hypothesis is to an experiment. For a scientist, a hypothesis dictates which facts are to count and serves as a selecting device. The controlling question is less restrictive than a hypothesis, though, for the hypothesis must also be empirically testable in a carefully defined way. In a broad sense, a controlling question must be testable, but the concept of testability in the humanities means that some available facts or accessible facts will make sense of one answer.

Here are some examples:

Fails criteria

1 Is *Hard Times* a successful novel?

2 What does Mr. Gradgrind do when he discovers his son is a thief?

3 To what extent is *Hard Times* representative of Victorian literature?

Satisfies criteria

4 What was the influence of the Preston Strike on the writing of *Hard Times*?

5 What was the contemporary reception of *Hard Times*?

6 Is the Gradgrind School a fair representation of utilitarian educational theories?

Question (1) fails the first test, for no material published on *Hard Times* can be irrelevant to it. Question (2) fails the second test, for it can be answered without doing more than reading the novel itself. It is too narrow a question. Question (3) fails the third test, for unless you are steeped in Victorian literature you are unlikely to have sufficient background knowledge of the period to deal with the question within one semester. Questions (4), (5), and (6) are all testable controlling questions because they provide a basis for selection of research materials, they require you to do research outside the novel itself, and they are plausible questions for an undergraduate to pursue within one semester.

To state a controlling question about Dickens is not the same as stating a topic. Your interest may be piqued by the status of women in the novel, but although naming the topic does limit what you need to read, you need to pose a controlling question before you can formulate research plans. You can turn a topic statement into a controlling question trivially, of course: "I intend to study the status of women in *Hard Times*" can be transformed into the question "What views of women are to be found in *Hard Times*?" When topics are merely rephrased as questions, the paper becomes a totally descriptive paper.

A good controlling question is fruitful to the extent that it suggests further, more specific questions which can be handled separately. Sometimes these further questions are suggested by key words in the controlling question ("Preston Strike"; "utilitarian"). But the more specific questions you can extract from the larger controlling question, the more fruitful the question. Thus, "What do the roles played by Louisa, Sissy, and Mrs. Sparsit show of Dickens's views of women?" leads you to three more specific questions about the role of each of these three characters as well as other more specific questions about Dickens's treatment of male characters: Are they contrasting or comparable? The question "What was the influence of the Preston Strike on the writing of *Hard Times?*" suggests further questions, such as: What are the dates of each? Is there any evidence that Dickens was aware of the Preston Strike? Is the evidence reliable? How does the account of the labor union in *Hard Times* compare with the facts of the Preston Strike? By contrast, the topic "industrialism" suggests less specific subareas than the controlling question: What were Dickens's views of industrialism? What was the contemporary state of industrial relations?

How do you generate a controlling question? By engaging in the strategies recommended in chapter 2 for generating ideas. Those strategies are designed to help you see what you already know. The controlling question builds on what you know to indicate what you need to find out. We will illustrate how some of those strategies might apply.

Classify your notes
Put them in separate piles. There will usually be an obvious basis for the initial classification for most of them (if you have kept them short). In an example such as ours, you should have notes relating to specific characters of the novel, descriptions of the setting, philosophical asides, imagery, internal cross-references, author's voice, and plot developments. In addition, you should have notes of your own thoughts as you read, some of which will relate to the categories mentioned above. Having separated your notes, analyze them. Is there a character on whom you have notes starting very late in the book? Why? Did you miss something? Or is it that the character plays a significant role only later in the novel? If so why? What characters resemble one another? Which contrast with others? Do you notice changes in the views of the characters over the span of the novel? Why? Look for the use of imagery (machines, smoke). Classify by theme (industrialism, education). Who tells the story? What is the function of the narrator?

Some other categories for classifying your notes should now be apparent to you, for the choices you made in selecting material on which to take notes is in effect the operation of a classification scheme of some kind, some general notion, perhaps implicit, of what was important and not. In a sense, the relationships that turn up when you classify in this first way are the discoveries you have made in your readings without being aware of them. (For example, you might find that all the comments made about Louisa are exactly the opposite of those made about Sissy. If so, are they mirror images of one another?)

There is more to be had from this strategy, for many of your notes will fit in several classifications. Force yourself to reclassify. This reclassification will unpack more information of a less obvious kind. Although you must dig for it, the result will be even more valuable in generating ideas for the paper. All disciplines relish surprise, and surprise comes from the non-obvious. Suppose you have a pile of notes for two characters, Bounderby and Gradgrind. It is easy to see that these two fit together in a category: they both represent the manufacturing class of Coketown, the local well-to-do. Less obvious is a classification under which fall both Blackpool (the honest weaver repudiated by all sides) and Thomas Gradgrind (born to advantage, the son of a wealthy factory owner). You ask yourself whether there is a way to complete the sentence, "Thomas and Stephen are the same in that they are both. . . ." You might decide they are both victims, or that they stand, in different ways, for the moral bankruptcy of the educational theories of Thomas's father. You might not use this similarity in your paper, but other more important relationships may be uncovered by the same method of reclassification.

One of the ways you generate ideas about a topic is by breaking it up into elements, by analyzing it. The strategy of reclassification is a way to do this. By finding difficult bases of classification you are slicing the novel up in different ways. The author chooses one basis of classification by arranging the novel in one order. You must devise other ways to slice it. This strategy of reclassification also applies to nonliterary works. If the author has chosen a narrative arrangement, then to analyze it you need to choose another way of seeing the book. Abstract the role of one character or trace the development of one relationship or of one idea. If a book of history is arranged chronologically, then you test your understanding of the book and reveal new relationships by reorganizing it for yourself. You might take out all the comments about economics, or about politics, or about religion, or about military affairs. In this way you make the material your own.

Figure 6.2 shows how you can come to see more by forcing yourself to reclassify. Suppose you find in your notes (figure 6.2) four quotations, which you have duly annotated with page number, source, context, and, possibly, brief interpretation. You would naturally have put (1) and (2) together, as indicated by the notation "imagery" on the two cards. You would also have initially placed (3) and (4) in the pile of notes relating to Louisa. But at some later point you should look systematically in the other cards to find imagery you might have missed, other notes that might be classified with (1) and (2). Then you are prepared to see as imagery Louisa's self-descriptions: "dried out" and a garden that has never bloomed (for lack of water?). And this in turn might lead you to look for other examples of these images.

① "little vessels... ready to have imperial gallons of facts poured into them until they were full to the brim"

HT p. 12. Narrator's voice describing teacher's view of students. (Imagery)

② "little pitchers"

HT p. 13. (Narrator's voice describing teacher's view of students. Imagery — see "vessels")

③ "Her remembrances of home and childhood were remembrances of the drying up of every spring and fountain in her young heart as it gushed out of her."

HT p. 197. Louisa's thoughts of herself.

④ "Where are the graces of my soul? Where are the sentiments of my heart?... What have you done, oh, Father, what have you done with the garden that should have bloomed once, in this great wilderness here."

HT p. 215. Louisa to Father in confrontation scene.

FIGURE 6.2
(on facing page)
*Notecards that can be
organized to reveal
patterns.*

As a beginner in the study of a discipline—and every student in an introductory course is to some extent a beginner—you may need to check your conception of what the discipline regards as important and relevant. An example of a wrong approach to a term paper in literature would be a straight narration of the events of Dickens's life, with no connections drawn between his life experiences and the writing of his novels. If you suspect you are picking out the wrong features of the primary text, or if you think your approach may be inappropriate, then you need to consult some basic library sources. (See chapter 4.)

For our example you would need to know the implications of considering *Hard Times* as a novel. What sort of comment or question can you appropriately make about a novel, either in describing it or evaluating it? For example, it is appropriate for a literary critic to ask why Louisa Gradgrind is a woman and not a man. That question would be a silly one for a psychologist or sociologist to pose about a real-life situation, but the question is proper for a literary critic, who is concerned with *Hard Times* as a work of fiction, something that Dickens made up to fulfill certain purposes. Louisa is after all a fictional character who is female because Dickens decided that she would be female. To understand the concept of the novel as a fictional world, you need to do some research on the elements of the novel.

To learn about the elements of the novel, you would follow the strategy of library search recommended in the last chapter. Start with the encyclopedia. If you follow the references to entries on Dickens in the *Encylcopaedia Britannica*, you will find one of the important references to him embedded in the analytical portion of an entry on "The Novel," specifically, in the subsection on the novel as propaganda. Examine the structure of the whole entry. Here is the portion of the outline in which the material on Dickens appears:

Elements of the Novel
> Plot
> Character
> Scene, or setting
> Narrative method and point of view
> Scope, or dimension
> Myth, symbolism, significance

Uses of the Novel
> As an expression of an interpretation of life
> As entertainment or escape
> As propaganda
> As reportage
> As an agent of change in the language and thought of a culture
> As an expression of the spirit of its age
> As a creator of life styles and an arbiter of taste[1]

1 "The Novel," *New Encyclopaedia Britannica: Macropaedia*, 1980 ed.

These are the most basic categories by which novels are analyzed. You might formulate a controlling question in their terms, a question *about* plot, narrative method, etc.

You can also get basic categories from more advanced bibliographies that annotate their references. For example, the table of contents of a bibliography of *Victorian Fiction* gives the following list for the chapter on Dickens:

Studies of Special Aspects	64
Characterization	65
Plot and Narration	67
Imagery and Symbolism	68
Style and Language	70
Comedy, Humor, Satire	71
Illustrations	72
Serialization	75
Dickens and Society	76
London	77
Industrialism	78
Women	79
Religion	80
Literary Predecessors, Contemporaries, and Successors	81
Notable Critics Criticized[2]	84

And looking further into the chapter on Dickens, you find a fully annotated bibliography that illuminates the significant topics and the controversies. Here is an example of the beginning of a paragraph from the bibliographical essay on Dickens:

Two particularly good essays on the rhetoric of the novel have appeared, David Lodge's in his *Language of Fiction* (1966) and Robert Green's *"Hard Times*: The Style of a Sermon" (*TSLL*, 1970). The tactics of its opening page are analyzed by Stanley Tick (*VN*, 1974). "Fancy," a theme of these essays, is critically assessed in another fine essay, David Sonstroem's (*PMLA*, 1969), and the imagery in several essays—J. Miriam Benn's (*DSA*, 1970), Mary Rose Sullivan's (*VN*, 1970), and most substantially in George Bornstein's (*NCF*, 1971). Anny Sadrin's "The Perversion of Desire" is a study of. . . . [3]

Reference materials can give you productive ideas for developing your paper, but do not depend exclusively on published lists. Try on your own

2 Reprinted by permission of the Modern Language Association of America from George H. Ford, ed., *Victorian Fiction: A Second Guide to Research.* Copyright © 1978 by the Modern Language Association of America.
3 Ford, *Victorian Fiction*, p. 100. Reprinted by permission.

to make sense of your notes. If you take your categories from a list given to you, the process of classification becomes a mechanical filling of a grid instead of the creative, interpretative process of discovery it can be.

Brainstorming You can brainstorm from almost any of your notecards, drawing out the implications of any notes you have written to yourself or free-associating on names (Dickens provides particularly good material for this associative thinking: "Coketown," "Bounderby," "Gradgrind"), or elaborating upon the relationships you uncover by the previous strategy of classifying.

Suppose you have noted a quotation from the novel, a description of the circus performers (figure 6.3), and added a note to yourself, "Doesn't this patronize them?" Studying the quotation, you begin to brainstorm— see figure 6.4.

Or you can consider your own associations with the phrase "hard times," but not merely your private associations. Perhaps you can draw on your knowledge of other historical periods when times were hard. Your brainstorming might then produce the notes in figure 6.5.

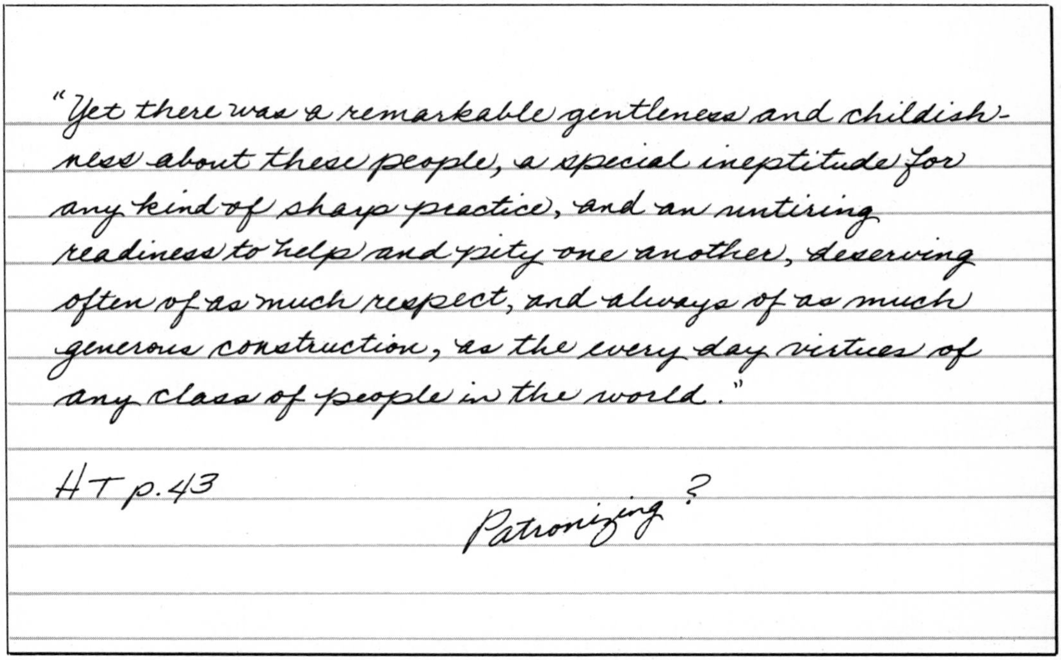

"Yet there was a remarkable gentleness and childishness about these people, a special ineptitude for any kind of sharp practice, and an untiring readiness to help and pity one another, deserving often of as much respect, and always of as much generous construction, as the every day virtues of any class of people in the world."

HT p. 43

Patronizing?

FIGURE 6.3
Notecard with your comment.

Why patronizing? Good to be gentle and ready to help one another. But is that supposed to go with being childish and inept? Is he saying only those who are childish and inept are capable of gentleness and generosity? As circus people they are outside society. They are also uneducated. Is he saying education, because it eliminated childishness, also eliminated gentleness and generosity? But Mr. Gradgrind, in his own way, is said to be generous and kind, and it is he who stands for the educational system. Or is it that his generosity does not emerge clearly until he has come to see how in Bitzer the educational system has eliminated finer emotions. Gradgrind early in the novel insists that everything can be weighed and measured in a utilitarian calculus. Calculus — calculating. That is just what Bitzer is. He is a calculator — ends up in the local bank dealing with money — and he is also calculating. He calculates his own interest and manipulates people, including his own mentor, Gradgrind, for his own interest. And he is supposed to be the successful student! But the utilitarians were supposed to be social reformers. Surely they did not intend the products of their education to turn out like Bitzer. Louisa once makes the mistake in the novel of saying, "I wonder." She is reprimanded by her father — "Never wonder." Could the utilitarians have regarded wonder as undesirable?

FIGURE 6.4
(on facing page)
*Brainstorming on a
passage from* Hard
Times.

A useful variant of brainstorming is the development of an analogy. In addition to helping you develop ideas, if you take a current reference you know something about, you may find the analogy will open fresh areas for you and allow you to say something original about the novel. If you have read some general accounts of *Hard Times*, you have discovered that it was published in segments in a journal called *Household Words*. You may also have noticed the references in the novel to industrial safety and found out in your general reading about the context of the novel that

---

Hard Times. Like the Great Depression. But this is supposed to be the middle of the Industrial Revolution. New wealth being created. New, more efficient manufacturing machines. So why hard times? Certainly the lives of the working people seem pretty bleak. But so do the lives of the owning class. Bounderby seems self-satisfied. But is he happy? We never see him enjoying himself. How can he enjoy himself without Fancy? So are we supposed to feel sorry for him too? His intentions are not evil. Neither are Gradgrind's. Muddle. That comes up several times. Stephen Blackpool thinks the problems come from muddle rather than malevolence. Of course this may be because he is simple minded and incapable of thinking ill of people. But does Dickens think of it as muddle? Are they all victims? Is this why Dickens is regarded as a social reformer and not a revolutionary?

FIGURE 6.5
*Brainstorming on your
associations with the
title,* Hard Times.

safety was a major issue of the day. So we have a connection: Dickens—journalist—industrial safety. Whom do you know living now who is also a crusader for industrial safety? Ralph Nader comes to mind. So take what you know of Ralph Nader and spin out the analogy: Dickens is like Ralph Nader in that they both. . . . Ralph Nader has created an organization that continually presses for consumer safety. Did Dickens? Ralph Nader engages in the political process, testifying before Congress and making speeches on behalf of candidates. Did Dickens? Nader is concerned not only with the safety of workers in the workplace but also with the safety of the products they make. Was Dickens? These questions will lead you to inquire into the political context in which *Hard Times* was written. The analogy is not perfect, at least in the sense that Nader is not a novelist. Do you know any current novelist who has done journalistic projects? Norman Mailer has. So has Truman Capote. These may be fruitful models for thinking about the journalist-novelist Dickens.

Here is another example of using an analogy to generate ideas: It is a basic tenet of the Gradgrind school that the reason should be educated "without stooping to the cultivation of the sentiments and affections." Reason, for Gradgrind, excludes the emotions. If you were a viewer of *Star Trek*, Mr. Spock, the Vulcan, should come to mind. He was incapable of feeling emotions. Contrast Bitzer, the successful product of Gradgrindism, with Mr. Spock. Mr. Spock could not feel, but he knew right and wrong; he was never dishonest; he knew the meaning of loyalty. Can the failure of Bitzer as a moral person then be explained on the basis of an undeveloped emotional capacity? Would Mr. Spock not be the perfect embodiment of the Gradgrind school?

These analogies are not intended necessarily to appear in the final paper. They are intended to help you explode the topic into various components which can be pursued further.

On the basis of these techniques you should now be in a position to write down a controlling question that will lead you to further material in the library. If you were interested in Dickens considered as a journalist-novelist-social reformer, then you might form the following question: "To what extent does *Hard Times* reflect the concerns of the social reformers of the day?" Then, in your library search, a title like "*Hard Times*: The News and the Novel" (by Joseph Butwin) will signify a relevant article, as will "Dickens and the Factories" (by Patrick Brantlinger) or "*Hard Times* and the Factory Controversy" (by K. J. Fielding and Anne Smith). If you decide to pursue the educational theme of *Hard Times*, then "The Gradgrind School: Political Economy in the Classroom" (by Robin Gilmour) will strike you as relevant, and if the Fact versus Fancy aspect of Gradgrind's educational system interests you, "Dickens and the Passions" by Barbara Hardy) will be relevant. You then follow up the internal references of the articles you choose to read. For whatever controlling question you select, you will now be searching not so much for *the* answer to it but for the varieties of answers and for the kind of evidence presented for each.

Getting started on nonliterary topics

In this section so far we have been discussing a research assignment that involves a primary text. We have assumed that the generation of ideas becomes systematic at the point when you have read the text and have a pile of notecards on which to work. To illustrate the case where you have no primary text and where, nonetheless, you are expected to do research, we have chosen a different discipline and a different topic. Suppose you are assigned, or you choose, the topic "the rights of animals," for a philosophy class. Now you might very well have strong views on animals, but if you have spent any time in a philosophy class you will have come to realize that philosophers regard the expression of your views as mere biographical facts about you. When you are assigned a topic such as animal rights, you are expected to take a position on the topic and give reasons for your position. What you need to find out is what positions are possible and what counts as a reason for or against those positions according to the conventions of philosophy.

First consult a general encyclopedia and a specialized encyclopedia, in this case *The Encyclopedia of Philosophy*. The two key words in the statement of the topic are "rights" and "animals." You can regard the topic as the "rights" subtopic of the topic "animals," in which case you begin with animals. Or you can regard the topic as the "animals" subtopic of the topic "rights," and begin with rights. In following this route you find some material on the topic of rights, but with little application to animals; and you find an enormous amount of material on animals, but with little application to the treatment of animals. This situation is not unusual for a topic that has become widely discussed only relatively recently as a whole subject category to itself. For topics like this one, to get bibliographies you have to go to very recent sources, of which the most up to date are periodical indexes. In this case you consult *The Philosopher's Index*, and there under "animals" you find information on recent essays published on the subject. So this index is the logical starting point for your research.

Ordinarily you use an index only to get references to other material to read, and you can judge what to select only by the titles. Many indexes, though, do more than list titles. They also provide you with abstracts of many of the journal articles listed. These abstracts should be used to get an overview of what the controversies are, of what the positions are, and of who is on each side. Here are some examples of abstracts from *The Philosopher's Index*:

BURCH, Robert W. Animals, Rights, And Claims. *Sw J Phil* 8,53–59 Sum 77.
Animals do not have rights because they lack the proper characteristics of rights-bearers, videlicet moral agency and a capacity to exert a moral self-defense. These characteristics are necessary in rights-possessors owing to the nature of rights as special moral "commodities." Rights are claims with a kind of first-person orientation; their point is to provide for an agent's self-defense from the moral point of view, consequently for personal dignity.

SINGER, Peter. The Fable Of The Fox And The Unliberated Animals. *Ethics* 88,119–125 Ja 78.

Michael Fox has attempted to refute the arguments for the equality of animals in my book, *Animal Liberation*. Unfortunately, he mistakenly interprets the argument as one based on rights and an absolute prohibition on killing. This article corrects the interpretation and replies to the few remaining criticisms.

REGAN, Thomas and Jamieson, Dale. Animal Rights: A Reply To Frey's "Animal Rights". *Analysis* 38,32–36 Ja 78.

In his paper, "Animal Rights" (*Analysis* 37.4), R G Frey claims to refute "the most important argument" for the view that animals have rights. We show that no prominent defender of the rights of animals has argued, or should argue, in the way that Frey suggests. Furthermore, we show that there is a plausible argument for the view that animals have rights that is left undiscussed by Frey.

FOX, Michael. Animal Suffering And Rights. *Ethics* 88,134–138 Ja 78.

In this reply, I answer some of the criticisms of my article "Animal Liberation: A Critique" (*Ethics*, January 1978) made by Peter Singer and Tom Regan. Several ways in which they have misconstrued my position are discussed, as well as their charges that I have misrepresented theirs. My chief purpose here is to clarify and reaffirm, in most essential respects, my characterization of them as advocates of a doctrine of animal rights. I also reconsider the issue of the qualitative and quantitative equivalence of human and animal suffering, the notion of membership in a moral community, and the role of the capacity to enjoy and suffer in the ascription of moral rights.[4]

These abstracts are typical of how philosophers deal with ethical issues. Notice how argumentative they are. The Burch article gives a reason for denying animals have rights. The Singer article is a reply to another article, as is Regan's, and the Fox article is a response to a response. Reading these abstracts should give you a sense of where the controversies are and who represents the various positions.

The possible positions on whether animals have rights are limited: either they do or they do not, or else you might make some distinction that enables you to argue that some animals do and some animals don't, or that in one sense animals have rights and in another sense they do not. From examining some of the abstracts of the articles, you can make a list of the players on each side, dividing them into those who support animal rights and those who do not:

```
Proponents of        Opponents of
animal rights        animal rights

Regan    Haworth     Fox         Narveson
Singer   Feinberg    Frey        Burch
Clark    Salt        McCloskey
```

4 *The Philosopher's Index*, 12, No. 2 (Summer 1978), pp. 68, 95, 91, 75. Quoted with permission from the Philosophy Documentation Center, Bowling Green State University, Bowling Green, Ohio 43403.

You could do it in more detail by laying out the order of the controversy: first Singer's paper, then Fox's, response to Fox by Regan and Singer, and rejoinder yet again by Fox.

It is important to understand the order of the controversy, because philosophers are concerned with the logic of an individual's argument, not merely with his conclusion. Suppose philosopher A presents an argument in defense of granting animals rights. Philosopher B criticizes A, but usually the criticism goes not so much to A's conclusion as to A's argument. That is, very often B's criticism is that A's reasoning is mistaken, not that A's position is mistaken. Consequently, the fact that you can make a list of the philosophers on each side of an issue does not itself guarantee that these philosophers have argued their positions in the same way. You run the risk of ending up with a list of arguments on one side and another list on the other, with no way of comparing them. If you can find a series of replies, as in the entries above, you know the arguments of each will be directed at the other.

Once you have identified the adversaries, you read the material to discover in more detail what the arguments are. This further reading should lead to notes on another list: arguments in favor (and replies) and arguments against (and replies). Another useful list in moral questions is a list of principles defended by various authors. The ultimate goal of a research paper in philosophy of this kind is that you identify and display the alternatives and do some evaluation of them, that is, choose a side and give a reasoned argument for your side.

Now that you have determined the positions, you are ready to see where your own views fit into the picture. Use variants of the brainstorming and classification strategies described in this chapter and in chapter 2. After you record a number of your own ideas on animal rights, look for a principle that connects the items on your list. Thus, you might take a series of cases that involve the ethics of treatment of animals: animal experiments, hunting of animals, the use of animals for cosmetics or clothes, eating animals. You ask yourself what your attitude to each case is. Then look at kinds of animals—cattle, dogs, snakes, insects, birds, and so on—and ask yourself how you feel about each kind of animal. You now have two lists: one with your feelings about various animals and the other with your attitudes about ways of treating animals. Do you distinguish between scientific experiments performed on rats and those performed on puppies? If so, look for a principle that explains the distinction you make.

Earlier we suggested the use of analogy as a brainstorming strategy. In the case of the topic "animals and human beings," the analogy between them is part of the marrow of the issue: Are humans and animals sufficiently alike to justify extending rights to (some) animals? Or are they utterly unlike? Here the analogy is not employed to generate ideas; it can be the central issue of the paper on the topic.

The use of examples is another useful strategy that both allows you to introduce your own voice in the paper and is also a central philosophical technique. Given that disputes over ethical questions in philosophy are disputes about principles, these principles are assessed by inspecting what they have to say about a wide range of examples. In a sense, examples are to philosophy what empirical data are to science. But examples also clarify in philosophy, as well as provide a basis for evaluating the principles. For instance, if a possible principle led to the consequence that cats are as entitled to consideration as are retarded human beings, would you then reject the principle? There is opportunity for wide scope to your imagination in devising perceptive and convincing examples.

Writing the first draft

You have reached the stage of first draft when you are ready to translate your ideas and thoughts and notes into connected discourse, with full sentences and complete organized paragraphs. The distinction between the research stage and the first-draft stage would be clear and tidy if one could characterize the first stage as one of finding out what you want to say and then the second stage as one of saying it. It is true that you should focus your attention in the early stages of your paper on discovering ideas, but many writers may find it difficult to continue their research beyond a certain point until they write down a tentative thesis. Most experienced writers give at least some thought to their potential readers as they think about this thesis. At any stage in the composing process, you may find yourself talking to the walls, to plants, to dogs, to typewriters, to the windows, or, if you are lucky, to a sympathetic roommate or friend. Sometimes in this internal conversation—either oral or written—you may hear an inspired turn of your own phrasing. Once in a while full sentences may come almost unbidden to your pen. Such sentences may even launch a flight of creative thought.

So the writing of a thesis sentence may precede the time when you actually sit down to write a first draft. On the other hand, you may begin a first draft with a thesis that you actually reject by the time you see what you have said in the draft as a whole. Many good writers do not really know what they want to say until they have written it out. Sometimes you find in writing that you cannot adequately support what you thought you wanted to say. You may even find the difficulties of writing out a full defense of your thesis reveal such weaknesses in it that you may switch to the other side entirely. It is possible, for example, that although you set out to attack a particular critic's interpretation of *Hard Times*, you may end up agreeing with him. Writing a first draft can be just as much a matter of discovering what you believe as is the research stage. In a most important sense, therefore, the first draft represents your testing *for yourself* whether your thesis "will write."

Transforming research notes into connected sentences and paragraphs is a matter of personal style. Some writers like to work from detailed outlines. They divide the thesis into a series of steps, and perhaps those steps into further steps, each step to represent a point to be made in one paragraph. The value of a detailed outline is that it keeps the overall structure of the paper fixed in your mind at each stage. The danger of an outline is similar to the danger of trying to get the first draft to read like a polished final version. You may come to regard the plan as fixed and final. Other writers like to work from a rough outline, where each point of the outline represents a major section of the paper. And other writers again prefer to forego plans (except perhaps in their head), writing out the thesis statement and then seeing how it develops.

You should experiment with these various strategies to find one with which you are most comfortable. Your purpose is to generate a series of paragraphs, and it does not matter just how you do it. In particular it does not matter in which order you do it. If you are working from an outline, there is no reason why you cannot begin with the last section or with a paragraph from the middle of the paper. In fact, since it always helps to get something down on paper, it may be a good strategy to begin with the paragraphs and points you feel most strongly about or the points you think will write most easily. Many writers find that writing one section—any section—of the paper helps them to develop new points.

You will find yourself with more information than you can use in the first draft, and the first draft generates more than you can use in the final paper. If a point does not fit, or if it is redundant, then even if it is a favorite of yours, you must be ruthless in taking it out. Record some of these extraneous ideas in your journal. Or make an appointment with your instructor to tell him about all the good ideas that you had to leave out.

In sum, almost anything goes in writing the first draft if it is successful in generating paragraphs.

You might use your notecards systematically for the purpose of generating paragraphs. Pick out a series of quotations that make different points. It does not matter where the quotations come from, whether from primary source material or from secondary sources. Then construct a paragraph around each quotation. The paragraph may be a commentary on the quotation, an elaboration of it, an objection to the opinion it contains, or an illustration of an important point. Then, once you have finished, consider what kinds of connections exist among the various paragraphs, whether they overlap or are coordinate to one another or subordinate. The strategy you will follow is exactly the strategy we outlined above for classifying notecards.

Suppose you have on a notecard the quotation shown in figure 6.6. By building a paragraph around the quotation, we mean that you write a paragraph expanding it in some way, describing its context or its con-

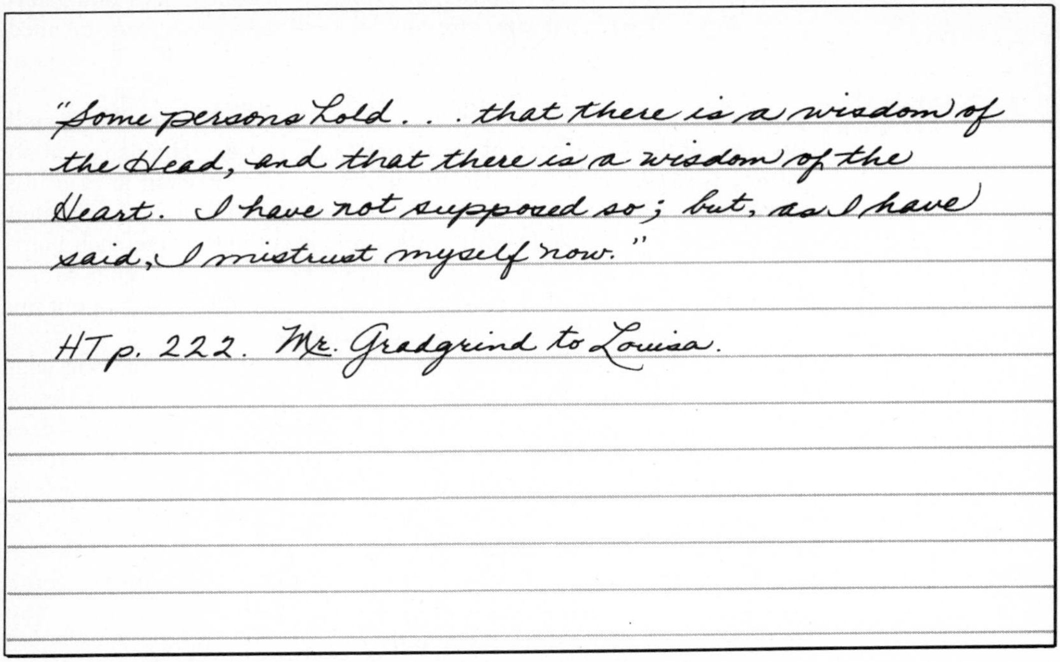

"Some persons hold . . . that there is a wisdom of the Head, and that there is a wisdom of the Heart. I have not supposed so; but, as I have said, I mistrust myself now."

HT p. 222. Mr. Gradgrind to Louisa.

FIGURE 6.6

tribution to the story, elaborating what it means for the novel (that is, what does it show?). It is possible that to get the writing going you might begin to narrate the context of the quotations, and then begin to draw some inferences from the material that you generate (figure 6.7).

Figure 6.8 is another example of a paragraph built around a quotation from a secondary source.

Another example inspired by some sentences you might have taken from a secondary source is shown in figure 6.9.

A second way to generate paragraphs is this: Suppose you choose to write about the Gradgrind school. Then there is an obvious list of people who illustrate the effects or lack of effects of an education such as this school offers. Some characters in the novel have been students (Bitzer, Thomas Gradgrind, Louisa, Sissy Jupe); some are teachers or officials (M'Choackumchild, Gradgrind). The other characters may also represent something about the Gradgrind school because they have developed outside its influence. Now it is possible for you simply to take each of these people and write a paragraph or more on each one, showing for each how the Gradgrind school functions or does not function.

But both of these strategies are adequate only for a first draft. By using these methods, you can generate the substance of many paragraphs that may appear in the final paper. Next you need to work on making the

FIGURE 6.7
First draft generated
from explanation of a
passage in Hard
Times.

The quote from Hard Times

Note the short reference in parentheses. You should have the full reference on a bibliography card.

Immediately a narration of the context in which the statement appeared — who said it, to whom, when? This is the easiest way to begin to write about a quotation.

The effect on Mr. Gradgrind.

Your interpretation of the relationship of this passage to the wider theme of Fact vs. Fancy.

Interpretation of the effect on Mr. Gradgrind, with another quote from your note cards taken from earlier in the book but related to the issue in this paragraph.

"Some persons hold . . . that there is a wisdom of the Head, and that there is a wisdom of the Heart." (HT, p. 222) Louisa's father says this to Louisa the morning after Louisa confronts him with his failure to give her an education in happiness. Mr. Gradgrind is shattered by the discovery of her extreme unhappiness and begins to doubt the educational theory of which he had been so certain. He is forced to consider that his earlier declaration to Bounderby, "The reason is . . . the only faculty to which education should be addressed" (HT 27), is mistaken. There is also a person's emotional life (the Heart) which he has neglected in Louisa. The opposition between the "wisdom of the Head" and the "wisdom of the Heart" is another version of the opposition made so much of in the earlier parts of the book--Fact (Head) vs. Fancy (Heart). He has failed his daughter's heart.

presentation sound less mechanical. No matter how hard the paper has been to write, you must work on making it easier to read.

Revising

When you move to the revising stage it is true that you know what you want to say. The emphasis now shifts to how successfully you communicate it to another person. A writer owes an audience sentences that are crafted carefully, precisely, and clearly. Thus, it is at the stage of revision that you should be concerned with individual sentences, writing and rewriting them as often as is necessary to communicate your meaning as directly as you can. The lament "But what I meant was . . ." is a symptom of a failure of the revision stage. Just as much a failure of revision is a

Quote from your notes on a secondary source. Only brief reference necessary—you should have full reference on a bibliographic card.

A statement of the general interpretation you are taking, with another quote that confirms your interpretation.

The significance of Butwin's quote, that is, what makes it depart from the general interpretation you have above.

Summary of Butwin's meaning, ending with another more elaborate passage from his paper, and a link to the general thesis.

"In order for the facts of industrial life to take hold they must be bodied forth in a fanciful way" (Butwin, p. 170). The theme of HT is Fact vs. Fancy, the serious vs. the playful, the Head vs. the Heart. (See Collins, p. 36: "One of the main themes of the novel--the contrast between the verbalized head-knowledge and the knowledge of the senses and the heart.") But in Butwin's paper another interpretation of the Fact vs. Fancy dispute appears. For he takes seriously the fact that Dickens was writing HT as a serial in a periodical which he edited, Household Words. Dickens was acting in effect as a political journalist. Then "Fancy" takes on the meaning of Dickens's art, his ability to recreate imaginatively for one class the experiences of another class. In this sense, Dickens can be read as claiming to present a truer account (that is, more factual) of the conditions of the day than the unimaginative, but factual, reporting of the daily newspapers. There is therefore a sense in which Dickens can be read as favoring Fact: "Hard Times is generally read as a denigration of 'hard facts' but at the same time it can be seen as Dickens' attempt to renew rather than reduce the status of fact. He sets out to reclaim fact from the hands of the statiticians by showing that much of what passes for fact in Coketown is really fiction" (Butwin, p. 175.)

FIGURE 6.8 *First draft of a paragraph built around a quotation from secondary sources.*

sentence that must be read more than once before the reader can decipher the meaning.

The cause of this kind of problem is very often the use of the passive voice, or the use of negative sentences where a positive sentence is possible, or the use of nouns where verbs are clearer. The surest way to deal with these problems is to find a friend or friends to whom you can read your sentences aloud. If they cannot understand your sentence, change it. And be prepared to change it completely if necessary, breaking one sentence into several if by doing so you clarify the meaning. Be especially wary of words and phrases that you particularly like because they sound imposing: "The genesis of *Hard Times* lay in the Preston Strike." Your friends may indicate that they do not understand this sentence. You may particularly like the opening "The genesis of *Hard Times*,"

A *quotation from*
Hard Times *to which*
Haberman draws
attention.

Haberman's view of
the passage.

Haberman's
interpretation of the
meaning of the
remark, with another
quotation from him.

A *thought that occurs*
to you—another
possible interpretation
of the dialogue. But to
decide which
interpretation is right
will require reading
beyond this passage.
You make a note to
yourself, and if it
should turn out to be
significant you should
try to assess which
interpretation is
correct. But as you
may not use it, it is
acceptable in a first
draft to continue and
leave a loose end.

"Are you in pain, dear mother?" "I think
there's a pain somewhere in the room," said
Mrs. Gradgrind, "but I couldn't positively say
that I have got it" (HT 198).
This sentence, "one of the most amazing
statements in the language," according to
Haberman (p. 40), encapsulates the effect of
living with a dedicated "Commissioner of Fact"
(HT 165) as Mr. Gradgrind. His fanatic insistence
that only facts are worth knowing has led Mrs.
Gradgrind to doubt her very experience of pain.
She knows there is pain, but is it hers? Her
state is desperate, as Haberman sees it: "So
withdrawn is she from her being, that she cannot
experience her own pain" (40). This is surely
Fact run rampant. (It is also possible to read
her statement as ironical, in which case she is
poking fun at Mr. Gradgrind's philosophy of Fact.
She is teasing him. Is there any other evidence
to show her role is ironic?)

FIGURE 6.9
First draft of a
paragraph generated
from a quotation from
Hard Times *and*
secondary sources.

and so you might try to mend it by revising the rest of the sentence. In
fact, the trouble lies in the use of "genesis." Less imposing sounding, but
clearer, is: "Dickens first thought of writing *Hard Times* when he read
about the Preston Strike." Notice also that not only is the revised sentence
clearer, but it commits you more specifically to a causal chain. The first
version of the sentence can mean almost any kind of relation between the
Preston Strike and the novel, excluding only the possibility of the novel's
being published before the strike took place. Impressive-sounding words
like "genesis" often lead to the suspicion that the writer is fudging, glossing
over a fact of which he is not sure.

Beyond the sentence level, writers owe their audience coherent and
unified paragraphs. Each paragraph should have a thesis statement and

a commentary upon, a development of, or evidence for that thesis. Ideally, each sentence within a paragraph should advance the argument or make a new point. If not, the paragraph is padded. You can test whether you are advancing the argument by the practice of "interviewing" each paragraph, as we explain that process in chapter 1. As you conduct these interviews, be alert to paragraphs that cover material already presented in other paragraphs.

Repeating yourself is not objectionable, however, when you are telling your reader what you propose to do or what you have done. Readers find it helpful to be given your interpretation of what you are doing while they read you do it. And this need for helpful repetition applies not only at the level of the paper, where you inform the reader in the introduction of what you propose to show and in the conclusion of what you have shown (these had better match), but also at the level of the paragraph, which might well conclude with another formulation of the main point.

When you move from first draft to final paper, you move from writer-based prose to reader-based prose. One particular danger in the transition is that you may fail to provide enough explanation for your points. You will have done sufficient research to be comfortable with distinctions or references that another person not as familiar as you are with the material may find mysterious. Again, check the reactions of your friends, and again, their responses should be taken as decisive. The context may be clear to you, but if your readers do not understand, consider some revision.

Everything we have said about revision to this point assumes a general audience. The obligations above are owed any audience. But when you write a term paper, you have to imagine a very particular audience. Although it is your professor who will read your final paper, you can run into trouble if you take your professor in his role as teacher as your final audience. You might then tend to make oblique references to experiences common to you both, such as classroom discussions, and neglect to provide sufficient context. Your instructor should be thought of as your audience only in the sense that he represents the world of scholars in his field. As he reads your final draft, he will assess it in terms of the standards assumed in his discipline. Defining the audience in this way means that considerations must operate beyond those of clarity and relevance. For one, you are expected to display competence in the conventions of whatever discipline your writing represents. You must take care to document properly, write bibliographies consistently, and follow the format recommended by the discipline. (See chapter 5.) Pay close attention to the style of the articles you read: to what degree is the writing done in the first person? How extensively do they use quotations? What is the typical format of first pargraphs: Do they declare their thesis right away, or lead up to it later in the paper? Do they announce their thesis as a problem they propose to solve or declare an interpretation they propose to defend? Do they begin with an engaging anecdote or an interesting and striking quotation? Or is the introductory paragraph a simple statement of how the paper will be organized? Thus, when you are taking an introductory course, read research materials for form as well as for content. The style of these articles by scholars in the discipline is the best guide for the form of the term paper.

Here are two paragraphs as they might appear in a revised paper. These paragraphs could have been generated from the examples of paragraphs we gave earlier in the first-draft section of this chapter:

John Holloway complains that in <u>Hard</u> Times the "creed Dickens champions in the novel . . . seems in the main to be that of 'all work and no play makes Jack a dull boy'."[1] It is, he says, the "standpoint of the mid-Victorian, middle-class Philistine."[2] These are strong words, and a radical attack on Leavis's famous judgment of <u>Hard</u> <u>Times</u> as a "completely serious work of art."[3] There is indeed much to Holloway's position. It is true that the portrayal of trade unionism in the novel is seriously defective, as House shows.[4] It is also true that the representatives of "Fancy," against the Fact of Coketown, are the circus folk, who live by playing. And that play, or amusement, was important to Dickens cannot be doubted, as the title of his first contribution to <u>Household</u> <u>Words</u>—"The Amusements of the People"—indicates.[5] Despite this bibliographical circumstance, the Fact versus Fancy theme in <u>Hard</u> <u>Times</u>, its main theme in the view of many commentators,[6] is more complex and subtle than the contrast of Coketown with the circus seems to indicate. Fancy is more than amusement.

Consider, for example, the scene in which Mr. Gradgrind, originally the representative of Fact,[7] is forced to confront the failure of his educational theories in the person of his own daughter, Louisa. To express her anguish, Louisa uses not the language of Fancy but the language of the Heart: "Where are the graces of my soul. Where are the sentiments of my heart?" (215). In response, her father concedes that those who believe in the wisdom of the heart may be right, and he, a believer in the "wisdom of the Head," wrong. It is not lack of amusement of which

Louisa complains. By "heart" Mr. Gradgrind and Louisa mean the finer sentiments, such as compassion, sympathy, even gratitude, which according to his earlier beliefs should be abolished (283). The heart appears again towards the end of the book, when Mr. Gradgrind appeals to his prize pupil's sense of compassion: "Bitzer, have you a heart?" Bitzer's response is only too true to the Gradgrind philosophy: "The circulation, sir, . . . couldn't be carried on without one" (281). In Bitzer's cynical dismissal of any meaning beyond facts, Mr. Gradgrind is brought face to face with the narrowness of his younger self. The revelation of the barrenness of his philosophy, its exclusion not only of play but of all important values, is complete.

---

¹ John Holloway, "Hard Times: A History and a Criticism," Dickens and the Twentieth Century, ed. John Gross and Gabriel Pearson (London: Routledge & Kegan Paul, Ltd., 1962), p. 168.

² Ibid., p. 163.

³ F. R. Leavis, "Hard Times: An Analytic Note," The Great Tradition (New York: New York University Press, 1963), p. 227. Leavis reads the novel as a subtle "confutation of Utilitarianism by life" (p. 236), and a "moral fable" (p. 227).

⁴ Humphrey House, The Dickens World, 2nd ed. (1941; rpt. New York: Oxford University Press, 1960), pp. 205–211. Also see David Craig, "Hard Times and the Condition of England," The Real Foundations: Literature and Social Change (New York: Oxford University Press, 1974), pp. 125–127.

⁵ As cited by Joseph Butwin, "Hard Times: The News and the Novel," Nineteenth Century Fiction, 32 (1977), 171.

⁶ David Lodge, "The Rhetoric of Hard Times," Language of Fiction (New York: Columbia University Press, 1966), p. 157; K. J. Fielding, Charles Dickens: A Critical Introduction, 2nd ed. (1953; rpt. London: Longman's, 1965), p. 160;

Philip Collins, "Good Intentions and Bad Results," <u>Twentieth Century Interpretations of Hard Times</u>, ed. Paul Edward Gray (Englewood Cliffs, N.J.: Prentice-Hall, Inc., 1969), p. 36.

[7] Mr. Gradgrind is introduced as "A man of realities . . . ready to weigh and measure any parcel of human nature." Charles Dickens, <u>Hard Times</u> (New York: The New American Library, 1961), p. 12. Hereafter the numbers in parentheses will refer to page numbers of this edition of <u>Hard Times</u>.

Notice that the particular instances of the theme Fact versus Fancy have now been generalized in an attempt to provide a deeper interpretation of the theme than any single critic is prepared to allow. Notice also the structure of the two paragraphs: First, the writer presents the view of one critic and contrasts that view to one of another critic. Then the writer attempts a preliminary evaluation of the first critic's view. The writer makes some concessions to the truth of the second critic's position and cites some evidence to support the second critic's thesis. Then the writer introduces his own thesis, that the theme is in fact richer and more complex. The writer next indicates that he has selected an important topic, since many commentators regard the theme in question as a central one.

In the second paragraph the writer explains two incidents from the novel as evidence for the thesis outlined in the first paragraph. Notice how the transition from the first to the second paragraph is made. By the use of "for example," the first sentence of the second paragraph signals that the thesis set forth at the end of the first paragraph is about to be made more specific. These transitional devices are ways of avoiding having to say at the beginning of each paragraph, "What I propose to say in this paragraph is. . . ."

Notice also how the documentation is done. Footnotes (1) and (2) are merely reference footnotes. See in (1) the differences between double quotes and single quotes. In footnote (3) the writer fills out the position of Leavis beyond what is said in the body of the paragraph. A writer provides this special kind of footnote when he wants to give the reader a little more information than he can conveniently provide in the text. Footnote (4) is an example of how a writer deals with material that is important but not directly related to the central theme. Footnote (5) is an example of how a writer cites from secondary sources. Footnotes (6) and (7) are examples of explaining allusions, and (7) also exemplifies what a writer does with a primary text to which he expects to make many references. It would be tedious to put a number and a footnote each time he makes a reference to *Hard Times*, so the first time he makes a reference to the novel, he gives the full bibliographical information and says that subsequently numbers within parentheses following a quotation will always refer to this edition of the primary text. (See chapter 5.)

The writer of this excerpt from a term paper in the humanities has learned a great deal about Dickens and about the critical history of *Hard Times*. But the writer is not simply presenting the information for its own sake. He has made selections, and he has shaped the research material to focus on the development of his own thesis. In summary, he has shown that he understands the function of research in the humanities: not to drown out the human voice with obscure references, but to give the individual voice the authority of a scholarly tradition.

QUESTIONS
1 What specific academic skills do you use when you write a research paper in the humanities?

2 What are the three distinct characteristics of a term research paper as opposed to other types of papers?

3 What is brainstorming? How is it useful in preparing a research paper?

4 What are the major criteria for developing a controlling question?

EXERCISES
1 Decide which of the following are controlling questions for a humanities research paper:

a At what point in his writing career did Dickens write *Hard Times*?

b What was the influence of *Hard Times* on the British awareness of the condition of the poor?

c Is *Hard Times* one of the most carefully written books in the nineteenth century?

d In what ways can *Hard Times* be considered a useful historical source?

2 After you have identified the controlling questions, make lists of the more specific research questions that can be derived from each. Compare your lists with those of classmates.

3 As a class, select a topic that would be appropriate for a research paper. Each student should, individually, narrow the topic by creating controlling questions about the topic. Compare and discuss your questions.

4 As a class, identify those characteristics that distinguish a humanities research paper from research papers in other fields. Make a list of ten topics that are appropriate for a research paper in the humanities.

7 Analyses and Reviews

In the last chapter we discussed procedures for writing research papers in the humanities. Research requires wide reading on a well-defined topic. As a researcher, you are on a quest to learn as much as you can about your topic and then to draw inferences from the wide variety of material that you read. But often in your humanities courses you will be asked to do a *close* reading of a text, rather than a wide reading of secondary sources. Instead of asking you to do a research paper or a term paper on *Hard Times*, your instructor may ask you to do a "close reading," or an "analysis," or a "critical paper" on *Hard Times*. In that case, the most important part of your job will be to read and to reread *Hard Times*—to sit and think, rather than to run and search.

On the other hand, you are asked to think, not to emote or to free associate. You may want to make a private record of your emotional responses to *Hard Times* or to whatever artistic work you have been assigned to analyze, but your finished paper should focus on your ideas about the work of art, not on your personal feelings.

In both an *analysis* and a *review*, you are expected to do critical thinking; you must discern various qualities of the work of art under consideration. Despite the popular connotations of the word "critical," a *critical paper* is not necessarily supposed to be fault finding. When you write a critical analysis, you are not expected to focus on whether you like the work or not but instead on what you perceive about the parts of the work and their relationships with each other.

If you are asked to write a *critical analysis*, your professor probably wants you to avoid or deemphasize specifically evaluative commentary. In the case of an analysis, you should probably assume that the work in question is considered by experts to be worth the time you are asked to spend thinking about it. In a *review* or *critique*, on the other hand, you are expected to evaluate the work in terms of its successful or less successful features.

The function of all the papers described in this chapter is to allow you to explore an artistic experience in some depth. This direct intellectual confrontation with the works of the creative imagination is at the heart of the humanities. To fulfill the purposes of these assignments, you must focus your attention as completely as possible on the works of art in question. Resources in the library can help you identify words and images that you do not know, but unless your instructor tells you to do research, you should reflect on the work of art without looking up other people's opinions about the experience. In other words, your task is to contemplate the work of art directly, without using intermediary sources to tell you what to think about the experience. In both analyses and reviews, it is perfectly proper and even necessary to use "I." The sound of a human voice is especially appropriate in papers of this type.

It is wise to assume that you are analyzing the work in question for an audience that includes your instructor and your classmates. Most of the time, in an analysis you are expected to assume that your audience has read the poem or novel, seen the performance, or looked at the painting. Your role is to illuminate the work of art through an explanation of your own informed vision. In a review, you usually should not assume that the readers of your paper have read the book that you are reviewing. But you should check with your instructor on this point.

Analyzing a poem

Suppose that you have been assigned to analyze the following sonnet by William Wordsworth:

THE WORLD IS TOO MUCH WITH US

1 The world is too much with us; late and soon,
2 Getting and spending, we lay waste our powers;
3 Little we see in Nature that is ours;
4 We have given our hearts away, a sordid boon!
5 This Sea that bares her bosom to the moon;
6 The winds that will be howling at all hours,
7 And are up-gathered now like sleeping flowers;
8 For this, for everything, we are out of tune;
9 It moves us not.—Great God! I'd rather be
10 A pagan suckled in a creed outworn;
11 So might I, standing on this pleasant lea,
12 Have glimpses that would make me less forlorn;
13 Have sight of Proteus rising from the sea;
14 Or hear old Triton blow his wreathèd horn.

Many students, especially those who do not plan to be English majors, are needlessly intimidated by this assignment. Some students think that they do not like poetry, and even those who like it believe that they won't like analyzing it, especially not in a formal paper. Students object to "tearing the poem apart." But in this case, analysis involves looking at the parts only to get a better vision of the whole. Analysis means examining the parts and then putting them together, not tearing things apart.

Getting started   An analysis of a poem begins with a careful reading of it. Read the poem several times, at least once or twice aloud. Remember that the poet has taken great care in selecting and arranging these particular words in this special order to create a total effect of meaning, form, and sound.

Take a few minutes and jot down everything that you think of when you read the poem. You probably won't be able to use much of this material directly in your formal analysis, but the time you take to express your feelings about the poem will be important in the long run. A poem is written to reach you emotionally and intellectually. Even though your formal paper will be an intellectual discussion of the poem, your analysis will be more alive and meaningful if it has its roots in some feeling about the poem. Also, if you allow yourself to express feelings about the poem at first, you may find yourself more involved in the project than you thought you would be.

Although self-expression is important, your major purpose for this assignment is to think about the poem. But how does a person think about a poem? First of all, ask yourself what you know about this poem, from your textbook, from classroom discussion, from previous reading. The poem looks short, so you might as well count the lines, looking for the magic number fourteen. Sure enough, the fourteen lines indicate that you may be dealing with a special form, a *sonnet*. Now a trip to the library is in order, but not to look up other people's interpretations of the poem. Instead, look up "sonnet" in a glossary of literary terms, such as M. H. Abrams's A *Glossary of Literary Terms*. [1]

Here you will find a wealth of ideas for organizing your paper. You will learn, for example, that because of the way that Wordsworth's sonnet rhymes, it is an example of a Petrarchan sonnet, which usually discusses a problem or situation in the first eight lines and then presents some sort of resolution in the last six. Now you have something quite specific to put in your notes (figure 7.1). You just have developed a possible structure for your analysis. But you have only the skeleton at this point. Most important in a poem are the words, and you have to find out much more about the words of this poem. As Donald Hall says in *Writing Well*, [2] you have to get "inside" these words, to find out as much about them and their family relationships as the poet knew and felt.

Begin with the unfamiliar names, Triton and Proteus. A good desk dictionary will tell you something about these pagan sea gods. If you want to see them more clearly—as clearly as Wordsworth did on his pleasant lea—then look them up in the *Oxford Classical Dictionary* or in a dictionary of mythology.

1 3rd ed. (New York: Holt, Rinehart & Winston, 1971).
2 3rd ed. (Boston: Little, Brown, 1979).

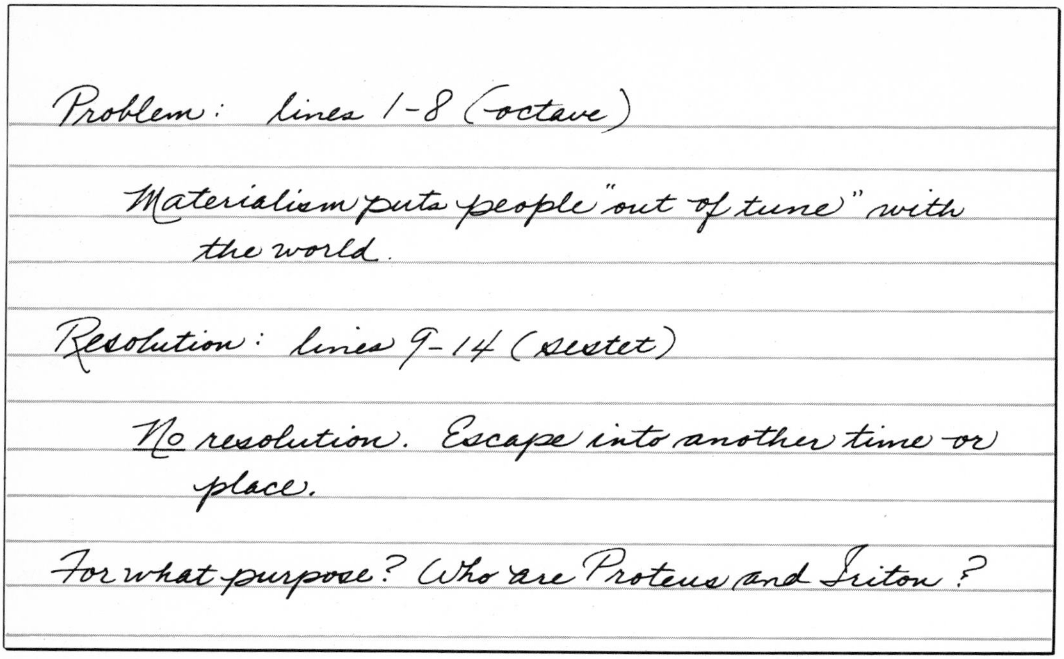

Problem: lines 1–8 (octave)

Materialism puts people "out of tune" with the world.

Resolution: lines 9–14 (sestet)

No resolution. Escape into another time or place.

For what purpose? Who are Proteus and Triton?

FIGURE 7.1
Preliminary notes in an analysis of a sonnet.

FIGURE 7.2
(on facing page)
An entry from The Oxford English Dictionary (*also called the O.E.D.*), *vol. XII, p. 300. Reproduced by permission of Oxford University Press. A supplement was published in 1933. A more up-to-date supplement is now in progress.*

Then look up "lea," "forlorn," "suckled," and other unfamiliar words in a good desk dictionary or, even better, in the *Oxford English Dictionary* (O.E.D.), which will give you the complete history of the word up to the time Wordsworth chose it. (See figure 7.2 for help in reading entries in the O.E.D.) *The Oxford English Dictionary* is a particularly good place to look up familiar words like "world" and "nature," especially if you get interested in why Wordsworth uses those two words in opposition to each other. Doesn't nature include the world, and doesn't the world include nature?

While you are thinking about the poet's use of familiar words, also look to see what words go together in categories. Sometimes it helps to list all the verbs in a poem to see what kinds of actions the poem describes.

Another way to categorize the words in a poem is to see which ones relate in meaning. "Bosom" in line 5 should thus be associated with "suckled" in line 10 and "howling" and "sleeping" in lines 6–7, since all these words relate to the image of nursing a baby. Imagery means simply word patterns that make us see pictures or hear sounds. Whether you are an English major or not, a close look at words will help you to understand imagery.

If you are an English major, you may wish to extend your analysis to metrics and to other more technical elements of poetry. In that case, you

World (wöⁱld), *sb.* Forms: a. 1 weorold, wuruld, worold, uoruld, wiarald, 1–3 weoruld, woruld, -eld, -old, 2 wurold, 3 we(o)reld. wæruld, *Orm.* we(o)relld. β. 1– world ; 1–3 weorld, 4–6 worlde (2 worlþ, 3 wurld, 5 whorlld(e) ; 2–3 werlþ, 3 *Orm.* werrld, 3–5 werld\e ; *north.* and *Sc.* 3- warld, 5–6 warlde, varld, (5 warlede). γ. 4–6 wordle, 5 wordel, wordil ; *north.* and *Sc.* 5–7 wardle, 6 wardill, vardil, wardel, vardel ; 3 werdle. δ. 3–6 word, 4–5 worde (6 woaude) ; 3–5 werd, 4–5 werde ; 4 wird ; *north.* 4, 6 ward. ε. 3 worl, 3–5 worle, 5 worlle, orlle, 6 worell ; 8 worl', *north.* and *Sc.* 5 warle, 8 warl', 9 warl. [Com. Teut. (wanting in Gothic): OE. *weorold, worold, world* str. f., rarely m., corresp. to OFris. *wrald, ruald, warld* (EFris. *warld*, WFris. *wröd*), OS. *werold* (MLG. *werlt, warlt*, LG. *werld*, MDu. *werelt*, Du. *wereld*), OHG. *weralt* (MHG. *werelt, werlt, welt*, G. *welt*), ON. *veröld* (Sw. *verld*, Da. *verden*) : a formation peculiar to Germanic, f. *wer-* man, WERE *sb.*[1] + *ald-* age (cf. OLD *a.*, ELD *sb.*[2]), the etymological meaning being, therefore, 'age' or 'life of man'.]

I. Human existence ; a period of this.

1. a. Chiefly *This world, the world* : the earthly state of human existence ; this present life.

To (unto, OE. oð) the world's end: as long as human things shall last, to the end of time (with admixture of senses 7, 9). Similarly in phrases such as *as as long as the* or *this world lasts*, and *in this world.*

832 *Charter* in Sweet *O. E. Texts* 447 Ðet he ðas god forðleste oð wiaralde ende. **c897** ÆLFRED *Gregory's Past. C.* xviii. 137 [Hi] ne dooð him nan oðer god ðisse weorolde. **971** *Blickl. Hom.* 57 We witon þæt ælc wi te..to ende efsteþ & onetteþ þisse weorolde lifes. **c1200** *Vices & Virtues* 17 'Andswere me'..he wile seggen, 'hwat hafst ðu swa lange idon on ðare woreld ?' **c1205** LAY. 5028 Þa wifmon þa þe a ðas weoreld iboren. **c1250** *Kent. Serm.* in *O. E. Misc.* 33 Þet ha yef us swiche werkes to done in þise worlde þet þo saulen of us mote bien isauued adomesdai. **c1250** *Gen. & Ex.* 32 Fader ..ðu giue me seli timinge To thaunen ðis werdes biginninge. **a1300** *Cursor M.* 91 Quat bote is to sette traueil On thyng ..þat es bot fantum o þis warld ? **c1300** *Havelok* 2335 Was neuere yete ioie more In al þis werd, þan þo was þore. **c1374** CHAUCER *Troylus* v. 1058 Allas of me vn-to þe worldis ende Schal noþer ben wretyn noþer I-songe No good worl. **c1400** *26 Pol. Poems* i. 123 They han here heuene in this world here. **1426** AUDELAY *Poems* 12 Ale the wyt of this word fallus to foly. **c1450** HOLLAND *Houlat* 43 Wa is me, wretche in this warld, wisome of wane I. **1451** *Paston Lett.* I. 189 In this werd that now is. **1513** *Life Hen. V* (1911) 22 Yearelie to be distributed..twenty poundis in pence to the poore people duringe the Worlde. **1570** *Satir. Poems Reform.* x. 36 He sall with vs rest, And we with him, sa lang as warld may lest. **1590** SHAKS. *Com. Err.* II. ii. 108 Time himselfe is bald, and therefore to the worlds end, will haue bald followers. **1597** — *2 Hen. IV*, v. iii. 104, I prethee now deliuer them, like a man of this World. **1670** T. BLOUNT *Acad. Eloq.* (ed. 4) 250 The Heir of a Knight in the right line shall be an Esquire to the worlds end. **1794** PALEY *Evid.* II. ii. § 8 A Christian's chief care being to pass quietly through this world to a better. **1797** JANE AUSTEN *Sense & Sensib.* xliv, 'As to that,' said he, 'I must rub through the world as well as I can.' **1856** DICKENS *Christmas Stories* (1874) 43 She was too good for this world and for me, and she died six weeks before our marriage-day.

b. With reference to birth or death ; esp. *to bring into the world*, to give birth to (see BRING *v.* 7 c) ; *to come into* (or *to*) *the world*, to be born (see COME *v.* 4 c) ; *fig.* (of a book) to be published ; *to go* or *depart out of this world.*

Beowulf 60 Ðæm feower bearn forð gerimed in worold wocun. **a1000** *Genesis* 2284 Þu scealt, Agar, Abrahame sunu on woruld bringan. **a1000** *Ælfst. Alex.* in Cockayne *Narrat.* (1861) 31 Ðin modor gewiteð of weorulde þurh scondlice deað. **c1205** LAY. 17235 He sæt stille alse þeh he wolde of worlden iwiten. **c1250** *Gen. & Ex.* 2284 Ic sal to min sune fare..or ic of werlde chare. **1297** R. GLOUC. (Rolls) 5116 & þe nyenteþe day of aueryl out of þis world he wende. [1382] *c1510* [see COME *v.* 4 c]. **a1400-50** *Wars Alex.* 2653 (Dubl.) Qwen he went of þis warld. **c1420** *Chron. Vilod.* 3953 Þaw y shulde now ouзt of þis worde gone. **1579** RANDOLPH *Let.* in Buchanan *Wks.* (S.T.S.) 56 The last little Treatise..that lately come into the World. **c1588** *Cath. Tractates* (S.T.S.) 250 Not doutand bot angels and sanctis depairted out of this wardle may and do pray for us. **1607** [see BRING *v.* 7 c]. **1784** BURNS *Addr. Illeg. Child* iv, My funny toil is now a' tint, Sin' thou came to the warl askient. **1914** 'IAN HAY' *Knt. on Wheels* xiii. § 3 Having been born into the world with a club foot.

Margin notes:

Various definitions of each word are listed chronologically with the earliest first. The earliest meaning of world *is a period of human existence, especially in the sense of the earthly state of human existence as opposed to the spiritual. (Wordsworth refers to this early sense of the word in his identification of the world with materialism.)*

These are the different forms and spellings of the word as it has appeared through the centuries. Deciphering this information will probably never be necessary for any undergraduate project.

Each definition is illustrated with a series of quotations starting with the first recorded use of the word in each sense. World *was first used in the sense defined in 832 A.D. You can get that piece of information even though you probably cannot read the Old English quotation that follows. Since this quotation is listed under the earliest meaning of the word, you can infer that the earliest recorded use of the English word* world *occurred in 832.*

may wish to consult a special text on the subject, such as James R. Kreuzer's *Elements of Poetry*.[3] Few freshman composition teachers expect you to write a technical analysis, and you should be able to create an A paper for most classes without consulting a special source on sophisticated poetic techniques.

You may want to find out something about the poet and about the time that the poem was written. Usually you do not have to look beyond your own textbook to find the date that the poem was first published—in this case, 1807. That piece of information will save you from talking about the poet's view of our materialistic nuclear age. The *Dictionary of National Biography* and other general reference works will tell you something about Wordsworth. You should consult these sources only to provide a context for your interpretation, not for research on other writers' views of the poem. You should use only those library materials that will help you to understand the words of the poem. You are then prepared to write your own interpretation.

Writing the first draft

You now have lots of notes, more than you probably ever expected to have on this short poem. You should also have recorded some ideas about patterns that you now see within the poem. In your first draft, you may find it useful simply to record in connected sentences all that you have learned about the poem. For example, one student wrote this first paragraph on an early draft:

```
"The World is Too Much With Us," by William
Wordsworth, is a traditional Italian or
Petrarchan sonnet. The Italian sonnet usually
consists of fourteen lines, divided into an
octave and a sestet. An octave is usually used to
raise a question or present a problem, and a
sestet resolves or reflects on the problem.
```

The above paragraph, although it won't do for a final draft, is an adequate way to get moving on a first draft. By writing up the information from his notes, the student is also reflecting on this information.

It is probably a good idea in an early draft to discuss the poem line by line, quoting two-line segments and then discussing each segment. In this way, you will record your thinking about the poem. You can go back to select, rearrange, and connect on later drafts.

If your own habits of writing make it difficult for you to push ahead to the end of a first draft without revising, don't worry about your stop-and-go method of working. You may find that you need to go back and try a first paragraph as soon as you find what you want to say about the

3 New York: Macmillan, 1962.

poem. Whether you are a full-first-draft writer or a stop-and-go editor, your goal should be to find your thesis—the major point that you want to make about the poem—at least by the time you are ready to do your later-stage revisions.

Revising   The student who drafted the above paragraph discovered that his major point was that Wordsworth used the form of the Petrarchan sonnet to express feelings about the world. The student then revised the pargraph:

> William Wordsworth in his poem "The World is Too Much With Us" has chosen the form of the traditional Petrarchan sonnet to express his feelings about the disheartening and declining condition of his world. The problem presented in the octave is that of being "out of tune" with the world. We are so caught up with money and possessions that we cannot see the riches of the natural world staring us in the face. The final six lines, the sestet, does not resolve this problem but instead reflects on the poet's desire to be a heathen raised on outdated beliefs rather than a Christian caught up in the drudgery of the modern world.

The student writer has used the knowledge that he merely recorded in the paragraph from his first draft to help him to understand Wordsworth's use of the sonnet form in the poem. The student also sets up expectations for the rest of the paper. He will discuss the poet's structural and lexical choices only when he wants to make a point about the way that those choices elaborate the theme as it is identified in the first paragraph. Consequently, the writer can go through his draft with an eye toward omitting unnecessary discussion from the earlier line-by-line analysis. He can also work toward making explicit connections between parts of his paper, since a line-by-line analysis tends in first-draft form to be naturally disjointed. He can also check to see that his concluding paragraph reminds the reader of what he has already presented, reflects on those ideas, and then suggests a wider perspective on the material. Here is the student's concluding paragraph:

> When this poem was written, the Industrial Revolution was just beginning. The poem, in a sense, is in the nature of a warning. But if we look around today, we can see that very few paid any attention to what Wordsworth said so powerfully in this traditional poetic form.

> Perhaps the modern world can no more hear
> traditional sonnets than we can hear old Triton
> blow his wreathèd horn.

In this conclusion, the student has evidently drawn on his notes about when the poem was written. He may even have referred to his very early notes that helped him to verbalize his feelings about the poem.

Analyzing stories, novels, and plays

Getting started When you are asked to write an analysis of a literary work longer than the poem discussed above, you will have to adapt the techniques that we describe. In general, however, your procedures can be quite similar to the process just explained. Once again, reading and thinking will be most important. Finding out something about the definition of the literary structure you are dealing with will be helpful. A respect for the words of your source will be essential.

You won't, of course, be able to look up all key words in a longer piece, but you may want to look closely at the use of words in important passages. The first and last paragraphs of stories and novels are especially significant. The opening lines and the "curtain" lines of plays demand special attention. It is always useful to ask why a writer decides to begin and end his work the way he does. Titles are usually even more important. A thorough analysis of the words of a title can lead you to an understanding of the work as a whole.

Reading carefully is still your best strategy, whether the work that you are analyzing is long or short. You should write as you read and reread. When you come to a passage in a novel that looks important or one that you simply like for reasons that may not be clear to you at the moment, copy the passage word for word in a notebook or on a notecard. Be sure to mark the page number for later reference. First of all, copying passages can slow down your reading in a useful way, since you have to stop and think actively about what you have read so far and also about why this particular passage has caught your eye. Second, copying the author's sentences gets you inside the author's rhythms and style in a way that almost nothing else can.

If you use this method, you may finish a four-hundred-page novel and find that you have ten pages or so of recorded quotations. You can then look over these quotations to try to see why you decided to copy down these and not others. You will begin to see patterns that you did not consciously notice as you were reading the novel or story or play.

Writing the first draft Often you will discover the focus for your literary analyses by looking carefully through the passages you have recorded. Several recorded passages from Joyce's "The Dead," for example, may refer to water in its various forms: snow, ice, tears. You may then decide to write about water imagery in "The Dead." You may then go back to the story and look consciously for passages that refer to water. You may also make random interpretative notes as you record pertinent passages. Then try a draft that moves through the story sequentially, discussing the water imagery as it appears page by page through the story. This procedure will produce a draft that is probably too detailed and fragmented, but at least you have something to shape and rework as you revise.

Revising The major job at this stage is to look for categories that transcend the page-by-page sequence of presentation in your first draft. You may decide to consider patterns of reference to water in its varying degrees of solidity— water, snow, ice—wherever they appear in the story to see how Joyce connects all these related images. Once you have discovered a conceptual, rather than sequential, pattern of organization, you are ready to write a thesis paragraph that articulates a controlling idea, which will then limit the detail that you choose to include throughout the paper. Try to summarize your major idea about the story as you would if you were teaching the story to someone else.

Writing an analysis of a performance

Sometimes you will be asked to write a paper about a performance of a play, concert, dance, or film. This sort of assignment can be exciting because of its immediacy, but the assignment can also be dismaying because you will not be able to return to the performance as you write about it. In fact, you will miss the most important and enjoyable part of the activity if you worry too much about your paper as the performance is in progress. Do not try to take notes in the dark. Use the assignment simply as a motivation to remain especially alert as the performance proceeds.

Getting started Remember the communal aspect of attendance at public performances and make it a point to discuss what you have seen and heard with friends. This is a time when a dormitory bull session is most appropriate. Your friends will have seen and remembered things that you missed, and you will no doubt be able to return the favor. Their reactions will stimulate your agreement or disagreement and may even make you want to write out your immediate responses when you return to your own room.

Before you go to bed, write as much as you can about the performance and your responses to it. Write as much as you can remember about the details of action, dialogue, costume, and set. You may not use very much of this material for your paper, but without some remembered details, you won't be able to write anything but vague generalities. If you have a printed program, use it to aid your memory. At least, all the characters and scenes are listed here. Also, keep in mind who has responsibility for what in any performance. If you recall, for example, that it is the director who has final responsibility for most decisions in the production of films and plays, you will find a subject for many sentences that you might have been inclined to write in the passive voice.

Writing the first draft Figure 7.3 shows some notes that a student recorded immediately after attending a performance of "The Moor's Pavane," performed by the Pennsylvania Ballet Company. The student used these notes to draft the following paragraph:

The ballet primarily tells Othello's story of a man driven by consuming and uncontrollable passions within the framework of a pavane, a stately and ritualistic dance of the sixteenth century. Consequently, the dancer who portrays the Moor dominates the action on stage from the instant the lights go on, and he moves with deft, sure steps in his long, flowing red robes that split mid-thigh revealing red hose. Looking like a Moor with swarthy, nut-brown skin and flashing

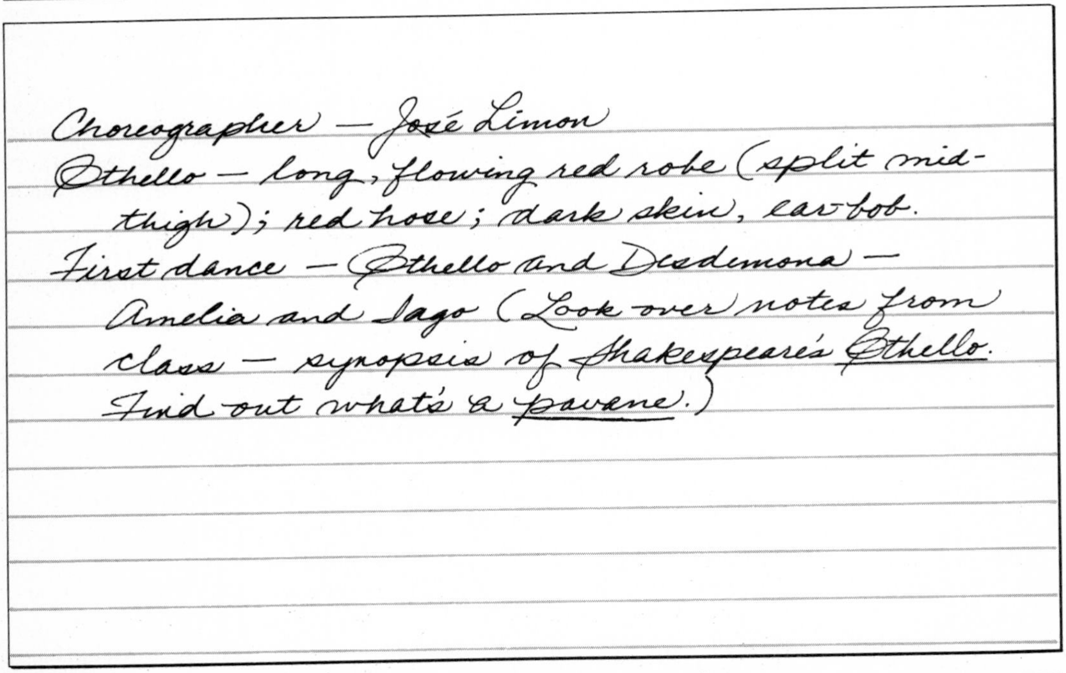

Choreographer — José Limon
Othello — long, flowing red robe (split mid-thigh); red hose; dark skin, ear-bob.
First dance — Othello and Desdemona — Amelia and Iago (Look over notes from class — synopsis of Shakespeare's Othello. Find out what's a pavane.)

FIGURE 7.3

diamond ear-bob, his appearance strongly suggests
that of a scorching flame.

The writer has made a good start here. He has generated a paragraph
full of vivid detail. He hasn't yet decided on the focus for his paper, but
he may not be ready to find a focus until he begins connecting sentences
and paragraphs. Some of his sentences need reworking, but he can get
the syntax under better control on a later draft.

Revising   After trying a few drafts, the student decided that he wanted to focus on
the way that the ballet conveys emotion through physical movements and
theatrical effects. He then revised the above paragraph.

"The Moor's Pavane," choreographed by José
Limon and presented by the Pennsylvania Ballet
Company, presents the story of Othello, a man
driven by consuming and uncontrollable passions.
The pavane, a stately, ritualistic dance of the
sixteenth century, provides the framework for the
intense emotions of the characters. From the time
that the Moor first appears, even his costume
reflects his passion. He wears long, flowing red
robes that split mid-thigh to reveal red hose.
Because of his appearance and his movements, he
dominates the action from the beginning.

The student's revision eliminates some detail: the flashing diamond
ear-bob, the nut-brown skin, the scorching flame. The detail that he has
retained—the red of Othello's costume—is used to highlight the point
about the Moor's passion. The student may have needed all the recorded
detail at an earlier stage in order to help him decide on a focus. Now that
he has chosen his main point, he can be more selective and economical
throughout the final draft.

Analyzing a painting or other graphic work

Suppose you have been asked to write a descriptive analysis of the watercolor that appears facing page 176. Students who do not plan to be fine
arts majors may be as intimidated by this assignment as non-English
majors sometimes are by the task of analyzing a poem. Once again it is
important to remember that it is not necessary to write a highly technical
analysis. Your major task is to look carefully and to classify what you see
in the painting.

Getting started   As you look closely at the painting, record your observations and your
feelings. In every painting look at the artist's use of space. Is there a focal

FIGURE 7·4
(on facing page)
*Preliminary notes on
the Blake watercolor.*

point? In other words, do parts of the work radiate out from a center of interest? Record ideas about shape and color. Note the proportion of objects and shapes. Write down your impression of the mood evoked by the painting.

The Blake watercolor clearly has narrative content, too, and you should find out something about the story that the painting tells. The subject is obviously biblical, but where in the Bible should you look? Now might be the time to check a few secondary sources for information on the artist, William Blake. You would then discover that Blake frequently based his paintings and lithographs on scenes and symbols from the Book of Revelation. In fact, in chapter 4 of the Book of Revelation, the depicted scene is described poetically in a way that must have inspired William Blake.

You may want to learn more about the significance of the Christian symbolism depicted in this scene. If so, look up some of the painted items—the elders, the rainbow, the seven seals—in a biblical dictionary. You might also want to look at chapter 4 of the Book of Revelation in the *Anchor Annotated Bible.*[4]

Figure 7.4 presents excerpts from some preliminary notes that one student recorded. This student has begun by noting down more detail than he will probably use in his paper. He has also summarized the narrative content of the painting, as it appears in the Book of Revelation. (Not all paintings have a narrative content.) In any case, most fine arts instructors will expect you to demonstrate your ability to *see* the visual elements in the work of art. So your notes on space, shape, color, and proportion are just as important as any background material that you find in the library.

In the case of this painting, the background material will probably help you to see the graphic elements of the painting in a context. For example, the focal point of this painting is obvious both from your seeing and from your reading. Everything depicted in the painting brings the eye to the divine throne. As a consequence, you may decide to organize your analytic description by beginning with the focal point or center of interest and then discussing the parts that radiate out from it.

In other works of art, other systems of organization may prove more useful. Edgar V. Roberts, in *A Practical College Rhetoric,*[5] suggests the following possible organizing principles: right, center, and left; up and down; foregrounds and backgrounds; earth, water, and sky.

Writing the first draft   You will discover the best structural procedure as you review your notes. Sometimes you will have to begin writing connected sentences before you will find a suitable organizing principle for your descriptive analysis. Since

4 (New York: Doubleday, 1964), pp. 69–82.
5 Cambridge, Mass.: Winthrop, 1975.

A picture of God sitting on a gold throne (center of picture). God has on white and light red robe. He has a long white beard and hair. There is light radiating from behind his head and shoulders. His arms are partially out-stretched and in one hand he is holding what looks like a scroll with seven red stones running down it (possibly the seven seals?). The expression on his face seems rather sad and forlorn as though he has given up hope.

On each side of God there is a row of kings bowing and placing their gold crowns at his feet. All of the kings are dressed in white gowns, white hair and white faces — like ghosts.

God's throne looks as if it is placed on a slab of white marble or stone. The stone seems to be floating on water (gray). Below the slab at the bottom of the picture are the faces of seven young children. They are in the water but only their heads are above it. They appear to have wings though. The face, hair, and wings of the children are all white. The expression on their faces is, like God's, rather sad and unhappy.

Described in the Book of Revelation, chapter 4

According to Revelation, the figures of the ox, lion, eagle, and man are constantly saying, "Holy, holy, holy Lord God Almighty who was, and who is, and who is coming."

Whenever the four praise and honor God the kings cast their crowns before the throne. Seven angels hold the seven plagues that God sends to earth.

The Book of Revelation describes how John the Apostle witnessed Judgment Day. Blake's painting is what John saw when he first was called to heaven. It is the scene preceding the fore-telling of Judgment Day.

the organizing principle of the Blake painting is so clear, our student wrote the first draft shown in figure 7.5.

To write this first draft the student has made some choices, as he sorted through his notes. He is focusing on the center of interest, the divine throne. But after mentioning the obvious placement of the throne in the center of the painting, he selects color as his primary area of discussion. As is often the case in first drafts, he has not provided a context for the descriptive analysis. The paragraph quoted above will not be the first paragraph of the final draft, but even in this early draft the writer has connected close observations of details of color to ideas about the general composition of the painting. In the process of revising, he can provide readers with enough background to make the analytic description more readily comprehensible.

Revising In the revision of this analytic description, the writer draws on his reading of biblical background material to establish the narrative significance of the painting, since the rest of the discussion will focus on the graphic methods employed to convey that meaning:

> William Blake's painting "The Four and Twenty Elders Casting Their Crowns before the Divine Throne" is a description of the scene preceding the breaking of the seven seals in the Book of Revelation. Because the breaking of the seven seals signals the end of the world and the onset of the Day of Judgment, God on his divine throne is the center of attention in Blake's painting of this apocalyptic scene.

In this new first paragraph, the writer also immediately identifies the painting that he will describe. He then refers the reader to the Book of

---

Red and white contrasted against blue and gray.

> The focal point of the painting is God seated on a gold throne. The two features that serve to make him the focal point are his position in the painting—the center—and his coloring. The predominant colors in the painting are blue and gray. God's coloring is pure white and pale red. He is wearing a white gown with a red robe over it, but the thing that is most noticeable about him is his white beard and hair, and the pure white light radiating from about his head.

FIGURE 7.5

Revelation, which is the source of the painting. In the last sentence of this paragraph he prepares for a transition to a discussion of focal point that he will develop in the next paragraph.

The second paragraph is a rewriting of the first paragraph of the student's earlier draft.

```
Not only does Blake place the divine throne in
the center of the painting, but he also uses
color to direct the viewer's eye to this focal
point. God's red robe contrasts with the
predominant blues and grays of the rest of the
painting. But Blake's use of white is most
dramatic. God's white beard and white hair lead
the eye to the pure white light radiating from
his head.
```

This revised paragraph illustrates other principles of revision. The sentences in the earlier draft are disjointed. The writer recorded those earlier sentences as he thought them. In the revised draft the first two sentences of the earlier draft are skillfully combined into a *not only . . . but also* construction. The writer effectively uses sentence variety; for example, a short simple sentence at the pivotal point in the paragraph: "But Blake's use of white is most dramatic."

The writer is in better control of sentence construction and of the structure of the paragraph as a whole. The revised paragraph has a direction, from least to most dramatic use of color.

Control is the byword on a finished draft. As you check through your own, be sure that you are in complete control of the direction of your paper as a whole. As always, check to see that matters of grammar, punctuation, and mechanics are also under control.

Book reviews

In many humanities courses and also in courses in other disciplines, you will be asked to write book reviews or critiques. The book will sometimes be a novel, but more often it will be a work of nonfiction. The book review involves procedures of analysis, but in this case the analysis is usually used as a means of evaluation.

Getting started Since analysis is a way of examining a problem by breaking it down into its parts and studying these parts in relation to each other and to the whole problem, you should familiarize yourself not only with the parts of the book (chapters, themes, arguments) but with their relationships. You should ask the following analytic questions:

- What are the purposes of the author in writing this book?

- What are the parts of the book? That is, how does the author try to accomplish his purposes?
- Does each part accomplish its purpose?
- Do the parts, collectively, accomplish the author's purposes?

Since the purpose of analysis in this case is evaluation—"to determine the worth of"—it is your responsibility to draw conclusions about the book. The type of evaluation you will make will vary with the assignment. You may, for example, be asked to evaluate the usefulness of a book for a particular audience or within a certain discipline. You may be required to critique the book on its own merits or in relation to other books on the same subject. At a minimum, you will need to determine the book's value to you. Do you think that the book is useful or important? In what ways does it please you or fall short of your expectations?

We emphasize the word "your" because a book review should represent your analysis and your evaluation. Many student reviews are unsuccessful because the writer is intimidated by having to critique a published work ("What can I possibly say about the work of a professional on this topic?"). True, you may not be able to review a book by assessing its validity and accuracy within the context of all that is known about a subject, or evaluate its use of unfamiliar sources or research methods, but you can decide if the book's purpose is meaningful to you and if that purpose is accomplished to your satisfaction. You can come to some conclusions about the strengths and weaknesses of a book in light of your reactions. Your views and opinions, if rendered thoughtfully and supported capably, are just as valid as those expressed in professional reviews.

A beginning point for writing a book review is to read some book reviews. Ask your instructor for advice on journals that contain good examples of reviews, or see chapter 4 of this text for how to find book reviews. You may not be able to emulate those professional reviews in style or sophistication of analysis, but they will give you examples of form.

Before you even begin to read the book to be reviewed, examine it. Find out when it was published. Study the table of contents to familiarize yourself with its organization (scope of the topic, chapters, subheadings, number of pages devoted to each element of the topic). Read the acknowledgments, preface, and introduction, for they are short essays in which the author speaks to the reader about the book. Find out if the author has included footnotes. If so, study the types of sources used. Look at the appendices, if any, to discover what the author felt was important enough to reproduce or discuss in more detail. Finally, scan the index to get a sense of what topics or persons appear most frequently in the body of the work.

As you examine the book, write notes to yourself about any features that strike you as possibly important. You will not yet know what you are going to write about, so keeping notes will preserve your impressions for your later analysis—after you have read the book. For example, assume you are assigned to review Thomas S. Szasz's book *Ideology and Insanity*. By examining the book before you read it, you can learn valuable information that will allow you to direct your reading to specific topics and important themes. In the introduction to his book, Thomas Szasz offers a clear, concise statement of his purpose:

In short, I shall try to show that the claims and practices of modern psychiatry dehumanize man by denying—on the basis of spurious scientific reasoning—the existence, or even the possibility, of personal responsibility. . . . psychiatry is . . . an ideology and a technology.[6]

From the index you can discover that the topics to which he probably gives the most attention are psychiatry, mental hospitals, freedom, and moral values. From the book cover you can learn that Thomas Szasz is himself a psychiatrist. This information will certainly affect your reading of the book.

As you read, keep notes! Even if you own the book and thereby have the luxury of writing in it, you should not rely on underlining passages or taking notes in the margins. Note keeping on cards or separate sheets of paper not only preserves significant parts of the book but, more important, preserves a running record of your reactions to those parts and the reasons you chose to record them. Remember, your review is going to be an analytical essay. You need to record your analysis of each of the parts of the book before you are able to analyze the entire work.

Your note taking, therefore, should be purposeful. First of all, you should not spend valuable time paraphrasing the entire book. What should you record? You will want to identify the author's purposes so you can refer back to them as you read. And you will need to record the most important ways the author tries to accomplish these purposes. Pick out a few salient themes and follow them through the volume, noting both the arguments and the proofs used to support the main thesis. You should build your analysis around these major points.

As you record parts of the book, you will also need to write down your impressions of how these parts are presented and the reasons why you developed your impressions. Good note taking is little more than keeping a running dialogue with yourself. Are you impressed with a certain argument? Do you wish that the author had given an example to support a certain point? Does the author make statements of importance without evidence or authority to back them up? Why does the point being made

6 Excerpts from *Ideology and Insanity* by Thomas S. Szasz. Copyright © 1970 by Thomas S. Szasz. Reprinted by permission of Doubleday & Company, Inc. p. 11.

contribute or fail to contribute to his developing argument? These and similar responses need to be recorded as you proceed. If not, you may well forget why you recorded whole parts of the book.

When you finish reading the book you should have a complete set of notes containing the major themes of the author, examples and details that illustrate strengths and weaknesses, comments explaining your reactions to these parts of the book, and your analysis of them. These notes will make it easier for you to move from reading to writing the review. Instead of rereading whole parts of the book and trying to find relationships, you should be able to put your essay together from your notes with only occasional time-consuming references to the book. Among the few tasks more frustrating than rereading an underlined portion of a book and trying to remember why you underlined it is realizing that a marked passage relates to another in the book and not being able to remember where the other passage is. Notes can be arranged, rearranged, kept in piles according to shifting topics, and annotated with directions and explanations.

For example, a student who is developing an analysis of one of Szasz's major theses—that psychiatrists make their evaluations on spurious criteria—might spend hours trying to find these two related, but physically separated references in *Ideology and Insanity*:

It may be recalled that the American poet Ezra Pound had been . . . incarcerated in a mental hospital in Washington, D.C.

In all, 2,417 psychiatrists [polled on Barry Goldwater's fitness to be president one week after his nomination in 1964] responded. By a vote of 1,189 to 657, the psychiatrists declared the Republican candidate unfit for the Presidency.[7]

Or a student might have notecards as shown in figure 7.6.

These notes, along with others on the general theme of spurious criteria, provide the material for the argument eventually to be presented.

Writing the first draft   With your ideas formed, your major concern at this point is ordering them and connecting them in a cogent essay. Creating a structure for a book review poses special problems. Too often a review simply follows the structure of the book ("First the author discusses. . . . He then turns his attention to. . . . His next point. . . . He concludes by. . . "). Writing from your own notes frees you from the tyranny of the author's organization and allows you to create your own ("The most important thesis of this author is. . . . It is not a convincing argument because. . . ").

If organization is the first requirement of structure, coherence is the second. Your structure must not only be logical; you must make very

7 Szasz, *Ideology and Insanity*, pp. 30, 204.

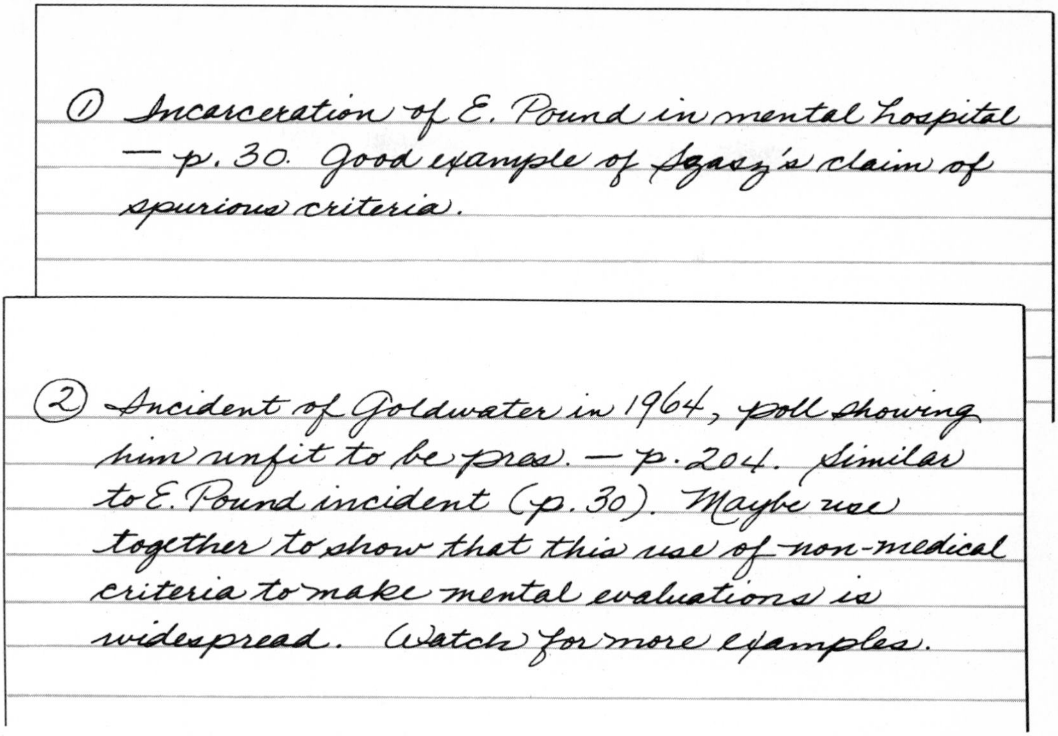

① Incarceration of E. Pound in mental hospital — p. 30. Good example of Szasz's claim of spurious criteria.

② Incident of Goldwater in 1964, poll showing him unfit to be pres. — p. 204. Similar to E. Pound incident (p. 30). Maybe use together to show that this use of non-medical criteria to make mental evaluations is widespread. Watch for more examples.

FIGURE 7.6

clear the connections among the various parts. Your first draft should be used to develop individual ideas with paragraphs and to relate these paragraphs to one another. In the first draft you are writing for yourself, so experiment. You may wish to begin by developing what you consider to be your most important argument or observation and then proceed to your other themes in order of importance. Or you may concentrate on developing your topic paragraph and relate other paragraphs to it. However you approach the problem of creating a whole paper, write and arrange until you are satisfied that all the points you wish to make are clear and can be followed by another person. If you can, have someone read your draft to tell you if your purposes are apparent and fulfilled. Tell whoever is reading your review not to worry about sentence structure, use of language, spelling, or punctuation (unless errors or imprecision detract from their understanding of your ideas), for these elements of writing are not your primary concerns in the draft stage.

Revising Now turn your attention to rewriting your paper to make your readers' experience with it as comfortable as possible. Once again, as in the papers of analysis, you should assume that your audience includes your instructor and your classmates. But this time assume that your readers have *not* read the book but want to know if they should and if so, why, and if not, why not. Keeping these needs in mind, you have specific obligations to fulfill: you must decide exactly how to integrate a summary of the book into your review; you must refine your sentence structure and word usage for maximum readability; and you must make explicit your overall evaluation in your conclusion.

You will need to fine tune your case before you take it public. Base your generalizations on concrete evidence. It is not enough to write, "Dr. Szasz indicts modern psychiatry for eliminating moral considerations from essentially moral decisions." What are "moral considerations" and what are "moral decisions"? Look inside these code words to find out what Szasz means by "moral."

You also must decide the extent to which you are going to quote the book directly. Reviews that simply string long quotations together are unsatisfactory. Reviews that contain no quotations from the book deprive the reader of experiencing the tone and general flavor of the author's prose. Select the direct quotations sparingly and use them only when such use will enhance or illustrate points you are making. For example, the force of Szasz's indictment of psychiatry can be communicated effectively by using this sample quotation from his book: "Psychiatry is a moral and social enterprise." His own words convey the reasons why he is concerned about the problem: "In America, when the ideology of totalitarianism is promoted as fascism or communism it is coldly rejected. However, when the same ideology is promoted under the guise of mental health care, it is warmly embraced."[8] It is not easy to capture the intensity of his concern in paraphrase.

Lastly, the revising stage is the place to develop your conclusions. In a book review the conclusion should contain your specific responses to the requirements established by the instructor in the assignment. At a minimum, this response should involve an evaluation of the book's usefulness. Your analysis within the essay of the book's strengths and weaknesses needs to be pulled together into an evaluation of the overall worth of the book for the type of reader for whom the book is intended.

Since this evaluation, however subjective or idiosyncratic, must follow logically from your review, you might consider writing your conclusions last. They represent your final summation of the parts of the review and how they lead to the evaluation you are presenting. End strong! Do not simply repeat your earlier analyses. Draw them all together into a specific, concrete recommendation. Keeping the needs of your audience in your mind until the very end will allow you to avoid closing with that all too familiar undergraduate last line: "All in all, I liked the book very much."

8 Szasz, *Ideology and Insanity*, pp. 47, 48.

1 What is meant by a paper of analysis or review? How does this kind of paper differ from a term paper?

2 Why is it often necessary to do research for a paper of analysis or review? How do these research activities differ from the research activities necessary for a full term paper?

3 What are your major responsibilities when you review a book?

4 What are the major similarities and differences between analyzing a poem and analyzing a painting?

1 Select a poem and analyze it according to the suggestions in this chapter.

2 Copy a poem or a brief but important passage from a short story. Did you feel that you became more familiar with the work after you copied it? Why or why not?

3 Select a book and write out a list of everything you could learn about the book before you actually began to read it for content.

4 The analysis below is of a poem by William Blake. Analyze the analysis. What is right with it? What is wrong with it? After completing your reactions to the student paragraph, write your own analysis of the poem.

The SICK ROSE

O Rose thou art sick.
The invisible worm,
That flies in the night
In the howling storm:

Has found out thy bed
Of crimson joy:
And his dark secret love
Does thy life destroy.

Blake's poem "The Sick Rose" is a symbolic poem in two stanzas of four lines each. It is about beauty and ugliness. The first stanza is creepy and hard to understand. It uses a lot of negative words to convey a feeling of sickness, darkness, a storm and a worm, which stands for ugliness. The second stanza, in contrast, represents beauty through such words as bed and crimson joy, but ends on a negative note with ugliness winning out. The rose is destroyed by the worm, which is the way it is in life when the ugliness within us destroys our beauty. I didn't like the poem.

8 Papers of Contemplation

Could all life be a dream? Does a blind person understand red? If Stalin were to return, would he be able to rule the USSR as he did in his own lifetime? College students typically ponder questions of this sort, not just in dormitory bull sessions, but in their philosophy and history classrooms. These questions require contemplation, the act of thinking about something intently. The word contemplation derives from the Latin *cum* (with) and *templum* (temple) and means literally to mark out a temple where augury, prophecy, is performed. In modern higher education the closest we get to prophecy is the contemplation of interesting questions, and writing is one of the best methods of systematic contemplation.

Frequently, instructors in the humanities and in the humanistic branches of the social sciences will assign contemplative papers. In fact, the analyses and reviews described in the preceding chapter are also essentially contemplative papers, with the contemplation directed in each case to a particular book or work of art. The activity of contemplation is central to the humanities. Some would say that this centrality distinguishes the humanities from other disciplines.

The human element is definitive in humanistic writing. The results of contemplation differ from individual to individual. The problems posed in contemplative papers are open ended. The questions dealt with do not have single right answers but instead require you to reflect and speculate on issues. This type of paper requires you to state a thesis or opinion on a subject, but the instructor's concern is not with his agreement or disagreement with the thesis you present, but with the defense you construct for your thesis.

To write a satisfactory paper of this type, you may not necessarily engage in research, but you will be required, on the basis of material learned in the course, to think through and reflect on a problem, to formulate a response, and to present your case with skill and clarity. Since you are being asked to rely so heavily on your own abilities to reason logically and to argue convincingly, you may find that this paper is difficult to do, but is especially satisfying when done well.

William Blake, *The Four and Twenty Elders*, c.1805
THE TATE GALLERY, LONDON

The most helpful way of identifying the contemplative paper is to think of it as lying on a continuum between expressive writing, which emphasizes the capacity to express your feelings on a topic, and research writing, which tests your ability to seek out information and to put it together in some coherent order. Like the expressive paper, the contemplative paper assumes that you already know all you need to know; like the research paper, it demands that you offer reasons and evidence for the views that you choose to defend.

Most of the problems raised in contemplative papers come from questions that originate in the classroom and from assigned reading. Thus, the assignment "Evaluate Berkeley's criticisms of Locke's theory of primary and secondary qualities," if posed in a context in which the class has read and discussed Locke and Berkeley, will require a contemplative paper as a response. But if you have not read and discussed the issues, the paper calls for research on the two philosophers. The context of the questions will help you determine what kind of paper is called for. Similarly, the context will also indicate the criteria for giving an acceptable answer. If you have read four Shakespeare plays and you are asked to write on Shakespeare's view of women, you need not read all the other plays by Shakespeare. You should develop an interpretation that can be confirmed in the four plays you have read and then specify those plays in the title of your paper. If, on the other hand, you are asked to address the same question as the topic of a term paper, you will be expected to do research on the issue, including other plays and what critics have written on the matter.

Finally, the open-ended nature of the questions leads to two consequences. First, you have considerable freedom in formulating your approach to the topic and in drawing conclusions. The questions are almost always those about which scholars in the disciplines disagree. Your instructor may value highly two papers that come to opposite conclusions— if they are both argued and defended well. Second, you must establish and explain what you are attempting to accomplish in the paper, but you must also tell the reader what you are not going to do. The professor will evaluate your paper partly on what you say the problem is and on the criteria you establish for a satisfactory answer. For example, let us suppose that the problem is: "Nietzsche said that the will to power is the essence of human nature. What are the implications of this theory for society?"

This problem can be broken down into the following areas of responsibility. The major question around which your thesis must be organized is "What are the implications for society of Nietzsche's belief that all of us possess, as our primary trait, the will to power?" You will need to identify the general implications of the theory and the general characteristics of society. These are the limitations within which you must work. You are not responsible for certain areas which, at first glance, seem important. For example, you do not have to write about Nietzsche himself or assess whether he accurately identifies the essence of human nature.

"I think he is wrong" is not a proper response to a question that asks you only to describe the implications of his theory.

In the rest of this chapter we will discuss four types of contemplative papers and offer some models of each. In every case we will identify the responsibilities you undertake by choosing to do a paper of that type, and we will suggest some strategies appropriate for each category. We will begin with the least difficult and proceed to paper assignments that require an increasing number and variety of skills. So, if you are assigned a paper of analytic or speculative inquiry, you will find it useful to review the discussions of the first two categories before proceeding.

There are four types of reflective and speculative papers:

1 the paper that asks you to attack or defend an author's view

2 the paper that asks you to compare, contrast, or choose between two competing views

3 the paper that asks you to solve a puzzle or resolve a defined problem

4 the paper that asks you to speculate on the probable or the most acceptable outcome from a given set of circumstances.

These classifications represent ideal types, and there is overlap. Moreover, they call for skills that shade over into one another. The comparison between two views, for example, will require the ability both to defend and criticize. Nevertheless, it is useful to identify the distinguishing characteristics of each type of paper.

Criticize or defend an author's view

Here are some examples of assignments that require you to attack or defend an author's view:

- React to Becker's interpretation of the Enlightenment.

- Attack or defend the view that Shylock in *The Merchant of Venice* is a symbol of justice.

- It has been argued that the belief in free will is not inconsistent with the belief that human behavior is predictable. Attack or defend this view.

In writing this type of paper it is your responsibility to identify completely and fairly the view to which you are reacting; decide upon your response to this view; decide how you propose to accomplish your purpose; and defend your own thesis, your agreement or disagreement with the author's view.

Getting started   Much of the success of your paper will depend on what you do before you begin to write. The prewriting stage is where many papers fail, for writing is too often attempted before planning is well enough underway.

The result is often frustration, which is frequently dissipated only by those last-minute meanderings produced to meet a 9:45 A.M. deadline.

You need a plan. And you need to begin to search for that plan well in advance of the due date for your paper. A good starting point for a defense of an author's view is to clarify for yourself the author's ideas. When planning a paper on Carl L. Becker's interpretation of the Enlightenment, for example, you should begin by summarizing his view of the Enlightenment. (See chapter 5.) Writing out Becker's view is important. Having it in front of you on paper allows you to study his ideas and refer to them as you continue to plan for your paper. Summarizing the thesis you plan to defend may appear an obvious first step, but many papers are unsuccessful because they are based on an incomplete or faulty understanding of the ideas to be discussed. For example, your writing of a summary of Becker's thesis might be just a few sentences, such as:

FIGURE 8.1

18th century not modern. Age of Reason really an age of faith — more like medieval society than modern society. They fooled themselves — were not liberated from the past. See pages 29, 144, 149 for quotes to use.

At this point, you may wish to jot down some of your own reactions to Becker's ideas, but be sure to indicate clearly in your notes what ideas are Becker's and what ideas are your own. When you use your notes to draft your paper, you will save yourself much time if these distinctions are clear.

Before you begin to write, you also need to develop a clear idea of whether you are going to attack or defend Becker's view. You need a goal, and to this end you may have to reread all or part of Becker's *Heavenly City of the Eighteenth-Century Philosophers.* [1] Take careful notes not only of his ideas but of those arguments that support or weaken his ideas. (See chapter 3 for help on taking notes from a text.) As you take down information, make notes to yourself on why you are recording certain items, whether you feel they are positive or negative, or how you think they relate to Becker's view. Figure 8.2 shows the sort of material you might have at this stage.

[1] New Haven: Yale Univ. Press, 1932; paperback reprint 1959.

Becker's view

For	Against
A lot of medieval patterns of thought in the 18th century	They believed in reason
Nature — God	Believed in heaven, but here on earth
They had faith (see p. 8)	Becker thinks that all these attitudes are medieval — they're not necessarily.
Believed in authority — just not God	
They wanted good society a. ideal of service b. morality	Just because they weren't really atheists or objective doesn't mean they're not modern.
They saw utopia	

Note: These are all like medieval people — they weren't different — that's how they fooled themselves.

Note: Most of his arguments are OK, but he doesn't use them properly.

FIGURE 8.2

Having the arguments in writing allows you to think on paper. Not only can you study your ideas, add to them, rank order them according to importance, and jot down your developing thoughts on them, but you are also creating a written record of your thought processes for later reference.

As your arguments develop you should become aware of what kind of attack or defense is best suited to the author's view. There are, basically, two types of attack you can bring against an author's view: the view is false; or it is insufficiently supported or unproven. The first kind of criticism attacks directly the central ideas of a given view; the second treats the arguments or proofs of a view without necessarily attacking the view itself. To take the first approach, you will present contradictory evidence to demonstrate that the view is either not factually true or cannot be logically true. In taking the second approach, you will not have to show that the author's view is wrong, but only that it is not true as presented. Your emphasis, therefore, will be on careful reasoning, addressed almost entirely to the internal logic and evidence supporting the author's view. You will need to show that the reasoning used to uphold the view is either wrong or does not necessarily lead to the validity of the view; or that the evidence is wrong or insufficient to permit acceptance of the view.

Conversely, there are three general types of defense that can be offered for any given view:

1 You might prove the view by independent arguments. Creating your own arguments, independent of those used by the author of the view, you can add to the case already made. The only constraint is that the arguments you develop do, in fact, provide good reasons to believe the view.

2 You might clarify the view. By cleaning up the language or by evaluating what is important and what is not, you can distinguish between the essential features of an author's view and its nonessential elements. This strategy allows you to evaluate the weight and validity of the objections to the view. Redefining and clarifying will sometimes be the best defense to the extent that it removes criticisms or renders them unimportant.

3 You might find it necessary to list the objections to the author's view and show that they are not valid or decisive. This procedure constitutes a defense of an author's view by attacking the criticisms of that view, even though you do not discuss the author's position directly.

By studying the arguments you have created in the context of these approaches, you should be able to decide if and how you are going to attack or defend an author's view. If these methods of invention do not enable you to choose a side with confidence, you might try pulling an outline out of both sets of arguments. Outlines are best used when you have generated some ideas and would like to impose a structure on them.

Once you have made up your mind, draft a statement of purpose, a plan of what you intend to accomplish in your paper. With this plan in front of you, you can make your notes on how the approach you selected will help you fulfill the plan and what evidence and arguments are best suited to your plan. You may then find it necessary to rearrange the arguments. This rough statement of purpose might appear like this:

Attack Becker's view because his arguments don't support his conclusions.

a. Characteristics he gives to philosophes are not necessarily medieval, but can be modern.
b. Doesn't define modern——so I don't know what he means by it. .
c. He twists words around so that "nature" becomes "God" and traits such as "faith" and "morality" have to be medieval.

or

I will defend Becker's view on the grounds that the comments on them in my textbook (that the philosophes were rational skeptics) were wrong.

a. Can't look at their words but what they meant by their words.
b. They wanted the same things as medieval people.
c. Thought a lot like medieval thinkers.

Those are concrete plans of action. Note that they contain a perspective to take (the attack is a dissection of Becker's methods, while the defense concentrates on Becker's conclusions). Also, the arguments are listed in order of importance. This order may well change while the paper is being written, but having a plan lets you begin your paper with definite goals. You also begin with good notes to remind you of why you made the choices you did.

Writing the first draft The process of organizing and composing a draft from your plan is a very idiosyncratic stage. Some people need to write two or three drafts before they are satisfied with the product; others are almost ready to go public with their first draft. However many drafts you do, you should reorganize and rewrite until you are satisfied with the execution of your plan.

Your main task at this stage is to move your ideas from rough notes to connected discourse. Your concern, therefore, is with the construction of sentences and paragraphs, and with strategies for using written language to relate your ideas to one another.

The best beginning point is to try to get a sense of what the whole paper will look like, what the major parts are, and how they fit together. You need a structure to work with. An informal outline or some other vehicle for trying to envision the whole will be useful. If you created a rough outline during the invention stage, you can build upon it; if not, begin by identifying the major responsibilities you have in writing your paper. Here is a sample plan:

I To show what Becker's view is

II To give my reaction to it

III To demonstrate why my reaction is sound.

These responsibilities translate into:

I Statement of Becker's view

II Statement of my intention to defend his view

III Defense of his view.

Remember, at this stage your major purpose is to clarify the relationship for yourself. As you go along, you can rearrange these large blocks until you are satisfied with their relationship to one another. For example, another way to fulfill your plan is:

I Textbook statements about the philosophes

II Objection to these statements

III Becker's view

IV Reasons his interpretation is more satisfactory.

When you are satisfied with the overall order, you can begin to flesh out your outline with component parts of each major heading, that is, the reasons you have to justify your selection of these goals. Here is a sample outline:

```
 I. Textbook statements about the philosophes
    A. They were rationalists
    B. They introduced modern skepticism
    C. They rejected Christianity and medieval
       heritage.

II. Objections to these statements
    A. These statements take philosophes at face
       value
    B. One-sided discussion
```

III. Becker's view that philosophes were more medieval than modern
  A. Their rhetoric was modern; they were not.
    1. Words they used
    2. Medieval goals
  B. Were skeptical only of certain ideas
  C. Claimed to reject Christianity, but did not reject religious view of life
    1. Faith
    2. Morality
    3. Perfection

IV. Reasons Becker's interpretation is more valid
  A. He looks at behavior and not just writings
  B. Philosophes are logically products of their own past
  C. Have more in common with medieval people than people today
    1. Goals similar to medieval people
    2. Would not understand today's relativism and lack of direction and purpose.

V. Conclusions

It is time to generate sentences from notes. Once you are satisfied with the sequence of arguments, you should give your attention to developing the relationships between the various parts of your paper. The purposes of the sentences and paragraphs you construct are to lay out your individual illustrations and arguments, and to discuss connections. It is important to remember that you are still writing primarily for yourself, although keeping in mind the requirements of your eventual readers may help you to make choices even at this early stage. But don't allow yourself to get locked into an unalterable plan. If you cannot make the relationships clear, do not hesitate to change your outline until your argument flows from point to point. Your emphasis at this stage, therefore, should be on giving coherence and cohesiveness to your plan.

Take stock of what you already have written. You should have:

- a rough summary of the view to be discussed,

- arguments criticizing or defending it,

- notes on the reasons for taking your stance, and

- notes from your readings and a working outline.

Organizing these notes, adding new thoughts to them, perhaps writing independent sentences that develop from your rereading of them in light of your plan may suggest to you the point in your paper at which you can most productively begin writing.

Many writers prefer to start at the beginning of a paper and work through. This strategy is possible if your outline adequately reflects a workable plan. In the outline above, this procedure allows you to set up your points, the interpretations you are going to argue against:

```
The standard interpretations of the Enlightenment
identify the philosophes as the first modern
thinkers. They argue (or it is argued) that the
philosophes rejected medieval ideas or created
modern ones (discuss them according to outline).
```

At this stage, you need not pay careful attention to actual sentence structure. Do not get caught up trying to write a brilliant first sentence. Make marginal notes to remind yourself to rewrite parts or insert possible alternative ways to express an idea, but you should not let worries about language usage interfere with the necessity to write the paper through to the end.

If you develop "writer's block," you may need to change the angle from which you approach the paper. Remember, you are free to return to techniques explained in "Getting Started." In fact, experienced writers shift back and forth frequently between planning, writing, and revising.

The key in the drafting stage is to establish relationships, so you might begin writing the most important sections first and build up a solid core to which you can attach the other parts of the paper. The heart of the contemplative paper is the defense you construct to prove your general line of argument. It may be useful to you, in the outline above, to start by developing part IV. The first connected sentences you write might look like this:

```
Carl Becker's perspective doesn't allow him to be
(taken in or seduced) by the modern ring of the
kinds of words used by the philosophes. Voltaire
might have written about toleration but he was
intolerant (find out what Becker means by
toleration--see if I can find an example from
Voltaire). This intolerance was medieval.
```

This example represents a central type of paragraph in a contemplative paper. It contains an important argument with a concrete example and relates explicitly to other parts of the paper, in this case, to the textbook writers who were "taken in" and to the statement of Becker's thesis, which will probably precede this paragraph.

The process of writing, rewriting, cutting and pasting to rearrange whole parts, of drawing arrows and making marginal notes to yourself continues until you have a rough, but whole draft. If at all possible, you should arrange to have it read by another person because by this time you are too close to the topic and too knowledgeable about your plan to see where gaps or inconsistencies exist. All you are trying to find out from a reader is whether your plan is apparent, if your perspective is clear, and if your structure is successful in executing your plan and proving your thesis. The job of the reader is not to evaluate your draft but to tell you where problems exist. If your instructor has a policy of discussing drafts, take advantage of the opportunity. If school policy does not prohibit it, give your draft to a friend. Tell your friend not to bother with word usage or sentence structure, but to concentrate on the argument as a whole.

Revising   Revising is too often thought of as a tidying-up chore consisting of proof-reading and editing if time permits. In fact, the revision stage is of enormous importance for the completion of a successful paper. Your draft is an incomplete paper. It may contain some excellent sentences, and you will almost certainly have revised parts while you were writing, but the purpose of your draft was to write for yourself, to execute your plan. Now you need to communicate that plan effectively to an audience.

The consideration of audience is critical to revising. It will help to insure the completeness and unity of the paper. Thinking of the instructor as your audience has certain drawbacks. Students, assuming that the instructor knows all about the topic, may leave out information or connections that are necessary to make the argument self-contained and self-explanatory, or they may deemphasize careful organization in favor of masses of information with the belief that the instructor will put it together. Write your final draft for intelligent readers who do not know about the topic, but might like to—if you can win their attention.

Determination of audience is only one of several decisions you will make. You have a draft. You should ask questions of that draft which will help to eliminate irrelevant material and finely tune the material you use. The primary question to ask of every argument, paragraph, and sentence is: "Does it serve my purpose?" Your purpose at this stage is to convince a defined audience that your point of view on the problem is plausible.

The suggested strategies for revising given below are not separate steps carried out sequentially, but are overlapping procedures in a complex process. We cannot propose a strict order for rereading your draft for word usage, sentence structure, paragraph construction, and transitions. Generally, you can expect to have to move back to some strategies from the "writing a draft" stage just as you did revisions while you were assembling an acceptable draft. We have isolated some revising procedures for the purposes of illustrating useful ways to shape a draft into a paper.

In the attack or defense of an author's view, your audience will expect your paper to present the author's view in a precise, accurate, and clear way, to take an unambiguous stand on the view, to give substantial reasons for your perspective, and to show how these reasons are valid and sufficient to substantiate your perspective. Readers are product oriented; they are not concerned with good intentions, but with a complete and well-argued paper.

A careful summary of the thesis to be discussed is important for the reader because this summary offers the concrete foundation upon which everything else is based. For example, unless the audience has read Carl Becker's book—and you should assume that your audience has not read the book—your summary constitutes their only knowledge of Becker's view. A finished rendering of your working summary might look like this:

```
Carl Becker argues that it is a fallacy to
believe that the eighteenth century was "modern."
Called the "Age of Reason," the Enlightenment
was, in fact, an age of faith not too different
in outlook from medieval Europe. The philosophes
"demolished the Heavenly City of St. Augustine
only to rebuild it with more up-to-date
materials."
```

Note that this summary captures Becker's argument, presents certain key words you will be using, and reproduces a short quotation from the book, just for flavor.

Tell the reader whether you are going to attack or defend the thesis and how you are going to proceed. It is usually best to let the reader in on your plan near the beginning of the paper so that the reader is able to read your paper with an understanding of your purposes and, consequently, can put your individual arguments into the context you define. You might write:

```
Becker's interpretation is sound. I agree with it
because it demonstrates the many parallels that
exist between medieval and Enlightenment
thinkers, proves that these similarities are
important, and shows that the intentions of the
philosophes are a better guide to understanding
them than their rhetoric.
```

You should also indicate the ways that you are qualifying your approach. For example, you may wish to let the reader know the following:

```
It is neither necessary nor possible to discuss
all of the many parallels Becker draws between
medieval and eighteenth-century thought patterns.
I will discuss only three--faith, authority, and
morality--to demonstrate his thesis.
```

This disclaimer may prevent second guessing on the part of the reader. As pointed out earlier, the contemplative paper gives you great latitude in defining and limiting the areas of your responsibility; if you omit discussion of parts of the author's view, the reader may wonder why, unless you specifically acknowledge the omission as deliberate, giving your reasons.

Most of your attention, however, should be given to the arguments you create and connect to support your thesis. As you examine each sentence and each paragraph, ask yourself a series of questions:

1 Does this sentence (or paragraph) support my main point?

2 Have I related it to the main point?

3 Must I add to it to clarify its function in the paper?

4 Does it contain parts that are not relevant?

A sample paragraph, developed from the draft, appears in figure 8.3. This paragraph carefully develops the ideas outlined in the draft. It supports the larger argument that parallels existed in the thought of the two periods, and explicitly tells the reader of this purpose. It includes a concrete example and relates it to the argument being developed.

The revised paragraph also shows careful attention to syntax and word choice; to matters of standard written usage, spelling and punctuation; and to the subtleties of tone and rhythm—all appropriate and necessary considerations in the revision stage. After the writer of the example on page 185 has filled in the informational gaps in his draft, he has done much more than a mere proofreading for spelling and punctuation.

Central to your concern about making connections are transitions. Your individual arguments may be sound, but unless they flow from one to another, they may not serve your purposes. You do not want the reader finishing a paragraph and saying, "So what?" Since each part of your paper marks another step toward your goal, explain how the step was taken and its significance for your argument. Transitions need not be long, but they must be explicit. For example:

```
Clearly, the textbook interpretation that the
philosophes were modern thinkers is wrong, but
this conclusion does not necessarily mean that
Becker's thesis is right. An examination of his
ideas, however, will show that his interpretation
should supplant the standard textbook
understanding of the Enlightenment.
```

This short passage sums up the conclusion you want your reader to draw about textbook interpretations and gives a sense of direction to the next part of the paper as it logically develops out of the earlier parts.

Like transitions, the conclusion to your paper should reinforce the unity of your argument. The conclusion is totally reader-oriented and

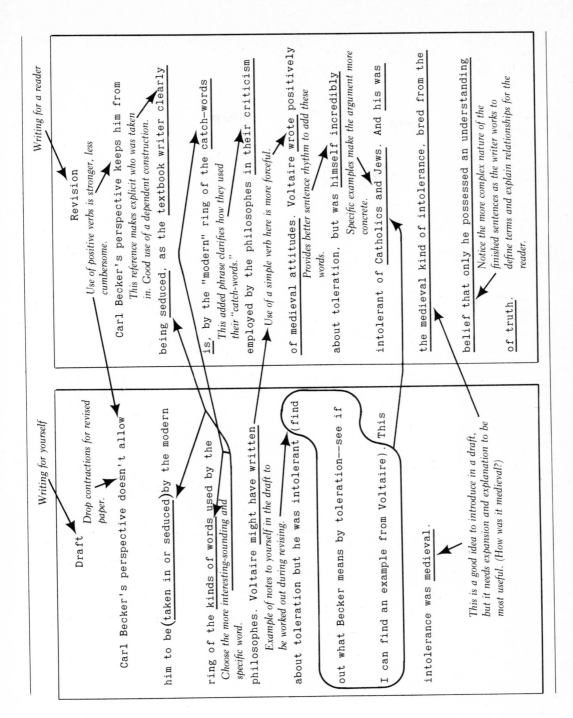

Writing for yourself

Draft   *Drop contractions for revised paper.*

Carl Becker's perspective doesn't allow

him to be (taken in or seduced) by the modern

ring of the kinds of words used by the   *Choose the more interesting-sounding and specific word.*

philosophes. Voltaire might have written   *Example of notes to yourself in the draft to be worked out during revising.*

about toleration but he was intolerant (find

out what Becker means by toleration—see if

I can find an example from Voltaire). This   *This is a good idea to introduce in a draft, but it needs expansion and explanation to be most useful. (How was it medieval?)*

intolerance was medieval.

Writing for a reader

Revision   *Use of positive verbs is stronger, less cumbersome.*

Carl Becker's perspective keeps him from   *This reference makes explicit who was taken in. Good use of a dependent construction.*

being seduced, as the textbook writer clearly

is, by the "modern" ring of the catch-words   *This added phrase clarifies how they used their "catch-words."*

employed by the philosophes in their criticism   *Use of a simple verb here is more forceful.*

of medieval attitudes. Voltaire wrote positively   *Provides better sentence rhythm to add these words.*

about toleration, but was himself incredibly   *Specific examples make the argument more concrete.*

intolerant of Catholics and Jews. And his was

the medieval kind of intolerance, bred from the

belief that only he possessed an understanding   *Notice the more complex nature of the finished sentences as the writer works to define terms and explain relationships for the reader.*

of truth.

FIGURE 8.3

need not even be written until you have finished revising. It should grow out of your completed paper and, at the same time, go beyond it.

Reminding your audience of what they have read is only one function served by a good conclusion. This section should not simply be a re-wording of your thesis paragraph, but should demonstrate how that thesis was developed into the whole paper your audience has just read. Your conclusion should also anticipate one large, final "So what?" from the audience. Reread your paper with this question in mind and reflect on the significance of what you have written. For a paper on Becker's view, a possible explanation of significance might read:

> The point is not just that Becker's thesis is right, in my opinion, but that the textbook interpretation is wrong. Textbooks are invaluable in introducing students to historical periods, but may not be reliable sources of interpretation. For one thing, they are necessarily general and cannot offer enough examples or evidence to prove the statements they make. This quality of textbooks influences the student to accept broad generalizations on faith. Historians must push interpretations beyond the point of faith.

Many parts of your paper lead logically to such a conclusion, but because your orientation is toward Becker's view, this comment fits no-where else in the body of your paper. Your conclusion should be implicit in the body of your paper, but implicit ideas should be verbalized and made explicit at the end. Your readers then feel satisfied that they have indeed followed your line of argument because they share with you a sense of closure in your conclusion.

Lastly, you might use your conclusion to suggest to the reader the questions that your paper raises. Making yourself aware of the implications helps you to put your effort into a larger perspective; making your reader aware of them enhances the usefulness of your paper. What are the implications of the paper on Becker's view for the study of history or philosophy or literature? A final passage might read:

> It is not a judicious practice to read a book without probing beyond the author's words. Were Renaissance humanists really the individuals they tell us they were? Did the Victorians really believe that women were asexual? Becker's methods could profitably be used to understand more critically every age in history.

When you write the other types of contemplative papers, you will use many of the strategies we have just explained for the defend-a-thesis paper. As you read about papers that compare and contrast competing theses, solve a puzzle, and speculate, be sure to refer to general strategies explained above. The following sections of this chapter will explain procedures distinctly helpful to the particular types of papers under consideration.

Compare and contrast

Here are some examples of assignments that ask you to compare, contrast, or choose between two competing views.

- Compare and contrast Descartes' and Hume's view of personal identity.

- Stalin and Hitler represented two opposing ideological systems, yet some historians see their methods of rule as strikingly similar. Compare and contrast their actual methods of governing. Do you agree or disagree with these historians?

- Compare the image of the future in Zamyatin's *We* with the image of the future in Orwell's *1984*.

In writing this type of paper it is your responsibility to: state the two items to be compared accurately and fairly; identify the specific areas to be compared and contrasted; identify the similarities; identify the differences; and develop a thesis and present your point of view on the similarities and differences.

Getting started In the first paper discussed, the attack or defense of an author's view, you had to understand one major idea, so a simple summary of that idea was enough to begin your analysis. In a compare-and-contrast paper, you are always dealing with at least two topics. Therefore, getting started is a bit more complicated.

Since you are working with combinations of specific ideas, people, or events, you need to begin by understanding the topics separately. If you are dealing with the thought of two writers, summarize their ideas. If you are analyzing two events, groups, or individuals, treat each separately. Act, at this point, as if you were writing two papers explaining the two topics. You will not know what specific points you will be comparing or contrasting in your paper, so do not get caught up in details at this early stage. You should develop a general understanding of the separate topics which will serve as a basis for your comparative analysis.

Your separate explanation of each topic is merely a way to get started. In later drafts you will work to synthesize ideas. Too often students submit what amounts to two separate essays that not only fail to relate to each other, but do not deal with the same specific areas. At early stages you are writing to find the connections which you will explain clearly later on.

Once you have a good understanding of the topics and have a set of notes on both of them, you need to identify the areas to be analyzed. Although you may not incorporate into your paper all of the areas you identify as being related, a careful search for such areas will help give structure to your thinking. For example, before you plunge into evaluations and judgments on the views of Descartes and Hume, you should identify the specific areas which you will evaluate: their theories of knowledge, their intentions, their views of human nature, their views of freedom. For each category in this list, you should jot down your notes of supporting material so that you will have a running record of the reasons you selected the category.

Your notes should also give you some indications of which categories are important. In the case of Descartes and Hume, the most important category, of course, is each writer's view of personal identity, but you may decide that to get to an understanding of this central area you will need to compare and contrast the two thinkers' views on the nature of knowledge, human nature, and language. Once you have made your choices, you need to decide in which areas similarities exist and in which areas there are differences. Generate two lists, one of similarities, the other of differences. As you identify possible areas of agreement and disagreement, record them under the appropriate classifications. A beginning list might look like figure 8.4.

By making lists and then drawing conclusions, you will greatly increase the chances that your paper will focus on the important areas that need to be compared to answer the question. Lists also allow you to rank-order the categories you select according to their importance to the question. But remember, while lists can help create the eventual structure for your paper, simple lists cannot convey the reasons you made the choices you

---

FIGURE 8.4

Similarities	_Differences_
Intentions	Theories of knowledge
The way they view self/body	Views on human nature
The way they view self/soul	Uses of introspection
	Views on mind
	Use of language

---

did. Lists are working outlines for specific purposes. At every step of the process by which you select the categories you are going to compare, write out your reasons for the choices and the evidence that supports your choices. You will need all of this material when you put your lists into connected prose.

At this point you are still left with a major decision to make before you begin writing. Although the assignment will usually require you to compare and contrast two topics, you should decide if the similarities or the differences between the two are greater. Almost invariably, a compare-and-contrast question requires you to state a point of view and argue it. Your essay will probably be evaluated not only for your success in discovering relationships, but for your success in analyzing and evaluating those relationships. At a minimum, the instructor will want to know which set of relationships is stronger. Therefore, your essay may well emphasize the similarities or the differences at the expense of the other. This emphasis should be communicated to the reader early in the paper. A concise, unambiguous thesis statement will help you to organize your essay as well as allow your reader to read your paper in a context. Examples of such thesis statements are:

```
Despite similarities in their concepts of self,
Descartes and Hume disagree in almost every other
important area, including personal identity.
```

or

```
It would appear at first glance that Descartes
and Hume disagree on the nature of personal
identity, but a close examination of their
thought reveals striking similarities that
overshadow their methodological differences.
```

At this stage, you should have in writing all of the materials you need to prepare a first draft.

Writing the first draft   Reread pages 182–186 of this chapter before proceeding, for a review of general draft-writing procedures. The comments given below are designed to apply specifically to a compare-and-contrast paper.

The major choice you will face in writing this type of paper is how to integrate the four different parts of your answer into one cohesive paper. Two model plans are offered here as possible approaches.

Model A   Linear Model

I Your thesis paragraph

II Statement of topic 1

III Statement of topic 2

IV Comparisons and contrasts between topics 1 and 2

V Evaluation and conclusion

or

Model B   Integrated Model

I Your thesis paragraph

II Similarities between topics 1 and 2

III Differences between topics 1 and 2

IV Evaluation and conclusion

If you adopt model A, you may find it most useful to begin writing part IV first, for what you choose to compare and contrast will determine how much of topics 1 and 2 you describe. A common problem in the execution of a compare-and-contrast paper is the tendency to write three separate essays that do not touch at all points. You might describe much more in steps II and III than the reader needs to know to understand the comparisons you make in part IV, or you may compare aspects of II and III that you did not describe. Another pitfall to avoid in model A is repeating yourself too much. Descriptions given in parts II and III need not be repeated when they are picked up again in part IV. Executed well, model A offers a logical, clear progression from description to analysis to evaluation.

Model B represents a more complex approach, for the organization of the paper is not based on your initial description of the topics, but on the relationships themselves. The focus is on the categories of similarities and differences: theories of knowledge, intentions, language. Each time a comparison is made you need to give the reader the information (description) required for the relationship to be seen clearly. This approach insures that the areas of comparison are explicit and at the center of the essay. The major problem of model B is the tendency to give too little description and evidence.

Since you are dealing with complex organization in both types of papers you may find it useful to generate two outlines with more detail than the examples above. Keep in mind that these outlines are tentative guides to creating a workable structure. You may need to flesh them out, rearrange them, or even try writing from them, until you are satisfied that you have a plan. Expanded outlines from models A and B could look like this:

Model A   Linear Model

I Thesis statement

II What Descartes thinks

   A Theory of knowledge

B Theory of the self
    1 in relation to body
    2 in relation to soul
C Human nature
D Identity

III What Hume thinks
  A Theory of knowledge
  B Theory of the self
    1 in relation to body
    2 in relation to soul
  C Human nature
  D Identity

IV Comparisons
  A Theories of knowledge: they are different
  B On the self
    1 in relation to the body; they are similar
    2 in relation to the soul; they are similar
  C Human nature; they are different
  D Identity; they are different

V Evaluation and conclusion

Note the absolute symmetry in steps II, III, and IV.

Model B Integrated Model

I Thesis statement

II Similarities between Hume and Descartes
  A On the self-soul
    1 Descartes
    2 Hume
  B On the soul-body
    1 Descartes
    2 Hume

III Differences between Descartes and Hume
  A Theory of knowledge
    1 Descartes
    2 Hume
  B Human nature
    1 Descartes
    2 Hume
  C Identity
    1 Descartes
    2 Hume

IV. Evaluation and conclusion

Note that at every stage both Descartes and Hume must be discussed in conjunction with each category.

We strongly discourage you from trying to write a comparison-and-contrast paper by giving all descriptions and evaluations of topic 1 and then repeating the process for topic 2. Although this method seems easiest at first, these dual essays rarely parallel each other.

Revising Once you are satisfied with your organization and have produced paragraphs that fit together into a coherent unit, you need to give your attention to the clear, economic expression of your ideas for an audience. In addition to previous suggestions on revising, you will need, in a compare-and-contrast paper, to pay special attention to two reader-oriented tasks.

The introduction of thesis paragraph. It is useful to think of this paper (and almost every paper) as moving at two levels. At one level you are developing your thesis, and at another level you are building in signposts so that readers can follow your procedure. You must not only state your thesis, you must make the reader aware of how you intend to demonstrate your thesis. It is usually appropriate to provide a clear signpost in your opening paragraph. For example:

```
Despite similarities in their concepts of
self, Descartes's and Hume's views of personal
identity are fundamentally different. I intend to
show that Hume and Descartes differ because their
theories of knowledge and their views of human
nature are diametrically opposed to one another.
```

In this short introduction you have stated your point of view, how you are going to proceed, and what your primary areas of discussion are going to be. You have prepared your reader to read your paper.

Transitions. Transitions are especially important in a paper that asks the reader to follow and understand a series of relationships. Your organization in draft form may be workable, but you still have to make sure that you connect the several parts effectively. This connection is most easily accomplished by being direct and honest with the reader. Point out relationships even when they appear obvious to you. Assume that your audience is not familiar with the two topics to be compared. This assumption will encourage you to be explicit. For example, in model A, when moving from part III to part IV, you might write:

```
The preceding discussions of the ideas of
Descartes and Hume expose minimal similarities,
but many differences. Moreover, the similarities
exist in relatively unimportant areas, while
their differences are significant. These
```

> differences, especially their opposing views on
> identity, arise from a fundamental disagreement
> over the way we receive knowledge.

This paragraph, then, leads directly into a discussion of their theories of knowledge.

In model B, in moving from IIIA to IIIB, the transition might read like this:

> While Descartes is a rationalist and saw
> introspection as a source of understanding,
> Hume's rigorous empiricism caused him to search
> elsewhere for an understanding of human nature.

This transition can lead to a discussion of their respective points of view.

Note, in both of these examples, the constant attention given to summing up and restating earlier conclusions as a way to maintain the connection between that which has been discussed and that which will be discussed.

The puzzle or problem paper

Here are some examples of papers that ask you to resolve a puzzle or explore a defined problem.

- Could all life be a dream?

- Does a blind person understand what "red" means?

- If human beings have free will, does this mean that their behavior is unpredictable?

In writing this type of paper it is your responsibility to explain what the problem is; explain why it is a problem; formulate, state, and defend criteria for an acceptable solution to the problem; and present and defend your solution.

Getting started This type of paper is encountered most frequently in philosophy courses. It is one of the most mysterious paper types, for it requires critical, analytical thinking and sensitivity to words and ideas. In approaching this paper you are left alone with your reasoning powers and the knowledge you have gained from class and from earlier studies. With papers discussed earlier in this chapter, your beginning point was a book or the thoughts of others. Starting this paper can be more difficult because you must first generate the raw materials with which you work.

The starting point is your realization that the question asked is supposed to be a puzzle, without an easy or obvious answer. The data you are given are all in the question itself, so to discover the exact intent of the question, begin by analyzing the different senses in which the most important words are used. Your solution to the puzzle may well depend on how you define the key words. For example, in the question "Does a blind person understand what 'red' means?" you have to decide how you are going to define the word "understand." One might argue that blind people cannot understand what "red" means because they lack the experience of red, the visual sensation we associate with red and, hence, are unable to identify an instance of red. On the other hand, there are facts about "red" which blind people know: frogs are not red; a red flag means danger; sunsets are red; and so on. Thus, blind people can use the word "red" in many contexts, just as seeing people do. It is true that they lack the visual sensation, but is that necessary to understand "red"? Your answer to this sample question depends on how you use the word "understand."

If a puzzle paper has no obvious solution, neither does it have a "wrong" answer in the traditional sense. In fact, your answer may not be as important as your explanation of what you think the question means. Philosophers put a heavy emphasis on method, on the identification of the problem, and on the explanation of why it is a problem. Therefore, you should spend a large part of your "getting started" time on formulating your understanding of the question. You will find free writing in your journal (chapter 2) to be a constructive way of thinking about what lies behind the question, what the key words mean, and what the implications of those words are.

Do not shy away from seemingly strange or exotic answers. These are often the most fun and the most productive in terms of learning to think critically. While studying possible interpretations, write down every thought, every reaction. Remember, your notes are the only materials you have to refer to when it is time to write. You will need an accurate record of why you eliminated options, why you chose to make certain choices, how you defined key words. It is surprisingly difficult to reconstruct your thought processes without a written record. Figure 8.5 shows sample notes on the question of blind people and red. Write down all questions and ideas for both sides, whether or not they seem important.

One of the purposes of a puzzle paper is to get you out of your mindset, to explore a problem in creative ways. You may end up by answering yes or no, but you may also decide that sighted people do not really understand what red means. Play with all possible ideas on paper until you feel that you have explored all options.

By that time you may well have a sense of your solution to the puzzle. If not, then begin organizing your free-writing notes into categories according to the possible solutions (figure 8.6).

For each solution note the objections that can be made against it. If you find all but one has objections against it, that is your solution, and you defend it by showing that objections exist for all other possible solutions. If you find that all have objections to them, as is often the case,

Understand — we understand what electrons mean without seeing them. There is a sense in which I understand a word without experiencing it. A slave knows what freedom is; we know what a vacuum is. Also explore other analogous questions such as do deaf people hum? What other ways to approach the word understand? Color-blind people who cannot distinguish red have a sense of color, but not of red itself. So they know that red is a color, but have not experienced it directly, etc.

FIGURE 8.5

and you can think of no other possible solution, then it is your option to advance the most acceptable solution or to argue that no solution is acceptable.

Writing the first draft
First review the procedures for writing a first draft on pages 182–186 of this chapter. For a puzzle paper, you will need to pay special attention to creating a format or a structure that will allow you the widest latitude for discussing your thinking processes, to raise questions, and to describe your methods as well as your conclusions. The most direct organization for a puzzle paper with a clear solution is:

I Present the problem

II List the possible solutions

III State the objections to the solutions

IV Present your solution

V Defend your solution

If a definition of the problem is the focus of the paper, the following is a possible organization:

I Present and analyze the question
  A various meanings of the question
  B implications of the different meanings
  C key words

II State the criteria for an acceptable answer

FIGURE 8.6

1. *Yes, blind people can understand what "red" means.*

2. *No, they cannot understand.*

3. *It does not matter if blind people can or cannot understand what "red" means.*

4. *Nobody can understand what "red" means.*

III Are there any acceptable solutions?
   A If not, explain why not
   B If so, proceed to IV
IV Present your solution
  V Defend your solution

Revising   Some general procedures for revising a contemplative paper are given on pages 186–191 of this chapter, but you should be aware of some special conventions of philosophical writing as you revise a puzzle paper.

A paper of this type should contain an explicit, running commentary on procedure as well as content. From introductory paragraph to conclusion, tell the reader what you are saying and why you believe it is important for your argument to say what you are saying. In other words, explain the "warrant." (See chapter 2.) Instead of building up to one major conclusion, the puzzle paper is strewn with conclusions as you eliminate alternatives and make assertions about individual words and ideas. Conclusions are based on earlier premises and, themselves, become new premises. You might find it useful to make liberal use of those words that indicate logical transitions (*therefore, such as, so, because, since, accordingly, for, so it follows that*), and those that signify countervailing reasons (*but, however, in spite of the fact, despite*).

Finally, during the revising stage of this paper, as in all papers, you need to choose your words carefully for exact meaning. Since in a puzzle paper you are trying to convey meanings of words that are separated from other meanings by nuances, the words you select to express these subtle differences can determine the success of your effort. In general, it is best to avoid metaphor in philosophy papers, such as "ship of state." If you cannot avoid ambiguous words (*real, determine, meaning, concept, idea*) or words for which there are several meanings (*freedom, voluntary, understanding, objective, subjective*), you should define them carefully within your paper.

The speculative paper

Here are some examples of assignments that ask you to speculate on the probable or the most acceptable outcome from a given set of circumstances:

- If Stalin were to return, would he be able to rule the U.S.S.R. as he did in his own lifetime?
- Hobbes said that we are obliged to obey the state only so long as it guarantees our security. How would he react to compulsory military service in time of war?
- How would George Orwell react to B. F. Skinner's *Walden II*?

In writing this type of paper it is your responsibility to understand completely the information given within the question, that is, the topics you have to work with; develop a prediction; state the prediction; and defend your prediction.

Getting started   The speculative paper introduces a "what if" dimension. It is of the first importance to grasp the purpose of a paper of this type before you begin. You are being asked to display your knowledge and understanding of two topics by describing an imaginary confrontation between them. This confrontation requires you to make judgments and choices based on your understanding. By asking you to apply your knowledge to an entirely novel situation, the instructor is testing your ability to use the material you have learned.

Consequently, your instructor will grade this paper on the power of your argument. Have you convinced the reader that your prediction could come true? It is more important to be logical than it is to be imaginative. Your prediction should be a logical extension of documented belief or behavior. In assignments of this sort the etymology of the word "contemplation" is most applicable. You must feel so comfortable in the temple of learning that you can perform augury there.

Take, for example, the question about Stalin and the U.S.S.R. This question requires you to show how, based on historical experience, Stalin would probably try to rule the Soviet Union today, and the ways that the Soviet Union—the party, the government, the military, the people—would probably respond. The tension between the two parts of the question arises from the changes that have taken place in the Soviet Union in the quarter century since Stalin's death. Are these changes real and extensive enough to prevent a return to Stalinistic rule? Or are they only superficial and easily reversed?

To answer this question you need to know how Stalin ruled, what the Soviet Union is like today, and where the areas of compatibility and incompatibility exist. Your prewriting, therefore, should begin by summarizing for yourself Stalin's policies and the main characteristics of his rule, and the salient features of Soviet society during his rule. Since you cannot possibly note everything, limit your notes to areas that seem relevant—general categories (the economy, war, political methods) and obviously important policies (collectivization, industrialization, and regimentation). A second set of notes on the Soviet Union today is necessary for the comparison.

Reducing your notes to lists may help you see relationships and omissions. Such lists, like lists 1 and 2 in figure 8.7, will also help you select the areas you will work with, thus limiting your area of responsibility to manageable proportions. Having decided on the important areas to discuss and possessing a general sense of similarities, you will need to add a third list, the characteristics of Stalin's rule (list 3 in figure 8.7).

History has shown that the items on lists 1 and 3 are compatible. The question is, can the items on list 2 be substituted for list 1 with the same results? Your answer depends on several choices you make. For example, the majority of items on lists 1 and 2 are dissimilar. These discrepancies may lead you toward a negative answer to the question. However, you may wish to weigh the items. Despite the differences between the two lists, one variable is the same: all political power continues to reside in the party. You could argue that if one man gains control of the party again, he could reverse the changes in all of the other areas. The test is to relate the items on list 3 to the characteristics on list 2. (Is rule by terror, force, and purges probable in a strong, stable society that is at peace?) However you weigh the data, these facts will be the basis for your prediction and will constitute a major portion of your paper.

One reminder: the lists you work with are not entities in themselves. They are useful tools to help you visualize data and relationships. The more important parts of your notes, as you plan your first draft, are the pieces of information you have written about the topics and your thinking about the topics and their relationships as you progressed towards your thesis.

Writing the first draft Review the steps in writing the first draft presented in the first part of this chapter. The organization of the speculative paper will depend on your topic and thesis, but you will need to construct a plan that integrates evidence and analysis. A paper that argues that Stalin could not rule today could, for example, begin with a description of Stalin's policies and methods, then move to the Soviet Union he ruled and the Soviet Union today. A paper that argues that Stalin could rule today might well begin

List 1: _Soviet Union, 1929-53_
rural economy
isolated, weak
one man rules
regimented society
war
party has all power

List 2: _Soviet Union Today_
urban, industrial economy
a world power
collective leadership — one man dominates
still regimented, but areas where control relaxed
peace
party has all power

List 3: _Characteristics of Stalin's Rule_
terror/fear/purges
collectivization of agriculture
forced industrialization
total command economy — heavy industry over con-
    sumer goods
socialist realism — regimentation of the arts

FIGURE 8.7

with a comparison of the Soviet Union, past and present. There are several other possible organizations for this type of paper. You, of course, should use any structure that helps you translate your plan into connected prose. As usual, be ready to change anything at this point in your paper development.

Revising   Again, review strategies for revising presented earlier in this chapter and also in chapter 6 and 7. Collectively, these sections have discussed writing for an audience, but editing and proofreading have not yet received sufficient attention. Revising, as you know from earlier discussions, is more than editing and proofreading, but review of the paper for punctuation, spelling and grammar is an important last step to any paper. A good idea can be diminished in the eyes of a reader if it contains distracting errors.

Convention dictates the proper ways to construct and punctuate sentences and spell words. When you revise, always keep a dictionary and an English handbook nearby for quick reference. If you are not sure how to spell words or where to place commas, look them up!

By the time you are proofreading your paper you will have read it perhaps too many times; whole parts of it will be fixed in your memory. This intimate knowledge of your essay makes proofreading for spelling, grammar, and punctuation a difficult chore. Often you will inadvertently skip over a part you know well or read for meaning again instead of for accuracy. Try reading your paper differently, from another angle, perhaps from end to beginning. Such a technique will allow you to break out of your earlier reading patterns.

Correctness and neatness, in themselves, do not make good contemplative papers, but as your instructors contemplate your grade, you do not want them to be distracted by an outside form that is not correct and neat.

QUESTIONS

1 What are the four major categories of papers of contemplation? How do they differ from each other?

2 How are papers of contemplation different from papers of analysis and review? In what ways are they similar?

3 What does the term "open ended" mean when it pertains to questions asked in papers of contemplation?

4 Why do instructors assign papers of contemplation?

EXERCISES

1 A professor assigns the following question: "What are the major ethical implications if scientists perfect cloning?" How can you tell if this question is intended to be answered in a paper of contemplation or in a research paper? How would the papers differ?

2 A professor assigns the following question; "Which painter do you think best represented the Expressionist school before World War I, Matisse or Picasso?" What does the question require you to do? What are the areas of your responsibility? What factors do you need to consider before you can answer the question?

3 Briefly identify the major differences among the four categories of contemplative papers. In which category would each of the following questions go? Explain your choices.

a Is television the most significant influence on our life-styles?

b What are the relative strengths of television and radio?

c It has been said that television is a "vast wasteland." Attack or defend this statement.

d If television did not exist, what would happen to American society?

e What would Benjamin Franklin think of television?

f Is television or the automobile the most significant technological influence in our society?

g What are the major problems with the way television is managed in America today?

4 Without actually concerning yourself with the answer to the following question, work out a list of subordinate questions and a strategy for developing an answer: "Can we know what is evil and what is good?"

of a
par
Kan
par
—
7
Bet

ame menta

e memory is

Memory does

imination f

de. in cont

Writing in the
Social Sciences

9 Term Papers in the Social Sciences

The social sciences—psychology, anthropology, political science, sociology, education, and economics—are all concerned with the systematic study of people and how they behave and live together as families, tribes, communities, and nations. With all of this emphasis on *people*, why must social science students spend so much time every semester alone in the library with a term paper assignment? The answer is that the library is the place where students have access to the most important work that has already been done in the social sciences. Through the process of surveying the state of knowledge on a particular topic, students learn more than merely what social scientists say about that topic; students learn how social scientists behave.

Social science research papers are usually assigned to allow students freedom to select and pursue a topic in some depth; to teach students to find and use social science library materials; and to teach students to evaluate and write about those readings in a coherent and contemporary social science framework.

Before you go on with this chapter, you may wish to reread chapter 4 on library resources (especially the section on resources in the social sciences), chapter 5 on using library resources, and the introduction to chapter 6 on the research paper in the humanities for a general overview of writing a paper from library materials.

Getting started

Assume that you have been assigned to write a term paper for a freshman psychology course, and your instructor has told you to look in your textbook to select a topic that interests you. At first, your interest in a topic may be overwhelmed by your fears of inadequacy in dealing with any topic in a field that you have been studying for only a few weeks. It may be comforting to remember that you have been asked to do the term paper assignment to give you an opportunity to learn about a topic, not to expound expertly on it. Through the process of researching and writing, you will learn more than a specific body of subject matter. You will learn general procedures within the field.

But do begin with a topic that has in some way piqued your interest. We have assumed in the social science section of chapter 4 that our sample student developed some curiosity about the topic of autism. Perhaps when this student was reading his textbook the disquieting image of a small child in total retreat from the world stimulated a desire to learn more about this mystery. Perhaps this student had written expressively in his personal journal about this situation and then found in this private writing the seeds of an interest that he could sustain through a semester of research. When you are looking for ideas for a topic, read through your private journal. (See chapter 2.)

We will assume that you have followed the procedures for a library search and that you are now ready to get started on writing up what you have recorded from your library work. Good research always results in more material than you can or should use. You will have to resist the common undergraduate tendency to use all of your information. This compulsion usually arises from one of two causes: either you want the instructor to know how much work you have done; or you begin writing without first deciding how to focus your paper, and consequently, you have no guidelines to aid you in determining what details you need. You can overcome the first difficulty by remembering that an instructor will be more impressed with how you integrate your research into a coherent presentation than with how much research you have done. The second difficulty can be avoided by focusing on a problem for your paper before you begin to write.

By focusing on a problem, we mean, simply, identifying or creating a real question within your broad topic area. The existence of a problem, or a controlling question, allows you to establish a direction in which to work in constructing arguments and selecting evidence. Your writing will then be goal-directed.

There is no magical point at which a writer begins to narrow a topic in a goal-directed way. Some writers begin with a series of questions that they keep in mind all through their library search. Frequently these questions are suggested to them by their reading of general reference works on the topic. Then, as these students proceed with their research they select from these questions and further refine their perspective. Other students need to accumulate many inches of notecards before drawing up a list of productive questions about a topic. Here are seven general questions to help you to categorize your accumulated information about a social science topic. Our sample student would substitute autism or the autistic child for X in each case. But these questions will work with a wide variety of topics.

1 What are the causes of X?

2 What are the theories about X?

3 What are the characteristics or symptoms of X?

4 What are the capacities for and likelihood of change in X; and what are the effects of any change in X?

5 What are the characteristics of the family or social group of X?

6 What are the similarities or differences in X depending on the environment?

7 What is the history of X?

Begin by organizing your notecards about autism according to these questions. Keep in mind that in your actual paper you will probably deal with no more than one or two questions. But for a start take a look at your notes in terms of these categories. At the least, you will have a better sense later of what you can, in good conscience, omit. Some students will find these questions useful much earlier in the process, possibly as they begin their library research. What information do you have about causes of autism? How are these theories related? What descriptive material do you have about autistic children? Then look for possible connections between the answers you have written down. For the topic of autism, you may find that questions 1, 2, and 3—those about causes, theories, and symptoms—are most productive. What are the connections between theories about the causes of autism and the way that various theories describe the symptoms?

Disciplines are defined by the problems that are appropriately posed within them. Table 9.1 provides examples of four controlling questions, each one appropriate within a different social science field, on the general topic autism.

As you formulate your controlling question you will, by necessity, begin to make choices. This process of selection reflects your understanding of the field you are studying. Your social science term paper is not expected to contribute new knowledge to the field; you are selecting and synthesizing the published material of others. Your controlling questions create a structure for your synthesis, and the structure that you create is your contribution to this term paper assignment.

Writing the first draft

Once you have formulated a controlling question you are ready to select and order your collected information to address that controlling question. A good starting point for the example above would be a definition of autism. But even here you face a difficulty. How can you distinguish a definition of autism from a description of its symptoms? To some extent autism is defined by its symptoms. Moreover, your sources may disagree on which symptoms are central to the condition.

You may want to address this controversy head on by beginning your paper with an overview of various definitions of autism and various de-

Field	Much too broad	Too broad	Still too broad	Controlling question
Psychology	Autism	Description of autistic children	Symptoms of autistic children and emotionally disturbed children.	What are the theories explaining autism? How well do the symptoms fit the theories?
Sociology	Autism	The role of autistic children in society	Autistic children in different societies.	Are autistic children found in all social classes and in all societies? Why or why not?
Political Science	Autism	Autistic children in U.S.	Laws about the schooling of autistic children.	What impact has the required education of autistic and other disturbed children had on local school budgets?
Education	Autism	The education of autistic children	The behavior of autistic children in the classroom.	What do the characteristic symptoms, emotional and cognitive, require in remedial teaching?

TABLE 9.1
Sample controlling questions in various social science disciplines

scriptions of symptoms. You should not feel uncomfortable about presenting your perception of controversy early in your paper. Divided opinion is a hallmark of the social sciences. Whether you address this controversy early or later in your paper, as background material or as part of your central focus, you must always take account of a variety of views, some of them mutually contradictory.

Another way to begin the first draft of the autism paper is to abstract from your sources the simplest and most generally acceptable definition and then to write that out as a start for your draft. The student quoted below has tried this strategy:

Autism is a childhood psychosis characterized
by withdrawal from reality and a refusal to
communicate and deal with people. It is
considered the most severe mental illness among
children and occurs more frequently in boys than
in girls. Psychiatrists believe the condition is
present from birth but is usually not noticed
until the third or fourth month and is also
influenced negatively or positively by the home

environment. Characteristics of autism are:
severe disturbance of language functioning;
skillful relationships with objects; queer
mannerisms and repetitious movements such as
rocking; abnormal desire to preserve various
objects in the environment in an unchanged state;
occasional phenomenal memory; and unusual
mechanical and musical genius.

This writer can always go back later, after he sees his whole first draft, and establish a broader context for his general definition. The most important thing about the paragraph quoted above—especially for a first draft—is that it can generate further paragraphs. The catalog of symptoms leads to a number of choices.

No theory or theoretical controversy has been mentioned yet. You now must decide whether to focus on one theory or on several theories of autism. Given your controlling question, you are under no obligation to write a paper that presents a comprehensive treatment of all theories. But which theories should you leave out? And how do you indicate that you have chosen to omit some theories? While you don't want to overwhelm your readers with excessive research, you do want to show that the omission of important theories was a deliberate choice and not an oversight. The notecard shown in figure 9.1 presents the major theories that could be addressed in this paper.

Once you have categorized the various theories recorded in your notes, you are ready to decide and to explain your particular focus. Here are two paragraphs, from two different first drafts. Each one provides a different focus for the paper's treatment of theories of autism.

Sample draft—student X:

This paper will not cover all of the varied
theoretical explanations of autism. Psychogenic
theories of Bettelheim and Kanner, as well as the
behaviorist position articulated by Krasner and
Ullman, cannot be covered here. Instead, the
focus of this paper will be on organic theories
such as those of Rimland, or Knobloch, or Rutter.
The paper will describe several of the organic
theories in some detail and determine how good a
fit those theories make to the symptoms of
autistic children.

Sample draft—student Y:

There are many individual theories which
attempt to explain autism. Space limitations

Many viewpoints about causes of autism.

1. Kanner originally tho't it was inborn disturbance of affect, different from childhood schizophrenia, partly because of early appearance.

2. Kanner later gave greater emphasis to coldness of parents as a cause, w. minimum effect from in-born — psychogenic).

3. Bettelheim also psychogenic).

4. Problems of making the definition too broad, includes too much.

5. Behaviorists: autism environmentally determined (Krasner & Ulkman) — faulty learning, differential reinforcement — parents at fault.

6. Organic views: Bender — diffuse encephaly. Knobloch — brain damage at birth or pregnancy.

7. Organic — more specific: Rimland — reticular system. Many others — abnormal responses to stimuli, lack of responses to sounds (Rutter) — could be form of mental subnormality.

Rest of chapter looks more completely at these points.

FIGURE 9.1

prohibit an examination of all of them, but one theory from each of three main orientations will be described and compared. Thus, the psychogenic position of Bettelheim, the behaviorist position of Lovaas, and the organic view exemplified by Rimland will be presented.

Each of these paragraphs informs the reader of what limitations have been placed on the scope of this paper. Telling the reader what is not covered in the paper puts the paper in its broader context without writing an encyclopedic study.

Remember that at this stage you are writing paragraphs to test thoughts. You can go back and revise the material later into finished prose. Whatever approach you select for categorizing the theories of autism, you will have to go on to explain the theories that you select and then, in response to your controlling question, show how the symptoms of autism do or do not fit various theories.

As you compose your paragraphs, you may find it useful to jot down in the margins a few one-word reminders to yourself about how you will proceed. Remember also that you are not locked into any choice you make along the way. You can always go back and change the beginning to conform with a better idea that occurs to you later.

As you write your first draft, you should return to reassess choices that you made in a general way when you were doing your research. Do you intend your paper to be comprehensive, representative, or argumentative? (See table 4.1 for definitions and uses of these characteristics of a paper.) Your decision on these characteristics helped to guide choices during your research. Think about these characteristics again as you select material from your research to write your first draft. Whatever else you intend your social science paper to be, you should always make it as up to date and authoritative as you can. Consequently, during your research you have collected some material from the most up-to-date and authoritative sources—scholarly journals.

You may encounter some difficulty, however, when you try to incorporate material from scholarly journals into your draft. You may have notes from a number of journal articles, but you may not know whether the research presented in a particular article is important or esoteric. You may also be unaware of which journals are prestigious and which are not. You may find some clues to the status of an article by looking it up in *Scientific Citation Index* to determine whether the article has been referred to by others. (See chapter 4 for a description of how to use this index.)

Journal articles represent the day-to-day workings of social science. An individual social scientist does research that replicates, extends, or refutes the efforts of other researchers. Thus, in a series of small steps, information about a phenomenon is compiled, forming a composite picture of the causes and limits and relationships of a phenomenon of human functioning. As you work with your scholarly material on autism, think of how the particular subject matter of the article fits in with the wider framework that you are developing. Then connect the highly particular material from the journal article to the emerging structure of your paper as a whole. For example, let us say that you have written a notecard (figure 9.2) from an article in the *Journal of Abnormal Psychology*.

This article reports on the varying ability of autistic children, children

Litrownik, McInnis, Wetzel-
Pritchard, and Filipelli

Study on 7 autistic, 7 Down's and 7 normal kids,
all with same mental age. Match-to-sample task
used because memory is not a factor in this discrimination task. Memory does influence performance in traditional discrimination paradigm used in previous studies.
In this study, in contrast to previous one, autistic
children performed as well as normals when matched
for mental age; Down's children inferior performance.

FIGURE 9.2

with Down's Syndrome, and normal children to perform a task that
involves making discriminations. Your first impulse may be to reject this
material as too narrow for your paper, but actually these experimental
data can be integrated into your paper to explain further the lack of
attention frequently observed as a symptom in autistic children. The
researchers selected an experimental task that did not involve memory and
found that when memory was minimized as an influencing factor, autistic
children performed as well as normal children of the same mental age.
Thus, you might suggest in your own paper that problems with memory
might influence the generally observed inattention of autistic children.

Once you have selected appropriate material from your notes and
tentatively organized this material into sentences and paragraphs, you
have written a useful first draft. Don't worry about composing an opening
or closing paragraph until the next stage of your writing.

Revising

You now have the body of your paper in first-draft form. Next, go through
and try to outline this material. This outline provides a visual overview
of your paper. If your outline does not work well, that is, if the topics are
not organized to your satisfaction, then begin moving around topics and

categories in your outline. Working with your outline at this point is faster and less cumbersome than working with your draft. Once you are happy with the order of topics in your outline, then turn to rearranging material in your paper.

Many writers use the cut-and-paste method; they actually cut apart their first draft, rearranging paragraphs, adding and deleting material, and then pasting the whole thing together again, like a jigsaw puzzle. If you use this method, be sure to photocopy the original of your first draft before you take a scissors to it. You may decide that, after all, you prefer parts of the original structure, so you will need a record of the way things were.

As you restructure your paper in this revising stage, you should focus your attention on the needs of your readers. As we have suggested for a number of other papers, you should assume that the audience for your term paper is composed of your classmates and your instructor. You must make your topic comprehensible to classmates who do not have the same background on the topic as you do, but you must write in a style more formal than one you would use if writing only for classmates. Most experienced writers do not wait until the revising stage to consider the needs of their audience. In fact, considerations of audience can serve as a heuristic throughout the writing process. But in a first draft, you can feel much more free to write with the primary purpose of testing and clarifying your ideas for yourself. When you are revising, you must give much of your attention to communicating ideas and information to others.

Especially if you use the cut-and-paste method of rearranging material in your first draft, you may have a fragmented paper. As you revise, give special attention to the transitions that you make between paragraphs. Transitional words—*consequently, thus, therefore, nevertheless*—must be used accurately (see chapters 2 and 6), but even their correct use is not enough. As your readers move from paragraph to paragraph, they need signposts to indicate the function of each paragraph as part of the whole logical structure. If signposts are really to serve their function of making readers feel comfortable about the road that they are traveling, these signposts must depend to some extent on repetition. Don't be afraid to reiterate an earlier point to show its connection to a later one. Repeat key phrases to connect two different situations to the main ideas in your paper.

At appropriate places in your paper, insert a tabular presentation to summarize material for your readers. These graphic presentations can serve as the best signposts of all, since they can clearly demonstrate relationships that you have been developing in your discourse. You should develop a table of your own, rather than reproducing one from another source. But tables do not need to be complex. Table A is an example of a table from the final draft of a student's paper on autism. The table gives clear visual form to the relationships of various theoretical positions about proposed causes of autism. Although a tabular presentation is an excellent signpost, it should not hang in midair. You should discuss the material

TABLE A
Theoretical Positions and Proposed Causes of Autism

Theoretical position	Theorist	Proposed cause
Psychogenic–functional due to stress	late Kanner	"emotional refrigeration" of parents
	Bettelheim	parental cause
Behavioral–environment	Krasner & Ullman	faulty learning from parents
	Lovaas	inability to learn appropriate responses
Organic	early Kanner	inborn defect
	Rimland	underactive reticular system
	Rutter	relative inability to comprehend sounds

in the table as part of the body of your paper. Use tables as clarifications and connections. *Never* let them stand alone.

As you revise, keep reminding yourself that your audience has not read all the background material that you have. Try to remember that not so long ago you knew very little about the topic and revise your term paper into the sort of presentation that you would have been grateful to read when you first started your research.

Your introduction, in particular, should be designed to help or at least to interest your readers. One way to engage your readers is to make them see your topic in concrete terms. A well-chosen quotation may be useful here. For instance, you might begin your paper on autism this way:

"We can't understand why Michael isn't like
other children. His father and I live with a
constant sense of guilt and fear. Last week,
without warning, Mike bolted out the front door
and ran right into the street. A car just missed
him because the driver slammed on the brakes.
Even so, I had to drag Mike screaming back into
the house." The mother of a six-year-old autistic
child described this situation to me.

Or you might prefer to open with this quote from Bruno Bettleheim's *Love Is Not Enough*:

    The most important of all skills, that of
    living well with oneself and with others, can be
    acquired only by living in an emotionally stable
    and satisfying human environment. If too many
    families no longer provide it, a vicious circle
    is created because parents convey to their
    children what they have never learned
    themselves.[1]

Both of these quotations create a vivid opening, the first because of the concrete situation described and the second because of the power of Bruno Bettelheim's language. Although direct quotations may provide a memorable way to begin or end social science term papers, direct quotations should be used sparingly at other points in your paper, probably even more sparingly than in a humanities paper. The norms of social science writing are in this way different from those of writing in the humanities.

At the beginning of your social science paper you may want to provide an overview of your topic rather than a dramatic opening. The student who began his first draft with a definition of autism decided to insert the following paragraph to precede that definition:

    What is early infantile autism? What symptoms
    does an autistic child display? What are the
    conflicting theories about autism? Do the
    theories adequately explain the syndrome? The
    topic of early infantile autism raises these
    questions, which will be addressed in this paper.

In fact, it is better to use a clear, straightforward, unembellished style like that of this paragraph than to reach too far for flair. In social science writing, as in any kind of writing, keep your *aim* foremost, and your aim is to be in control of a body of social science material and to communicate your understanding of that material to your peers and your professor. You also want to show that your research has helped you to intuit some of the conventions—the etiquette of social science. Social scientists value factual writing presented with some sense of authority.

Even though you are just a beginner in the field, you can show your growing authority in small ways as well as large. For example, you might

---

1 Reprinted with permission of Macmillan Publishing Co., Inc. from *Love Is Not Enough* (p. 375) by Bruno Bettelheim. Copyright 1950 by The Free Press, a Corporation, renewed 1978 by Bruno Bettelheim.

remember that most articles that you have read during your research used headings and subheadings as a standard feature of their format. You should divide your own paper into sections and use appropriate subheadings. Properly used, subheadings can function usefully as signposts for your reader. The use of subheadings is distinctive to the social and natural sciences. Most professors in the humanities do not want to see subheadings in the papers that you write for their classes. As we have said throughout this book, traditions are different in different academic fields.

In writing, as in life, through experience students develop a sense of tact. Perceptive students learn not to confuse the objective with the evasive. They understand that factual prose need not be dead prose. If, for example, you have done some field work with autistic children, you could integrate relevant parts of that experience with your research presentation. One student strengthened her paper with the following paragraph:

> There is also a desperate need for sameness. I worked with a little girl who had an obsession with the way she wore her garments. For example, whenever she wore a sweater she insisted it be buttoned to the top button. Not only this, but it had to be done from the bottom up, and yet when she chose to take it off it had to be done from the top down.

Some students might hesitate to include this interesting piece of information, not only because it is anecdotal, but because the writer must use the word "I" to relate it. It is true that the word "I" is used less frequently in the social and natural sciences than it is in the humanities, but in an instance like the one above, most instructors will approve the use of "I."

In order to convey the impersonal tone of science, students too often use passive sentence constructions. Good social science writing, on the contrary, conveys factual information in an objective tone without heavy reliance on the passive voice. In the example below the sentence in the active voice is just as objective and factual as the sentence in the passive voice, and the active sentence actually conveys more information in a more direct manner:

Passive: It was thought that autism and mental retardation were mutually exclusive.

Active: Early theorists thought that autism and mental retardation were mutually exclusive.

As you revise, check your passive sentences and see if you can provide them with a subject and transform them into active, forceful sentences.

Also look to see if you are using too many nouns—especially nouns that end in *-tion, -ment, -ing, -ion, -ance*—and too many weak linking verbs: *is, has, were.* Change them to strong verbs.

You should also check to see that you are using technical vocabulary clearly and appropriately. Since your audience is composed of other social science students, you should use specialized vocabulary when that vocabulary expresses a concept more precisely than you could do with more popular terms. For example, you may write that autistic children characteristically fail to "modulate sensory stimuli." The word "modulate" means quite specifically to adjust the level, and "sensory stimuli" again refers quite specifically to things that activate any of the five sensory systems. The phrase "modulate sensory stimuli" is thus an example of useful technical language, not of jargon. Jargon is characteristically imprecise and evasive. A writer would be using jargon if he wrote, "Autistic children are known for persistent, percussive abuse of the cranial structure vis à vis a lateral environmental barrier." What the writer means to say here, simply and precisely, is that autistic children sometimes bang their heads against the wall, and no social scientist would object to the phrase "bang their heads against the wall." Good writing in the social sciences is precise, not evasive. If you do use a technical term like "modulate sensory stimuli," you should probably go on to explain and illustrate the term to connect it to the context of your paper.

Finally, go through your paper and check carefully for errors in usage, spelling, and typing. After all the time and effort that you have expended to establish your authority to review writings on autism, you don't want to blow it by submitting a paper littered with errors. After you have worked for a semester on a project, each error is far too expensive. Proofread meticulously. Some students read their papers backward at this stage so that they have enough distance to spot spelling and typing errors.

Check also that your references are in the correct form. (See chapter 5 for APA style, which most of your social science instructors will want you to use.) Check, too, that you are listing only those works that you have actually read. For instance, the majority of material that you have read on autism refers to a 1943 paper by Kanner, which is a classic because of its early definition of the syndrome. But unless you read Kanner's original paper, you must not use it as a reference, although you certainly can write about Kanner and cite the author who cites him.

At some point in this challenging process you may begin to feel a bit autistic yourself. But if you sequence your activities so that you actually spend the whole term on this term project, you will learn a great deal about the workings of the social sciences from your thorough research on a particular topic.

QUESTIONS 1 What skills is the term paper in the social sciences designed to help you practice?

2 Why are references to other social scientists so important in the social science research paper?

3 What are the important rules for and limitations on using direct quotations in a social science research paper?

4 Identify the ways that considerations of your audience can help you at every stage in developing a research paper.

EXERCISES **1** Substitute a topic for "X" in the questions on pages 209–210. In your journal work out all of the possible questions you might follow up if you wrote a paper on that topic.

2 Identify the major differences between research papers in the humanities and those in social sciences. What are the most important similarities?

3 Select a topic, like the autism example, and try to develop it in the manner illustrated on page 211.

4 Avoiding jargon or excessively technical language, rewrite the following paragraph in clear, expressive English.

The limited parameters of our study preclude serious generalizations beyond suggesting that the continued availability of grain depends significantly upon favorable environmental influences. It is believed that forecasts subsequent to this study which indicate prolonged drought in the impacted area are based on too many variables to be meaningful. Precipitation is anticipated with a consequent increase in grain-producing capability.

10 The Case Study Paper

Teachers, social workers, and congressional assistants often must write case studies. When you are asked to write a case study in your introductory social science course, you are getting practice in an important professional skill. In social science, the observation of behavior is basic to other more sophisticated skills. Psychologists, sociologists, anthropologists, and political scientists are trained observers and recorders of the behavior of individuals and groups. They know how to see detail and to record what they see with great accuracy. When you write case studies for your social science courses, you will practice skills of close observation and accurate record-keeping.

Here are some examples of case study assignments:

- In your visits to a nursery school or child-care center, select one child for observation. Describe that child's language, social behavior, and motor and perceptual-motor capacities.

- Describe and analyze a small group to which you have belonged or belong now. Some areas you may discuss are the group's norms and values, subcultural characteristics, stratification and roles, ethnocentrism, and social control techniques.

- Describe the behavior of the patient you have been assigned as he/she interacts with you each week, both on the ward and in recreation areas.

- Describe the case history of HR1457 from its inception to its passage as a law.

The last example, a political science assignment to write the case history of a bill in Congress, requires certain specialized procedures that we will explain at the end of this chapter. The other tasks all involve direct observations of human behavior, while the political science assignment requires applying observational techniques more indirectly. But in all the assignments, your responsibilities in writing a case history include the following:

1 to decide what items of behavior to observe

2 to record the relevant behavior in detail and with a minimum of subjective judgment on your part

3 to group all of the observations into categories for a more careful study and discussion of them

4 To apply theoretical concepts to the categories for the purpose of explaining the observations.

Getting started

When you observe, you record objectively the details of what you actually see. You do not try to explain, interpret, or judge. Your eye is a camera. Only after you have made an accurate and complete record of observations can you begin to draw inferences from your data. As you read in chapter 2, inferences are conclusions. You cannot draw conclusions until you notice and record very carefully what the facts are.

Let us suppose that you are observing the behavior of a class of preschoolers. You see one child pull a toy away from a second child, who then cries. What should you record? Do not record that two chldren who don't like each other are having a fight. If you do, you will lose many valuable facts. Later observations may show that the first child always pulls that particular toy away from any other child who happens to have it. You may then want to draw a very different inference from the facts of the first observation combined with those of other observations. Also, if you establish a mindset too early, you may try to fit all of your observations into a pattern that is not really adequate to explain what is happening. You might pay too much attention to the interaction of the two children you first observed and miss other activities of both children.

Accurate observations are essential starting points for your case study paper. But in our everyday life we are not accustomed to seeing things keenly, and we rarely record what we see. To accustom your own eye to the sharper vision necessary for this assignment, try the following stratagem. Pretend that you and one of your classmates are working together as a team to observe this preschool class. You and your partner have read the same textbooks and have heard the same lectures, so you are bringing the same conceptual framework to your observations. But your partner is blind. As you both prepare to write your case study papers, you scrupulously tell your blind partner only what you see, not what you think the observation means. After all, you do not want to influence your blind partner with your conclusions. You want to give him an opportunity to form his own. You are conscientious about communicating only accurate, objective observations. You do not initially describe behavior as "lazy," "dependent," or "kind." Instead, you describe in detail what the people do and say. Only later, after the observation period, do you draw inferences about what you have recorded.

But even for your blind partner you can legitimately refer to concepts in your textbooks to help make your observations something more than random. As we have explained earlier, academic disciplines are defined by the questions that they ask. Do not overlook your textbook as an aid to your vision. Chapter headings and subheadings may indicate general questions to bring to your observations. If you are writing a case study for a course in early childhood education, you should recall that the authors of your textbook have raised questions about the development of children. They categorize this development into motor, language, social, and cognitive. You should try the same categories. The authors of your sociology textbook have raised other questions: the size and composition of social groups, the degree and kind of social control, the definitions of standards (norms), and the consequences of norm violations. If you are writing this paper for an introductory sociology course, bring these categories to your case study of a small social group.

Even with the help of organizational principles from your textbook, you may have difficulty in focusing your observations without missing the obvious. Let us suppose that you are assigned in a psychology course to observe a litter of young animals periodically over a four-week period. At each observation you record such behavior as sucking, moving, and sleeping. But remember that the purpose of the assignment is to watch the process of development. Ask yourself what signs of growth you might see over a four-week period. Then record the appearance of the fur, for example, at each observation. Is it growing? At your first observation were the pups' eyes always closed? When was the first time that you saw them open?

Since your major goal in your observations is accuracy and objectivity, whenever you can count something, by all means do so. A frequency count involves recording the number of occurrences of a specific, narrowly defined behavior. For example, you might record the number of times a particular child addresses a comment or question to the teacher in a classroom. Or you might count the number of teacher-directed questions asked by several different children. In a description of social group behavior you might count the number of times the women on their way to market stop to greet people. Later, when you look over your recorded observations, you can base your inferences on something more than vague impressions.

After you have decided on the behavior to be observed, organize your notebook in columns or by pages so that you provide separate space for each category. Write on only one side of each page of paper. As you observe items in each category, record them in sequence, by date, time, or stage of development, in the proper space. You may find yourself developing, consciously or unconsciously, a shorthand system for recording observations. Whatever shorthand systems you develop, make sure that you can decipher them accurately days or weeks later, and that they are, in fact, symbols for observations and not inferences.

Force yourself to record something about each category during each observing session. Write as much as you can. You should not assume that you will remember items without writing them down. You may wish to develop a checklist on which each item has to be checked after a record is made of the observations. A checklist, in column form, will show, in a dramatic, visual way, areas for which your record is incomplete.

During your recording periods, do not worry about recording too much. It is always possible to write a paper from too much information, but sometimes impossible to write one from too little data. In fact, at the end of your recording period you will probably possess an abundance of data that will not find its way into your paper. It is better to have this throwaway material than not to have sufficient material on which to base solid conclusions. Just as you have to be careful not to infer while you are observing, so you have to take care not to edit while you are recording. Especially when your paper is based on material collected from a series of observations, you must take very detailed notes. You may not know at first what areas of behavior will become interesting as your observations proceed. Without a written record of routine, boring, or seemingly unimportant observations, you cannot go back to make comparisons when a startling event occurs. Edit out useless material only after you have completed your observations, since only then will you be in a position to make decisions about what is important and what is not.

The final activity in getting started is to fit your grouped observations into the theories required to explain them. Now you can make inferences about the data. Try spreading all of your observation sheets out on the floor and grouping them by category into the concepts that you are studying in the course. One of the instructor's purposes for this exercise, remember, is for you to explain theoretically the behavior that you observe. Examples of concepts or theories in social science courses are: in child development—sibling rivalry, attention-getting behavior, motor skills, language development; in sociology—alienation, conformity, deviance; in psychology—identity diffusion, depression; in political science—single-issue campaigning, fear mongering. This list is merely illustrative. The concepts with which you are to work—from which you are to choose—will be presented in the course.

Your task is to select the explanation or explanations that best account for the observed behavior. It is possible that some behavior will fit several theoretical explanations. For example, a boy's response to a teacher's question about the number of children in his family might be, "My parents have one son and one daughter" when, in fact, there are two boys and a girl. This observed remark might be illustrative of sibling rivalry, attention-getting behavior, inadequate understanding of the concept of number, or semantic confusion of the words in the question. You may not be able to decide which theory or theories best explain an instance of behavior at this point, but there are tests to apply. It might be possible to eliminate potential explanations if they are not consistent with other observed behavior. In the case above, if the boy did not display attention-getting behavior in other areas, or if he demonstrated facility with numbers, you might decide to eliminate these explanations. Similarly, different categories of behavior, when compared, might disclose a pattern that is best understood when a certain theory is applied. You may not, however, be able to explain a particular behavior after looking over your data. If not, simply note that some observations may fit into several categories and begin writing your first draft. Writing sentences and paragraphs is often a useful way to make connections and to generate ideas. The shape of your paper will help you to decide how best to account for your observations.

Writing the first draft

The first draft of a case study paper may be easier to begin if you start writing on each of the behavior categories, neglecting, at first, the introduction or opening paragraphs. Write on each category as if you were writing separate papers, on separate pieces of paper. You will probably find that you fill some pages and move on to second sheets for some categories, while you are able to write only a few sentences about other categories. You may find some sections easier to write than others. Concentrate on those. Do not worry, at this point, about finishing one section before going on to another. Your primary task is to get your ideas and connections down, to discover areas of difficulty, and to begin to make assertions.

When you have written what you can in all categories, it is important to go back to your observation sheets to make sure that you have thought about every relevant item in your notes. An example of notes prior to their being transformed into a first draft appears in figure 10.1. These notecards illustrate student observation of children in a preschool classroom. (T stands for teacher and A, B, C, D, and E are children.) You will see that a number of words have been abbreviated for rapid note taking. The student's first-draft attempts at converting the notes in figure 10.1 to prose are as follows:

Socialization
    In socialization, A seems less mature than the other children. On one occasion she screamed for no apparent reason, but was happy when the teacher came over. She was seen pushing the other children who returned the push, but they were never seen initiating pushing against A. A did not share well. A spent a lot of time near the teacher. The other children were better able to

FIGURE 10.1
(on facing page)

Free play period

A screamed when B appr.

T came over — held A

T return to gym group w. A

A stayed w. T

A push E, E hit A, T intervene

Paper cutting for kites

T gave directions — kids talking

Kids cut on lines easily, except D

Must share paste among 3 kids —

    A grabbed it 3x

    C grabbed it 1x

D needed no help w. paste

All children tacked pix on wall themselves

Story time

A push E, C push A in lining up

A push chair near T

A wiggles, talks to D (didn't hear what they said)

T review story and ask ?s.

B, C, D, E raise hands — T choose D and E to answer

and ?— D and C raise hand — A calls out answer

Children all sing and march at end of story

A reminded to march, not skip by T.

follow the teacher's directions for sharing,
completing a task, or raising hands to answer a
question than was A.

Does wiggling = unsocialized behavior?

<u>Motor coordination</u>
In large—muscle activities the children do not
differ much. They all march and move chairs
pretty much the same way. Cutting and pasting
with construction paper was harder for D than for
the other children.

Does wiggling belong in this section?

Don't panic if your first bout of writing does not produce insight.
Inspiration is usually the result of diligence. Read again through your
drafts of the different categories, not to edit them, but to discover meaning.
Ask yourself, "So what? Why did I make all of these observations?" Reread
your assignment sheet and ask, "Why would the professor assign this task?
What am I supposed to learn?" How would you explain the children's
behavior to your roommate if he asked about your case study? In fact,
you might read an observation aloud and ask, "Now, why would X behave
this way?" Another useful way to generate connections and explanations
is to try to write out different explanations for each instance of behavior.
When you actually press yourself to write justifications for each theory,
you will find it easier to select the more plausible theories. Eliminate the
ones that you cannot write about and try to develop, for each instance of
behavior, the explanations that are left. Don't be afraid to jot down
questions about inconsistencies. Your instructor may be willing to clarify
areas of difficulty.

Once you feel comfortable with your conclusions and think that they
are sufficient to explain your observations, you need to write an introduction that presents the general rationale for your paper. If you can write
out a statement of purpose—the reason you are writing the paper, the
behavior observed, and what you intend to demonstrate about this behavior—then you are ready to revise your paper for presentation. One student's introduction looked like this in draft form:

<u>Introduction</u>

~~This paper~~

~~A child's strengths in one area.~~

This paper describes several instances of
behavior in a preschool child. The behavior

observed can be grouped into motor coordination,
language, cognition, and socialization. Although
the children are all the same age--four years
old--and the same social class, they are not
alike. Some children are better in one area, or
poorer in another

Revising

In the first draft you are primarily interested in working out your ideas.
The purpose of subsequent drafts is to write the paper for a reader. The
final draft should be designed in form and language so that another person
will understand explicitly what you are trying to say. A reader's interests
are different from yours. For example, you may write your first draft as
a narrative by following your observations from the first one to the last
one. This sequence is natural because you went through the observations
from beginning to end and remember the points at which you made
discoveries. Also, you may be tempted to select the easiest principle of
organization—chronological order. The reader, however, is not interested
in the history of your observations. The reader wants to know what patterns
you observed and what inferences you drew. Therefore, the proper form
for your paper is not a narration about making observations, but a description and summary of the results of observations. Following are examples of narrative prose and explanatory prose of the same observations.
The narrative paragraph, organized according to the time sequence in
which the events took place, is all right for a first draft because chronological order frequently provides the easiest way to get thoughts on paper.
The explanatory paragraph is organized with the main idea first, the
remainder of the paper presenting details from the observations to support
the explanation.
 Here are notes translated into literal narrative prose:

Socialization
    During free play time, I saw A scream when B
came near her, and after that A stayed near the
teacher. A didn't get into any real problems
next, during the kite making, although she didn't
share the paste well. When they had story time I
saw A push somebody and be pushed back. She sat
next to the teacher and talked quietly to another
child. The teacher asked questions after the
story, and A never raised her hand although she
did call out an answer once.

    Does wiggling belong in this section?

And here is a non-narrative revision of the above paragraph:

Socialization

```
    A's behavior seemed less mature socially than
the other children's. When another child came
near her, A screamed for no obvious reason. She
spent a lot of time near the teacher, both during
free time and story time. The other children
followed the teacher's directions to share paste,
or to raise hands, or to march and sing better
than A did. A pushed others and was then pushed
in return. No one initiated aggressive behavior
toward A.
```

It is important to remember that when you move from narrative to explanatory prose, you are not necessarily moving from a less formal to a more formal prose. Students sometimes tend to write in a stilted, artificial style when they organize their papers topically. The passive voice does not sound more scholarly. ("The observation was made . . .") Use the first-person "I" if it helps you achieve a clear, direct style.

As you revise, edit out value-laden, unsupported generalizations. When moving from description to inference, a writer has to move from descriptive words to evaluative words, and this shift increases the risk of choosing words that are not supported by the data as given in the paper. Keep the observations themselves as free as possible from value-laden descriptions. You will probably present your inferences and conclusions as generalizations. Do not be afraid to generalize, but make sure that your generalizations are built on solid detail. Here is an example of unsupported evaluations:

```
    Our current president is a (very attractive)
(down-to-earth) person and her leadership qualities
are (without question) (Unfortunately,) she will
soon leave this position.
```

We have circled the writer's value judgments. If such words appear in your descriptions, you must be sure that they are not just "fillers," but grow out of the details of your observations.

One reason that your instructor assigned the case study paper was to help you learn theories and concepts in a particular social science discipline. Check your paper to be sure that you have used specialized language appropriately. Avoid extended definitions. Incorporate specialized vocabulary into the paper in a manner that shows an understanding of these terms. For example, the following paragraph contains the word "ostracizing," a term especially useful in explaining behavior in anthropology, sociology, and education, but the writer does not help the reader to understand "ostracizing," nor does the writer show that he understands the term:

```
    Ostracizing is something she will not
tolerate. Instead, she believes in stressing
possible achievements. If a mother or child
accomplishes something, you can be sure that Irma
will give praise to them.
```

Any number of words could be substituted for "ostracizing" without changing the meaning of the assertion. Irma may be equally intolerant of "gossip," "rumor," or "mean talk." What is "ostracizing" in this context and why won't Irma tolerate it? The reader can't tell. The reader has no way of telling whether the word is understood by the student or is, in fact, the right word for the observation being made.

In the following example, in contrast, the student shows a clear understanding of "ostracizing" by creating a context in which the meaning of the word is unambiguous. The writer also has developed an accurate sense of the audience for whom he is writing. This writer does not assume that his instructor is his only reader. If the student had made that limited and misleading assumption, he might have stopped his description after the first, short paragraph, for certainly the instructor would understand how the terms apply to the situation. By thinking of peers, classmates, or roommates as his audience, this student has had to explain how the concepts apply to an actual situation. Because the writer has imagined a wider audience, he has written with the necessary degree of clarity and detail.

Social Control Techniques

```
    Like all primary groups, we expected
conformity to the norms of the group in dress,
speech, social behavior, and values. And like all
groups we developed ways to enforce this
conformity. The four ways we handled violations
were sarcasm, gossip, physical punishment, and,
as a last resort, ostracism.
    Of these, sarcasm and gossip were the more
used and less severe. If, for example, a member
got his hair cut too short, the others would make
sarcastic remarks about his ears, the shape of
his head, and so on. Gossip was used to correct
behavior in such areas as girls and dealing with
money. If a member was "hen-pecked" or "too
tight" with his money, the others began to speak
about these to each other until the offending
```

party found out. This form of reprimand was usually effective.

Physical punishment was employed to correct continued violations of minor values or first—time violations of major values. If, for example, a member was "too tight" with his money after the use of sarcasm and gossip, then he might be hit by one of the members of the group. If, as Rich did when he "ganged—up" on another person, a member violated an important norm, he might be physically roughed up or engaged in a full—scale fight. Usually, this form of correction occurred spontaneously without any member passing judgment verbally or formally.

Ostracism was the last resort in response to a member's deviant behavior. If any member knowingly violated one of the group's major norms, and continued to do so, the other members simply stopped associating with him.

Your conclusion, as well as your introduction, must be carefully constructed, for it is the part of your case study paper which ties together the disparate categories. Your final draft should be a unified paper. The conclusion should be used to reinforce this unity, but also to go beyond that which has already been stated to discuss the implications of your observations and explanation.

The case history of a bill in Congress: HR1457

Few undergraduates have the opportunity to go to Washington, D.C., to make first-hand observations about how a congressional bill develops into the law of the land. Sometimes this process takes several months or even years. Nonetheless, students of political science can, to some extent, bring techniques of close, systematic observation to the behavior of Congress, just as sociologists can bring these tools of the social sciences to their observations of more accessible social groups.

The *Congressional Record* provides a full, daily transcript of everything that transpires on the floor of the House of Representatives and the Senate. If you are interested in HR (House of Representatives bill) 1457, you would have available to you the full record of everything that was said and done about this bill on the floor of the Congress. The committees and subcommittees of the House also publish detailed reports of their hearings and deliberations. Few college libraries store the full *Congressional Record* and the reports of congressional committees, but with enough lead time, your college reference librarian can help you gather the printed information that you need. Besides these primary sources, you can also read more indirect accounts in newspapers and in other printed material, both official and unofficial.

Although you are looking at words rather than at actual behavior, you are performing a task worthy of an apprentice political scientist, and you have responsibilities similar to those of the sociologist and the anthropologist who observe behavior first hand. You must decide what to focus on from the voluminous detail provided in the official transcripts. You must categorize your observations without leaping too quickly to subjective judgments. Finally, you must apply theoretical concepts to the categories for the purpose of explaining the observations.

Your first draft of the case history of HR1457 may describe the following sequence of events: Representative Alison Gray (Republican, Rhode Island) and Representative Joyce Kempner (Democrat, Pennsylvania) introduced HR1457 into the House on April 14, (year?). The Speaker of the House (name?) assigned the bill to a standing committee (which one? who are the members?). The chairperson (name?) of the committee gave the bill to a subcommittee (which one? who are the members?) for study and hearings. After debating the bill, the members of the subcommittee held hearings to allow experts and other interested parties to provide testimony to the subcommittee. The subcommittee finally returned the bill to the full committee with a recommendation to pass it. The committee accepted the subcommittee report and voted to send the bill to the floor of the House. On July 28, (year?) debate began. Several representatives (who?) proposed amendments (what?), but the full House accepted only two (which ones?) before passing the bill by voice vote. Senator Carol Waldman (Republican, Idaho) and Senator Louis Plaskow (Democrat, Maryland) had introduced a similar bill into the Senate on April 25, (year?). The Senate bill followed a similar course to passage, but the resultant legislation did not contain the two amendments, so the leadership in both houses appointed members (who?) to a conference committee to work out a compromise version to be sent to the president for his signature.

Now that you have systematically categorized your factual observations, you are in a position to ask questions that will lead to inferences about why the bill passed and what the bill actually means. Why did the Speaker select one committee rather than another to debate HR1457? Was the chairperson known to be sympathetic to the bill? How did the chairperson of the subcommittee select the witnesses who appeared at the hearings? Who lobbied for and against the bill? Was the purpose of the amendments to improve or to kill the bill? What were the significant divisions in the voting on the bill? What was the composition of the conference committee?

Only by answering such questions can you transform observations into inferences and write an essay that has a thesis ("The Congress passed HR1457, but hostile members of the conference committee undermined the original intent of the bill by accepting two House amendments which effectively removed all enforcement mechanisms"). Without careful observation of the progress of the bill or without your application of theoretical concepts to explain the observations, you might be misled into asserting simply that the Congress passed HR1457 into law, when the crucial observation is that the law was significantly different from the bill.

Seeing and writing like a social scientist can help all of us to observe more carefully. We rarely take the time in everyday life to look at one another. In contrast, when we behave like social scientists, we must record observations systematically as preparation for drawing cautious inferences. Writing the exercises explained in this chapter can help us to see and to think more clearly.

We are reminded of a story that appeared in the press a few years ago about a first-grade teacher who wrote the following on the permanent record of one of her students: "Has unstable family life." This remark followed this child through his school years, affecting the way his teachers treated him. Finally, when the first-grade teacher was asked to reconstruct the observation that led to her inferences, she said that the boy's mother could never come to the school for daytime appointments and that on one or two occasions the child had come to school with broken shoelaces and his shirt on inside out. She had recorded only her conclusion, "unstable family life," without any supporting observations. Other teachers might have reached different conclusions from the same observations, but the first-grade teacher's omission of supporting data compromised the right of other readers of the record to draw their own conclusions. Her shaky inference took on the appearance of fact.

The reader of any case study has the right to object to your inferences. You must present enough carefully observed detail to make such objection possible.

QUESTIONS 1 What is a case study paper? What skills can be practiced by writing this type of paper?

2 What are your major responsibilities in "getting started" on this paper?

3 What are the important differences between observing and inferring? Why is it necessary to distinguish between them?

4 In what ways is the case study of a bill in Congress similar to a case study of individual human behavior?

EXERCISES 1 Along with some of your classmates, observe the behavior of a person (ideally one of your classmates acting out a role) and write down what the person does. Then write down what you believe the person was actually trying to do or communicate. Compare your observations and inferences with others. Account for the disagreements.

2 Write your own paragraph from the data in figure 10.1. Compare your paragraph with the examples provided in the text.

3 Select an event that is currently in the news, preferably one that is on-going, such as the campaign of a politician, and collect daily news articles on the topic for a period of time—a week, a month, or two months. Using the material in this chapter, write a case study paper on the event.

4 Analyze and evaluate the following paragraph from a case study paper.

> Michael is a preschooler who does not like to be away from home every morning. He comes reluctantly to nursery school and, the minute his mother leaves, begins to act aggressively. Sadly, he has no siblings to interact with at home, so he has not learned how to relate to other children. He is unhappy, bored, and doesn't even like the cookies at midmorning break. He doesn't respond to our gentle encouragement and might be better off at home with a sitter.

5 See the Appendix for a set of extended instructions for "The Mama Rat Project," a case study that is assigned annually to freshmen in Psychology 101 and English 101 at Beaver College. Your own psychology department may be willing to set up a similar observational opportunity.

11 Reporting Findings in the Social Sciences

The social sciences are disciplines based on empirical observations. Researchers in these disciplines collect data and report them to others. Each discipline has methods peculiar to itself and differs from the others in the problems it identifies as within its domain. Despite these differences, however, each discipline has a common commitment to collecting information in an objective, scientific manner. This chapter will deal with the conventions that govern the ways in which you are expected to write up your data.

Here are some examples of assignments that require you to report findings:

- How fast is the world population increasing and what will it be in the year 2100? Or 2200?

- What is a desirable growth rate for the economy and how can that rate best be achieved?

- How does a "fence" avoid arrest for possession of stolen goods?

- What is the special significance of gift giving in Japanese society?

- Do handicapped children learn better in special classes or when integrated in regular classes?

- Will the recently launched advertising campaign for Brand X significantly boost sales?

When you write papers to answer questions like these, you must use the skills described in other chapters as well as the new ones described here. But it is not the purpose of this chapter to teach you how to collect data— you will learn that in your social science course. The focus of this chapter will be on how you write your report of your findings.

Getting started

Reports of findings follow a pattern that is similar for all the social science disciplines. According to the pattern, a paper has four parts: an introduction, a description of the methods used in gathering data, a description of the findings, and a statement of the conclusions. Disciplines vary in the degree to which they expect the pattern to be explicit and rigidly adhered to. In fact, experimental psychology requires you to follow the more formalized natural science procedures explained in chapter 14. Some disciplines require that you name each section with a specific subheading. In other disciplines there is a general implicit expectation that the substance of the four parts should be in your paper, but the pattern need not always be explicit. In all cases you will be expected to introduce your paper, describe your methods and findings, and draw some conclusions.

By reading the appropriate professional journals you can learn the degree of formality required for your paper, but you should not be misled by these journals. What appears in them is the final version of a paper, so its structure is that of a final product. The order in which the various elements are presented in the paper need not be the same as the way in which they were initially drafted. Very few social scientists begin writing with a clearly conceived introduction and then move serially through the writing of the paper to the results and the conclusion. Instead, they know generally what kinds of information each section will contain. Knowledge of this general scheme frees them from trying to write the whole report from top to bottom. In fact, professional social scientists often start in the middle. So although we will now describe each part in the order in which it is supposed to appear in the final paper, you should not assume that you must follow this sequence in your own writing process. But whatever order you follow in the composition of your paper, you need to know the purpose for each part of the pattern.

The *introduction* of a report is supposed to accomplish two goals. First, it states the question to which the paper is intended to be the answer. This statement of the question is necessary in the introduction to any paper of a problem-solution format. The second goal is more specific to a social science paper: to show how the question is relevant and important in the context of the social science for which the paper is written. You need to show why a psychologist, a sociologist, or an economist specifically should be concerned with the question. We have earlier discussed ways of generating a controlling question (chapters 6 and 9), and what was said there applies here also. But particularly significant to the introduction section of this kind of paper is the necessity for a general indication of how the question you choose is manageable by the methods of the science within which you are working.

In the *methods* section of the paper you describe how you went about collecting findings or doing the work of the study. Such a description is essential to any scientific study, for one of the fundamental principles of the scientific community is that studies be capable of replication. It must be possible for someone else to repeat your study to check its results. Your description of the methods must be precise enough so that someone else could do the study again, exactly as you did.

Thus, if you observe human subjects, you should describe all the characteristics pertinent to the study: age, intelligence, ethnic group, social class, income level, education, medical history, and so on. If you have used questions in an interview or in a test procedure, then you should list the questions. (If you did not, how could another person replicate the study?) But the finished description of what you did should not be an autobiographical narrative that proceeds step by step through all your activities. Limit the description of methods to what your reader must know to replicate your procedures. The actual historical process by which you came to your conclusions is of little interest to your reader, so plan to revise a first-draft narrative. The reader needs to know what questions you used in your interview; the reader does not need to know when and how it occurred to you to ask question 3.

In some social science projects you will not be collecting information directly from human subjects. Instead, you might consult the census bureau, voting records, statistical abstracts and yearbooks, or presidential reports. The compilation of data from these sources has the same requirement of replication, so you must cite your sources.

The *results* section presents the information you have discovered. The actual form of the presentation can vary, from verbal descriptions to complicated statistical calculations. Later in this chapter we describe in detail the uses of tables and figures to organize your data. You must distinguish between these organized presentations of results and the raw data. If you have carried out a statistical calculation using a computer, the raw data of the study will include the computer printouts and the data you fed the computer. If you have used interviews, your raw data will include the answered questionnaire forms. You do not present these cumbersome items in the results section. You must categorize, classify, or tabulate these raw data in some standard way.

Conclusions are the interpretations of those results. These interpretations explain the importance and relevance of the findings to the rest of the field. In order to write a conclusion, you must draw upon the background presented in the introduction.

To sum up the special purpose of each of these four sections of a paper: The introductory section should answer the question "What led you to do this study, and why is it important?" The methods section should answer the question "How did you go about studying this matter?" This question should be answered in a way that allows the reader to repeat what you have done. The results section should answer the question "What did you find out?" The concluding section should answer the question "What do the results mean?"

Writing the first draft

Sitting down and writing the paper that describes your findings may seem almost anticlimactic after all the work that you have done in collecting your findings. You have already planned your research question, looked up some background on it in the library, gathered your data or findings, and armed yourself with knowledge about the different parts of this paper. If statistical analyses are required, you have done them already. And here you are at the beginning again. But if you start your task of writing with the methods section, you may find that you can quite painlessly report your procedure and, by doing so, complete a whole section of your first draft.

Drafting the methods section

This section of the paper describes how you collected the findings. Understanding the method appropriate to each discipline gets you to the heart of the discipline itself. We do not intend to present an exhaustive classification of methods. But we do present below two examples of widely differing methods for approaching questions in the social sciences:

1 How fast is the world population increasing and what will it be in 2100? In 2200?
Method: A mathematical prediction based on statistics, data from demography, and demographic laws.

2 How does a "fence" avoid arrest for possession of stolen goods?
Method: Field work with a fence and/or other persons knowledgeable in the area, for example, detectives. Description of method would include characteristics of persons talked to, circumstances in which interviews took place, questions asked, retest strategies, and so on.

Students often find the methods section the easiest one to write because it is based on very concrete elements. On your first draft do not be afraid to use writer-based prose (chapter 1). You can make the transformation to reader-based prose on subsequent drafts. The following passage will serve for a first-draft attempt:

```
I decided to use the Navajo Indians as my native
group because they were the best integrated while
still maintaining a separate identity. Then I
determined which social role was. . . .
```

When you revise, you will abstract from this narrative only what the reader needs to know about the effect of your methodological decisions. Your reader does not need to know how or when you decided to do what. In your revision you might simply identify the Navajo Indians as an integrated group that still maintains a separate identity. But the first-draft account of your discovery process may be necessary to you. Once you record your activities in an order that is meaningful to you, you can more easily rearrange these elements in a form that is useful to a reader.

Drafting the results section

This section contains the description of the findings. The form of presentation and the very definition of findings vary as widely as the content of the disciplines in the social sciences. Findings may be presented in words, graphs, numbers, tables, flow charts, and formulas. We describe below the most commonly used forms for the report of your findings.

Words. You might be surprised to find words included as a form of presentation in a scientific paper. Sometimes students assume that to be scientific is to be numerical, but this is a mistake. It is quite possible to do research and collect information and then present it entirely in prose. The idea that words are somehow unscientific is not only false—for it rules out a great deal of perfectly respectable social science—but this misconception leads to a serious flaw in writing scientific papers: the appearance of uninterpreted numbers and diagrams. When you present your findings in numerical form, you must also explain them to your reader in words. Words are not just an alternative form of presenting the same results. Prose and diagrams and tables of numbers serve different purposes and communicate differently. If you want your reader to grasp the relationship between, say, inflation and war, then it is best to present the data in a graph. If you are presenting geographical information, then the reader needs a map. But neither the graph nor the map can stand by itself. It is an error to present findings in prose alone when a map is called for. The map will communicate more effectively part of the information you wish to communicate. It is equally an error to present the map or graph without sufficient verbal interpretation. The forms should be seen as complementary rather than as exclusive alternatives.

We present below an excerpt from a criminologist's case study of a "fence" (a receiver of stolen goods). Although the criminologist spent two years on his research, nowhere in his book does he use charts, tables, or even percentage points to present his findings. He conducted systematic interviews with the fence and with thieves who dealt with the fence. The criminologist also systematically observed and recorded a full range of pertinent activities. These written records and interviews constitute the criminologist's findings, which must in this case be reported in words. If your own findings are based on close observations and interviews, you may decide to report your findings in words only. If so, reread chapter 10 on case studies, since you will use many techniques similar to those described there.

Vincent is a businessman; he buys and sells merchandise in order to make a profit. Some of his merchandise is stolen; some of it is not. There is only one advantage to trading in stolen goods: one can buy them cheaper than legitimate goods and thus make a greater profit.

At any given moment, roughly eighty percent of the retail stock on Vincent's shelves is legitimate. This does not mean that the merchandise costs the same as it would in a department store. Rather, Vincent prides himself in buying dead stock, damaged merchandise, factory close-outs, overruns, and the like at especially low prices. Having traded legally and illegally for more than twenty years, Vincent enjoys a large number of contacts in the business world whom he solicits for such buys. For example, Vincent recently bought three cases of name-brand wigs from a friend in a drug distribution center. In drugstores the wigs normally sold for $7.99, but the drugstores that bought them found them difficult to sell even when they were marked down to $5.99. Thus the supply house found itself stuck with cases of wigs no one would buy. Vincent bought three cases for $125. At 120 wigs per case, that represents a wholesale cost to Vincent of 35¢ per wig. Although the price tag on them in his store reads $6.00, Vincent is selling them quickly at $4.00.

Vincent has a number of explanations for why he is able to sell legitimate merchandise that a neighborhood drug, clothing, variety, or general merchandise store cannot sell.

• • •

Vincent's aggressive but pleasant salesmanship and his lower prices on legitimate merchandise are important factors in keeping his customers coming back. The fact that his customers know he has stolen merchandise to sell at prices lower than at any legitimate outlet also figures importantly in his trade in legitimate goods.

• • •

Far more important to Vincent's business than the psychological edge his trade in legitimate goods gives him in dealing with retail customers are the multiple advantages that such a legitimate business identity gives to his trade in stolen merchandise. Collectively, these advantages are commonly referred to as a "front." To explain the interplay between illegal and legal trade which constitutes the front, it is necessary to explicate the legal elements of the offense of receiving stolen goods.

Receiving stolen goods can be legally adjudged a crime if and only if it is proven that (1) the goods in question are in fact stolen goods; (2) the accused did in fact have them in his possession; and (3) he had reasonable cause to know they were stolen. In running his fencing business Vincent constantly employs procedures that render the discovery or proof of one or more of these elements difficult or impossible.[1]

The above extract comes from a book that, although directed to other criminologists, was of interest also to a larger audience. The combination of these facts—that it comes from a book and that it has a wider audience—means that its form of writing is not typical of the writing scientists do when addressing one another in professional journals. There the prose is typically more dense than in the above example, and it also typically contains more technical terms. When writing for journals, authors tend to be more conscious of restricted space and so pack their sentences with

1 Reprinted with permission of Macmillan Publishing Co., Inc. from *The Professional Fence* by Carl B. Klockars. Copyright © 1974 by Carl B. Klockars. Pp. 77–80.

information. Here is an example from a specialized journal in anthropology (the definitions were provided as part of the results of the study):

Examination of residence histories indicates that most couples follow one of three main residence possibilities: (1) a couple establishes immediate neolocality at the outset of marriage and lives in a house separate from their respective families of orientation throughout their marriage. (2) A couple lives in uxori- or virilocality for a number of years and then eventually moves into its own home. (3) A couple lives uxori- or virilocally at the outset of marriage and remains so permanently until the parents die; the younger couple then has the house to itself. In turn, when the next generation marries, one child in each household almost always follows the last pattern of permanent residence at home, while other children will follow pattern 1 or 2 of immediate or eventual neolocality. . . .

• • •

1. Neolocality: a couple lives in a house separate from the families of either spouse.
2. Uxorilocality: a couple lives with the wife's family (i.e., in the home of the wife's parents).
3. Virilocality: a couple lives with the husband's family (i.e., in his home).
4. Ambilocality: a couple may live either with the wife's or the husband's family, depending on personal choice (which does not preclude the possibility of a later shift to some other form of residence.[2]

Diagrams using words. Prose, as exemplified in the previous section, describes the relationship between ideas linearly. That is, you must read from beginning to end, line after line, left to right, over and over again, until you understand the ideas presented. The relationships being explained might take a paragraph or a page to present. For some prose, with long complicated sentences, understanding necessarily comes slowly. Social science writers often aid the reader's comprehension of prose by adding visual representation. A diagram, like a map, shows what items or ideas are related to other ideas. The visual representation alone cannot explain the ideas, but when added to the prose explanation, the visual form illuminates relationships and provides a means of understanding and remembering. The visual presentation may be a diagram, a table of organization, a flow chart, or a schematic drawing. Usually boxes containing words stand for the concepts, and the particular layout—directional arrows, columns—indicates the relationships among the concepts. In the example below, an article on unemployment includes this sentence: "The total population was divided into three categories: those not in the labor force, those under the age of 16 years and in school, and those in the

2 May Ebihara, "Residence Patterns in a Khmer Peasant Village," in *Anthropology and the Climate of Opinion*, ed. Stanley A. Freed, (New York: The New York Academy of Sciences, 1977).

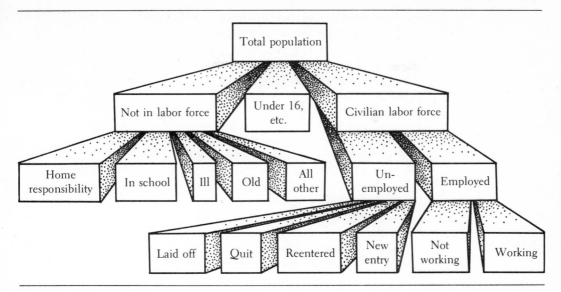

Total population

Not in labor force | Under 16, etc. | Civilian labor force

Home responsibility | In school | Ill | Old | All other | Un-employed | Employed

Laid off | Quit | Reentered | New entry | Not working | Working

FIGURE 11.1
*Population in various
employment
categories. (From*
Macroeconomics:
Understanding
National Income,
Inflation, and
Unemployment *by
Edwin G. Dolan with
the collaboration of
David E. Lindsey.
Copyright © 1977 by
The Dryden Press, a
division of Holt,
Rinehart and
Winston. Reprinted by
permission of Holt,
Rinehart and
Winston.)*

civilian labor force, whether working at present or not." The information communicated by this sentence is also presented in the diagram in figure 11.1. In little more space than is taken by the sentence, the diagram presents not only the three classes mentioned by the sentence, but also two other levels of classification and thirteen further classes. The diagram provides an instantaneous representation of the concepts, and the reader can see the relationships among concepts all at once.

You may decide that the concepts presented in the above example are simple enough to be explained without the aid of a diagram, and indeed you should be selective about the number of diagrams that you finally present. You will want to use only one or two at most in your finished paper. But, as we point out in chapter 2, diagrams, flow charts, and tables can be useful to you in the draft stage, even if you decide not to use a particular diagram or table in your finished paper. Sometimes you need to see the pertinent relationships graphically before you can write connected prose. Diagrams, flow charts, photographs, maps, tables, graphs, and charts may be helpful to you or to your reader in clarifying complex relationships. Although you do not need to devise a graphic representation for every set of relationships in your findings, you do need to explain every graphic representation in words.

Photographs and maps. Social scientists sometimes present findings in the form of photographs and maps. Anthropologists, economists, and, of course, geographers are more likely to use these illustrations. Social scientists use photographs for accurate descriptions, not for aesthetic pleasure, so students must limit the number to a few and use them only when photographs are the best means for clarifying a description. Although you may see large numbers of photographs or drawings in social science texts, especially in introductory courses, the text has aims different from your paper. The numerous photographs in texts do more than illustrate the content; they are presented to catch the eye of the reader. Do not use photographs or drawings in a report merely to interest the reader. You must assume instead that the reader is interested in the clear presentation of the findings themselves.

The two photographs presented in figure 11.2 illustrate a study of ritualized gift giving in modern Japanese society. In the first picture we see that although the analysis is of present-day activities, the women are wearing the traditional robes, not modern dress, and the gifts are being presented in a ritualistic pose. That pose would be difficult to describe without a picture. In the second photograph we can look at the wrapped packages and try for ourselves to guess the contents of each before we read what the subjects of the experiment guessed. When we do read these findings, they will mean more to us because of our experience with the photograph. Before you read the caption, try to guess the contents of each gift.

As a second example, figure 11.3 is a schematic drawing of a cave, called Shanidar IV. This drawing comes from a paper of just four pages. In earlier papers the author, Solecki, had reported the existence of the cave. In this paper he argues that the inhabitants of the cave must have had a form of religious life because he found materials with pollen content among the Neanderthal remains in the cave. If there were flowers in the cave, he says, then there were funerary rites, and therefore religion. It becomes critical, then, to show exactly the relationship between the location of the bones in the cave and the location of the pollen samples. He shows this relationship with the drawing in figure 11.3.

Tables. Tables are the most common form for presenting findings. They are used in all disciplines, although their use is greater in economics than in anthropology. Researchers use tables to summarize their findings in numbers or percentages of items in a category. These tables vary in degree of sophistication and complexity. Newspapers or newsletters may publish a table describing the number of children enrolled in each grade in a school district, intending that table to be read by lay people. Or a journal article in the social sciences may publish descriptive research findings in tabular form to communicate with peers in the discipline.

Suppose you have collected data about the occupations pursued by graduate students of history after they received their bachelor's degree but before they entered graduate study. You would present those findings as shown in table A. A second example, one that you might present for an economics course, reports the effects of sex and education on income (table B). Tables are used to divide information into various categories; tables A and B use columns and spaces for six occupations, six levels of education, and the two sexes.

One purpose of a table is to help you to make comparisons between

FIGURE 11.2
Two uses of photographs to report findings. The top photo is a recreation based on a photograph in the study. The bottom photograph is from the study and shows wrapped gifts whose contents were guessed by the Glasgow sample. A, Gift box containing tea; B, luxury bath soap; C, small bottle of whiskey; D, box of chocolates; E, large bottle of whiskey; F, bath towel. [From Helmut Morsbach, "The Psychological Importance of Ritualized Gift Exchange in Modern Japan," in Anthropology and the Climate of Opinion, ed. Stanley A. Freed (New York: The New York Academy of Sciences, 1977). Used with permission of Dr. H. Morsbach, Glasgow University, Scotland.]

various columns of information. If you had conducted a study of ritual gift-giving like Morsbach's, then you would have collected data on the accuracy with which selected individuals from Tokyo and from Glasgow guessed the contents of the wrapped gifts. You might have percentages of the accurate guesses from each sample group. You would then construct a table showing the percentages of accurate guesses. The table would also show the results of a statistical test determining the significance level of

245   *Reporting Findings in the Social Sciences*

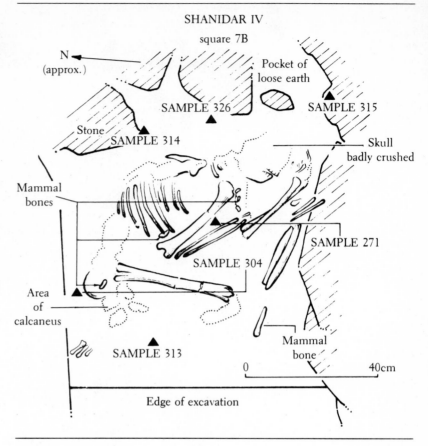

FIGURE 11.3
Using a map to report findings. [From Ralph S. Solecki, "The Implications of the Shanidar Cave Neanderthal Flower Burial," in Anthropology and the Climate of Opinion, *ed. Stanley A. Freed (New York: The New York Academy of Sciences, 1977), p. 116. Used with permission from The New York Academy of Sciences and from Ralph S. Solecki, Columbia University.]*

SHANIDAR IV

square 7B

N (approx.)

Pocket of loose earth

SAMPLE 326

SAMPLE 315

Stone

SAMPLE 314

Skull badly crushed

Mammal bones

SAMPLE 271

SAMPLE 304

Area of calcaneus

Mammal bone

SAMPLE 313

0   40cm

Edge of excavation

TABLE A
Occupation Preceding Entry to
Graduate School in History (in %)

Occupation	Male	Female
Unemployed	11	38
Waiting Tables	14	14
Other Blue Collar	33	24
Clerical	5	8
Professional	7	5
Self-employed	30	11

(The numbers presented here do not represent real data.)

TABLE B
Median Earned Income of People 22 and Older
(Rounded to the nearest $100)

Level of Education Completed	Male	Female
1–8 years	3,900	3,400
9–11 years	9,700	6,300
12 years	13,700	9,200
1–2 years of college	14,000	11,600
3 years	18,300	13,200
4 or more years of college	20,400	15,100

(The numbers presented here do not represent real data.)

the difference between the groups. The statistical test indicates whether the differences are statistically significant or not. Table 11.1, which comes from Morsbach, is a model of a table you might have constructed from your findings.

The table you construct must have two labels: the table number corresponding to the sequence of tables in the paper, and the title of the table. Also, each column has a subtitle describing it. Even though the table presents a great deal of information, you must explain that graphic information in the body of your paper. You must not assume that the table is self-evident. A table should never stand alone. Sometimes a reader just wants a quick look at your tables to determine, for instance, how your groups differed. Sometimes the reader may want to read a description of all your results. In your results section you might provide a prose explanation of your table:

As table 11.1 indicates, the Japanese adults guessed more accurately than the Scots the

TABLE 11.1
Accuracy of guessing the contents of wrapped gifts

| | Percentage correct | | | |
| | Tokyo sample | Glasgow sample | | |
Items	*(n = 26)*	*(n = 38)*	*Significance level**	*Group more accurate*
Large bottle of whiskey	92%	69%	$p < .001$	Tokyo
Gift box containing tea	4%	3%	n.s.	—
Bath towel	92%	24%	$p < .001$	Tokyo
Small bottle of whiskey	12%	42%	$p < .10$	Glasgow
Luxury bath soap	73%	32%	$p < .01$	Tokyo

Source: Helmut Morsbach, "The Psychological Importance of Ritualized Gift Exchange in Modern Japan," in Anthropology and the Climate of Opinion, *ed. Stanley A. Freed (New York: The New York Academy of Sciences, 1977), p. 106.*
*Chi-square test or Fisher exact probability test.

packages containing the large bottle of whiskey, the bath towel, and the luxury soap. In contrast, the Scottish adults guessed the small bottle of whiskey slightly more accurately than the Japanese, and the tea was not guessed accurately by either group. The Japanese had a particularly high (92 percent) level of accuracy when guessing the large whiskey and the bath towel; the Scots did not guess any gift at the same high rate, although their most accurate guessing was on the large bottle of whiskey.

Graphs and charts. Researchers also make extensive use of graphs to present their findings. Graphs show the relationship between two or more variables. Suppose you were studying the relationship between historical time and world population. First you want to show the steady population figure for many hundreds of years and then the rapid increase since 1900. Then you want to project the world population in the year 2000. You would present the information you accumulated in a graph with one variable, years, on the horizontal axis and the other variable, world population, on the vertical axis. The relationships between these two variables are described by the line, increasing very, very gradually at first, and then extremely rapidly. See figure 11.4.

The visual representation of the dramatic change in population at the turn of the century can best be presented by a graph, not by words alone.

FIGURE 11.4
Using line graphs to present findings.
[*Based on UNA-USA National Policy Panel on World Population,* World Population: A Challenge to the United Nations and Its System of Agencies *(New York: United Nations Association of the USA, 1969), p. 12.*]

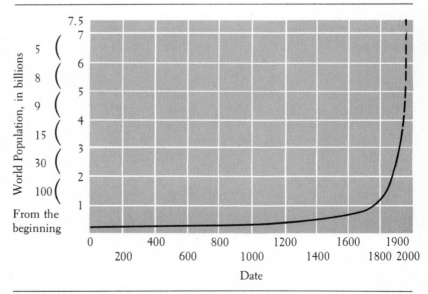

In a single rapid movement of the eye as we look at the graph in figure 11.4, we see the dimensions of change in world population, a concept that would require many words to describe.

Researchers also use a figure known as a bar graph to show relationships between variables. If you were comparing population and gross national product in developed countries and less developed ones, you would have obtained information that you could present in percentages or fractions. (See figure 11.5.) Using a bar graph with differences in the shading and length of the bars, you could show that developed countries have a smaller percent of the world population and a much larger percent of the gross product of the world. In contrast, the less developed countries have a larger percent of world population and a very small percent of the world's gross product. Thus, compared to the developed countries, the less developed countries have more people sharing a much smaller gross national product. This comparison of the countries gives us an inverse relationship. Even a reader not accustomed to interpreting graphic figures can understand these obvious differences in shading and length. A bar graph can clarify your findings.

After you have made a preliminary decision about the verbal and graphic means that you will use to present your results, you should next examine your findings in comparison with your original expectations. When you look at your original hypothesis, which should be carefully recorded in your notes, you may discover that your findings do not fit exactly with your earlier expectations. Don't worry! Even in the work of professional social scientists, findings don't fit expectations exactly. If

FIGURE 11.5
Using bar graphs to present findings.
[*Based on UNA-USA National Policy Panel on World Population,* World Population: A Challenge to the United Nations and Its System of Agencies *(New York: United Nations Association of the USA, 1969), p. 27.*]

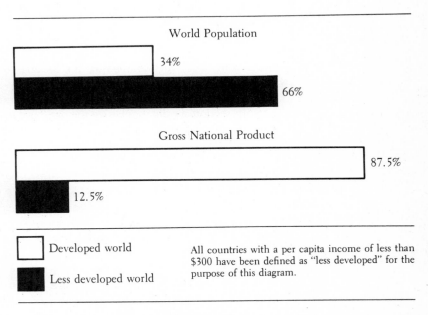

World Population

34%

66%

Gross National Product

87.5%

12.5%

☐ Developed world

■ Less developed world

All countries with a per capita income of less than $300 have been defined as "less developed" for the purpose of this diagram.

social scientists could predict human and societal behavior perfectly, they would design crystal balls, not research techniques.

Then you must examine your raw data again. To gain a new perspective, try some of the strategies explained in chapter 2. Reexamine the findings from a viewpoint different from your original research question. Focus on another variable, for example. Frequently, students have raw data that they do not use fully, so be sure you have been thorough in converting pertinent findings into paragraphs, tables, graphs, or statistical analyses.

As you begin writing the *results* section, make a list of the findings. You have several options in presenting them. You may want to group those that are most closely related. If you have extensive findings, they may call for subtitles and subsections. You may decide to present the more mundane findings first and build up to your most important or surprising results, devoting more space to what is more important. Or you may prefer to begin with what is most important and then go on to present the rest of your data.

If you have used statistical tests on your findings, subordinate the description of these tests. When you first try a social science report, you may be tempted to make the statistical test the focus of the results section. This tendency is understandable because it is natural to feel that the correct application of a statistical test is by itself a significant achievement. Still, that inappropriate focus is a subtle violation of the conventions of scientific reports. Here is an example of a student's first attempt to record his use of statistical tests:

```
Several chi—square tests of differences between
samples were performed comparing the Scottish and
Japanese samples for each gift.
```

More experienced writers emphasize the findings and use a more subtle way to present the statistical test.

The following example conforms to the convention that the prose in the results section should emphasize the data, not the statistical tests. The chi-square statistical test can be put in a footnote or in a subordinate part of the sentence.

```
    Table 11.1 shows that the guesses of Japanese
students about the contents of 3 of the wrapped
gifts were correct significantly more often than
the guesses of the Scottish students (χ² = a, p.
< .05).* In contrast, the Scottish students
were significantly more adept at guessing the
contents of the packages containing the small
bottle of whiskey. Both groups were inaccurate in
their guesses about the contents of the packages
```

which contained tea. Here the difference between
the two groups was not significant.

---

*χ^2 means the statistical test used to calculate
the degree of difference in the responses of the
Scottish and Japanese groups. a is the number
obtained by performing the χ^2 tests on guesses
for each gift. p means the probability that a is
not this large merely because of chance. This
probability must be less than 5 chances out of
100 (< .05). When researchers obtain a
probability level < .05, they consider the
difference to be "significant."

Drafting the introduction   First write a statement describing the purpose of the study. Many students overlook this step, probably because their purpose is so obvious to them. But consider your readers. They need a clear statement of purpose right away if they are to have a context in which to read your paper.

You must next present a review of relevant background material. It may help to view your introduction as a mini term paper, presenting what other researchers have found about the problem that you address in your study. Consequently, rereading chapter 9 may be useful at this point. Before you collected your own findings, you did a great deal of reading and recording in the library. Now that you know the results of your own study, use your own findings to guide you in selecting and ordering this library material. You may even have to return to the library to look up background information on findings that you did not expect to have and about which you therefore did not collect any background material.

Drafting the conclusion   This section has two purposes. One is to summarize your findings in a sentence or two without all the more technical aides—visual and statistical—you used in describing them in the results section, which precedes this one. The second purpose is to discuss the implications of your findings. What do your results mean? Why are they important? In discussing the implications, you are concerned with linking your particular results to the background information you cited in the introduction. You should suggest that your findings give further support for and/or disagree with some previous research. In addition, you should link your findings to the theoretical orientation from which both your work and the other cited work grow. In making this connection you may use techniques of comparison and contrast, discussed fully in chapter 8.

And finally, you should put both the theoretical position and the findings in some larger social science context. Reread pages 201–204 of chapter 8 on papers of speculation. As you write your conclusion, you are actually speculating about the relevance of your own work to general problems in the discipline.

Revising

You have written a first draft of four different sections of a paper. Now you must shape these fragments into one coherent paper. Although we have emphasized the four separate sections of this paper to make writing the first draft a more manageable task, the paper must be a readable single unit when you complete the finished product.

Frequently papers of this type are not long. Papers that report findings do not include (unless they are doctoral dissertations) an exhaustive review of the literature on the subject. Rather, you are writing the paper to report and explain your own findings. In revising your paper, be sure that everything in the paper is related to those findings. You may be particularly tempted to include too much in your introduction. Avoid going off on tangents—even interesting ones. Be sure that you show the relationship of all background material to the study at hand.

Be sure that you convert writer-based prose to reader-based prose (chapter 1). Check your methods and results sections in particular to transform the narrative of what you did and why you did it into an account of what the reader needs to know about your procedures and about your findings.

Next check for the following courtesies, which will convey to your reader that you know how professional social scientists behave when they present their research:

1 Use headings for your tables, graphs, and photographs. Use both "Table 1" or "Figure 1" numbered sequentially throughout your paper and a *title* for your graphic representation, e.g., "Present-day gift exchange."

2 Be sure that you explain all tables and figures in the body of your paper. Like the bride on the wedding cake, tables and figures never stand alone.

3 Title your paper in a way that makes clear what your study is about.

4 Use section titles. Instructors in almost all social science disciplines expect to find subheadings for at least the main sections of your paper: Introduction, Methods, and so forth. In some disciplines, you are expected to divide each section further with pertinent subheadings. Look at the form of the papers you have read during your research. The actual practice of these social scientists is a helpful guide for your decisions.

5 Use the proper form of documentation (chapter 5) to write your reference list.

6 Write a brief (often only a 100-word) summary, using the guidelines in chapters 5 and 13. Instructors in many social science fields will expect this abstract to accompany your full paper.

7 Use your dictionary and grammar handbook to check your paper for accuracy in typing and spelling, punctuation, and conformity to standard usage. You may have been meticulous in the procedures you used for collecting your data, but you will finally look sloppy if your finished draft is sprinkled with many misspellings and typographical errors.

Drafting and revising your report in the ways we have described will help you to analyze what you have found and then to report that analysis to other apprentice social scientists.

QUESTIONS   1 What is the standard structure for writing up your findings in a social science paper? Why is it often useful to draft the sections in an order different from the final order?

2 What are the differences between the results section and the discussion section?

3 When are visual presentations most useful? Give examples.

4 What is accomplished by the use of the photographs in figure 11.2?

EXERCISES   1 Consider the six sample questions given at the beginning of the chapter and try to identify the research methods that would be required to answer each.

2 Read the selection on the "fence." From reading this passage, can you tell anything about the methods that the researcher used?

3 In this chapter we have drawn inferences from figures 11.1, 11.4, 11.5, and tables 11.1, A, and B. Study these visual presentations and try to infer other information from them. Make a list of the inferences that you think can be made from the figures and tables and compare them with lists made by classmates.

4 Using the definitions that are provided, rewrite the passage from the journal article on page 242 so that a classmate could easily understand it.

Cancer (
G. Scat
(1949).
V. L. W
J. Gilbe
48, 119 (
W. L. M
docrinol
A. B. Ol
1975).
A. B. O
1977).
J. Solom
p. 875.
R. H. Sh
Fed. Am

drocannabinol wi

trogen Receptor

periments with Δ^9-tetr

th rat uterine cytosol

rtheless significant, co

se data support, at the

estrogenic activity (at

trogen-like binding su

causes a primary estro

Writing in the
Natural Sciences

Med. 28
Found.
R. C. K
Engl. J.
M. A. A
. Solom
uck, A.
. Solom
Med. 291
R. C. K
rds, J.
New Yor
R. M. V
Rawitch,
1976).
A. Jakut

Competition of Δ⁹-
Estrogen in Rat U

Abstract. *Direct com
nd estradiol in bindin
hat Δ^9-THC was a wea
oplasmic estrogen rec
ations that Δ^9-THC h
strogen receptors). M
t the level of estrogen*

12 Recording Observations in the Natural Sciences

The types of writing that you do in a science laboratory have more in common with writing tasks in the humanities and social sciences than you might think. The topics are different, of course, but for many science assignments you can use modes of writing that you have learned and employed in other courses. For example, as you make notes in your laboratory notebook, you are mainly narrating procedures and describing results. Later, when you write up your lab report, you will classify and analyze your findings in order to draw inferences from them. In the laboratory, however, these writing tasks are used to facilitate a particular method of problem solving, the scientific method.

To understand the role of writing in the laboratory, you must first understand the processes and purposes of the scientific method of investigation. This method is a way to examine and understand the physical world by asking questions and answering them through empirical investigation. In the sciences we derive knowledge from observation and experimentation, and the purpose of the knowledge is to establish (to confirm or disprove) principles by which we understand the physical universe. This method usually begins with an idea or a question, for example, the speculation, which we develop in later chapters, that perhaps the reason that men who are heavy marihuana users develop enlarged breasts is that marihuana acts like a female hormone. This idea must be molded into a hypothesis, or a working thesis ("Let's see if the active ingredient of marihuana attaches to the same chemical binding in the uterus as the female hormone estrogen"). Scientists then test the hypothesis in the laboratory under carefully controlled conditions. They construct an experiment which is designed either to prove or disprove the hypothesis; if successful, this experiment is reported to other scientists (chapter 14).

Writing is central to this discovery and testing process. Without writing, a scientist could not get to the end of an experiment and remember it accurately enough to describe it in the detail necessary for other scientists to replicate it. A report of findings must include an accurate description of the experimental design and a careful narration of the working out of the design in addition to an account of the findings. These essential parts of the report must be constructed from notes.

College freshmen are almost never required to carry out the entire process from formulating a hypothesis to reporting the results of an experiment, but college entry-level courses in science usually include a laboratory experience to introduce students to the methods that scientists use to solve problems. In the first instance, laboratory exercises are designed to acquaint students with course content. By requiring students to report classic experiments or observations, these courses also teach the skills an experienced scientist needs, especially careful technique and thorough recording. These emphases are continued through upper-level courses.

The evaluation of laboratory technique reflects the priorities that instructors attach to the experience. At a minimum, the instructor compares the student's results with expected results (Does the compound synthesized in chemistry lab melt in the correct temperature range, indicating that the synthesis was successful? If not, has the student adequately explained the discrepancy?). In most introductory courses, however, instructors evaluate students' notebooks not only for results, but also for thoroughness and accuracy in describing the experiment. Also, it is common for students to have to study the material recorded in their notebooks so that they can take special quizzes called "lab practicals." These tests are designed to discover whether students are familiar with the procedures as well as the results of laboratory exercises. In brief, science stresses method as well as results, and students need to give attention to understanding and remembering laboratory technique as they carry it out.

It is the purpose of this chapter, and of chapter 13, to familiarize you in detail with the writing demands of laboratory work in the sciences and to prepare you to use writing to become a more effective science student.

Purpose of the laboratory notebook

All experimenters, from entry-level undergraduates to professional scientists, keep a record of laboratory work. This record, regardless of its format, is called a laboratory notebook. Its purpose is to provide a complete and accurate account of the testing of a hypothesis in the controlled environment of the laboratory.

For professional scientists, the laboratory notebook acts as an aid to memory and will eventually provide the details for their research reports (chapter 13). Not only do scientists need a complete and well-organized record of each different experiment, but as they change one variable in the same experiment, they must have detailed records to compare results. Furthermore, research can take months or years to complete, so scientists often have to go back to their early notes to finish a project. Since notebooks are often shared with co-workers, scientists need to give attention to recording in a fashion that can be quickly and easily understood by others. A carefully prepared laboratory notebook may make all the difference in certain legal situations, when the notebook may have to serve as proof of a discovery. In short, working scientists invest great care in their laboratory notes.

While undergraduate notebooks do not serve as many purposes, they are, nevertheless, critically important in their own contexts. They assist you in carrying out, understanding, and explaining your laboratory experiences. They are an invaluable record for review, since you may be studying the material weeks or months after the experience. Your instructor will read your lab notebook to see if you understand the techniques of working scientists. Consequently, it is in your interest to invest time and care in the laboratory notebook.

Writing in the laboratory notebook

Your laboratory notebook might be a commercially produced fill-in-the-blank workbook or a regular notebook in which you record information according to your instructor's directions. Whatever the style, notebooks share a common requirement: all are designed for your original, on-the-spot records of your laboratory activities. As you carry out the assigned procedures, you should record the results immediately. In a workbook, space will be provided; in your own notebook, you should record your notes in complete sentences. Resist shorthand record keeping. Writing complete sentences will ensure that you understand the concepts with which you are dealing. Later on, when you study your lab notebook, full sentences will provide a clear, unambiguous record of your procedures and results. The importance of complete sentences is illustrated in figure 12.1, which shows a sample page from a chemistry workbook.

FIGURE 12.1
(on facing page)
A *sample page from a chemistry workbook.*
[*From* Laboratory Manual for Chemistry: Basic Concepts and Contemporary Applications *by Leonard S. Wasserman.* © *1974 by Wadsworth Publishing Company, Inc., Belmont, California 94002. Reprinted by permission of the publisher.*]

Notice that the two-word answer "universal solvent" has been marked incomplete. While these words may seem very clear when written, especially in a workbook format, which has a discussion paragraph right next to the question, the meaning will fade, and at exam time you may well have to waste time in deciphering notes that you lazily recorded in abbreviated form. Make your notes complete in themselves.

Writing in complete sentences has another, more immediate advantage. Doing so allows you to know, before you leave the lab, if you understand completely the purposes of the assignment. A complete sentence has a structure that connects ideas and imparts meaning, and scientists, like English majors, need to make and understand connections. Forming your responses in connected discourse reveals gaps in your understanding while the instructor is still available, and allows you to ask intelligent questions about unclear procedures or other difficulties. For example, this question appears in a chemistry lab exercise on solubility: "Why is CCl_4 used to remove nonpolar oils and grease?"

A student who had read the appropriate material in his textbook could be fairly certain, from the wording of the question, that the answer should

Unit 6

A Study of Solubility, Water Pollution, and Water Purification

Discussion

This series of experiments is concerned with water pollution and purification. Pure water is a colorless, odorless, tasteless liquid. Because it is a universal solvent, natural waters contain a variety of dissolved compounds, including oxygen, carbon dioxide, and, in many areas, even undesirable substances (pollutants). The properties of solutions must be considered to understand both the pollution and purification of water.

Solutions are mixtures of dissolved substance (the *solute*) and the dissolving substance (the *solvent*). Solutions are generally characterized by:
1. homogeneity
2. absence of settling
3. the non-separation of the solute from the solvent by filtration

When a substance is dissolved in water, depending upon the nature of the solute:
1. the individual molecules may be separated and become hydrated (alcohol in water);

$$C_2H_5OH \xrightarrow{H_2O} C_2H_5OH_{(aq)}$$

2. the ions may be separated and become hydrated (NaCl in water);

$$NaCl \xrightarrow{H_2O} Na^+_{(aq)} + Cl^-_{(aq)}$$

3. each individual molecule may be separated into ions and the ions become hydrated

$$HCl \xrightarrow{H_2O} H_3O^+ + Cl^-$$

Polar water molecules pull apart the ions of ionic compounds and separate them from the crystals. The ions are kept separated by additional water molecules which prevent the positive and negative ions from recombining. In a similar manner, the molecules of polar covalent compounds are also separated and kept apart by the polar water molecules.

Prelaboratory Discussion Quiz

Incomplete answer.

1. Why is water readily polluted?

universal solvent

Complete answer.

Water is a universal solvent and consequently many compounds, including pollutants, dissolve in water.

2. What are the characteristics of a solution?

3. What occurs when a substance is dissolved in water?

be, "Carbon tetrachloride is used to remove nonpolar oils and greases because it is also a nonpolar compound and, therefore, can dissolve the solid greases. CCl_4 is also miscible with liquid oils." But, at the same time, part of the lab experiment that yielded this answer would also show that soap mixed with water could also dissolve oils and greases. Does this discovery require a more complete, complex answer in which soap and water are compared with carbon tetrachloride? This question should be asked of an instructor before class ends, but to ask it, a student needs to have thought about his responses completely enough to know that a problem exists. Writing provides that occasion.

To make your written answers most useful for immediate understanding or later reference, you should give particular attention to two characteristics of good writing. The first is to write with as much detail as possible. As we said in chapters 2 and 10, observation (and experimentation) should result in concrete and explicit record keeping. Do not estimate; do not leave blank spaces to be filled in later; do not cut corners. The scientific method demands exactness, because scientific theories are based, finally, on hard data.

Second, when narrating procedures, use connecting words to show relationships wherever necessary. Just as philosophers have to show sequence in logical arguments (chapter 2), so scientists must give careful attention to cause-effect relationships and the cumulative nature of scientific experimentation. If appropriate to the format of your lab notebook, you should use words such as *then, consequently, next, because,* and *therefore.*

Revising and correcting the laboratory notebook

Since your notebook is supposed to provide a record of what actually went on in the laboratory, you should make every effort to record the results correctly the first time. Your results should never be copied over to make them neater or better organized. Copying not only wastes time, it introduces the possibility of copying error. Even worse, if your instructor sees a copied version, he may have cause to wonder if you wrote a new version to change results after you realized that the original results failed to confirm the hypothesis.

If you do make errors while recording in the laboratory, correct them as clearly as possible either by erasing or by crossing out and rewriting on the original sheet. If you are uncertain about your on-the-spot composing skills, work out your answer on a piece of scrap paper, then, before you leave the laboratory, copy the answer onto your lab sheet.

If you do make an uncorrectable mistake in your lab notebook, do not tear the sheet out. Simply fold the sheet lengthwise and mark "omit" on the face side. Similarly, if you need to add sheets to your notebook (physiograph tracings or data-laden note sheets), attach them permanently to the appropriate pages. Do not use paperclips.

Format for the laboratory notebook

For many laboratory notebooks, especially in entry-level courses, the formats are already developed by the publisher of your workbook or by your instructor. You will receive instructions for that sort of lab sheet in class or in the lab.

If no format is provided, or if your instructor asks you to develop your own, your obligation is to work out a format that allows you to communicate all major features of an experiment. Every report of an experiment is divided into at least five sections: *title, purpose, materials and methods, results,* and *conclusions.* If your task is a multiple-experiment exercise, you will have to decide whether you should treat each experiment separately or subdivide the major sections within a single report.

Develop a title that describes your experiment. Thus, "The Relationship between Human Pulse, Blood Pressure, Respiration, and Exercise" is a better title than "Experiment #9, Circulation." Next, state briefly, in complete sentences, the purpose of the exercise. Often you can copy the title and purpose directly from your lab manual, giving due credit, of course, to the author of the manual. You will learn more, however, if you record the purpose in your own sentences.

The materials and methods section contains a summary of the procedures used in the experiment. Write out these procedures in complete sentences and organize them into logical paragraphs. Then describe your equipment. You should identify the major pieces of apparatus, unusual chemicals, and laboratory animals. Your identification should also be detailed enough to allow a reader to distinguish between sizes or types of the same equipment (instead of "physiograph," write "physiograph, Grass model 7B"). Drawings illustrating complicated equipment setups and notes on the particular settings used to obtain results from equipment are sometimes useful additions to your lab notes. Professional scientists characteristically record this kind of detail. Figure 12.2 illustrates a page from a physiology notebook showing a record of how equipment was set up and the dial setting that was used to obtain the data.

Sometimes you may paste in a photocopy of the methods section from your lab manual, and you should certainly incorporate any special lab handouts into your notebook. In both cases, read through the material and record any changes you made in the methods. For example, if the chart paper from your physiograph recorder can be set to run at either 1 cm per second or 5 cm per second, but not at any speed in between, you would obviously have to change a statement in your photocopied lab manual methods that says, "with the paper speed at 2 to 3 cm/sec."

The results section is the core of your laboratory record, and it usually consists of a combination of tables or figures and written explanations. Whenever possible, you should make preparations before you enter the lab for tables on which you expect to record data. You can then easily fill in the raw data.

pulse - pressure expt (cont.)   3/31/81

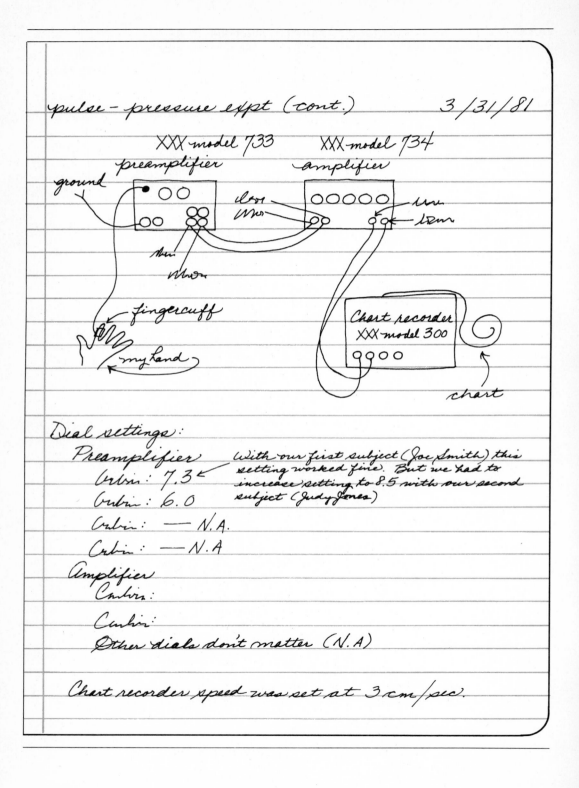

Dial settings:
  Preamplifier
    (dial): 7.3 ← With our first subject (Joe Smith) this setting worked fine. But we had to increase setting to 8.5 with our second subject (Judy Jones)
    (dial): 6.0
    (dial): — N.A.
    (dial): — N.A
  Amplifier
    (dial):

    (dial):
  Other dials don't matter (N.A)

Chart recorder speed was set at 3 cm/sec.

FIGURE 12.2
(on facing page)
*A page from a student
physiology notebook,
showing details needed
in the materials and
methods section.*

You cannot always anticipate events in the laboratory, so no matter how carefully you prepare in advance, there may be times when you find yourself jotting down notes on any convenient piece of scrap paper, even on a paper towel. In that case you should permanently attach these notes to the results section, along with the table you develop to present data. If you use data from chart recorders, then it is appropriate to attach the printout to the results section (figure 12.3).

The conclusion section includes a general summary of the outcome of the experiment (Did the results confirm previous results? Were the results what you had expected?) and possible reasons for the results if they were not what you expected. If your results did turn out as expected, you should comment on that fact. For example, in a discussion of a physiology experiment on pulse pressure, the student included a photocopy of the lab manual's figure illustrating a typical pulse-pressure record and commented on the similarity between the illustration in the manual and the actual recording he had made in the lab. The questions posed in your lab manual should also be answered in this section.

The research notebook

The research notebook is the most advanced form of lab notebook. It contains the complete record for a program of original research, from the development of a hypothesis to the rationale, methodology, results, and conclusion for each experiment. These notebooks are introduced and used primarily in upper-level courses. Although the general procedures used in the research may be described in technical manuals or published research reports, the advanced science student often makes specific changes in methodology necessary for that individual research project. Also, the advanced science student is always on the lookout for unexpected results. Therefore, it is especially important that a research notebook be complete and up to date. In addition, undergraduate research notebooks should be reasonably neat and well organized, for they are usually shared with a faculty adviser.

The format for the research notebook is variable, not only because of individual record-keeping styles, but also because of the physical characteristics of the data. For example, three-ring binders or even manila envelopes are more appropriate than composition-style notebooks if the data appear as long, unwieldy tables and figures. Students, however, usually select a combination of a chronological notebook (a day-by-day account of research activities) and the lab notebook format described in the preceding pages.

We have discussed at several points in this chapter the purposes and uses of laboratory notebooks. In entry-level courses, most of the uses are instructional. However, laboratory notebooks are also indispensable sources for other types of scientific writing. Like research notecards in history or philosophy, lab notebooks can provide the foundation for a full-

electrocardiogram expt (cont)   4/17/81

The QRS complex of the electrocardiogram

This recording done at faster paper speed (25 mm/sec) than previous recordings so that the electrocardiogram would be more spread out for easier labelling.

This recording done at lead V_6 (subject = Joe Smith)

    left arm ⎫
    rt. arm ⎬ — terminal
    left leg ⎭
    chest electrode, + terminal

Selector switch in the $V_1 - V_6$ position

→ put on midaxillary line, even with left nipple

fledged paper. The next chapter will describe such a project, the laboratory report.

QUESTIONS   1 What is the scientific method of investigation?

2 Why is the strict adherence to the scientific method so important in laboratory experiments?

3 What are the primary purposes for keeping a laboratory notebook?

4 What are the most important rules for keeping a laboratory notebook? Identify the purpose for each rule.

EXERCISES   1 Write out in prose form a laboratory experiment that you have recorded in a preprinted laboratory manual. What advantages and disadvantages do you find with each method?

2 As a class, discuss the major similarities and differences between observing in the social sciences and in the natural sciences.

3 Write prose answers to questions two and three on the sample page from the chemistry workbook in figure 12.1.

FIGURE 12.3
(on facing page)
A page from a student physiology notebook, showing information recorded in the results section.

13 The Laboratory Report in the Natural Sciences

The laboratory report is written to describe, document, and communicate the completion of an experiment in a natural science laboratory. When written by a professional scientist, the report presents the results of an original research project, whereas student laboratory reports more commonly present the results of research projects that repeat classic experiments. The report is more often expected of upper-level science students, whereas the laboratory notebook described in chapter 12 is assigned in beginning science courses. Science instructors frequently ask students to write laboratory reports on the following types of questions:

- What are the effects of four different sodium chloride concentrations on the germination of radish seeds?

- How does vigorous exercise affect heart rate and breathing rate in young adult humans?

- What happens when magnesium metal reacts with HCl dissolved in water?

- What is the relation of centripetal force to mass and velocity?

- What amount of work is needed to pull an object varying in mass up an incline varying in height?

Getting started

Before writing the laboratory report you have already accomplished a great deal in the laboratory. You have completed your experiment, and you have kept detailed notes in your laboratory notebook (chapter 12). Now, before you begin writing your laboratory report, you should have an idea of what this report will look like when complete.

The typical lab report is divided into seven sections:

1 Title

2 Abstract

3 Introduction

4 Methods and Materials

5 Results

6 Conclusions

7 References Cited

The laboratory report in the natural sciences has a great deal in common with the report of findings in the social sciences, so you will benefit from reading chapter 11. But note that the natural sciences expect more formalized procedures and format than do the social sciences. The natural sciences are in this way more traditional. And there is indeed a longer tradition of doing and writing up experiments in the natural sciences than in the younger social sciences, where there is more flexibility.

Briefly, the sections of the laboratory report may be characterized in the following way:

Title	Your title need not be a complete sentence, but it should be very explanatory, making clear exactly what was tested in the laboratory exercise.
Abstract	The abstract is a brief summary of your report, not to exceed approximately 250 words.
Introduction	The introduction provides background information and explains the particular problem addressed in the lab exercise.
Methods and Materials	The section on methods and materials is a straightforward explanation of how you did your experiment, including a description of subjects, apparatus, and methods of collecting data.
Results	The results section is a clear, comprehensible description of your data in an organized form. Raw data are rarely presented in a laboratory report, except possibly in an appendix.
Conclusions	This section is a discussion of your results, noting significance and accounting for any discrepancies from predicted results.
References Cited	This section lists all literature cited, including your lab manual or text.

A good lab report should begin, not only before you think about the form of your final paper, but even before you begin the experiment. Before walking into the laboratory, you should know the methods you will use and, if possible, the results you can expect. With this preparation, you will be able to carry out the experiment smoothly, describing the details of your method and recording the appropriate data in your lab notebook. You should begin to write your lab report as soon as possible after the experiment because even with the aid of a lab notebook, memory fades, and certainly you ought to capitalize as soon as possible on your enthusiasm for telling the scientific community about your results.

Writing the first draft

The section on methods and materials is the most straightforward section in your lab report. Here you explain exactly how you did the research. Your explanation should be detailed and clear enough so that another undergraduate could duplicate the experiment, or so that you could duplicate it five years later. While this latter expectation might seem remote to you now, you may be surprised to learn that your professor almost certainly once or twice found himself, years after the fact, referring to one of his own undergraduate laboratory reports. Whether his experience was bad or good, it has almost certainly influenced him to be a demanding judge of the methods and materials section of your lab report. Nonetheless, this section, like the procedures section in chapter 11, is still probably the easiest part of your lab report to write, and we recommend that in your first draft, you write methods and materials first.

The methods section is always written out in complete sentences using the past tense. Although scientists have long favored the passive voice ("Five chemical tests were performed on each unknown compound"), the active voice is now becoming increasingly popular ("I performed five chemical tests on each unknown compound"), and you should try to use both voices in your writing. Remember that it is acceptable to use "I" or "we" in your lab report, if you are objectively reporting what you did. Statements of feeling are inappropriate, but the word "I" is not the culprit here. In fact, the use of the first person makes your style more direct and, therefore, more scientific. Again, as in writing a laboratory notebook, you should exercise some judgment in deciding which details to report. Do mention details such as the brand and model of complicated apparatus ("Grass polygraph, model 7B"), but omit obvious details, such as the brand or size of common laboratory equipment ("Kimax test tubes, 10 ml").

Unless the lab exercise is relatively brief, you may find that a complete recounting of materials and methods is tedious. Ask your instructor if it is acceptable to cite the directions in your lab manual and then to summarize these directions in your laboratory report. Be very careful to note any differences between the materials or methods in the lab assignment "procedure" and those materials and methods that you actually—either purposely or accidentally—employed in your execution of the experiment.

The methods and materials section is often divided into appropriate subsections. For example, in a biology lab report you might divide this section into "subjects" (the animals used in this experiment) and "apparatus" (the equipment used in the experiment). You will probably want to include figures and tables to clarify approaches and experimental design.

Drafting the results section

In this section you present in a clear, easily comprehensible fashion the data that result from your experiment. Usually, you both write out the results and present them in the form of tables or figures. A figure differs from a table in that a table consists only of words or numbers, whereas a figure includes other graphic forms, such as a drawing, graph, picture, flow diagram, or a computer representation. Well-designed figures are generally easier to comprehend and evaluate than tables because of the visual impact. Be very careful in your design of bar or line graphs, since there are rigid conventions dictating their format. Consult your lab manual and if necessary check your preliminary design with your professor to be certain that you have not misinterpreted any of these conventions. Read chapter 11 for suggestions about graphic presentations of data.

Your written statement of results should highlight the most important or interesting findings shown on your figures or tables. Although you should not draw conclusions about your results in this section, it is perfectly acceptable and even desirable to point out trends or identify special features in the data. You should always give a brief explanation of the experiment that yielded the data you are reporting. Scientists tend to read only sections of research reports, so you should become accustomed to supplying context for each section. Even those reading your whole report will appreciate signposts along the way to let them know where they have been and where they are going. Usually a sentence, or just a part of a sentence, will clarify the source of the data (see figure 13.1).

If you have used statistical procedures to analyze your data, you should present key numbers from your calculations as part of your written section on results. Chapter 11 discussed the inclusion of these analyses in your paper. Again, there are specific conventions governing the presentation of these numbers, and you should either consult your lab manual or ask your professor if you are uncertain. Remember that the word "significant" is not used to describe differences in data unless you have carried out accepted statistical procedures and can specify the level of probability ($p < 0.05$) associated with your use of the word "significant."

Drafting the introduction section

The main body of the lab report begins with an introduction, which provides background information and explains the particular problem addressed in the laboratory exercise. In undergraduate lab reports, the background information is usually found in either the course textbook or the lab manual, and the purpose of the lab exercise is explained in the lab manual or assignment sheet. Therefore, the introduction is usually just a rewriting, in your own words, of the material available in your text.

Your tendency in the first draft of this section may be toward the autobiographical; you may want to say something about what this laboratory exercise means to you. Writer-based prose of this kind will not be

Weak wording: failure to write out results; failure to orient reader by restating the experiment.

Better wording.

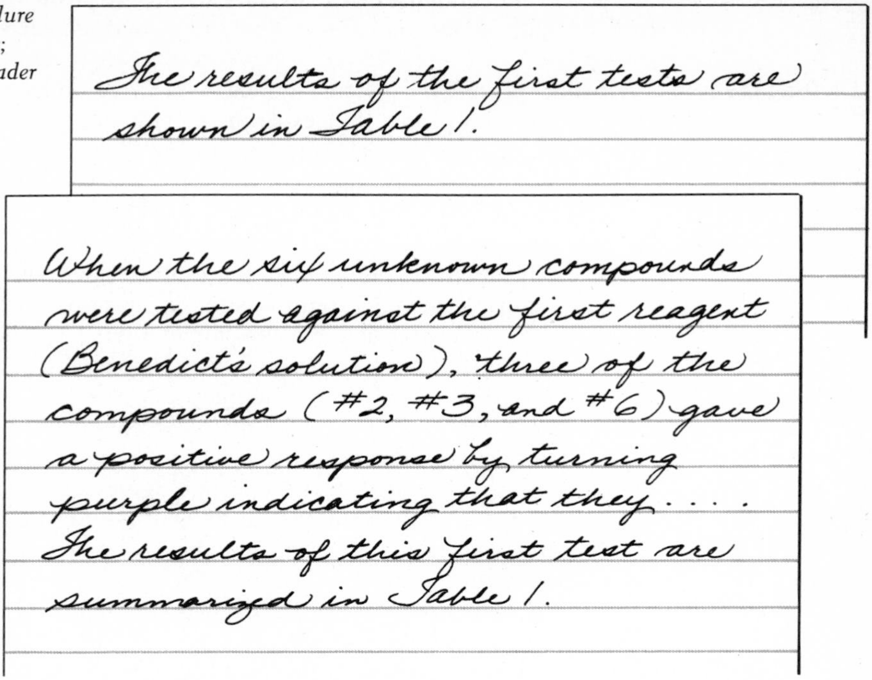
The results of the first tests are shown in Table 1.
When the six unknown compounds were tested against the first reagent (Benedict's solution), three of the compounds (#2, #3, and #6) gave a positive response by turning purple indicating that they. . . .
The results of this first test are summarized in Table 1.

FIGURE 13.1
Providing context in the results section.

appropriate in your finished draft. Even though your own major purpose in doing the lab exercise is to make yourself familiar with a particular laboratory technique, do not say so in your introduction. Keep in mind the broader aim of the laboratory report: to convey information about your work in the laboratory, the why and how, in a form that is clear, explicit, and detailed enough for your readers, who are other apprentice scientists. These apprentice scientists—your classmates—expect you to behave like a scientist, in your writing as well as in your laboratory technique. Your attention to the courtesies of the profession in format and style communicates to your audience that you are learning how scientists behave when they report their research.

As you work to find a clear and explicit form for your introduction, you might try one of these two common sequences:

1 General information; specific information; purpose of the experiment: Begin by presenting the background information and by locating the laboratory exercise within this background information. Close the introduction with an explanation of the purpose of the experiment.

2 History; specific information; purpose of the experiment: Begin by reviewing the historically important research development that led to the

present state of knowledge and by locating the laboratory exercise within these developments. If you choose this strategy, you might also mention additional developments that go beyond the state of knowledge represented by your experiment.

For example, suppose you were introducing a physiology laboratory exercise in which you had measured the number of red blood cells in a given volume of whole blood. If you had enumerated the red blood cells using a special slide (hemocytometer) and a microscope, you might want to mention in your introduction that more sophisticated and entirely automated instruments are now routinely used to do red cell counts in hospitals. Again, close your introduction with a final paragraph explaining the purpose of the experiment. By delaying an explanation of the purpose until the final paragraph, you will have a nice transition to the next section, which will describe the materials and methods that you used in your particular experiment. Although the use of subheadings such as "Materials and Methods" partially relieves the need for transitional sentences, the very best lab reports still prepare the reader for each new section. The resulting clarity is a hallmark of a well-written report.

Your introduction should also reflect a familiarity with both the format and style of writing used in professional research reports and with the more immediate needs of your audience of fellow undergraduates for thorough explanation and clear writing.

The most common writing difficulties in laboratory reports are failures to cope successfully with these demands. Figure 13.2 presents an example of writer-based prose that should eventually be edited.

Drafting the conclusion section

In this section, you present the conclusions you have drawn from your results. You also discuss the importance of your conclusions and try to account for any discrepancies that might have arisen between your results and the predicted results.

In laboratory reports of original research this section is fairly extensive because the new research must be put into the context of previously reported research. In student lab reports, the discussion may be briefer when the results repeat a classic experiment. If your experiment was entirely successful, you can merely report that your results, like the lab results of other science students, again confirm a classic and well-established principle. Be careful to summarize and to cite the statements in your lab manual or textbook that predicted the results. If your professor expects a more extensive discussion section, then you might expand your section by mentioning additional, more detailed information obtained from outside reading. Information of this sort is identical to information used in your introduction, and it is often possible to shift information between the introduction and discussion until a nice balance is achieved.

If your results did not come out as predicted, then you have more to discuss. First you must again justify the validity of your predictions by

no longer used routinely in most hospitals. Instead, the procedure has been mechanized. The blood sample is put in a machine that sends the blood through a small hole, and as the individual cells pass through the hole, they are detected and counted.

Good section that presents the most modern methodology in terms that are easily understood.

Now let's look at the equipment and procedures that I used to do this experiment.

Too friendly. The reader is never addressed directly, or even indirectly, in formal scientific writing.

This entire sentence is a waste of space and might be interpreted as an attempt to pad the report. Even worse, it is patronizing to assume that the reader is unable to see the heading MATERIALS AND METHODS which appears next in the report. Although this sentence might have been well-intended as a transitional sentence, it is too obvious and is best omitted from the final report.

FIGURE 13.2
Writing the introduction to a laboratory report.

locating, summarizing, and citing appropriate material in either your lab manual or in your text. Then you must explain what has caused your particular results rather than the expected results. Unless your own responses are specifically requested by your professor, you should avoid commenting on the pedagogic or entertainment value of the experiment. A comment like, "This experiment was really fun and I learned a lot" is not appropriate.

Drafting the abstract

When the body of your report is complete, you are ready to write your brief abstract. Summarizing your report is a very useful thinking exercise. Abstracts are usually limited to 250 words, and they consist of a single tightly organized paragraph. Your abstract should answer these questions:

1 What methods were used? You should mention important details about the experimental subjects, the approaches, and the procedure. Write these sentences in the past tense.

2 What variables were measured? Use the past tense.

3 What results were obtained? Use the past tense.

4 What conclusions can be drawn from these results? Use the present tense.

A sample abstract from a student laboratory report is illustrated and annotated in figure 13.3. Also see chapter 5 for more general help with summarizing.

Writing a title   The final step in writing your first draft is to provide the report with a title. Avoid simplistic titles. ("Biology Lab Report" or "Radish Seed Experiment") and beware of humorous titles ("How Much Salt Can a Radish Take?"). Because of long-standing traditions in scientific reporting, attempts at humor sound strained and inappropriate.

Revising

After you have written the first draft of the various sections, you can get an impression of the final lab report. If it seems too skimpy, search out additional information from more advanced textbooks or even from the original research articles cited in your lab manual or text. You are not usually expected to locate up-to-date research articles, however.

Now your report can be treated like any other first draft, either by sharing it with fellow students or by putting it away for several days. When you return to it with a fresh perspective, consider these questions: Does your title explain the experiment? Does your abstract provide a concise summary of the experiment? Does your introduction thoroughly explain the experiment so that another undergraduate would understand what was done and why? Is your "Materials and Methods" section complete enough so that another person could duplicate your experiment? Are your results clearly written out so that your reader knows what results are particularly interesting? Are your graphs or tables thoroughly labeled, properly titled, and presented in the most comprehensible format? Does your discussion section explain why certain results could be expected? Does it go on to compare your results to these expected results?

Check your draft for correct details of syntax, punctuation, and spelling. Make sure you have used appropriate organizational structure and paragraphing. Use the subheadings for sections described in this chapter. Remember that scientists are often especially sensitive to sloppy presentation.

Now you are ready to add the references section. Although this paper will have fewer references than the scientific review paper (chapter 14), the references are arranged in the same way. As a bare minimum you need to cite your lab manual or the instructor's handout and your textbook. Of course, if you have read additional references, you should summarize them and cite them in your lab report.

Now prepare final copies of your figures or type out tables. To produce professional-looking figures, draw them first lightly in pencil. Then, when you are certain that they are accurate and correctly drawn, go over them with black ink and erase the pencil lines. Avoid using color whenever

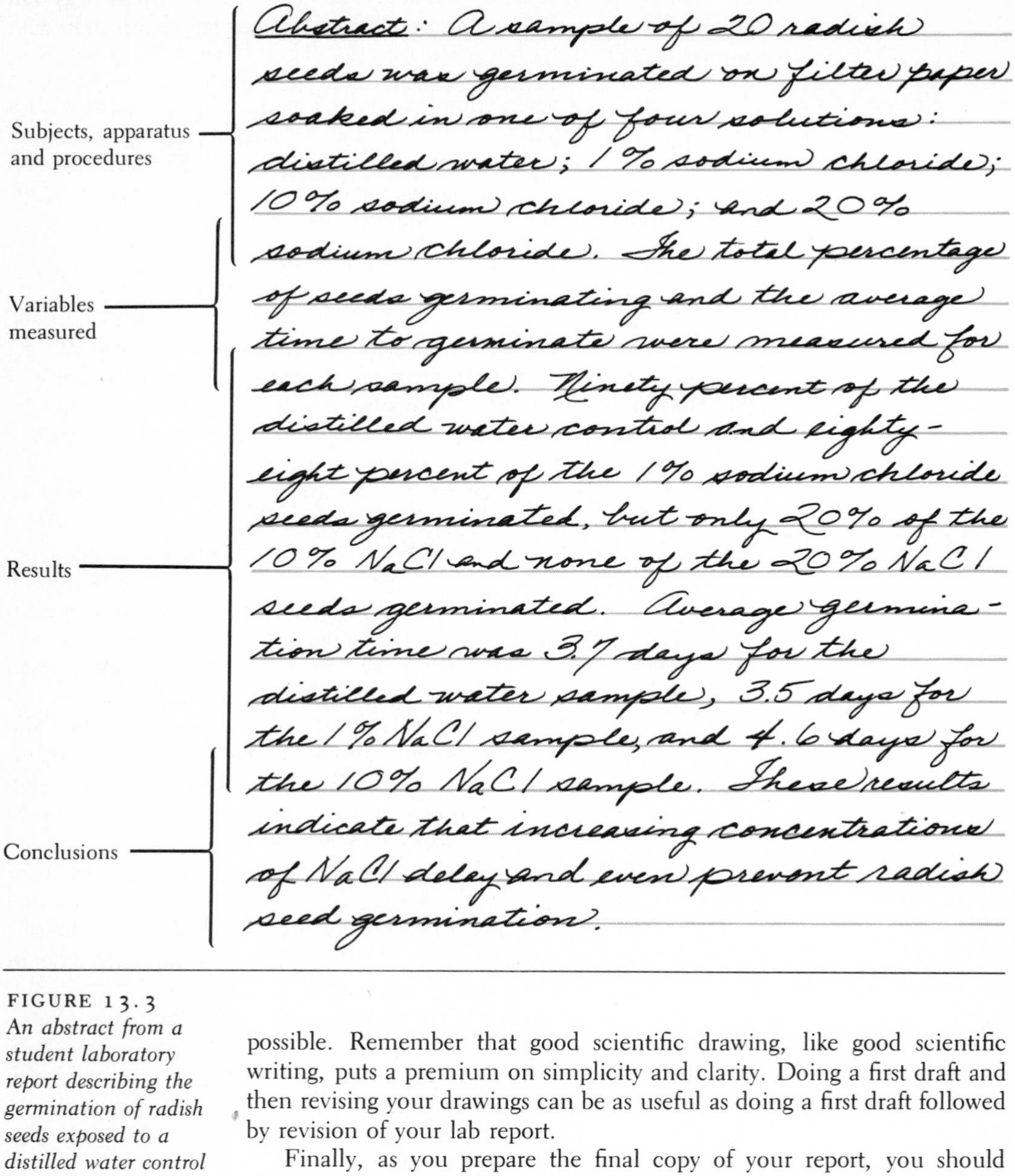

Abstract: A sample of 20 radish seeds was germinated on filter paper soaked in one of four solutions: distilled water; 1% sodium chloride; 10% sodium chloride; and 20% sodium chloride. The total percentage of seeds germinating and the average time to germinate were measured for each sample. Ninety percent of the distilled water control and eighty-eight percent of the 1% sodium chloride seeds germinated, but only 20% of the 10% NaCl and none of the 20% NaCl seeds germinated. Average germination time was 3.7 days for the distilled water sample, 3.5 days for the 1% NaCl sample, and 4.6 days for the 10% NaCl sample. These results indicate that increasing concentrations of NaCl delay and even prevent radish seed germination.

Subjects, apparatus and procedures

Variables measured

Results

Conclusions

FIGURE 13.3
An abstract from a student laboratory report describing the germination of radish seeds exposed to a distilled water control and three concentrations of sodium chloride (NaCl).

possible. Remember that good scientific drawing, like good scientific writing, puts a premium on simplicity and clarity. Doing a first draft and then revising your drawings can be as useful as doing a first draft followed by revision of your lab report.

Finally, as you prepare the final copy of your report, you should follow the rather rigid conventions of the profession. The title is usually centered on a title page, which also includes your name, the course number, laboratory section, and the date the paper is due. When you use either figures or tables, remember that the figures are consecutively numbered, with an explanatory figure legend below them, and that tables are also independently consecutively numbered, with a centered title above them. Also remember to mention in the body of your report the presence of all figures that you have put on separate sheets of paper, each with its title above (for tables) or legend below (for figures). Then insert each page into your lab report as the page immediately following the mention of the table or figure in your writing. While this procedure requires that you delay numbering your pages until you have almost completed your report, it is much easier than trying to leave appropriate space on the typed pages of your report.

All this effort will produce a permanent record of your work in the laboratory. Through this activity you will practice skills essential to the scientist. Science proceeds not merely because people do research but because they meticulously publish their procedures and findings to the scientific community at large. Clear and effective writing is more than useful to you as a scientist; it is your obligation.

QUESTIONS
1 What are the seven sections of a laboratory report?

2 What materials belong in the introductory section? Why?

3 What is the purpose of an abstract in a research report?

4 Why is it important to consider your classmates as the audience for a laboratory report?

EXERCISES
1 Compare and contrast the style for reporting findings in the social sciences (chapter 11) and reporting findings in the natural sciences.

2 Using the data from figure 12.1, write a title and introduction for a laboratory report.

3 Using the data from figure 13.2, write a results section and a conclusion section for a laboratory report.

14 Review Paper in the Natural Sciences

The scientific review paper consists of a clear and understandable explanation of the state of knowledge in a limited scientific area. The best review papers summarize the present situation in an ongoing field of research. Your review paper should bring your readers up to date, saving them the effort of locating, reading, and comparing original research publications. Your paper should also present the information at an appropriate level of technicality so that your readers can understand it, even though they might have trouble understanding the original research publications.

Because the purpose of the scientific review paper is to inform an already interested reader as efficiently as possible, the paper has a characteristic "scientific writing" style which emphasizes conspicuous organization, clarity, and brevity.

Some strategies that you can use effectively for term papers in the humanities are inappropriate for the scientific review paper. Remember that your contribution in writing a scientific review is in the organization, explanation, and clear presentation of complex concepts. Additional personal commentary on your topic frequently backfires by undermining your reader's confidence in your explanations. For example, you should not take a position on your topic; that is, you should not argue that one group of researchers is right and another group is wrong. Your paper is not designed to be argumentative (chapter 4), especially since any discrepancies will eventually be resolved by additional research. Also, you are not expected to come up with a new or original way of looking at the material. Only a scientist with many years of experience even attempts to do that.

In writing this type of term paper it is your responsibility to:

1 Select a topic that is appropriate to the course and suitably limited in scope. The best topics deal with problems under active investigation, rather than with problems that have been solved.

2 Identify and read the recent literature on the topic. The amount of literature may compel you either to expand or (more likely) reduce the scope of your topic to produce a paper of the desired length.

3 Organize the information into a meaningful pattern, using subheadings and sometimes an outline.

4 Paraphrase and simplify the information in the original articles and integrate it into the structure of your paper. (See chapter 5.)

5 Complete the paper using a format and writing style that are appropriate for a scientific review paper.

Getting started

Discovering a workable topic is the single most important determinant of the success of your review. Even before you begin to speculate on potential topics, look through your science textbook to ascertain the scope of acceptable topics. If you already have a topic on which you want to work, make certain that it falls within the subject matter covered in the course. Some topics are not wise choices even if they fall within the scope of the course. Sometimes a topic that has stimulated your interest because of its coverage by the popular media will present hidden difficulties when you try to use it as a topic for a scientific review. For example, the topic may be too complex: a paper on the development of a better flashlight battery becomes a chemical nightmare as you try to describe topochemical reactions of lithium and transition metal compounds. Or the topic may be too diffuse: a paper on the cause of infant crib death becomes a listing of the twenty or so most likely causes for this vaguely defined syndrome. Or finally, the topic could be too speculative: a paper on the use of pickled bats' feet as a cure for cancer becomes a futile search for recent journal articles because no reputable research has been done on the problem. Also, your library facilities may limit your topic. For example, unless you have access to a medical school library, you will find it difficult to obtain information on medical topics.

While you should be genuinely curious about your topic, be sure that your curiosity concerns the scientific features of the subject, not the emotional. In a course in the philosophy of science, in the history of science, or in freshman composition, you can find opportunities to write about the ethical and historical implications of popular topics, but for hard-core science courses, focus on the current state of scientific knowledge in the area defined by your research questions. If you have any doubts about your topic choice, check with your professor before investing time in library research.

As you begin to select a topic, consider using one of these three strategies, all designed to produce a rewarding and impressive review paper:

1 Look carefully at recent research reports, select one, and use it as a basis for your library search.

2 Look at the bibliography in your textbook, select a reference, and use it as a basis for your library search.

3 Look for a professionally written scientific review, select part of it as your paper topic, and then do a library search for up-to-date information.

Looking at recent research reports

By going to the recent issues of respected scientific journals, you will be able to identify a topic that the experts consider an exciting area of ongoing research. Writing on such a topic will let you share in the excitement of scientific research in progress.

This strategy has the distinct benefit of simplifying your library search. If you use a recently published journal, then you will have the most up-to-date information, complete with a list of appropriate references. On the other hand, the drawback to this method is the difficulty of understanding the writing in specialized scientific journals. To overcome the complexity of scientific research reports, you should select research journals appropriate to your level. If you are writing a relatively short paper assigned in a freshman-sophomore course, you might consult scientific journals aimed at the educated public. Such journals include *Scientific American, American Scientist, Bioscience, National Geographic, Smithsonian, Natural History,* and *Science 80.* Even the weekly magazine *Science News* and the weekly supplement (Tuesday) of the *New York Times* can get you started on current topics. If you are writing a more sophisticated paper for a junior-senior course, you should go directly to the recent issues of the more scholarly scientific journals intended for professional scientists, for example, the prestigous weekly journals *Science* and *Nature.* In addition, scientific disciplines have their own specialized journals. For a discussion of these publications, see the natural science section of chapter 4.

FIGURE 14.1
(on facing page)
Comments produced by a methodical second-semester sophomore biology major seeking a paper topic in vertebrate physiology. The comments assume two semesters of general biology, one semester of cell biology, and a semester of comparative anatomy. [*Contents page from* Science, *vol. 197 (16 Sept. 1977).* Copyright © 1977 by the American Association for the Advancement of Science.]

As you consult the table of contents in a recent issue of an appropriate journal, you will see articles that can serve as the basis for good paper topics. If you are using a journal written for professional scientists, it is especially important to be patient and thorough, for interesting articles are often obscured by titles made up of technical terms and cautious wordings. For example, one student read carefully the table of contents from *Science* (figure 14.1). Rather than skim scores of titles, this student decided to dissect a few, and gained for his efforts some good possible topics that might have been passed over by a student who could not get beyond the difficult first reading. Here in figures 14.2, 14.3, and 14.4 we illustrate three of these dissections, and we evaluate the potential of each title as a source for a paper topic.

Careful reading of the title in figure 14.2 indicates that this paper concerns a blood test for alcoholism. An understanding of the exact chemicals measured is not important to the overall concept, although

[Handwritten annotations at top:] ocean waves? Sounds like geology. WRONG TOPIC! / "Review" indicates cell tie. or biochem topic. "membrane" indicates cell tie. TOO HARD! TOO SPECIALIZED!

ANNUAL MEETING

Call for Contributed Papers: A. Herschman; Instructions for Contributors. 1173

BOOK REVIEWS

Social Anthropology and Medicine, *reviewed by D. Landy;* Europe's Giant Accelerator, *A. Roberts;* Chemical Pharmacology of the Synapse, *R. E. Zigmond;* Books Received and Book Order Service 1174

REPORTS

Carrier-Mediated Photodiffusion Membranes: *J. S. Schultz* 1177

Long Waves In the Eastern Equatorial Pacific Ocean: A View from a Geostationary Satellite: *R. Legeckis.* 1179

Timekeeping by the Pineal Gland: *S. Binkley, J. B. Riebman, K. B. Reilly* 1181

Ratio of Plasma Alpha Amino-*n*-Butyric Acid to Leucine as an Empirical Marker of Alcoholism: Diagnostic Value: *M. Y. Morgan, J. P. Milsom, S. Sherlock* . . . 1183

Lectin Release by Soybean Seeds: *D. W. Fountain et al.* 1185

Aluminum Absorption and Distribution: Effect of Parathyroid Hormone: *G. H. Mayor et al.* 1187

Competition of Δ^9-Tetrahydrocannabinol with Estrogen in Rat Uterine Estrogen Receptor Binding: *A. B. Rawitch et al.* 1189

Long-Term Unit Recording from Somatosensory Neurons in the Spinal Ganglia of the Freely Walking Cat: *G. E. Loeb, M. J. Bak, J. Duysens* 1192

Technical Comments: Electrochemical Growth of Organic Charge-Transfer Complexes: *D. F. Williams;* Metric of Color Borders: *R. W. Rodieck; B. W. Tansley and R. M. Boynton* 1194

[Handwritten marginal annotations:]

"? hormone?" *(near Parathyroid Hormone)* ; "!!!" *(near Estrogen)* ; "neurophysiology" and "neuroanatomy" *(near Spinal Ganglia)*

"pineal gland" – function discussed in physiology timekeeping is a difficult concept. POSSIBLY, BUT ONLY IF NOTHING EASIER

"Alcoholism" – an interesting medical topic. Sounds like it has COMMON INTEREST.

"soybean" – sounds like ecology or plant physiology. WRONG TOPIC.

"parathyroid hormone" – function discussed in physiology – but aluminum not mentioned. POSSIBLY, BUT ONLY IF NOTHING EASIER.

"cannabis is marihuana plant; Δ^9-tetra-hydrocannabinol is an important ingredient in marihuana. This topic certainly has COMMON INTEREST!!!! GOOD TOPIC

"somato-sensory neurons" – obviously a neurophysiology topic. Neurophysiology is a review subject. Too HARD! TOO SPECIALIZED!

FIGURE 14.2
*Analysis of title of
article about
alcoholism.*

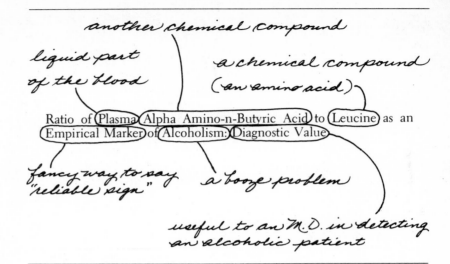

another chemical compound

liquid part of the blood

a chemical compound (an amino acid)

Ratio of (Plasma) (Alpha Amino-n-Butyric Acid) to (Leucine) as an (Empirical Marker) of (Alcoholism:) (Diagnostic Value)

fancy way to say "reliable sign"

a booze problem

useful to an M.D. in detecting an alcoholic patient

these happen to be rather simple organic molecules that most students with a year of chemistry recognize.

In figure 14.3 you probably realize that Δ^9-tetrahydrocannabinol is the major active ingredient in marihuana. You also recognize estrogen as an important female hormone which acts upon the uterus. This article explores a relationship between the two compounds, a topic of personal interest to many students and a topic that has been covered in the popular press.

The article described in figure 14.4 obviously requires some back-

FIGURE 14.3
*Analysis of title of
article about
marihuana-estrogen
relationship.*

Read "successful competition" since scientific papers usually report successful experiments.

Cannabis is the marihuana plant!

major female hormone

Competition of Δ^9-Tetrahydrocannabinol with (Estrogen) in Rat (Uterine) Estrogen Receptor Binding.

the uterus (womb) is the target organ for estrogen

FIGURE 14.4
*Analysis of title of
article about DNA.*

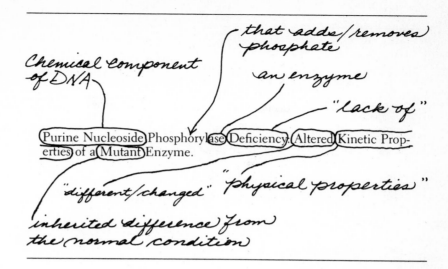

ground in biochemistry before it can be readily understood. If you **are** writing your review for a biochemistry course, this topic could be very productive. However, if your audience is less advanced, you will have to provide a minicourse in biochemistry before you can even begin to discuss this topic.

It is very useful at this point to try to write out in your own words the topics that interest you. The purpose of such an exercise is to make sure that you are clear on their meanings and to provide the occasion to write down your initial reactions. For example, a student considering the second article might write the brief note shown in figure 14.5. Such notes can be referred to later if other topics do not work out, and can be understood much more readily than if you had to begin again to look at tables of contents.

If, after careful analysis, the article looks interesting, your next step is to go to the article itself. Read the abstract and the introductory section. If they are filled with words that are unfamiliar to you and concepts that you do not understand, you should consider finding another topic, for you might spend too much time simply trying to learn enough to allow you to do the research for your paper. The abstract should give you a good understanding of the whole project, thesis, and results. The introductory section should give you, in more detail, some background information on recent research, so if you decide to work on the topic, the introductory section will be useful as a framework and guide for your own research. You will need, of course, to expand and to simplify the material, but this overview of a standard research work can provide you with a basic outline of what your paper might be like. Figure 14.6 shows the introduction of the marihuana article with comments by a student evaluating its usefulness for a possible outline of his own research paper.

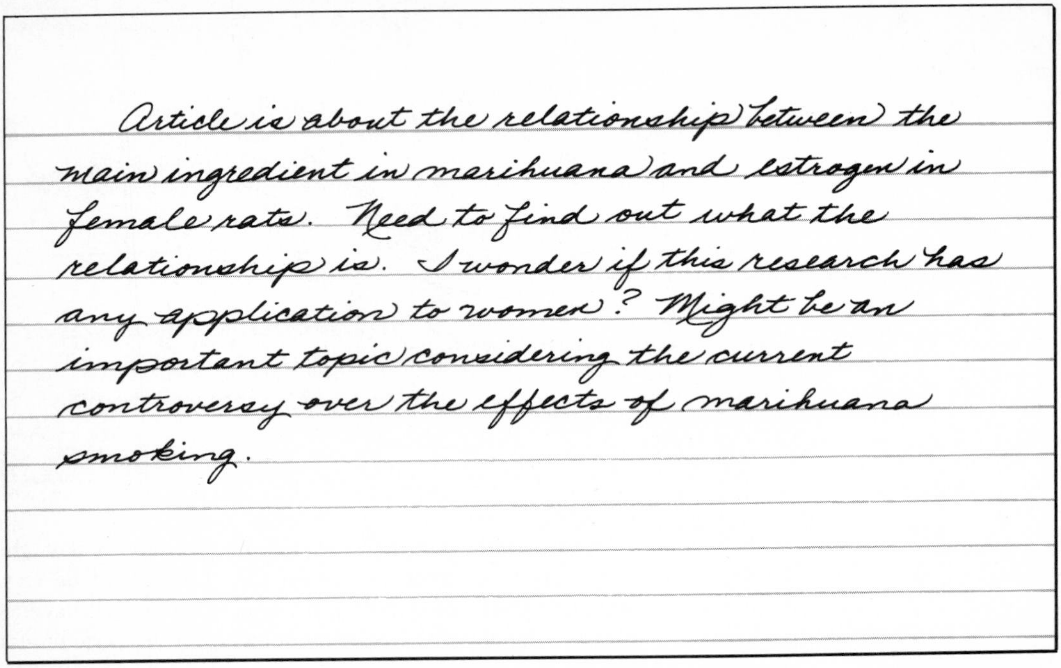

Article is about the relationship between the main ingredient in marihuana and estrogen in female rats. Need to find out what the relationship is. I wonder if this research has any application to women? Might be an important topic considering the current controversy over the effects of marihuana smoking.

FIGURE 14.5

Notice that in addition to obtaining additional references to consult, this student has begun to formulate questions that can be the basis for his own paper. It is important in this generative stage to think in terms of questions, for ultimately you are going to have to develop your own framework for your research paper.

In deciding whether the article does provide material for your paper, you should consult the final section of the article, usually called the discussion section. This section, again in more detail than the abstract, provides the conclusions as well as further references that might prove useful. Figure 14.7 shows how the student used the discussion section from the *Science* article to add to his own preliminary outline.

Using the bibliography in your textbook Another good starting point in your search for a suitable topic is your course textbook. Almost all upper-level textbooks in the sciences give references to the research reports and review articles that were used in writing the book. Read the reference lists and select articles that can serve as the basis for paper topics.

When you use this strategy for topic selection, you can be certain that you have chosen an important and appropriate topic. Also, the textbook will explain how the topic relates to the other subjects discussed in the course. However, you will still have to discover if the topic is an area of active research, and you will have to find up-to-date information on the topic.

You can locate recent research reports on your potential topic by using an indexing service like *Science Citation Index, Biological Abstracts,* or *Chemical Abstracts.* See chapter 4 for a more detailed discussion of these materials. A lack of recent research reports indicates that you have chosen a no-longer-active topic, and you should probably try again.

Updating and simplifying a professionally written review

Because you are writing a scientific review paper, it may already have occurred to you that you might look at professionally written reviews to get some ideas for good topics. As we suggest in chapter 4, you should begin by locating the annually published review series that specializes in your discipline. These professionally written scientific review articles are more comprehensive and complex than the review you have been assigned to do, so after deciding on an interesting looking article, use the subheadings to help you limit your topic. Usually one or two sections will provide enough material for your review. Next summarize the information in the section you have selected, using the suggestions in chapter 5 on how to summarize without plagiarizing.

Although the professional review will give you an organizational pattern, your eventual addition of background information and up-to-date research developments should transform the organization into something clearly your own. Since any published scientific review article will be at least two years out of date, you must still search for the most recent research reports on your topic. As discussed in chapter 4, a forward search using *Science Citation Index* or a subject-oriented search using an appropriate index like *Biological Abstracts* or *Chemical Abstracts* will locate these reports for you. Although the information in these up-to-date research reports should dominate your review, you must connect this new information to the pertinent background material.

You may have noticed by now, if you have read the chapters on research papers in the humanities and social sciences, that topic selection in the natural sciences is based much more on a survey of the literature than on invention devices. Your topic must be current, and it must be the object of enough research to allow you to write about it. However, once you have identified a topic area, your responsibilities are those of any writer in any discipline: you need to narrow and define the topic so that it becomes a real question that you address and not just a broad subject. If, for example, you have decided on the topic of marihuana, you should pose a question about the subject. You need a controlling question that will provide direction to your research and organization for your paper when you are ready to write. Questions, such as the ones listed below, allow you to view your topic from a variety of perspectives, one or several of which might provide the framework within which you can work.

[Handwritten margin notes:]

MAIN POINT

I. Background Info?

II. Does Δ⁹THC have a feminizing influence?

A. Human
1. ♂
2. ♀

B. Rats
1. in vivo (in living ♂ rat)
♀
2. in vitro (in test tube)
♀ — this paper

III. Does Δ⁹THC cause cancer, esp. in women?

IV. Is Δ⁹THC dangerous to babies?
A. Before birth
B. While nursing

What's this?   *OK! 45 is explained in the methods.*

Competition of Δ^9-Tetrahydrocannabinol with Estrogen in Rat Uterine Estrogen Receptor Binding

[Handwritten: explanation required]

Abstract. *Direct competition experiments with Δ^9-tetrahydrocannabinol (Δ^9-THC) and estradiol in binding assays with rat uterine cytosol estrogen receptors showed that Δ^9-THC was a weak, but nevertheless significant, competitor for binding to cytoplasmic estrogen receptors. These data support, at the molecular level, the observations that Δ^9-THC has a weak estrogenic activity (at least the ability to bind to estrogen receptors). Moreover, estrogen-like binding suggests that Δ^9-THC, acting at the level of estrogen receptor, causes a primary estrogenic effect rather than an indirect or secondary phenomenon.*

[Handwritten: INTRODUCTION]

There has been increasing speculation (*1*) and some experimental support (*2, 3*) for an estrogen-like biological activity associated with heavy, long-term marihuana smoking in man and with the administration of Δ^9-tetrahydrocannabinol (Δ^9-THC) in male rodents. Because most of the data have been obtained from experiments in vivo where specific hormone-sensitive organs were examined for stimulation (*2, 3*) or repression (*4*), the conflicting results may be due to indirect effects in the whole animal.

The reports of uterine stimulation in castrated female rats by Solomon *et al.* (*3*), and of lowered levels of luteinizing hormone, follicle-stimulating hormone, and testosterone in men by Kolodny and co-workers (*2, 5*) after the long-term administration of Δ^9-THC have also focused attention on the estrogenic nature of the drug. Since it has been demonstrated that Δ^9-THC may be transferred across the placenta to the developing fetus (*6*), and that it appears in the milk of lactating animals (*7*), the question of deleterious effects on fetal and newborn offspring must be addressed. Estrogen and estrogenic compounds may play an important part in the development of several forms of carcinoma in human females and their offspring (*8, 9*), and they are potential suppressors of male hormones and of androgen-dependent tissues (*4*). Moreover, it has recently been reported that estrogen receptors occur in both human prostate (*10*) and rat testes (*11*). To test the hypothesis that Δ^9-THC acts as an estrogen in a direct experiment, we have examined the extent to which Δ^9-THC competes with estrogen for sites on rat uterus estrogen in vitro. We have also experiments with rat uterus pon...

[Handwritten: same journal (Science)]

References and Notes

1. J. W. Harmon and M. A. Aliapoulis, *N. Engl. J. Med.* **287**, 936 (1972); T. W. Hill, *Addict. Res. Found. Ont. J.* **4**, (No.1), 2 (1975).
2. R. C. Kolodny, W. H. Masters, G. Toro, *N. Engl. J. Med.* **290**, 872 (1974); J. W. Harmon and M. A. Aliapoulis, *Surg. Forum* **25**, 423 (1974).
3. J. Solomon, M. A. Cocchia, R. Gray, D. Shattuck, A. Vossmer, *Science* **192**, 559 (1976).
4. J. Solomon and D. X. Shattuck, *N. Engl. J. Med.* **291**, 308 (1974).
5. R. C. Kolodny, in *Marijuana and Health Hazards*, J. R. Tinklenberg, Ed. (Academic Press, New York, 1975).
6. R. M. Vardaris, D. J. Weisz, A. Fazel, A. B. Rawitch, *Pharmacol. Biochem. Physiol.* **4**, 249 (1976).
7. A. Jakubovic, R. M. Tait, P. L. McGeer, *Toxicol. Appl. Pharmacol.* **28**, 38 (1974).
8. S. B. Gusberg and R. E. Hall, *Obstet. Gynecol.* **17**, 397 (1961); B. S. Cutler, A. P. Forbes, F. M. Ingersoll, R. E. Scully, *N. Engl. J. Med.* **287**, 628 (1972); A. Voss, *Am. J. Obstet. Gynecol.* **58**, 748 (1949); M. Feinleib, *J. Natl. Cancer Inst.* **41**, 315 (1968).
9. A. L. Herbst, H. Ulfelder, D. C. Poskanzer, *N. Engl. J. Med.* **284**, 878 (1971).
10. E. F. Hawkins, M. Nijs, C. Brassinne, H. J. Tagnon, *Steroids* **26**, 458 (1975).
11. J. Kato, T. Onouchi, S. Okinaga, N. Ito, *Endocrinology* **94**, 902 (1974).
12. W. L. McGuire, P. O. Carbone, E. P. Vollmer, Eds., *Estrogen Receptors in Human Breast Cancer* (Raven, New York, 1975).
13. G. Scatchard, *Ann. N.Y. Acad. Sci.* **51**, 600 (1949).
14. V. L. Wittliff, D. G. Gardner, W. L. Battema, P. J. Gilbert, *Biochem. Biophys. Res. Commun.* **48**, 119 (1972).
15. W. L. McGuire and M. DeLaGarza, *J. Clin. Endocrinol. Metab.* **36**, 548 (1972).
16. A. B. Okey and G. S. Truant, *Life Sci.* **17**, 1113 (1975).
17. A. B. Okey and G. P. Bondy, *Science* **195**, 904 (1977).
18. J. Solomon, M. A. Cocchia, R. DiMartino, *ibid.*, p. 875.
19. R. H. Shoemaker and J. W. Harmon, *Fed. Proc. Fed. Am. Soc. Exp. Biol.* **36**, 345 (1977).
20. Supported in part by NIMH grant RO1-MH20558, NIDA grant RO1-DA00105, and NIAMDD grant AM 18896. A.B.R. is the recipient of research career development award AM 70473. A preliminary report of this study was presented at the FASEB meeting in Chicago, Ill., on 5 April 1977 [*Fed. Proc.* **36**, 780 (1977)].

[Handwritten: Science]

FIGURE 14.6
(on facing page)
The introduction of an article from Science, *showing how it has been used to generate topics and subheadings for an undergraduate scientific review paper.* [*From Allen B. Rawitch, Gregory S. Schultz, Kurt E. Ebner, "Competition of Δ⁹-Tetrahydrocannabinol with Estrogen in Rat Uterine Estrogen Receptor Binding,"* Science, *vol. 197 (16 Sept. 1977), pp. 1189, 91. Copyright © 1977 by the American Association for the Advancement of Science.*]

- What are the (mathematical, physical, chemical, astronomical, geological, biological) characteristics of X?

- Into what general category does X fit?

- How is X similar to or different from Y and Z?

- How is X related to A?

- What are the theories about X?

- What is the state of knowledge about X?

- What remains to be discovered or resolved about X?

- Why is X important to humans?

- What is the history of X?

- What are the ethical implications of X?

When you begin your research, such questions can provide categories for your notecards. These categories can be dropped, changed, or added to as you research, but in doing so you have to make conscious decisions which will help you to formulate plans for your paper. Your goal is to move from a broad topic to a one-or-two sentence controlling question. Table 14.1 provides examples of this movement, using the marihuana-estrogen problem. The rows in this table show how the topic of marihuana would be treated in the scientific fields of biology and chemistry as opposed to the way the topic would be treated in fields in the social sciences and humanities. Focusing on the ethics, history, or politics of marihuana use is interesting, important, and appropriate to courses in philosophy, history, or political science. We want to underline the point that only certain questions provide an appropriate focus for hard-core science courses.

Searching for a topic properly takes a great deal of time, but it is time well invested, for your search also produces an abundance of notes on the articles you read. These notes should consist of summaries—accounts that are written in your own terms but are nonetheless completely consistent with the articles. You need not hunt for quotable passages, for scientific review papers do not usually contain direct quotations. Instead, you should paraphrase or summarize all pertinent information. See chapter 5 for a review of these skills. When it is time to write, you will be able to incorporate some of these summaries directly into your paper.

After you have arranged your notes according to the questions that you asked of each article, you should be able to draw out an outline or an organization for your paper by using your questions ("What is the history of X?") as subheadings. By transforming questions into statements, you might come up with a tentative structure like this:

```
1. History of the marihuana—estrogen
   relationship: male heavy users developed
   breasts, etc. (female sex characteristics);
```

Taken together, our data demonstrate the capability of Δ^9-THC, and to a lesser extent 11-OH-Δ^9-THC, to compete with estradiol for binding to cytoplasmic estrogen receptors. The ability of the drug to occupy estrogen receptor appears to be limited under the conditions reported here (a maximum of 22 percent of the specific binding sites). It is clear, however, that the compounds responsible for the primary psychoactive effect of marihuana show significant estrogenic binding affinity.

These findings are opposite to those reported by Okey and Truant (16) who used a cannabis resin preparation to examine Δ^9-THC inhibition of estrogen binding to cytosol receptors. We have no explanation for their failure to observe competition between their cannabis resin preparation and estrogen receptor. These workers also reported that their cannabis resin had no effect on uterine weight (16) and, more recently, Okey and Bondy (17), using pure Δ^9-THC, obtained a similar result. It may not be appropriate to compare the effects of pure Δ^9-THC in vitro with those observed with cannabis resin (a mixture of many cannabinoid compounds and related natural products). Moreover, both Solomon et al. (3, 18) and Shoemaker and Harmon (19) provide data consistent with our observations.

While the demonstration of chemical binding to estrogen receptors (as judged from competitive displacement and direct binding experiments) is not, in itself, sufficient evidence to prove estrogenic activity in the full biological sense, recent reports by Solomon et al. (3, 18) of a uterotropic effect of Δ^9-THC in castrated female rats and by Kolodny et al. (2) of lowered testosterone levels suggest that this competitive binding may have biological significance.

ALLEN B. RAWITCH
GREGORY S. SCHULTZ
KURT E. EBNER
Biochemistry Department, University of Kansas Medical Center, Kansas City 66103
RICHARD M. VARDARIS
Department of Psychology, Kent State University, Kent, Ohio 44242

II. Does Δ^9 THC have a feminizing influence?
  A. Humans
    1. Males — Kolodny et al., 1974; Kolodny, 1975 (book)
    2. Females —
  B. Rats
    1. In vivo (inside living animal).
      a. male
      b. female — Solomon et al, 1976 Science   but Okey & Truant get opposite result
    2. In vitro (outside animal, using cell extracts)
      a. male — prostate and testes have estrogen receptors, even though they are ♂ sex organs.
      b. female — Rawitch et al., 1977 — this paper
         get opposite result   Okey & Truant, 1975   Okey & Bondy, 1977
    Solomon et al. 1976,
    Solomon et al. 1977 agree w/ Rawitch
    Shomaker and Harmon, 1977 agree w/ Rawitch

FIGURE 14.7
(on facing page)
*The discussion section
of a research report in
the journal* Science,
*showing how it has
been used to expand
on a student's
preliminary outline.*
[*From* Science, *vol.
197 (16 Sept. 1977),
p. 1191. Copyright ©
1977 by the American
Association for the
Advancement of
Science.*]

review structure and function of estrogen;
also mention dangers of estrogen (cancer).

2. Biologically active constituent of marihuana
   Δ^9—THC isolated as active compound——show
   structure
3. Laboratory evidence that marihuana acts like
   the hormone estrogen in rodents
4. Laboratory evidence that marihuana acts like
   estrogen in humans
5. Medical significance of a marihuana—estrogen
   relationship, if indeed it does exist,
   including reduced male fertility, increased
   incidence of cancers especially in females,
   and possible damage to fetal and newborn
   humans.

Writing the first draft

Developing a sense of organization is an important first step in molding
a paper from research. To decide whether your research forms a complete
paper, we suggest that you begin writing a first draft before your research
is finished. Writing connected prose, sentences and paragraphs, gives you
some idea of what a finished product might look like. Is your topic still
too broad to be written about in the assigned number of pages? Is it too
narrow to fill them? Are there gaps in your research or understanding of
the topic? You can better answer these questions after you have tried
various explanations and transitions to connect the parts of your research.
Don't worry yet about language or spelling or any writing task that will
deflect your attention from your purposes in writing this draft.

The advantage of writing a paper that is organized according to subheadings is that you can begin almost anywhere, for in most cases, these
sections are independent units. The summaries in your notes can provide
the beginnings of your draft; you can usually expand them or insert them
at appropriate points as you develop each section.

Because of the nature of note taking for a review paper in the sciences,
some students prefer to cut and paste a first draft. In fact, you can take a
scissors to the notes that you have just accumulated and use them directly
as part of the draft. Leave space for connecting paragraphs or instructions
to yourself about what is needed to tie your summaries together. But
whatever procedure you choose for the writing of your first draft, you
should write out the body of the paper while you still have time left for
more research if needed. Leave the introduction and conclusion to be
written later.

In writing about the marihuana-estrogen relationship you could group
together all research reports that tested the effects of marihuana (either
the active ingredient THC or the THC-containing marihuana resin) on

Field	Much too broad	Too broad	Still too broad	Controlling question
Biology or chemistry	Marihuana	Effect of marihuana on human users.	Damaging physiological effects of marihuana on human users.	What is the state of the research that suggests that the active ingredient of marihuana, Δ^9-THC, acts like the female hormone estrogen?
Philosophy	Marihuana	The ethics of marihuana.	Ethics of marihuana experimentation on humans.	What are the ethical implications of studying the long-term effects of marihuana on human subjects who volunteer for such a study?
History of science	Marihuana	History of marihuana use in the USA.	The accumulation of evidence suggesting that marihuana has negative side effects.	A history of the marihuana-estrogen relationship.
Political science	Marihuana	Legalization of marihuana.	The relationship between medical evidence on the safety of marihuana and the legalization of marihuana.	What are the political implications of legalizing Δ^9-THC, the active ingredient of marihuana, if it is known to do serious long-term damage to humans?

TABLE 14.1
How the topic of marihuana can be narrowed to a controlling question in four disciplines.

whole rodents. Below is a student summary of such a research report which, in itself, is a good beginning for a draft section of a paper.

Okey and Truant (1975) tested on female rats the effects of a cannabis resin which presumably contained the active ingredient THC. They found no estrogen—like stimulation of the uterus of these rats: 1. the uteri of cannabis—treated rats weighed the same as untreated control rats, and less than that of estrogen—treated rats. 2. the estrogen—receptor molecules found in the

```
cytoplasm of uterine cells had not been occupied
by a marihuana-resin molecule (such as THC) in
the resin-treated rats and could still attach to
a normal amount of estrogen.
```

This passage can be built into a draft in several ways. In this case, the student chose to paste the passage to a sheet of paper and to go on with a note about what he might add to expand the passage. In the note to himself, reproduced below, he also prepares to add the next summary to his expanding draft.

```
Use illustration in introduction to explain the
concept of binding; also maybe a diagram of cell
to show location of cytoplasm and the concept of
cytosol. Here, go on to summary of a follow-up
experiment to the one above.
```
```
Okey and Bondy (1977) tested the effects of pure
THC on female rats. Again they found that the....
```

After you have pieced together the body of a complete paper, ask one or two friends, preferably ones in the same course, to read it, provided that such a practice is allowed in your school. Tell your readers to ignore grammar and other surface features, and to read for total comprehension. Do they understand what you are writing about? Is the background information useful in understanding the paper? Is the importance of the research clear? Discuss the paper with them and decide which of their comments should be incorporated into the revision.

Revising

You should plan to make major changes in your first draft before you submit your paper for evaluation. If you limit your revising to correcting grammar or sentence structure, you will miss an opportunity to do other important reader-oriented tasks. Remember, you are writing your review paper for an audience of science undergraduates who require thorough explanations of unfamiliar terms, careful transitions so that they can follow the research, and, perhaps, diagrams to illustrate difficult concepts or structures. Your revising responsibilities must include everything that will help your audience to share your understanding of the problem.

Most of the tasks discussed in the revising sections of the other chapters in this book apply also to the science review paper. You should look particularly at chapter 9 for advice on the use and abuse of technical language and passive voice constructions. Also, you should strive for effective transitions to guide your reader through the complex, sometimes unfamiliar words and concepts that are so common in the sciences. But there are some special features of style and format that you should give particular attention to in this type of paper.

Tone of the paper. Your purpose in writing a scientific review is to inform your readers, not to persuade them. To accomplish this goal you must write with authority. Authority comes not only from the sources you cite, but also from your own confidence in your understanding of the subject matter. This confidence is conveyed in your skillful, dispassionate presentation of the material. The appropriate tone for a science paper is formal. The use of "I feel" or even "I think" is out of place in this kind of informational paper.

Use of subheadings. Most review papers have at least three subheadings, and it is common to have additional divisions within the subheadings. Conventions govern the placement of subheadings, so you should ask your instructor how they actually appear in a paper in your discipline. One common form of subheadings appears as follows: major subheadings appear in the middle of the page with the initial letter of each word capitalized; subheadings under these appear at the left-hand margin and are underlined, again with each initial letter capitalized; the next category is indented from the left-hand margin and in this instance only the first word of the subheading begins with a capital letter, while the whole subheading is underlined. See the example below:

A Centered Main Heading

A Flush Side Heading

An indented paragraph heading

Scientists are purposeful readers. They like to be able to locate and relocate particular information quickly. Titles for subheadings should be brief and informative. When you check the titles of each subsection, make sure that the material in each section belongs there.

Illustrations. Another characteristic of scientists is that they like illustrations and diagrams. These provide quick visual reference for subjects that would be difficult and cumbersome to describe in prose. Check to see if you can clarify any part of your topic by adding a visual representation. For example, on the marihuana-estrogen topic, your final paper could usefully include a drawing of an estrogen molecule (obtained from a table of steroid hormones in the *CRC Handbook*), and the tetrahydrocannibinol molecule (obtained from the *Merck Index*), so that your readers can see the similarities in structure. When you use illustrations, always refer to them in your writing to alert your reader to their presence.

References cited section. Instead of a bibliography that includes works on the topic, scientific papers have a section entitled "References Cited." For the proper format of scientific citations and the reference section, see chapter 5.

Other revision strategies. If, as you revise, you begin to wonder about the appropriate level of complexity for your audience, consult several *Scientific American* articles. These articles demonstrate how to move your audience of fellow undergraduates up to the level of complexity required by your topic. Your textbook will also demonstrate how to present complex material to an audience with a limited background.

When the body of your paper is satisfactory, you should write your introduction and conclusion. These are best left until last to insure that they reflect accurately the final version of your paper. Remember that we have advised you in your own reading to focus first on the introductions and conclusions of articles. Your reader may decide to read your paper in the same way. These are important sections and must be written carefully so that the rest of your paper is put in the correct perspective.

The introduction may be theoretical, setting out the problem, or it may recount recent research which has raised questions about earlier assumptions on your subject. Whatever it covers, it should establish the importance of the subject and point the way toward your emphasis in the paper. An introductory paragraph on the marihuana-estrogen relationship based on the outline shown above might begin:

A possible relationship between the physiological effects of marihuana and the female hormone estrogen was first suggested in a report by Harmon and Aliapoulis in 1972. This report noted the development of female secondary sex characteristics in adult male humans who were heavy users of marihuana. These characteristics, which paralleled those induced by the female sex hormone estrogen, included enlarged breasts and reduced fertility. Since these reports, the possibility that marihuana might have estrogen-like properties has been pursued in the laboratory both at a physiological and at a biochemical level.

This paragraph sets out the problem and the nature of the research very succinctly and sets the stage for two types of discussion, of the problem itself and of the studies of the problem.

When you write your conclusion, you should begin by reminding your reader of the major research steps that you have described in the body of your paper. For the marihuana-estrogen topic, mention the original observations that marihuana had a feminizing effect on male humans and then briefly summarize both the physiological evidence, pro and con, that marihuana, or at least THC, has estrogen-like effects on estrogen-target organs, and the biochemical evidence, pro and con, that Δ^9-THC competes with estrogen for the same binding sites in target-organ cells. After summarizing, tell your reader what these experimental results really mean and why they are important. You could comment on the increasing number of research reports from various laboratories testing the possible estrogen-like action of the active ingredient of marihuana. You could even mention how these results will be important in resolving problems about the use and legal status of marihuana. Again remind your reader of the dangers if, in fact, marihuana does act like estrogen. Here is the only place to consider the questions: Why is X important to humans? What is the history of X? What are the ethical implications of X?

Finally, you should remark on the problems remaining to be solved. For the marihuana-estrogen research there are two obvious problems: conflicting results and the possible damaging effects of both estrogen and Δ^9-THC. You should point out that these problems will have to be resolved through further experimentation.

When your paper is complete, proofread for surface errors. Be especially careful to put in symbols ("Δ") that are not on your typewriter. Proofreading is exceedingly important in a scientific review paper. Since scientists must be thorough and exact in the details of their laboratory work, scientists also expect the same precision in written work.

QUESTIONS **1** What is the purpose of a review paper in the natural sciences?

2 How does a review paper in the natural sciences differ from a research paper in the social sciences? How are they similar?

3 What are the most important limitations placed on you when writing a scientific review paper?

4 What are your special responsibilities when revising a review paper?

EXERCISES **1** Select and define a topic by using the methods discussed in this chapter and then test the topic by using the criteria given on page 283. Narrow the topic according to the guide on page 288.

2 Using the methods described in this chapter and in chapter 4, locate five up-to-date research reports on any one of the following topics:

  a Can gorillas "talk"?

  b How do birds know the correct destination when they migrate?

  c What is a "black hole"?

3 Using methods that you did not employ in your original search, add two items to the list that you compiled for exercise 2. Which methods produced the best results?

4 Select one of the research reports from the list you compiled in exercises 2 and 3 and write a summary of it.

5 In 1977, *Science* published the article, A. B. Rawitch *et al.*, "Competition of Δ^9-Tetrahydrocannabinol with Estrogen in Rat Uterine Receptor Binding." Using *Citation Index* and other methods explained in this chapter and in chapter 4, find several articles reporting research done since 1977 on the marihuana-estrogen similarity. Hint: You may find some research that casts grave doubts on the hypothesis that marihuana mimics estrogen in human males.

Appendix:
Student Papers Written in Response to Assignments in History, Sociology, Psychology, and Biology

On the following pages we present four sample student papers together with the assignments that evoked them. As you can tell from the professors' instructions, the papers have been written under varying circumstances and for different purposes. The first paper is a take-home examination for a history course. The assignment fits very neatly into the general type that we call papers of speculation (see chapter 8). The second paper is a case study of a social group, and for further explanation, you should look again at chapter 10. That chapter will also be helpful in understanding what the student is doing in the next paper, "Mama Rat," but the "Mama Rat" paper is a hybrid in a number of ways. It is more of an exercise than it is a formal paper, and it also depends on approaches presented in chapters 12–14, "Writing in the Natural Sciences." The last paper is a scientific review of current research on the songs of humpback whales. Of the four papers, the scientific review paper might pose the most difficulties because it requires beginning students to read rather sophisticated scientific sources. We think, however, that with the help of chapter 14, you could write a scientific review paper that is at least as good as our sample.

These papers are adequate examples of what beginning college students can do with the designated assignments. These papers are far from perfect, and we know that you will write better ones. Please send us copies of your best.

History 134: Take-home essay

The purpose of the following question is to encourage you to think about the changes within the Soviet Union during the past twenty-five years. Please answer the question in a clear, focused essay of not more than three typed, double-spaced pages. Assume that your audience includes your classmates and your instructor.

To answer this question you must develop a prediction. There is no right or wrong answer. Your paper will be evaluated on the power of your argument. Have you convinced your readers that your prediction could come true? It is more important to be logical than it is to be fanciful. Show that you understand Stalin's Russia, Stalin's view of leadership, present-day conditions in Russia, and the relationships among all of these factors. Essays will be evaluated on the consistency of your thesis and argument, the analysis of the data you select, and the general persuasiveness of your essay.

The question: "If Josef Stalin were to return, would he be able to rule the Soviet Union as he did in his own lifetime?"

TAKE—HOME EXAMINATION

Alan Marcus
History 134
October 31, 1999
Dr. Bette Landman

ACKNOWLEDGMENTS

Most of the information in this paper is derived from lectures, class discussions, and readings in History 134. I also asked my grandmother what she remembered about newspaper accounts of Stalin's Russia.

Alan Marcus
History 134: Modern
Russia

Were Josef Stalin to return, would he be able to rule the Soviet Union as he did in his lifetime?

Josef Stalin was the dictator of the Soviet Union from 1928 to 1953. His main policies included purges of all opposition, forced collectivization of agriculture, and massive investment in heavy industry. He furthered his

Description of Stalin's
policies. These are the
criteria that will be
used when comparing
the two periods (the
Soviet Union under
Stalin and now) in
the remainder of the
paper.

Thesis: introduction of
the line of argument
to be taken.

Description of the
USSR when Stalin
ruled.

Description of Soviet
Union today.
(Note parallelisms to
description of USSR
under Stalin).

Note the absence of
footnotes which would
be used if this were a
research paper.

policies at the expense of the people in whose
name he was supposed to be ruling. He destroyed
the peasant farmers and murdered between five and
six million people, including those in the party
or military who were in positions to challenge
his authority. Stalin was an egocentric madman
who demanded complete obedience in everything
from industrial policy to art and literature. The
penalty for failure to follow his policies was
usually death. He ruled to perpetuate his own
power. But if he were to return, he would be
unable to rule in the same manner. Too much has
changed within the Soviet Union.

Stalin's rule fit the age in which he lived.
When Stalin came to power in 1928, Russia was a
large, disorganized, rural nation, isolated from
the rest of the world and populated with people
who were used to absolutist rule. Russia was
militarily weak and existed in a hostile world
filled with capitalists and fascists, and, after
1933, Nazis, who openly talked of invading the
Soviet Union. In short, Stalin did have some
reasons for his extreme policies of force and
terror. In the name of necessity, he could demand
obedience to his policy of bringing Russia into
the twentieth century. It was a matter of
survival as well as an exercise in ego
satisfaction.

Today, circumstances in the Soviet Union are
totally different. The nation is a giant
industrialized superpower. It is militarily
secure and, obstensibly, at peace. Consequently,
since 1953, successive regimes have chosen to or
have been forced to relax the domination of the
party in many areas of life. Soviet citizens have
been given rights to own private land, to read
Western works, to make management decisions in
broad areas of industry. Moreover, the Russian
people have grown to expect more out of life than
they did under Stalin. Citizens have become
increasingly accustomed to more comfortable, if
still inconvenient, lifestyles, and the Soviet
system has had to adjust to providing more
consumer goods, especially Western goods.
Consequently, expectations have risen and
criticism and dissent have become widespread,

for people know that, within broad limits, dissent will not be punished by capricious purges or execution.

Shows consideration of main counter-argument and shows why the counter-argument is not valid.

I do not suggest that there has been any significant shift in the substance of power since 1953. In fact, the party and its apparatus continue to possess a monopoly of political and military power. The dictatorship that Stalin established is still intact so, theoretically, the party could rule as Stalin did. Such a possibility, however, is unlikely. The changes since Stalin's death are more than cosmetic. The circumstances of the people, their attitudes, and their expectations have improved dramatically. Moreover, the changes in the past quarter century have created strong vested interests within the bureaucracy and within the many new industries that have grown up. Stability is too ingrained in the Soviet Union to permit again the rule of another egocentric madman.

Analysis of what has been shown.

Restatement of thesis for strong ending.

Assignment sheet: Small group study—Sociology 100

Describe and analyze a small group to which you have belonged or belong now. Some areas you may discuss are the group's norms and values, subcultural characteristics, stratification and roles, ethnocentrism, and social control techniques.

In previous semesters students have written on the following groups: an informal group of camp counselors or campers; a high school clique; an informal friendship group formed on a dorm corridor or in a class; a church social group; an extracurricular club. Do not use your family as the small group.

Your paper must be submitted in draft stages: (1) proposal; (2) work-in-progress; (3) draft for peer review; (4) finished paper. (See your syllabus for due dates.)

Your finished paper should be no more than ten pages, typed, double-spaced. If you write a draft of the paper in English 101 or 102 or if you visit the Writing Center, please include this information on the acknowledgments page. Because we are using peer review, every student must write an acknowledgments page. I encourage you to discuss your paper with friends and other instructors. Sometimes other members of the group that you choose to analyze will remember a detail that has slipped your mind.

ANALYSIS OF A HIGH SCHOOL PEER GROUP

Theodore Freund
Sociology 100
December 6, 1999
Dr. Calvin Cameron

Acknowledgments

I want to thank the person who served as my peer reviewer (I don't know his name), because the review helped me see some ways I could improve my paper.

I did not use the Writing Center because after the peer review I felt fairly confident about my paper. But I am grateful for the opportunity that we had in English class to discuss this paper assignment. And I especially want to thank my friends, Sid, Rich, and Bart, because writing about our in-group made sociological analysis seem more relevant to me.

SMALL GROUP STUDY PAPER: A PRIMARY SOCIAL GROUP

Establishment of a general context for the paper.

Social groups are essential to the definition of human socialization. People belong to many social groups—family, church, school, neighborhood, club. Although, as individuals, we might like to believe that we are independent, free to act as we think and feel, the truth is that much of our behavior is influenced by our social in-group (Horton & Hunt, 1976). This paper describes a primary social in-group that I belonged to, along with three peers. The group was a primary group because the members came together as friends, not for a particular purpose

Definition of primary group as contrasted with secondary group.

as would be true in a secondary group like a college classroom or a church choir. Individual members of a primary in-group interact with each other on an intimate basis, with each group member interested in each other group member as a whole person not simply as a performer of particular social roles. In the specified secondary groups, people would regard each other as classmates or as singers. In a primary group, members regard each other as complete people. I will describe the constitution of my primary social in-group as well as the roles of each of the members. I will also give attention to the characteristics and values of the group, its ethnocentricism, and its means of social control.

These descriptions give the reader the criteria the author used to make judgment of "lower middle class."

This group consisted of four male friends, Sid, Rich, Bart, and me (Ted). All of the members lived within a four block radius of each other in the Oxford Circle area of Northeast Philadelphia. We were all members of the lower middle class. Sid's father was a fireman; Rich's was a security chief for a large firm; Bart's father drove a truck, and mine was a bus driver. With the exception of me, all of the members of the group were Catholic, although none was practicing his religion. Rich dropped out of school in the ninth grade. Sid and Bart graduated from high school, and I am the only one who has gone to college. We are now all either nineteen or twenty years old, but the group itself held together until we were seventeen or eighteen.

Subculture Characteristics: Norms and Values

Subheading created by combining two of the suggested areas from assignment indicates that the student has created his own organization instead of writing a simple narrative or following, without thinking, the topics as they appear in the assignment.

The most salient characteristics and values of our group are described below and summarized in Table I. Most features of our behavior were the same as those of other Northeast Philadelphia teenagers, but some characteristics, I am sure, were unique to us. The speech and slang of our group was similar to our peers, including extensive use of four-letter words. However, three of us, all except Sid, knew sufficient German to carry on short conversations. We often spoke in German in the company of others when we either did not want to be understood or we simply

Table I
Characteristics of Primary Group Evidenced in Culture and Subculture of Group

	Culture—Northeast Phila. teens	Subculture of Group
Speech	Includes profanity	—Some use of German in public —Adaptation of Monty Python
Clothes	Jeans, T-shirts, sneakers	Pea coats
Social ritual	Saturday night dances at area high schools or recreation centers	Obtain beer to drink before dance
Attitudes toward fighting	—Acceptable behavior —Fight to win	—Acceptable only if fight was initiated by non-group person —Fighting must be between equal numbers, no "ganging up"

Concrete examples presented without value judgments.

wanted to impress people. This private language was also a source of amusement. We especially enjoyed the curious looks of passengers on buses when we spoke in German. Our second "in" language consisted of expressions from Monty Python records and shows. It was quite common to call each other "a sniveling mound of parrot droppings" or "a slime."

Table I is a good way to illustrate for quick reference the points of similarity and difference between the primary group and their larger culture.

Our clothes were also pretty much the same as everyone else's in our age group. In the summer we wore jeans, t-shirts, and sneakers. For most dances we wore ties and jackets, but only because they were usually required. We did, however, all wear peacoats in the winter and this piece of clothing set us apart from the usual leather-coated groups. The main purpose for wearing old Navy coats was not related to status, however, but to practicality. They were cheap and warm.

Our primary ritual was the Saturday night dance at one of the local high schools or recreation centers: Father Judge, St. Hubert, St. Basil, and Jardel. We pretty much lived for weekends and for these dances. A typical Saturday usually began about noon with four hours of basketball or whatever game was in season. Then we would all go down to the corner store and put up $1.25 each, and wait for "Psyche Mike," the neighborhood runner. Mike was a twenty-six-year-old epileptic, almost always out of work, who purchased our usual two six-packs of beer in exchange for a dollar, which he would use to buy a beer or two for himself. We would stash our beer in Bart's basement for use later that night.

After dinner at our respective homes, we would meet back at Bart's at six-thirty, sit around and drink beer for an hour, and then leave for the dance. Our routine was upset if we were not able to find Mike in the afternoon, for we would have to meet about six o'clock at the local beer distributor's and try to get someone to go in and buy our beer. Occasionally this strategy did not work, and we had to go to the dance "dry." After we were sixteen and could drive, we sometimes varied our routine by driving over to the bars and clubs in New Jersey, where the drinking age was eighteen, and spending the night there.

Drinking alcohol was our primary way of getting "high." Especially near the end of our six-year association, we thought it acceptable to get drunk routinely once or twice a week. But we thought it a "pretty low life" when Bart once got drunk every night for three months. Drugs were not an important part of our group. Only Bart and I smoked marihuana, and then only for relatively short periods of time, about a year.

Of course, we never thought in terms of "ethical" systems. I believe that our standards and expectations were quite similar to those of other groups in our social class. They were simple and straightforward: you didn't let anyone push you around, especially girls; you never hit your mother, but at the same time, you never did much of what she told you to do; you tried never to show fear, or for that matter, love.

We did have two standards that may not have been totally distinctive but were not considered norms for similar social groups. One was that you never started a fight. Only "degenerates" did that. Of course, you never backed down if one was forced on you, and you always fought to win. On the one occasion that Rich tried to start a fight, Bart punched him and all three of us carried Rich away. The second strong conviction was that we, as a group, never "jumped" anyone. Our belief again was that only degenerates fought four on one because they didn't have the guts to fight fair. Rich violated this group value once by jumping into a fight that a friend was losing. We pulled him out and, although we didn't punish him, we threatened to do so. With us it was a matter of honor.

Roles, Status, and Leadership

This subheading is appropriate to this social group, although the instructor has not used this precise terminology in the assignment. The student has created his own analytic structure rather than merely presenting a narrative about a group of friends.

Much of the behavior of members of a group is defined and limited by the role of each member within the group. Although the roles of the members of our group changed somewhat over six years, we all had tacitly understood, if not articulated, roles.

Bart, for example, was generally regarded as the leader. He usually pioneered new fads or activities. His house was almost always the meeting place, and in the last three years of the group, he earned more money than anyone else. His position as host and money lender helped to keep him in an authoritative position with regard to our activities, our dress, and our interactions.

Sid was the "whipping boy," and, until near the end, Rich was the clown. We picked on Sid all of the time, but almost always in a kidding manner. For example, we teased him about everything from the size of his head to the way he pronounced his name. Rich, who always had a joke to tell, was the butt of our teasing when Sid was not around, but Rich gradually emerged from these minor roles because of his expertise with automobiles. As we all began to drive, we became dependent on Rich for the maintenance of our cars. To some degree his authority on cars carried over to other matters. We listened to Rich's opinions much more seriously at the end than at the beginning.

My role remained virtually unchanged for the

Note the attempt to explore the relationships beyond casual observations and to organize them within categories instead of presenting them without a structure.

years. Because I was acknowledged to be the smartest member of the group, I was the resident authority on intellectual matters and the person in whom the other members would confide if they wanted to discuss a matter that would not have been appropriate for full group discussion. We did not have many "intellectual" discussions as a group, but sometimes, in private, without fear of ridicule, individual members would talk seriously and candidly about something of interest to them.

Since I was the most aggressive and physically the largest group member, I was also considered the first to be called on in time of trouble. Once at a party we averted a physical confrontation with several troublemakers because of my actions. As Sid said, "I'm sure glad you were there." Since that incident the other members of the group have become more capable of defending themselves.

Overall, the pecking order of the group was: first, Bart; second, Ted; third, Rich; and fourth, Sid. In different areas, however, the status order was different. Below are rankings in several areas. Before writing this paper, I discussed these rankings with other group members.

Competition and Cooperation

Attempt to provide theoretical context from reading for the rest of the section.

Competition within a group occurs in order to acquire rewards—money, love, power—which exist in limited amounts. The only significant resource that existed in our group was leadership, for which the competition was sometimes intense. When we split, we split into two camps. One consisted

Table II
Status Order for Group Members for
Five Categories

This table illustrates points made in the text but expands the material covered to give more information than would be manageable in prose form.

Categories	First	Second	Third	Fourth
1. Meeting Girls	Bart	Ted	Rich	Sid
2. Mechanical ability	Rich	Bart	Sid	Ted
3. Physical ability	Ted	Rich	Bart	Sid
4. Finances	Bart	Sid	Rich	Ted
5. Intelligence	Ted	Bart	Rich	Sid

of Bart and Sid, the other of Rich and me. It was within this arrangement that most of the conflict within the group took place, and, consequently, a good portion of the conflict took place between Bart and me, especially over the question of who would lead the whole group. This interaction involved trying to win over the lesser member of the other camp (Rich or Sid). The competition did not involve physical tests of any kind, but did take the form of verbal harassment. The most common expression was criticism of the other leader. Bart would say to Rich, "Why listen to him. He's such an ass." I would respond, "Sid, you must be pretty stupid to follow him; he doesn't know what he is doing." This sort of competition was almost continuous for the full six years.

Example to illustrate the concept of competition.

Several times there were actual breaks within the group. Usually, however, these rifts lasted only for a day or two. Rich and I would go to a dance at St. Basil, and Bart and Sid would attend one at Father Judge. In general, Bart would control the group. I might wrest control for a few weeks, but then leadership would revert to Bart for months. During one period, Bart's control was so complete that I was, for a time, forced out altogether.

Student presents this information without emotional editorializing.

When Bart was in control, his domination over Sid was almost absolute. Sid followed Bart everywhere, regardless of whether or not Sid wanted to go. In contrast, Bart's authority over me was not very strong, and his control of Rich was somewhere in between. Rich could say yes or no. When I was in control, Rich followed me blindly, Sid shifted somewhat, and Bart acted pretty much as I did when Bart was in control.

Student draws inferences, does not merely list events.

Overall, however, we showed a great deal of primary group cooperation, derived probably from our ethnocentric feelings for each other. Group cooperation was particularly evident when we dealt with other groups. In times of emergency, especially when we had trouble with others, we became very cohesive. An example was the occasion when the six members of a gang called C & A attacked Sid one night, apparently for no reason. We considered it our duty to retaliate, and the

Example to illustrate cooperation.

next night we did. I went because Sid was part of our group, even though I never really liked Sid very much. It was "us against them."

Social Control Techniques

Paragraph designed to put this group into larger perspective of primary groups.

Like all primary groups, we expected conformity to the norms of the group in dress, speech, social behavior, and values. And like all groups, we developed ways to enforce this conformity. The four ways we handled violations were sarcasm, gossip, physical punishment, and, as a last resort, ostracism.

Student builds generalizations on solid detail.

Of these, sarcasm and gossip were the more used and less severe. If, for example, a member got his hair cut too short, the others would make sarcastic remarks about his ears, the shape of his head, and so on. Gossip was used to correct behavior in such areas as girls and dealing with money. If a member was "hen-pecked" or "too tight" with his money, the others began to speak about these matters to each other until the offending party found out. This form of reprimand was usually effective.

Physical punishment was employed to correct continued violations of minor values or first-time violations of major values. If, for example, a member was still "too tight" with his money after the use of sarcasm and gossip, then he might be hit by one of the members of the group. If, as Rich did when he "ganged-up" on another person, a member violated an important norm, he might be physically roughed up or engaged in a full-scale fight. Usually, this form of correction occurred spontaneously, without any member passing judgment verbally or formally.

Use of technical term, "ostracism," reinforced by explaining, in other words, the meaning of the term.

Ostracism was the last resort in response to a member's deviant behavior. If any member knowingly violated one of the group's major norms and continued to do so, the other members simply stopped associating with him.

Ethnocentrism

Our belief that our group was superior to others led, naturally, to ethnocentric feelings and behavior. The other groups were "fags" or "degenerates." This feeling that we were the best caused us, several times, to turn down invitations to parties because there would be too many "fags" there or because we didn't want to associate with "degenerates." One notable ethnocentric reaction occurred after the four of us met and began dating, collectively, a group of four girls. After about two months these girls began to cool down the relationship and then rejected us in favor of four members of a gang that lived about seven blocks from us. None of us could understand how these girls could drop us for them. We were cool, and those guys were "smacks." We finally decided that the girls were "screwed up." Why else would they leave us for them?

Concrete criteria for ethnocentric feelings.

These feelings of superiority came out with regard to any other type of group, whether we distinguished ourselves from them by class, nationality, or size. We were superior to the lower class groups in Fishtown because they were "scum." We were better than the "degenerates" of South Philadelphia. The upper classes in Parkwood Manor were beneath us because they were "snobs." Larger groups of boys were inferior to us because it took more "guts" to go to dances with only four in a group instead of ten or twenty.

Good attempt at analyzing reasons for the relationship.

Of course, there were some groups that we considered almost equal to us, primarily because we were friendly with them. One particular group, known as Posalie Street, were definitely our equals. We went to dances with them; we partied with them; we even dated some of their female members. Many times we went down to Posalie Street to "hang around," and often they came to Bart's to do the same. They shared our values and our norms. The only reason that we did not become closer together, I suppose, was simple geography.

Conclusion

At the present time the group does not exist, nor is it likely to again. Bart and I grew away from Rich and Sid. In fact, Bart and I are now closer than ever, and I think it is because there is no longer a power struggle between us. In some ways I outgrew the primary group, especially as I increased my contacts with members of a secondary group, Beaver College students. It was with this new association that I first began to realize that my primary group was really not so great. And, although they are an "in-group" for me, college students are definitely an "out-group" for the other three, even for Bart, who still gives me a bad time about the new direction of my life.

Although I have outgrown my primary group, I can neither forget it nor diminish its influence on me. My primary group served an important function during my adolescence. It provided me with "intimate, personal, and total involvement in others' lives" (Horton and Hunt, 1976, p. 155). In some respects it is sad that the primary group no longer exists, for I sometimes miss the easy interaction and the casual teasing that was so much a part of it. However, its displacement by the secondary group of college classmates was inevitable, and this more impersonal and goal-oriented group is appropriate for me at this stage of my life.

References

Horton, P. B. and Hunt, C. L. <u>Sociology</u>. New York: McGraw-Hill, 1976.

Psychology 101–102: The Mama Rat project

Beaver College
Dept. of Psychology
Glenside, PA 19038

Introduction   One of the major goals of this project is to show how the course of development follows an orderly sequence both in humans and other mammals. Another is to observe the behavior of mothers before birth and with their pups. You are probably more interested in children than in rats, but children develop much too slowly for the time we have available. Rats go through childhood in six weeks and are sexually adult in twelve weeks; the developmental process is short in time but is similar in many respects to that exhibited by humans. As you watch baby rats develop, you will have experiences in making behavioral observations, relating those observations to theoretical principles, and writing a short paper describing your observations and conclusions.

The theoretical interest of the project lies in two areas. The first is that of "instinct," or species-characteristic behavior. Your instructor and your text will give you some background for the ideas you will be examining in this area. Maternal behavior is often given as an example of an instinct. You will have a chance to watch a rat mother preparing for the birth of her pups and caring for them. You will then be able to check what you see against the criteria for species-characteristic behavior in the readings.

The other area is development. You will have a chance to observe the orderly changes in appearance and behavior of the pups as they get older and check these observations against the principles of development described in your readings and in class. If you want to read further, your instructor can direct you to material on reserve in the library.

Instructions for observations

You will observe the external anatomy and behavior of several litters of rat pups from the time they are born until they are weaned about a month later. You will also observe the behavior of the mothers from their last few days of pregnancy until weaning. Pregnant rats usually build nests a few days prior to parturition. With luck, you may be present while a female is delivering.

You should observe the rats for fifteen minutes per day, three days a week for four weeks; i.e., 12 observation periods lasting a total of three hours. If all the rats are asleep, you will have to stay longer than fifteen minutes or come back at another time. The animals are located behind a one-way viewing screen in Room 108. Rats are most active during the night so we maintain them on a reversed light-dark cycle. Since they are relatively insensitive to red light, such illumination simulates their nighttime which begins at 8 AM and ends at 5 PM. Try to make all of your observations at about the same time each day. Do not turn on the lights in the observation room. You must allow a few minutes for your eyes to adapt to the very dim light in the room.

The most useful way to record your observations is to make a large table or chart on several pages of your notebook with columns for each category of behavior. An example of the format for such a chart is attached. During each period you should be sure to record descriptions of at least several of the items about mother or pups from the list in Table 1. The more information you record, the easier it will be to write your final paper. Date every observation so that you see a progression, and you know the milestones, such as birth, eyes opening, beginning walking, first eating solid food, weaning, etc.

It sometimes helps to discuss your observations with your roommate or someone else in the class to increase the precision of your descriptions. You may find that you did not notice some details. After talking with

SAMPLE CHART

Date of observation	Mother's behavior	Pups: Physical development	Locomotion	Sensory development	Social behavior	Miscellaneous
Sept. 11						
Sept. 13						
Sept. 15						
Sept. 18						

someone else, you may be able to record your next observation with greater specificity.

Observation of mothers. Your observation periods will be divided between watching the mothers and watching the pups. In observing the mothers, you will look for the following categories of observations as listed in Table 1: nest building, retrieving the young, grooming the young, grooming herself, nursing, sleeping, feeding, walking. The last four activities you will observe simply to see the postures and movements which are characteristic of an adult rat, so that you can compare adult activities to those of the pups. Watch the mother particularly for her interactions with the litter: nest building, retrieving, grooming, and nursing. You should see changes during the four weeks, because at the end of that period the litter will be weaned and could be living away from the mother.

When you observe grooming, for example, record in as much detail as you can exactly how the mother does it. How does she hold the pups? Does she hold them differently at different ages? What parts of the body are involved? Is this grooming similar to her grooming of herself, of the pups' grooming of one another? When observing nursing, record details about time, postures, and methods of weaning. Be precise in all descriptions and set up your own subcategories. Look for changes over the four-week period. Table 2 presents examples of criteria for several categories.

Observation of pups. Spend two-thirds of each observation period observing the pups in any single cage. Observe the same cage during all 12 observation periods so that you may gain an appreciation of behavioral

TABLE 1
*Behavioral categories
for description of
mother rat and pups*

1. *Mothers*
   Nest building
   Grooming self, grooming pups (especially anal licking)
   Exploration
   Nursing
   Retrieving
   Rejecting pups at weaning
   Walking
   Feeding

2. *Pups*
   Sleeping (solitary, social)
   Feeding
      Suckling
      Solid food—eating behavior
      Drinking
   Locomotion: Stages include trunk movements or wiggling, twitching, freezing, sniffing, orienting, hopping, crawling with forepaws, righting movements, rising to erect position, walking, running, climbing, rising and swaying, jumping.
   Sensory behavior: Describe indications of response to visual, auditory, odor, tactile cues.
   Elimination: urination, defecation, anal licking
   Vocalization: quality of sounds (if audible), stimuli to sound production
   Grooming: face washing, licking, scratching (which paws, location of area scratched)
   Exploration: sniffing objects, making lateral head movements, digging in nesting materials
   Social behavior: Describe at each stage.
      —huddling, mutual sleeping postures
      —fighting over nursing position
      —general social activity such as running, jumping, chasing, wrestling, mutual grooming
      —fighting, including description of posture, length of encounter, acting of "victor" and "loser"
      —pseudo-sexual behavior, sniffing and licking of genitals, mounting

Stages of growth and physical development should be outlined on the basis of exact descriptions of skin (later fur), appearance of coloration, apparent length and weight, time of opening of eyes.

TABLE 2
*Sample criteria for
behavioral categories*

1. *Nest building*
   Mother rat pushes bedding material with nose, holds it in forepaws, heaps it in corner of cage (how high? how tidy or regular? what proportion of the bedding materials in the cage is included in the heap?). Mother lies on heap creating a depression in the center. Mother works at edges of heap. Mother picks up her tail and carries it to nest.

2. *Grooming self*
   Mother lies on back, paws extended, licks and bites at fur (where?). Mother scratches at head behind ears with fore or rear paws (which?). Mother rubs against sides of cage. (Describe position of mother while she is licking as precisely as possible.)

3. *Feeding behavior*
   Mother lies on side, belly extended (describe position exactly). Pup struggles for position on mother's belly with wriggling movements of trunk, treading movements of forepaws. Pup holds on to nipple, engages in coordinated sucking movements and treading of forepaws. Pup struggles to maintain position, squeals if displaced by mother's movements or by other pups. (Time length of suckling for several pups.) Describe actions as pup disengages when it is sated.

---

and anatomic development of rat pups. Table 1 provides a partial list of items to observe. For each item you must record in careful detail the components of each example of behavior. How do the rat pups sleep? In what position? How does walking develop? What parts of the body make what kinds of movements? Do the pups walk the way the mother does?

Be careful not to record your feelings or interpretation, but simply what *you see*. "The mother is taking time for herself," or "She hates her babies now that they are older," are *not* good observations. "Mother is sleeping on opposite side of cage from nest," or "Mother walks away from pups during nursing," are appropriate observations because they do not project human feelings onto the animals.

**Instructions for
paper**   Your paper has two components: (1) a chronological summary of your observations and (2) an interpretation or discussion of the important concepts demonstrated by your observations. Assume that your paper will be read by another member of the class who could not do the observations, but who has read the same material that you have.

Summary. In making your summary, first arrange all 12 observations of mother and of pups in order and read through them to see the chronology of feeding changes, or mobility, or grooming, or condition of nest, etc. You are to summarize material both about the mothers and the pups. A summary requires the omission of some of your details and the selection of more important observations. If your 12 observation periods show a continuous, detailed picture of growth of only some of the categories of behavior listed in Table 1, then emphasize those and ignore others. You see that the quality of your summary is dependent upon the quality of your observations. A graphic or tabular summary of your observations is helpful to the reader. Remember there are many details to be read about and understood, so give the reader all the help you can.

In summarizing your observations remember that you are providing scientific data rather than a report on your own feelings. For example, even if you had a strong emotional reaction to seeing a mother rat give birth, you should not include a report of that in this paper. (You might want to write an entirely different kind of essay for your English class on your feelings of pity, terror, or sympathy as you watched a mother rat give birth.)

Interpretation. The purpose of this section of the paper is to link the observations you have described in part 1 with the theoretical ideas and concepts discussed in the readings and in class. In a sense you are telling the reader why it was worthwhile to have made these observations. You should take several of the theoretical concepts about trends in development or about species-specific behavior and look for data in your observations which would help explain or illustrate these concepts. One example might be the concept that motor behavior progresses from mass responses to specific or differentiated responses. Look at your observations. Can you find examples of mass responses (generalized twitching might be one)? Can you find examples of specific responses (handling solid food is one)? Now check the frequency with which mass responses and specific responses occur early in the pup's development, later in development. Does the concept fit your observations? Are there more mass responses early and more specific responses late?

You should do something like this for two or three other concepts. The more ably you relate observations to concepts the more you will understand how scientists are able to draw important conclusions from observational data.

A few last words. In your final draft, check your paper for spelling (especially psychological terms) and punctuation. Errors of spelling and punctuation give a poor first impression of your writing skills. If your paper received a first reading in English 100, 101, or 102, you should write an acknowledgment of this. The Beaver College Style Sheet describes the form for acknowledgments and references for psychology papers.

The quality of your paper will not be judged on its length. A good paper has richness of detail, a presentation that allows the reader to "see" through your observations, and a thoughtful interpretation linking concepts to your observations.

Mama Rat

Karen Sykie
Psychology 101
October 15, 1999
Dr. Bernard Mausner

Acknowledgments

I want to thank my English 101 instructor,
Professor Peggy Horodowich, for giving me an
opportunity to work on drafts of this paper in
the English 101 course, even though the finished
paper was actually required in Psychology 101.
Not only did she provide class time for peer
group responses to my paper, but she conducted a
lesson on the precise recording of observations.
The whole class had a chance to see ways to make
sense of a list of details.
I also want to thank my roommate, Elizabeth
Czyszczon, for looking at the baby rats with me,
even though she said that they made her sick. She
was the one who noticed the emergence of the dark
spots on the rats' backs.
Finally, thanks to my boyfriend, Kenneth
Fairness, for typing my paper.

Mama Rat

During a four-week period I observed the
behavior of a laboratory rat mother and her
litter. I began my observations on the day before
the litter of eleven rat pups was born, and I
observed the rats for fifteen minutes for four
days of the first week, and three days during
each of the next three weeks—thirteen
observations in all.

*Student correctly
assumes her audience
is familiar with
laboratory cages and
does not describe
them. She does
explain observational
context.*

Behavior of the Mother

Nestbuilding

During my first four days the Mama rat spent one-quarter of the observed time in nest building. She picked up pieces of the nesting

material with her mouth and/or front feet, accepting some pieces and discarding others, and threw the selected particles on top of the nest. The nest was a large pile with a center indentation made by the litter, but because the nesting material was soft, the pile became flattened by the movement of the litter. She

spent less time rebuilding the nest during the second and third weeks, and she spent no time at all on the nest during the fourth week.

Grooming herself and the pups

The mother groomed (cleaned) her head by licking her front feet and then running them along her face and nose. She chewed at her tail and licked her anal area. She stood on her hind legs and licked her stomach and nipples. She

licked all the pups at the same time while they were lying in a huddle. She turned them over and moved them around with her front feet and licked other portions of their bodies including the anal areas.

Nursing and weaning of the pups

The mother nursed the pups continually during the first week, leaving the nest for only a few seconds at a time to scratch herself, or get food and water. Sometimes she chewed food while she was nursing the pups. She sat on top of the nest, and the pups nursed under her. Sometimes I could see a pup's leg protruding from the side of the mother's body. During the third week the pups would hang on the mother's nipples for a few seconds when she began to leave the nest. The pups would hang on and then fall into the nest as the mother walked on. During the third and fourth weeks, the mother gradually spent less

time nursing the pups. In fact, during the fourth week, she pressed her body against the walls of the cage to prevent the young from nursing.

Instinct

Instinctive behavior, that is, complex behavior which is specific to the species and appears in complete form without opportunity for learning or practice, characterizes most of the

mother's behavior. She built and rebuilt the nest, starting before the pups were born; she ate the afterbirth; she groomed herself and the pups. This complex behavior was made up of many component movements and seemed to have a similar pattern each time I observed it. Since this

litter was the first one for the mother, she could not have learned the behavior previously. As the weeks went on, the mother spent less time nursing, probably because the pups' needs and the mother's milk supply diminished.

Development of the Pups

Physical characteristics

The pups' skin was pink and wrinkled at birth. Their heads were more than half the total size of their bodies, in contrast to the mother's head which was about one-seventh the size of her body. Their limbs were short and stubby. Their ears were flat against their heads, and their facial features were undefined. After a few days the skin color turned to a darker pink, and by the

end of the first week darker patches were beginning to show on various places on their bodies. During the second week their heads were completely dark with dark spots clearly defined on their backs. The dark spots began to have fuzzy hair, while the undersides and limbs remained pink. By the end of the second week, the facial features, ears, and digits were clearly defined, and individual differences in the size of the pups began to show. The color differentiation of the pups was complete by the third week as the black and white hair grew

longer. The eyes opened during the third week. I could not tell whether the pups' sense of smell was developed or not. Their bodies and limbs grew into better proportion with their heads, so by the end of four weeks they looked like smaller versions of their mother, except for individual color differentiations.

Locomotion and motor skills

In the first days after their birth, the pups remained in a huddle and their bodies quivered and twitched. When one pup moved, a ripple of movement seemed to go through the mass of sleeping pups. Their major activity was nursing. When sucking at their mother, their front paws seemed engaged in a pumping action.

After a few days the pups were able to move a few inches by sliding along on their bellies and pushing with their hind feet and pulling with their front feet. By the second week the pups were able to lift their heads and upper bodies and were standing on their feet, although their bodies and limbs were shaky. Sometimes they would move several inches away from the litter. They could not yet see, so they may have gotten back by smell or possibly by sensing body heat. Sometimes they would be retrieved by their mother, who would pick the wanderer up in her mouth and return him to the nest after a thorough grooming.

The term "second week" rather than actual dates of events makes the paper easier to read.

The third week showed the greatest increase in the level of their activity. Their movements became more rapid and the pups were able to get up and walk away from the nest and return without assistance from the mother. The pups began putting their front feet up on the sides of the cage, and they were able to run about with quick, accurate movements. This substantial increase in locomotion occurred in the same week in which their eyes opened. Those two significant changes might be related genetically.

In the fourth week, the pups were running around the cage and hanging from the screen on the top of the cage. They seemed almost to hop or bounce when they moved. When a sudden noise or movement occurred, they would dart around. They were also capable of picking up things with their front feet and grooming themselves and their litter mates.

Rich detail in description.

The development of the rat pups' physical characteristics and motor skills clearly exemplified three trends in development: <u>cephalocaudal</u>, from head to tail; <u>proximodistal</u>, from near the trunk to far from the trunk; and <u>mass–to–specific</u>, increasing precision of movements. The rats were born with oversized heads and stubby bodies. Their first movements were with their heads and front legs. The cephalocaudal pattern, from head to tail, was exhibited as they began to use their back legs and could coordinate the movement of all four legs. The newborn rats had stubby bodies that appeared to be almost a single mass. But as the weeks went on, they developed more specific mobility in their limbs in the expected mass–to–specific pattern. Their developing skills in picking up food and other materials and holding these things while they ate exemplified their increased precision in specific movements. Their pattern of development was from the trunk to extremities in a proximodistal direction. Their increased skills in scratching and grooming were also examples of mass–to–specific and proximodistal development. All of these trends appeared simultaneously and overlapped.

Most mammals, including humans, develop according to similar trends. Infant rats and human infants have heads larger than their bodies and the growth of muscles and nerves proceeds downward; their appendages grow and develop dexterity after the trunk itself has developed to some extent; as they grow, they gain increased precision in their movements. Infant rats and human infants are also very different in the specific ways that they exemplify these general growth patterns. Each species has its own individual characteristics that are species specific. The age at which eyes open, for example, is a species specific characteristic. The litter of rat pups that I observed demonstrated these distinctive features as well as general trends of growth.

Biology 137 (animal behavior): Scientific review paper

Each student will research and write a review paper. The purpose of the paper is to summarize the present state of investigation in a well-defined area of scientific interest and on a topic of on-going research.

Please select and define a topic, which must be approved by me. Find at least 8 to 10 research materials (papers, articles, books) on the topic and, in your own words, synthesize the research into a review paper. You should write your review so that a classmate in Biology 137 can understand the existing research situation on your topic. Your audience is composed of your classmates who are interested in science but who are not familiar with your topic.

This paper must be submitted in draft stages: (1) topic; (2) preliminary reference list; (3) draft for peer review; (4) finished draft, 8 to 12 pages, typed, double-spaced, with citations and reference list.

See the syllabus for due dates.

```
                    THE STATE OF RESEARCH
                    ON THE "SONGS" OF THE
                    HUMPBACK WHALE




                                   Gillian Morton
                                   Biology 137
                                   April 28, 1999
                                   Dr. Myra Jacobsohn
```

```
                    Acknowledgments
     I want to thank my instructor, Professor Myra
Jacobsohn, for her encouragement throughout this
project. She helped me to see that even a
confirmed literary type like me can become really
interested in a scientific topic. I won't say
that the humpbacks will ever replace the sirens,
but I'm glad to know that song in some sense can
be an appropriate subject for a biology course. I
also want to thank the students in my peer review
```

group, Barbara Kearney, Masha Lande, and Morton Apfelbaum, for their very helpful comments on my draft.

THE STATE OF RESEARCH ON
THE "SONGS" OF THE HUMPBACK WHALE

Introduction serves to identify the object of the study. It discusses characteristics that a science student would need as a context for reading the essay. Notice that the description is not evaluative, for example, the student does not say, "the humpback whale is a beautiful animal."

Whales, like all members of the order Cetacea, are warm—blooded marine mammals. They breathe with lungs and give live birth to offspring, which they nurse. These characteristics make Cetaceans unique among sea animals and worthy of being studied more in the manner that we study primates rather than in the way we study fish. Like dolphins, Cetaceans on which extensive research has been done (Cousteau & Diolé, 1975; Lilly, 1975), whales are known to be capable of performing sophisticated mental functions (Cousteau & Diolé, 1975).

One whale which has intrigued researchers for nearly three decades is the humpback. Growing in length to nearly forty—five feet, the humpback is known for its giant, sculpted flippers which can grow to a third of the whale's total body length. Although found in all oceans of the world (McIntyre, 1974), the humpback population is concentrated primarily in the Antarctic Ocean. But even there they have never been plentiful. Perhaps once they numbered over thirty thousand, but the increase in whaling over the past forty years has reduced that number drastically (Payne & McVay, 1971). Even though the humpback has been overhunted in the northern hemisphere, small groups or herds gather in various areas of these waters to feed and give birth. The waters of Hawaii and Bermuda are most frequented. And it is in these areas that researchers have recorded their "songs" during their annual migrations.

History of Recordings

Subheadings are brief and descriptive, capitalized, and centered.

Research into the songs of whales was not possible until the development of sonar in World War I. But the first serious research was not done until 1952 when O. W. Schreiber made extensive recordings off Oahu, Hawaii. W. E.

Schevill later recognized the sounds recorded by Schreiber as coming from humpback whales. The most impressive recordings were made near Bermuda by Frank Watlington, who collected his sounds by hydrophone. His equipment and fortunate location allowed him to record humpback sounds during their spring migrations (1953–1964), without the usual interference of shipboard and cable noises and without the fear that he was disturbing the whales by the presence of an observer (Payne & McVay, 1971). Roger and Mary Payne then continued where Watlington left off. They made several hundred hours of recordings off Bermuda during the spring from 1967 to 1971. More recently, Clark and Clark (1980) have begun research on whale behavior when the recordings are played back to them.

History section provides the background for the research to be discussed.

Source and Nature of the Songs

These topics are neither technical nor controversial, so they are covered quickly and efficiently.

Physically, the sounds of the humpback whales are produced entirely by shuttling air within their heads. That is, no air is expelled from the whale to produce the sounds (Miller, 1979). Consequently, the songs can be and are produced while the whales are submerged. For the most part, whales are alone and relatively inactive when they start to sing. When a few whales begin to gather, the first stops singing, but then the group begins to produce various unorganized mumbling sounds. Gradually, they all join in to form a rumbling chorus. Cousteau and Diolé (1972) consider this behavior analogous to orchestra members first tuning their instruments, then, all at once, striking up their piece of music. Once they are singing together, whales, like professional musicians, breathe in staggered sequences so that they will not interrupt the song.

Analysis of the Songs

This is the main section of the paper.

On first hearing the songs of the humpback whale, one gets the impression of an almost endless variety of sounds. However, sound spectrographic analysis reveals that all of these sounds occur in particular patterns and that every few minutes long sequences are accurately repeated (Payne & McVay, 1971). Since bird sounds are called "songs" because they consist of a fixed pattern of sounds, it is also correct to call the sounds made by the humpback, songs. Unlike the songs of birds, which are high-pitched and last for only a few seconds, the songs of the humpback vary in pitch and can last for up to thirty minutes. Interestingly, if a whale song is recorded and speeded up fourteen times the normal playback speed, it sounds amazingly like the song of a bird (Payne, 1979). Payne and McVay (1971), analyzing humpback songs, discovered and described the parts of the patterns of the songs. The shortest sound of the song is called a "unit." Some units, when analyzed at slower speeds, actually turned out to be a series of rapid pulses which Payne designated as "subunits." A series of units create a "phrase," and a continuous sequence of phrases is called a "theme." Several themes combine to form a song. A "song session," that is a series of songs, can last for hours. In summary, a subunit, a unit, a phrase, a theme, a song, a song session comprise the sound repertoire of the humpback whale.

Payne and McVay's studies (1971) reveal the fact that the humpback has a definite species-specific song pattern and that individual humpbacks vary their songs. By studying and analyzing scores of recordings and spectrograms, Payne discovered that all songs consist of three main sections: the first contains rapidly repeated pulses that vary in tone; the second consists of many short units of high frequency; and the last is made up of lower and longer notes that are repetitious both in rhythm and frequency. Payne believes that these three basic sections make up a general species-specific pattern for the humpback whale. Clark (1980), for example, discovered that right whales "talked back" to recordings of other right whales but swam away and made few responses to the songs of the humpback.

Despite the existence of a pattern among humpback whales, individual whales vary their songs. Payne noted that an individual whale,

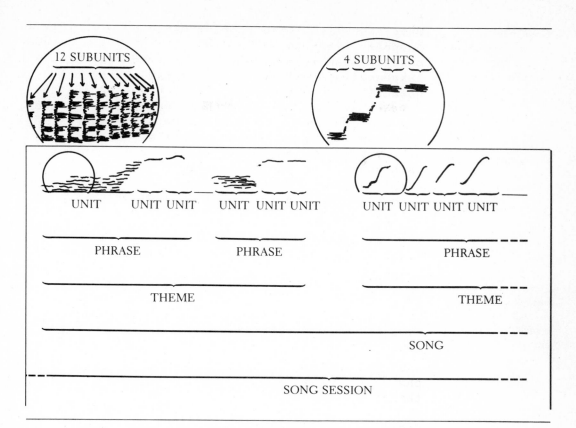

Most papers in the sciences and social sciences include graphic presentations of information.

Fig. 1. This diagram represents a whale sound spectrogram which depicts the different parts that make up a whale song. The circled marks are enlargements of patterns from the diagram. (Payne & McVay, 1971)

repeating its own song, will change the song length. He recorded two successive songs of one whale. The first lasted seven minutes; the other continued for twelve and one-half minutes (Payne & McVay, 1971). The spectrograms of the recordings revealed that the variations in length were due to differences in the number of times that individual phrases were repeated within a theme. In other words, whales do not simply sing mechanically, but compose as they sing.

This ability of humpbacks to change their songs sets them off from other singing animals.

Only man shares this complex behavior with the humpback. The Paynes, after twenty years of studying recordings, have discovered that the humpbacks not only vary individual songs, but change their song over a period of years (Payne, 1979). But, regardless of how frequent or complex the changes are, each whale apparently learns them. The recordings show that the "new" song, with the variations on it, is the only song sung each year.

"Composing" the Songs

Payne's research (1979) indicates that the musical talent of the humpbacks may be inherited. Payne compared the songs of humpbacks from Hawaii for a four-year period with those of the Bermuda whales for the same four years. He discovered that the two whale populations, which certainly had not been in contact, had the same song structure and functioned according to the same kinds of changes. This finding strongly suggests that the whales inherit the songs and the ability to improvise upon them. Since the whales do not sing at their summer feeding grounds, Payne (1979) first believed that it was possible that the whales simply forgot the song between seasons and then from fragments of the old song improvised a new one each year. However, after further study of humpbacks off the island of Maui, Payne (1979) discovered that the whales had not forgotten the previous season's song, since they were singing it when they first returned to Maui. Only later in the season did the changes in the song begin to develop (Payne, 1979). Payne's conclusion was that during the time between breeding seasons, humpbacks keep the previous year's song, without change, in memory.

Purpose of the Song

The actual function of the elaborate song still eludes scientists. Mrozek (1978) argues that the song may be a territorial proclamation, that it provides adequate spacing and prevents direct competition among males for females. Some researchers believe that the song may actually be

Student does not take sides but presents different theories objectively.

a love song. The best evidence for this theory is that the song is sung only in one season, suspected to be the breeding season, and is sung only by adults (Miller, 1979). Schevill (1964, as referred to by Payne & McVay, 1971) similarly argues that the song is related to pair formation. Humpback songs recorded near Puerto Rico were being sung in February, the beginning of the northward migration of the whales. This phenomenon suggests, according to Payne and McVay (1971), that the song, therefore, might serve as a flock call to hold together a loose cluster of individual whales.

Conclusion

The student concludes by discussing the implications of the research.

Note this reference to the introduction.

It has taken years of research to find and identify a pattern of communication in the sounds of the humpback whales. Perhaps further research, especially into the timing and accompanying behavioral patterns, will establish the exact purposes of the songs. Findings in this area may also have implications for the study of the sounds of other animals which may communicate in patterns that we do not recognize. At a minimum, continued studies will make us more aware of the intelligence of the humpback and may contribute to its preservation.

Reference List

The quantity and nature of the sources for reference indicate a freshman/ sophomore paper.

Clark, C. W., & Clark, J. M. Sound playback experiments with southern right whales. Science, 1980, 207, 663–664.

Cousteau, J., & Diolé, P. The whale. New York: Doubleday, 1972.

Cousteau, J., & Diolé, P. Dolphins. New York: Doubleday, 1975.

Lilly, J. Lilly on dolphins. Garden City, N.Y.: Anchor Press, 1975.

McIntyre, J. The mind in the waters. New York: Charles Scribners Sons, 1974.

Miller, J. A whale of a song. Science News, 1979, 115, 26–27.

Mrozek, C. Giant nightingales of the deep.
   Oceans, 1978, 11, 2–7.
Payne, R. Humpbacks: Their mysterious songs.
   National Geographic, 1979, 156, 18–25.
Payne, R., & McVay, S. Sounds of the humpback
   whales. Science, 1971, 173, 585–597.

Glossary

Academic disciplines Branches of learning that have developed different traditions, perspectives, and questions but that all depend on orderly intellectual habits of reason and consistency.

Acknowledgment An expression of thanks for help received during the composing process. This help might include responses to drafts, conversations about the evolving ideas, moral support, or typing. (See **Documentation** for the types of help that cannot merely be acknowledged but must be documented in a footnote or an author/date reference.)

Analysis A close examination and interpretation of an artistic or intellectual endeavor.

Argument In logic, a set of statements that include a **Conclusion** that is said to follow from or be supported by evidence, called a **Premise**.

Argumentation A form of writing or speaking that employs logic to support or refute a position.

Audience The intended readers for a piece of writing.

Bibliography A list of sources of information on a particular subject.

Case study (or history) A report of information derived from the close observation and recording of behavior.

Claim A conclusion, an inference that follows from evidence.

Cognitive style An individual's way of perceiving and thinking about experience.

Collaborative learning Studying together with classmates; learning from people who are at approximately the same level of learning as you are.

Conclusion An inference that follows from evidence. (See **Premise**.)

Controlling question A focused inquiry to which your paper will be an answer.

Critical thinking Thought processes that are characterized by careful analysis and discernment, not necessarily by faultfinding.

Critique A close examination, interpretation, and evaluation of an idea, experience, or work of art.

Description A form of writing or speaking that gives a detailed account of something, creating a mental image through appropriate use of words.

Discourse Communication of ideas or information by speaking or writing.

Documentation A record of sources used in research: direct quotations; other people's judgments, ideas, opinions, inferences; facts that other people have discovered; experiments performed by other people. This record must provide enough information so that readers can check the original sources. The two major forms of documentation are the use of footnotes and the use of the author-date method.

Draft A rough or preliminary version of a piece of writing.

Exposition A form of writing or speaking that explains and analyzes.

Expressive writing (reflective writing) Writing that has as its primary aim the private expression of feelings and responses; for example, diaries, private journals, reaction papers.

Figure A drawing, graph, picture, flow diagram, computer representation, or other graphic form used to present the results of research. (See **Table**.)

Ground A premise, the evidence on which a conclusion in an argument is based.

Heuristics Strategies to help you discover ideas and to learn more about a topic; opposed to rules in that heuristics can lead in many directions and do not guarantee a single right answer.

Humanities Branches of learning concerned with questions of human values; for example, history, philosophy, languages, linguistics, literature, archaeology, jurisprudence, history and criticism of the arts, ethics, comparative religion.

Incubation A period of rest or change of activity when you allow your ideas on a particular project to take form while you consciously do something else.

Index An alphabetical list that points to where books and articles are to be found; an alphabetical list that points to particular pages in a book.

Informative writing Writing that has as its primary aim the communication of information to others.

Journal (a) A notebook for private writing. (b) A scholarly periodical.

Lab practical A special quiz designed to discover whether science students are familiar with laboratory procedures and results.

Laboratory report A paper that describes, documents, and communicates the completion of an experiment in a science laboratory.

Liberal arts The branches of learning in an academic college program, including the humanities and the social and natural sciences; distinguished from more technical subjects by an emphasis on questions, rather than on fixed answers.

Literary writing Writing that has as its primary aim the achievement of beauty in language or form.

Long-term memory The capacity to store information, ideas, facts, and images in the mind for an extended period.

Memory The capacity to retain facts, ideas, or images in the mind. (See **Short-term memory** and **Long-term memory**.)

Narration A form of writing or speaking that tells, or gives a sequential account of something.

Natural sciences Branches of learning concerned with the systematic study of nature and the physical world; for example, biology, chemistry, physics, geology, astronomy, zoology, botany.

Peer criticism, peer review Exchanging helpful comments on work-in-progress with people who are at approximately the same level of learning. Students respond to the work of other students; scholars in a discipline review the work of other scholars.

Peer groups Several classmates meeting together to review drafts or to discuss ideas.

Pentad A heuristic developed by Kenneth Burke; five different perspectives for looking at a topic: as an action, actor-agent, scene, means, purpose.

Persuasive writing Writing that has as its primary aim convincing others to do or to believe something.

Plagiarism The act of using sources without documentation or of accepting help without acknowledgment; taking the ideas or writings of someone else and passing them off as your own. (See **Documentation** and **Acknowledgment**.)

Premise The evidence on which a conclusion in an argument is based.

Primary source First-hand direct account of information or experience; a work of art or original philosophical text. (See **Secondary source**.)

Private writing Writing that you do for yourself as a personal record or as an aid to learning, not as a form of communication to others.

Problems Focused questions to which you do not yet know the answer.

Reader-based prose Linda Flower's term for writing which centers on the needs of readers to understand concepts and information; usually structured analytically, with ideas developed and explained in a context; often a revised version of **Writer-based prose**.

Review A summary, close examination, interpretation, and evaluation of an artistic or intellectual endeavor.

Scientific method A systematic way to examine phenomena in the physical world through questioning, observing, and experimenting.

Secondary source An explanation, interpretation, or summary of a primary text; a second-hand account of information or experience. (See **Primary source**.)

Short-term memory The capacity to take in new information and to retain it briefly without practice.

Significant The odds are less than 5 to 100 that the results are due merely to chance.

Social sciences Branches of learning that are concerned with the systematic study of people and how they behave and live together as families, tribes, communities, and nations; for example, psychology, anthropology, political science, sociology, economics, education, business administration.

Summary A condensation of the substance or main idea of a longer piece of discourse.

Table A graphic representation that consists only of words, numbers, and lines. (See **Figure**.)

Warrant Stephen Toulmin's term for a general principle of inference that justifies the connection between a **Ground** and a **Claim** by showing the relevance of the ground to the claim.

Writer-based prose Linda Flower's term for writing in which you talk to yourself on paper, explain ideas to yourself; usually structured as a narrative, with ideas abbreviated rather than developed, centered on the writer's feelings and procedures, rather than on the needs of a reader. (See **Reader-based prose**.)

Zero draft, discovery draft A preliminary version of a piece of writing in which you generate sentences and paragraphs before you find a workable structure for your ideas.

Index

Abrams, M. H., 157
Abstract. *See also* Summarizing
  abstracting journals, 75, 81, 88, 94–95,
    141–42, 281–83
  section of laboratory report, 267, 272–74
Academic disciplines, 4, 30, 44–45, 211,
  224, 225, 236, 266–67, 288, 327
Academic problems, 22–37
Acknowledgment(s), 119–21, 296, 299,
  313, 314, 319, 327
Aim, 7, 9, 218, 270
Almanacs, 74, 85
Analogies, 27
  for animal rights, 143
  for *Hard Times*, 139–40
Analysis, 68, 155–74, 298–308, 327
  book reviews, 169–74
  of painting, 165–69
  of performance, 163–65
  of poem, 155–62
  of stories, novels, and plays, 162–63
Annual review, 82–86, 96–97, 283
Anthropology, 4, 208, 222, 242, 243–45
Argument, 37–45, 327
Argumentation, 37–45, 64, 98, 142–43,
  176–204, 214, 295–98, 327
Aristotle, 32
Audience, 7–9, 14, 327. *See* Revising
  humanities, 144, 147–50, 156, 174,
    186, 196
  natural science, 270, 289, 291, 319
  social science, 214, 216, 217, 220, 229,
    231, 241, 251
Author-date method, 116–21
Authoritative, 98, 214, 218, 290
Autism, 209–20
  library research on, 81–89

Bar graph. *See* Graph
Bazerman, Charles, 66
Beardsley, Monroe, C., 42
Becker, Alton L., 28
Becker, Carl, 178–90
Berkeley, George, 177
Bettelheim, Bruno, 87, 212–13, 217–18
Bibliography, 72–75, 79, 327. See
  Documentation
  annotated, 75, 136
  on Dickens, 136–37
  and indexes, 75
  MLA format, 110–16
  recording, 100–102
  reference lists, 110, 111, 117–20
Biology, 4, 268, 280–93, 319–25
Blake, William, 165–69, 175
Book review, 79–80, 169–74
Bracy, William, 9
Brainstorming, 20, 23, 137–39, 143, 163–
  64, 166, 170–71, 198, 202, 281
Burke, Kenneth, 28, 29, 31

Capote, Truman, 140
Card catalog, 76–77, 79
  entries for autism, 85–88
Case study, 222–35, 327
  sample, 298–308, 308–18
Category, 132–37, 224–26, 233, 238,
  244–48, 285, 300–308, 311–12
Cause/effect, 38–52, 260
Charles II, 22–30, 76, 127
Chemistry, 258–60, 288
Chi square, 250–51
Citation Index, 75–76, 214, 283
Claim, 43–45, 327

Class notebook, 20. *See also* Note taking
Cognitive style, 5–7, 327
Coherence, 9, 172–73, 232, 252
Collaborative learning, 62, 121, 173, 186,
    289, 296, 299, 313, 314, 319–20,
    327
Collage, 31
Comprehensive, 98, 214
Compare/contrast, 65, 67, 191–97
Conclusion
    in logic, 37–43, 200, 230, 327
    of paper, 161–62, 174, 190, 232, 237,
        238, 251–52, 263, 267, 271–72, 287,
        291, 308, 325
Congress (U.S.), 232–35
Context, 128, 212, 214, 251, 270, 299,
    314, 320
Controlling questions, 129–32, 136, 140,
    209–11, 233, 238, 273, 283–88
Copying, 21, 129, 162
Creative writing, 12
Criminology, 239–41
Critical paper, 155–75
Critique, criticize, 68, 155–75, 327

Data, 58, 236, 239–50, 256, 267, 269
Definition, 36, 66, 158–59, 210, 211,
    230, 300, 316, 322
Descartes, René, 191–97
Description, 66, 167–68, 210–11, 219,
    222–35, 236–55, 256–64, 266–75,
    298–308, 308–18, 320, 328
Diagrams, 32–35, 242–43, 323
    tree diagrams, 38–43
Dickens, Charles (*Hard Times*)
    library research on, 72–81
    summarizing notes on, 102–3
    term paper on, 128–54
Dictionaries, 74, 92, 157, 158, 159, 160
Discipline. *See* Academic disciplines
Discourse, 328
Discovery draft. *See* Zero drafts
Documentation, 107–110, 121, 153–154,
    252, 272, 328
    APA format, 110, 116–121
    MLA format, 110–116, 119–121
Draft(s), 10–14, 329, 330
    analysis of literature, 162–63
    analysis of painting, 166–68
    analysis of performance, 164–65
    analysis of poem, 160–61
    book review, 172–73
    contemplative papers, 182–86, 193–96,
        199–200, 202–3

humanities term paper, 144–47
natural science laboratory report, 268–73
natural science review paper, 287–89
report of findings, 238–52
social science case study, 226–29, 233
social science term paper, 210–15

Ebner, Kurt E., 285
Economics, 4, 208, 243
Editing, 15, 230, 253. *See* Proofreading
Education (discipline of), 208, 211, 224
Egocentric writing, 13. *See also* Writer-
    based prose
Elbow, Peter, 19
Emig, Janet, 19
Empirical, 236–53, 256–64, 266–75
Encyclopedia, 73, 74, 79, 82, 92, 135–36,
    141
Endnotes, 110
Error, 9, 15, 107, 220, 253, 260, 273
Evidence, 37–45, 128, 140, 181. *See also*
    Data
Exam writing, 64–70
    of applications and speculations, 67, 68,
        69
    compare or contrast, 65–67
    develop a point of view, 65
    information, 65–66
    key words, 66–67, 68–69
    timed exams, 69–70
    writing answers, 67–70
Experiment, 256–64, 255, 266–69
Expressive writing, 7, 8, 13, 19–20, 313,
    328

"Fence," 239, 240–41
Figure, 242–46, 248–49, 274, 323, 328
Findings, 236–53, 256, 261, 267, 269
First draft. *See* Draft(s)
First person. *See* "I"
Fitzgerald, F. Scott, 6, 109
Flower, Linda, 13, 329, 330
Flow chart, 22, 32–35, 242–43
Focus, 9, 10, 129–40, 161, 162, 165, 168,
    209, 212, 233
Footnotes, 110–14, 119–20, 152
    alternative format (APA), 116–17, 119–
      20
Format, 9, 10, 107, 110–20, 150, 219,
    237–38, 261, 266–67, 273
Freewriting, 20, 47, 48, 137–40, 157, 162

Ghandhi, Mohandas, 108
Genre, 8, 9

Geography, 122, 243
Getting started, 11
  analysis of literature, 162–63
  analysis of painting, 165–66
  analysis of performance, 163–64
  analysis of poem, 157–60
  book review, 169–72
  contemplative paper, 178–82, 191–93,
    197–99, 201–2
  humanities term paper, 128–44
  natural science laboratory report, 266–68
  natural science review paper, 277–87
  report of findings, 236–38
  social science case study, 223–26
  social science term paper, 208–10
Graph(s), 248–50, 252
Gray, Paul, 79
Ground, 43–45, 328

Hall, Donald, 157
Handbooks, 82, 92
Hard Times. See Dickens
Headings, 252. *See* Subheadings
Heuristic(s), 8, 11, 23–37, 216, 328. *See
  also* Controlling questions
History, 4, 11, 127, 201–4, 285, 295–98
Hypothesis, 131, 256, 263
Humanities, 5–6, 126–205, 176, 328
Hume, David, 191–97

"I," 156, 219, 230, 268, 290, 316
Illustrations, 290. *See also* Visual
  representations
Incubation, 12–13, 328
Index, 75, 80, 88, 93–96, 141–42, 283,
  328. *See* Abstract
Infer(ences), 225, 230, 234, 305, 316. *See
  also* Logic
Informative writing, 7, 328
Interview, 240
Introduction, 217, 218, 228, 232, 236,
  251, 261, 267, 269, 281–82, 287,
  291
Invention. *See* Heuristic
Irmscher, William F., 29

James I, 63–64
Janik, Allan, 43
Jargon, 220, 289, 306
Jefferson, Thomas, 108
Johnson, Edgar, 80
Journal, personal, 20–22, 198, 209, 328

Journal articles, 214, 241, 328. *See*
  Periodicals
Joyce, James, 162

Kanner, Leo, 220
Key words, 15, 65–69, 75, 76, 78, 91–92,
  94, 103, 141, 162, 198
Kinneavy, James, 7
Klockars, Carl B., 240–41
Kreuzer, James R., 160

Label, 247, 252
Laboratory report, 109, 236–52, 266–75,
  328
Lab practical, 257, 328
Langbaum, Robert, 108
Le Corbusier, 108
Lectures, 57–58
Levinson, H. C., 105
Liberal arts, 5–7, 328
Library
  card catalog, 76–77, 79, 85–88
  computer search for references, 78, 95–
    96
  periodicals, 76, 78, 80–81
  recording material, 100–102
  reference section, 73–76
  research in Natural Sciences, 89–97
  research on Dickens's *Hard Times*, 78–
    81
  research on Social Sciences, 81–89, 209
  research process, 71–73, 97–98, 100–
    102
Lists, 23, 192, 202–3
Literary analysis, 129, 135, 155–63
Literature, 7, 72–75, 77, 78–81, 126–40,
  144–53, 162–74
  literary writing, 7, 329
Locke, John, 177
Logic, 37–45, 260

Mailer, Norman, 140
Mama Rat, 235, 308–18
Map(s), 243–46
Marihuana, marijuana, 91–96, 280–93
Mathematics, 4
Mausner, Bernard, 30
Memory, 18–19, 56, 75, 257, 329
Metaphor, 27, 47–48, 201. *See* Analogies
Methods section, 236, 237, 238, 239, 256,
  258–60, 261, 263, 267, 268
Milford, Nancy, 109

Miller, George, 75
Morsbach, Helmut, 244

Nader, Ralph, 140
Narration, 14, 219, 229–30, 239, 252, 256, 298–308, 329
Natural sciences, 5, 89–97, 237, 255–93, 329
Nietzsche, Friedrich, 177
Nold, Ellen, 9
"Not only . . . but also," 169
Note taking, 55–64
  from book review, 171
  from class discussions, 59–60
  for humanities term paper, 132–44
  laboratory notebook, 257–64
  from lectures, 56–59
  in library, 100–102
  for natural science observations, 257–64
  for papers of contemplation, 179, 192–93, 198–99, 202
  from readings, 62–64
  in reading poem, 157
  for social sciences, 210, 223–25
  studying from, 60–62
Novel, elements of the, 135–36

Observation, 222–35, 236, 238, 240, 256–64, 268, 309–12
O'Neill, Eugene (*Mourning Becomes Electra*), 30
Outlining, 15, 145, 181–84, 193–95, 199–200, 216
Oxford English Dictionary (O.E.D.), 158–59

Painting, 165–69
Paragraphs, 15, 42, 145–47, 149–53, 161, 162, 165, 168–69, 184–85, 188–89, 196, 212–14, 216
Particle, wave, field, 28
Passive voice, 148, 219, 230, 268
Peer readers, 14, 173, 186, 289, 299, 313, 319–20, 329
Pentad, 29–31, 329
Performance, 163–65
Periodicals, 75, 76–78
  humanities, 80–81
  natural sciences, 93–96, 278–82
  social sciences, 88–89, 93–96, 214, 237, 241–42

Persuasive writing, 7–8, 329
Philosophy, 4, 11, 127–28, 141–44, 176–78, 191–201, 285
Physiology, 4, 271
Photograph(s), 243–45, 252
Pike, Kenneth, 28
Plato, 32–33, 109, 120
Poem, 156–62
Political science, 208, 211, 222, 225, 233–35, 285
Premise, 37–42, 329
Prewriting. *See* Getting started
Primary sources, 109, 128–29, 141, 153, 329
Private writing, 8, 19–22, 329. *See* Writer-based prose
Problem, 176, 329
  paper, 197–201
Problem-solving, 7–11, 150, 256
Proofreading, 9, 15, 204, 220, 253, 273, 292
Psychology, 4, 10, 75, 208, 211, 222, 224, 225, 237, 308–18
Puzzle paper, 197–201

Questions. *See also* Controlling questions
  for abstracts, 272
  for arguments, 38
  for book reviews, 169–70
  for contemplative papers, 177
  essay exams, 64–70
  flow charts, 34–35
  interviewing paragraphs, 15, 186, 188, 228
  and liberal arts, 6
  problems as focussed questions, 22
  for revising drafts, 186, 273
  and topics, 22–31
Quotations, 101, 129–30, 137, 145–46, 148–50, 162, 174, 217
  documentation, 107–10

Rawitch, Allen B., 285
Reader. *See* Audience; Peer readers
Reader-based prose, 150, 239, 252, 329
Reference(s), 110, 117–18, 220, 252, 267, 273, 290, 325
Representative, 98, 214
Research notebook, 263–65
Research paper. *See* Term paper
Results, 238, 239–50, 261, 263, 267, 269. *See also* Findings

Revelation, Book of, 166–68
Review, 96, 276–93, 330
Revising, 14–16
  analysis of literature, 163
  analysis of painting, 168–69
  analysis of performance, 165
  analysis of poem, 161–62
  book review, 173–74
  contemplative paper, 186–90, 196–97, 200, 203–4
  humanities term paper, 147–54
  natural science laboratory report, 273–75
  natural science review paper, 289–92
  report of findings, 252–53
  social science case study, 229–32
  social science term paper, 215–20
Rieke, Richard, 43
Roberts, Edgar V., 166

Schultz, Gregory S., 285
Sciences. See Natural sciences; Social sciences
Scientific American, 290
Scientific method, 256, 330
Scientific review paper, 276–93
  sample, 319–26
Scriven, Michael, 42
Secondary sources, 128–29, 330
Sentence, 9, 148–49, 169, 220, 253, 258, 273, 289
Shakespeare, William, 177
Shaughnessy, Mina, 15, 16
Significant, 251, 269, 330
  significance level, 250–51
Social sciences, 81–89, 207–53, 330
Sociology, 4, 208, 211, 222, 224, 225, 298–308
Solecki, Ralph S., 244, 246
Soviet Union, 201–3, 295–98
Speculative paper, 67, 201–4
  sample, 295–98
Stalin, Josef, 201–3, 295–98
Statistical tests, 250–51, 269
Steinbeck, John, 68
Story board, 31
Structure
  of book review, 172–73
  of literature, 162
  of poem, 161
Subheadings, 219, 224, 252, 273, 277, 287, 290, 300, 303, 308, 315, 320
Summarizing, 21, 56, 66, 102–7, 187,

202, 251, 252, 272, 277, 285, 288, 312, 319, 300
Szasz, Thomas, 171–74

Tables, 22, 35–37, 216–17, 244–48, 252, 261–62, 269, 273–75, 301, 304, 313, 330
  tabulate, 238
Term paper, 71–123, 126–55, 208–21, 251, 276–93
Thesis, 128, 129, 144, 149, 153, 165, 179, 187, 193, 196, 210–13, 233, 277, 296–98, 320, 324
  as hypothesis, 256
Title(s), 261, 267, 273, 274, 278–80
  of tables, 247, 252, 274
Tone, 219, 290, 324
Topic, 22, 277–83. See also Controlling question
  vs. controlling question, 131
  from notes, 133
  vs. problem, 22–37
Toulmin, Stephen, 43
Transitions, 9, 15, 40–42, 161, 169, 188, 196, 200, 216, 260, 271, 287, 289, 324
Treeing diagram, 12, 25–27, 38–43

Underlining, 62–64
Unity, 9, 172–73, 232, 252
Up-to-date, 98, 214, 278, 283
Usage, 9, 148–49, 169, 220, 253, 258, 273, 289

Value judgments, 230, 301, 305, 315, 320
Visual representations, 22, 31–35, 60, 216–17, 242–46, 251, 261, 274, 290, 322–23
Vocabulary. See Word; Jargon

Warrant, 43–45, 200, 330
Wasserman, Leonard S., 258
Whales, humpback, 319–25
Wiener, Harvey, S., 66
Winterowd, W. Ross, 29
Word, 9, 27, 200, 220, 230, 300
  in poem, 15, 161
  in sentences, 198–99
  words for findings, 240–42

Wordsworth, William (*The World is too much with us*), 156–62
Writer-based prose, 13, 14, 150, 239, 252, 269, 272, 330
Writer's block, 185
Writing center, 298, 299

Yearbook(s), 82, 85
Yeats, William Butler, 22
Young, Richard, 28

Zero drafts, 11, 330. *See* Draft(s)